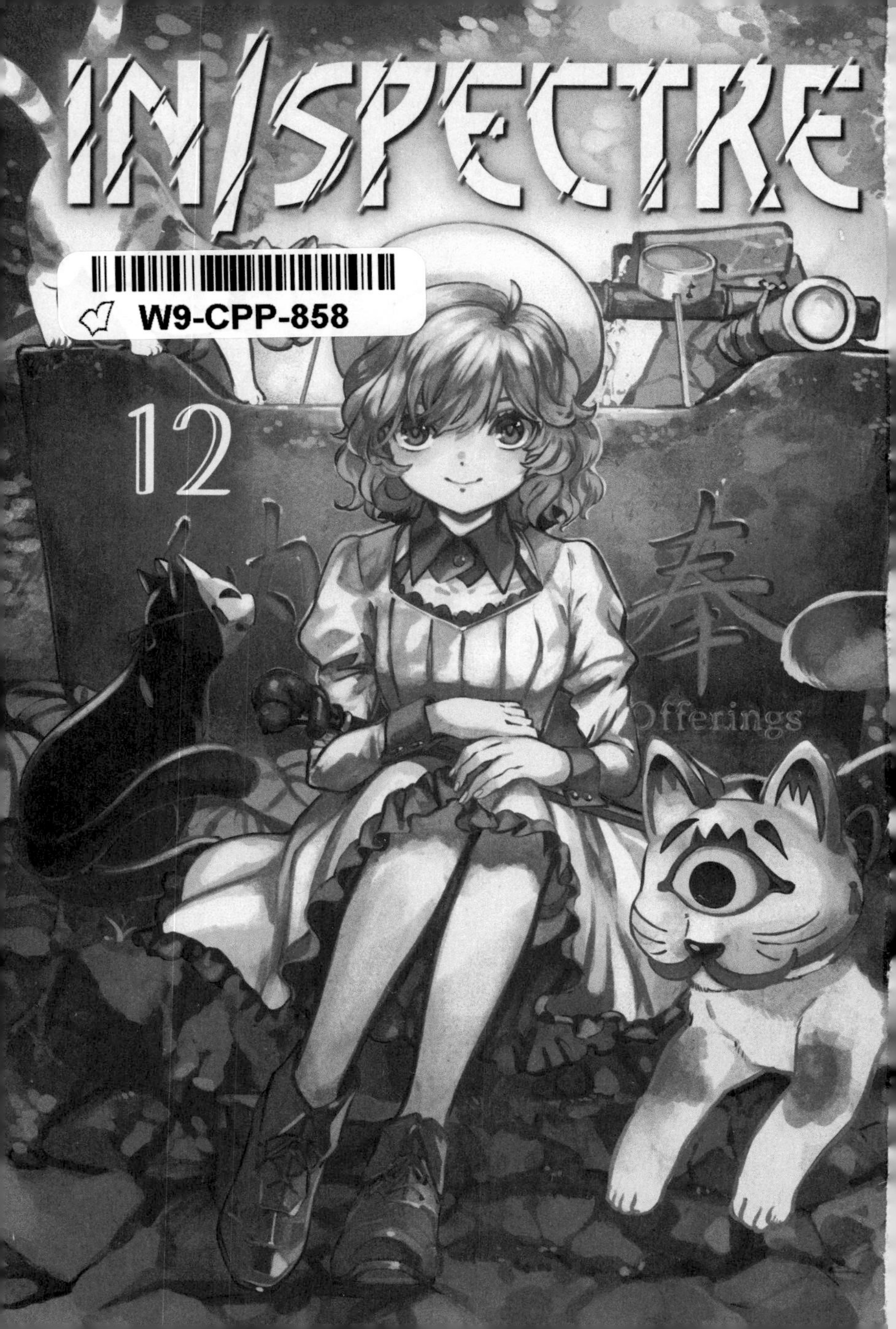
IN/SPECTRE
12
Offerings

CONTENTS

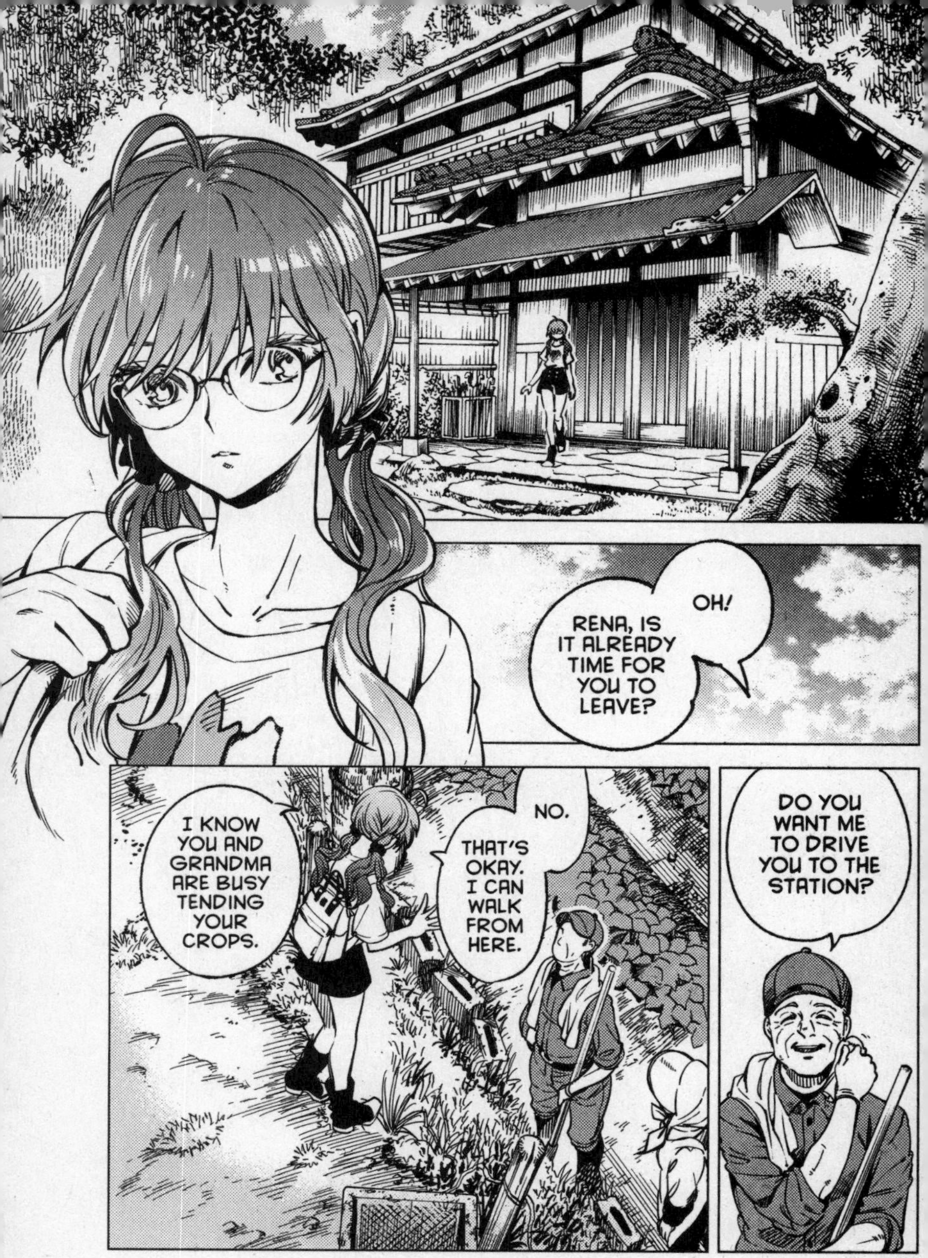
OH!
RENA, IS IT ALREADY TIME FOR YOU TO LEAVE?
DO YOU WANT ME TO DRIVE YOU TO THE STATION?
NO.
THAT'S OKAY. I CAN WALK FROM HERE.
I KNOW YOU AND GRANDMA ARE BUSY TENDING YOUR CROPS.

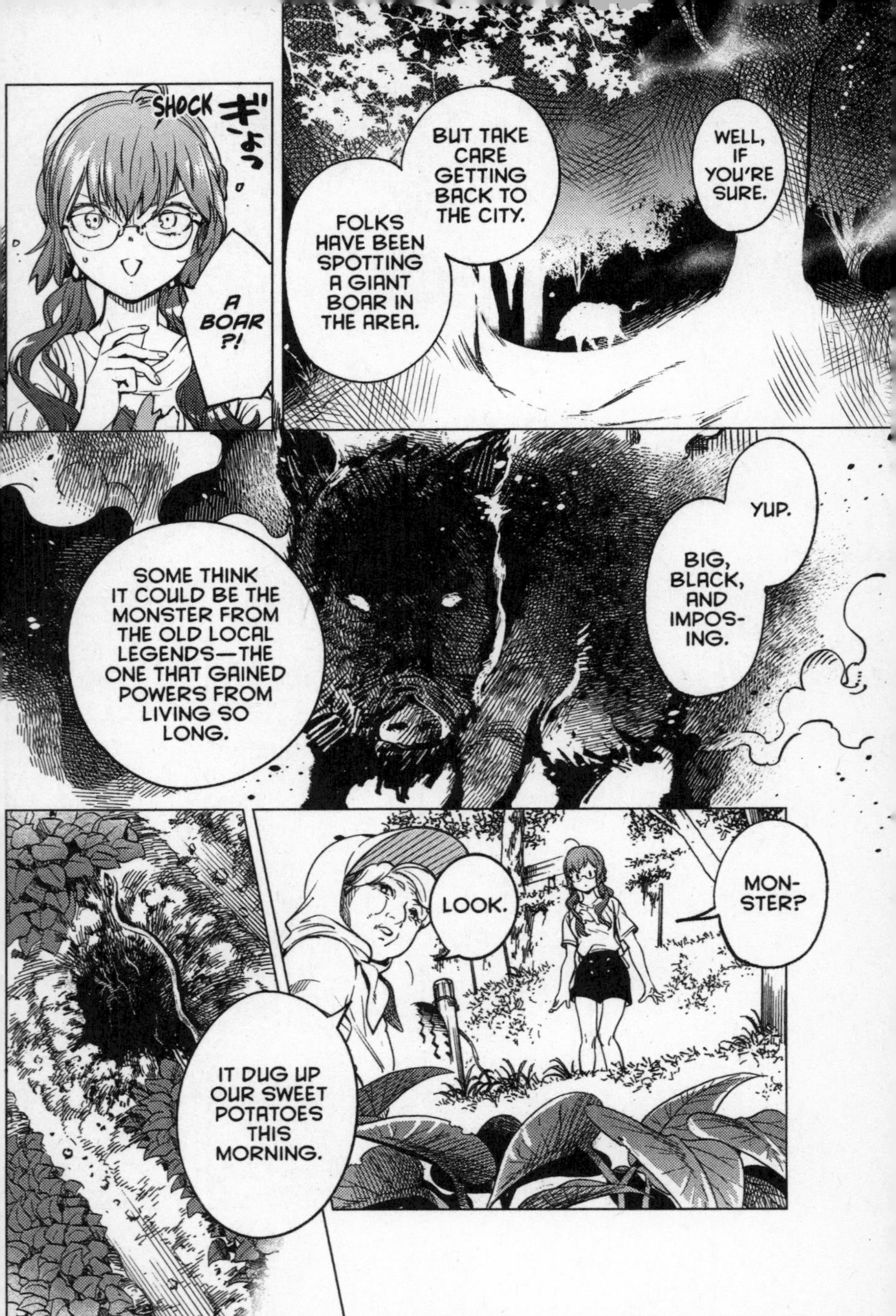
WELL, IF YOU'RE SURE.
BUT TAKE CARE GETTING BACK TO THE CITY.
FOLKS HAVE BEEN SPOTTING A GIANT BOAR IN THE AREA.
SHOCK ぎょっ
A BOAR?!
YUP.
BIG, BLACK, AND IMPOS-ING.
SOME THINK IT COULD BE THE MONSTER FROM THE OLD LOCAL LEGENDS—THE ONE THAT GAINED POWERS FROM LIVING SO LONG.
MON-STER?
LOOK.
IT DUG UP OUR SWEET POTATOES THIS MORNING.

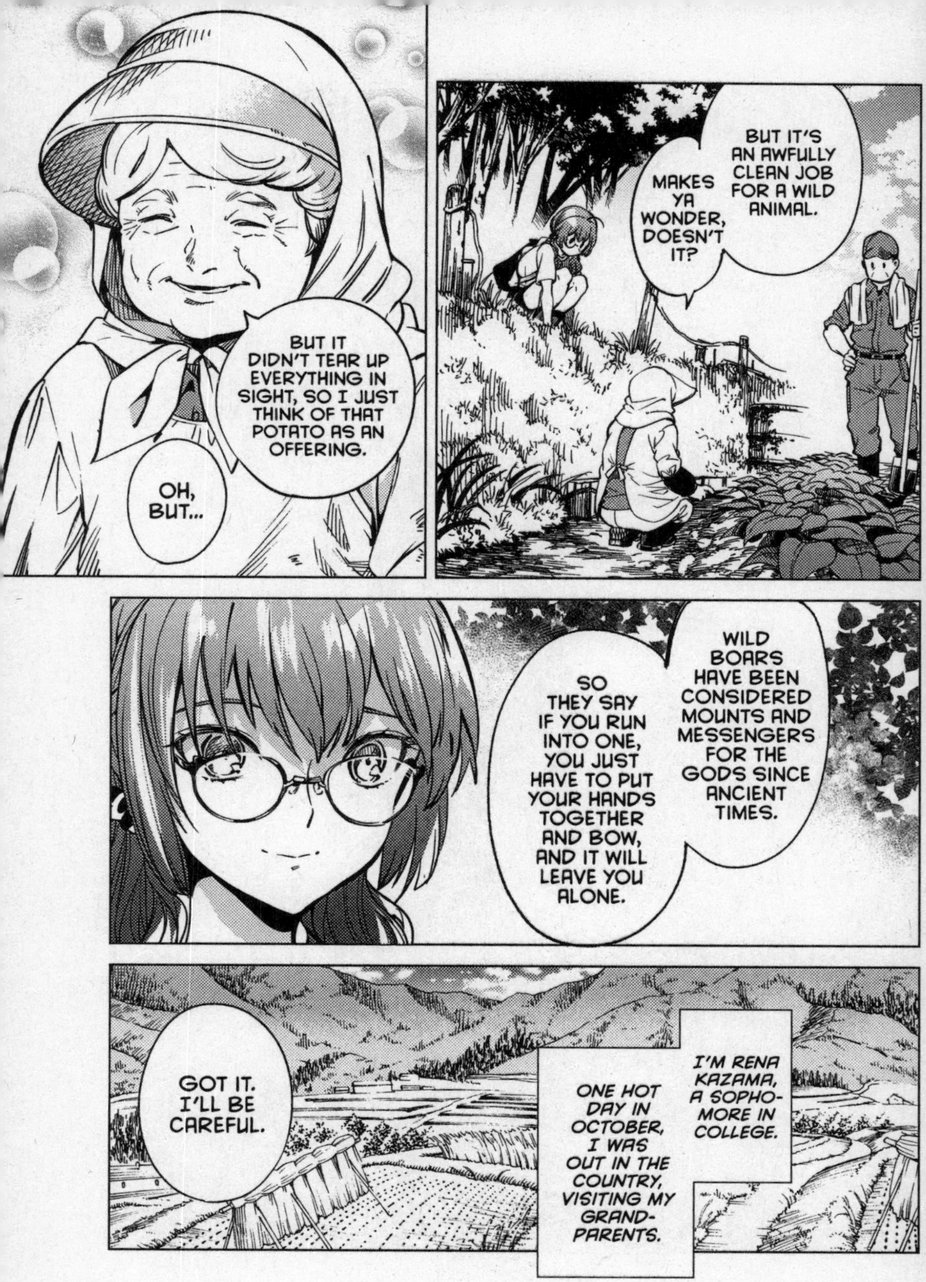
BUT IT'S AN AWFULLY CLEAN JOB FOR A WILD ANIMAL.
MAKES YA WONDER, DOESN'T IT?
BUT IT DIDN'T TEAR UP EVERYTHING IN SIGHT, SO I JUST THINK OF THAT POTATO AS AN OFFERING.
OH, BUT...
WILD BOARS HAVE BEEN CONSIDERED MOUNTS AND MESSENGERS FOR THE GODS SINCE ANCIENT TIMES.
SO THEY SAY IF YOU RUN INTO ONE, YOU JUST HAVE TO PUT YOUR HANDS TOGETHER AND BOW, AND IT WILL LEAVE YOU ALONE.
I'M RENA KAZAMA, A SOPHOMORE IN COLLEGE.
ONE HOT DAY IN OCTOBER, I WAS OUT IN THE COUNTRY, VISITING MY GRANDPARENTS.
GOT IT. I'LL BE CAREFUL.

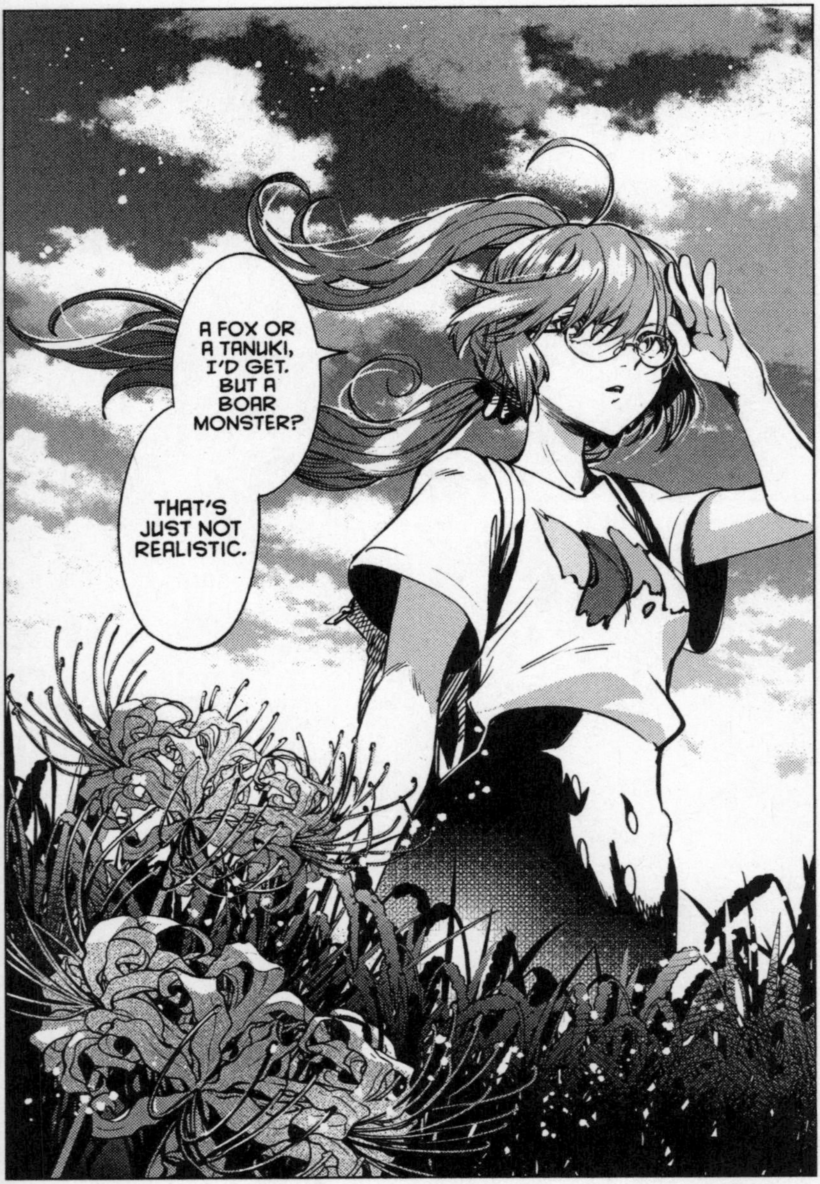
A FOX OR A TANUKI, I'D GET. BUT A BOAR MONSTER?
THAT'S JUST NOT REALISTIC.

CHAPTER 29:
"AN UNCERTAIN VOICE FROM BEYOND"

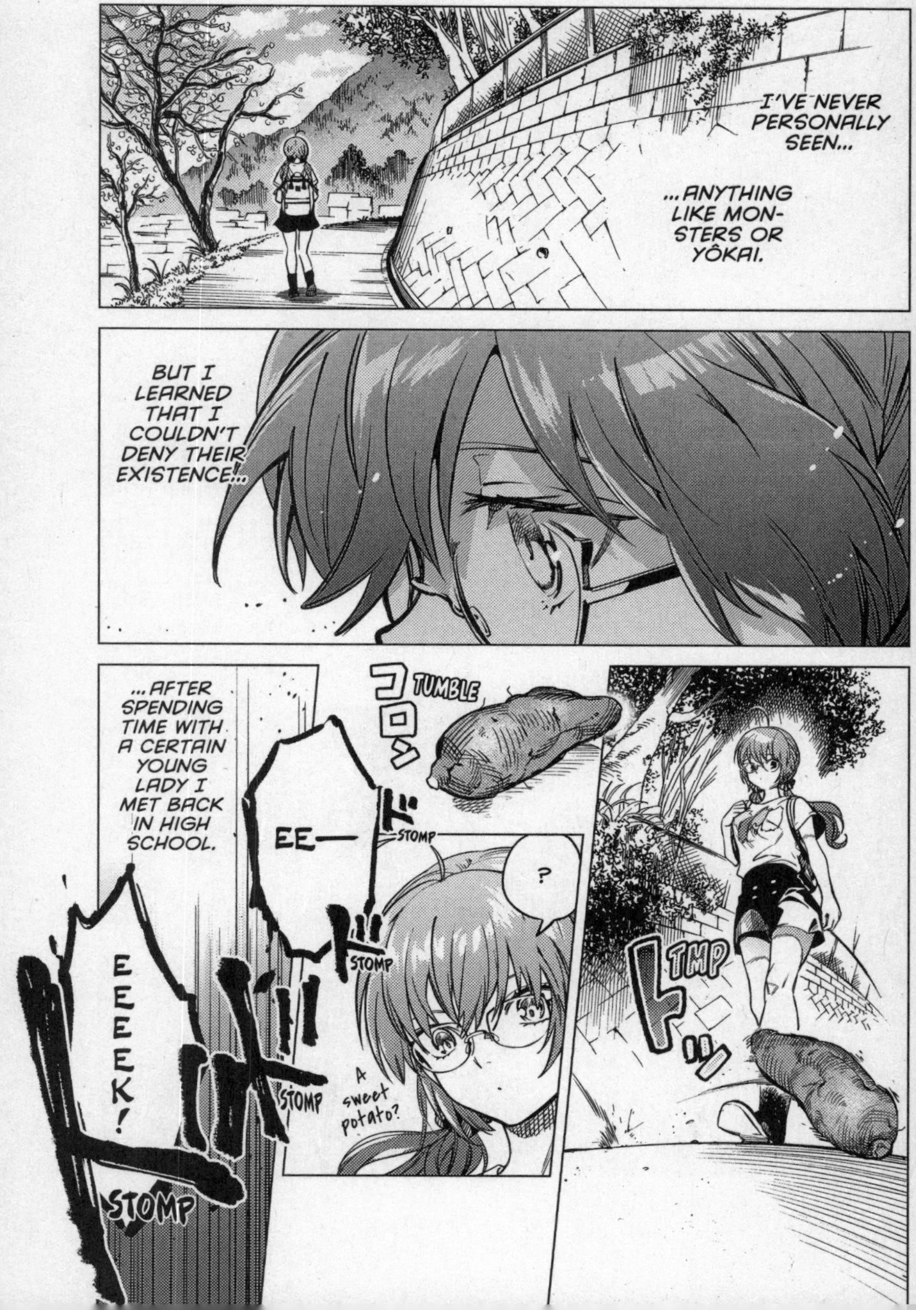
I'VE NEVER PERSONALLY SEEN...
...ANYTHING LIKE MONSTERS OR YÔKAI.
BUT I LEARNED THAT I COULDN'T DENY THEIR EXISTENCE...
コロン
TUMBLE
TMP
?
A sweet potato?
...AFTER SPENDING TIME WITH A CERTAIN YOUNG LADY I MET BACK IN HIGH SCHOOL.
EE—
STOMP
STOMP
STOMP
EEEEK!
STOMP

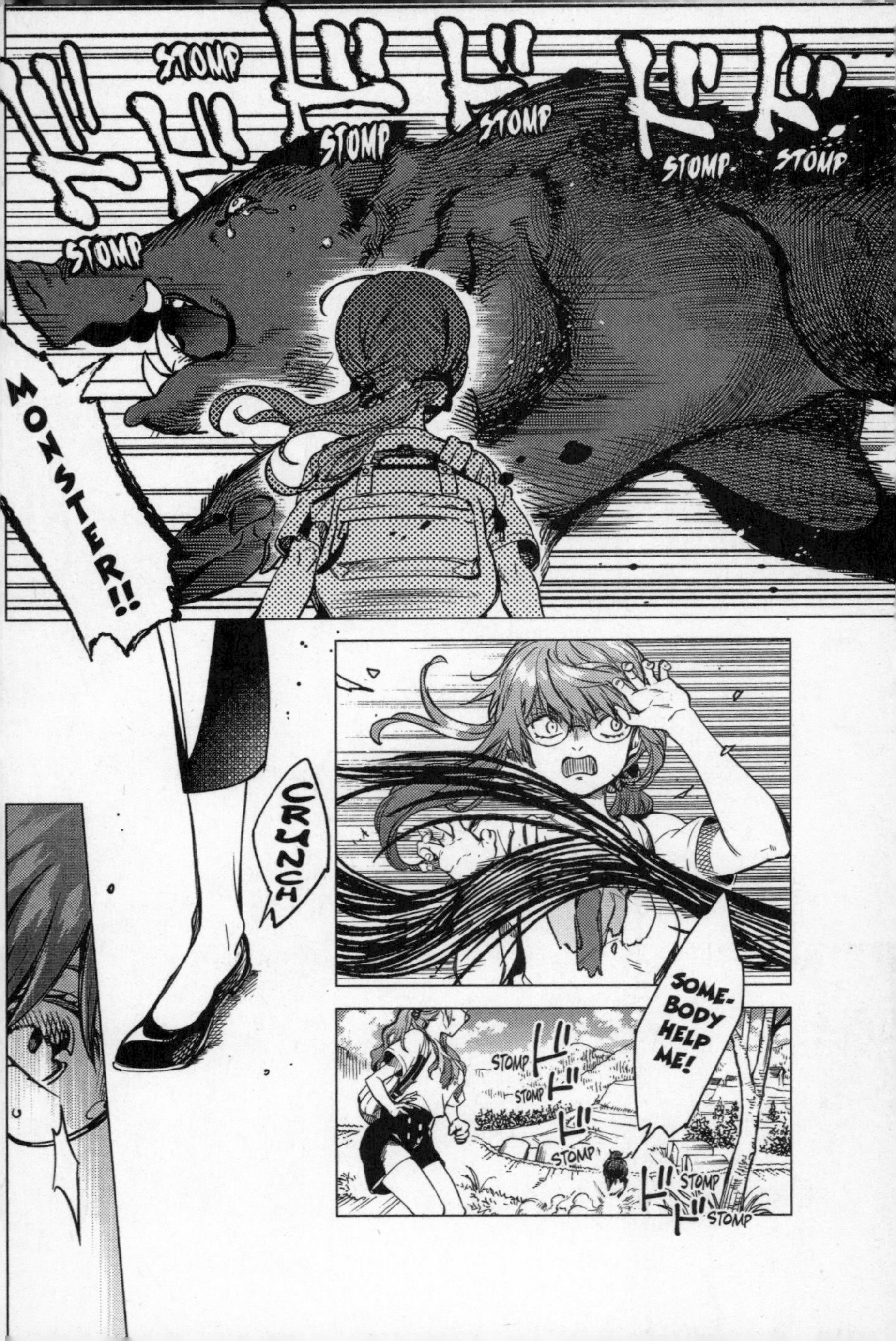
STOMP
STOMP
STOMP
STOMP
STOMP
STOMP
MONSTER!!
SOME-BODY HELP ME!
STOMP
STOMP
STOMP
STOMP
STOMP
CRUNCH

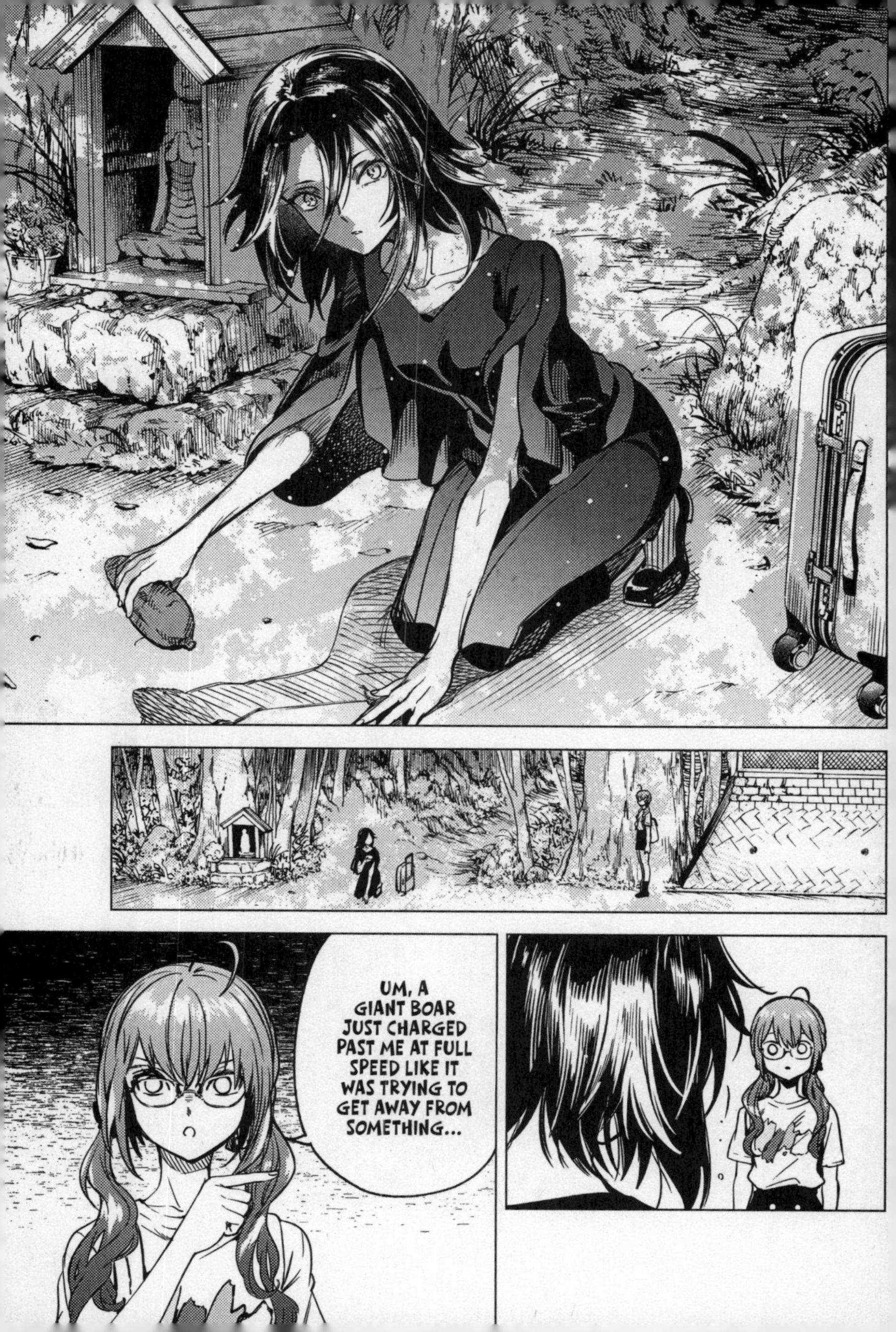
UM, A GIANT BOAR JUST CHARGED PAST ME AT FULL SPEED LIKE IT WAS TRYING TO GET AWAY FROM SOMETHING...

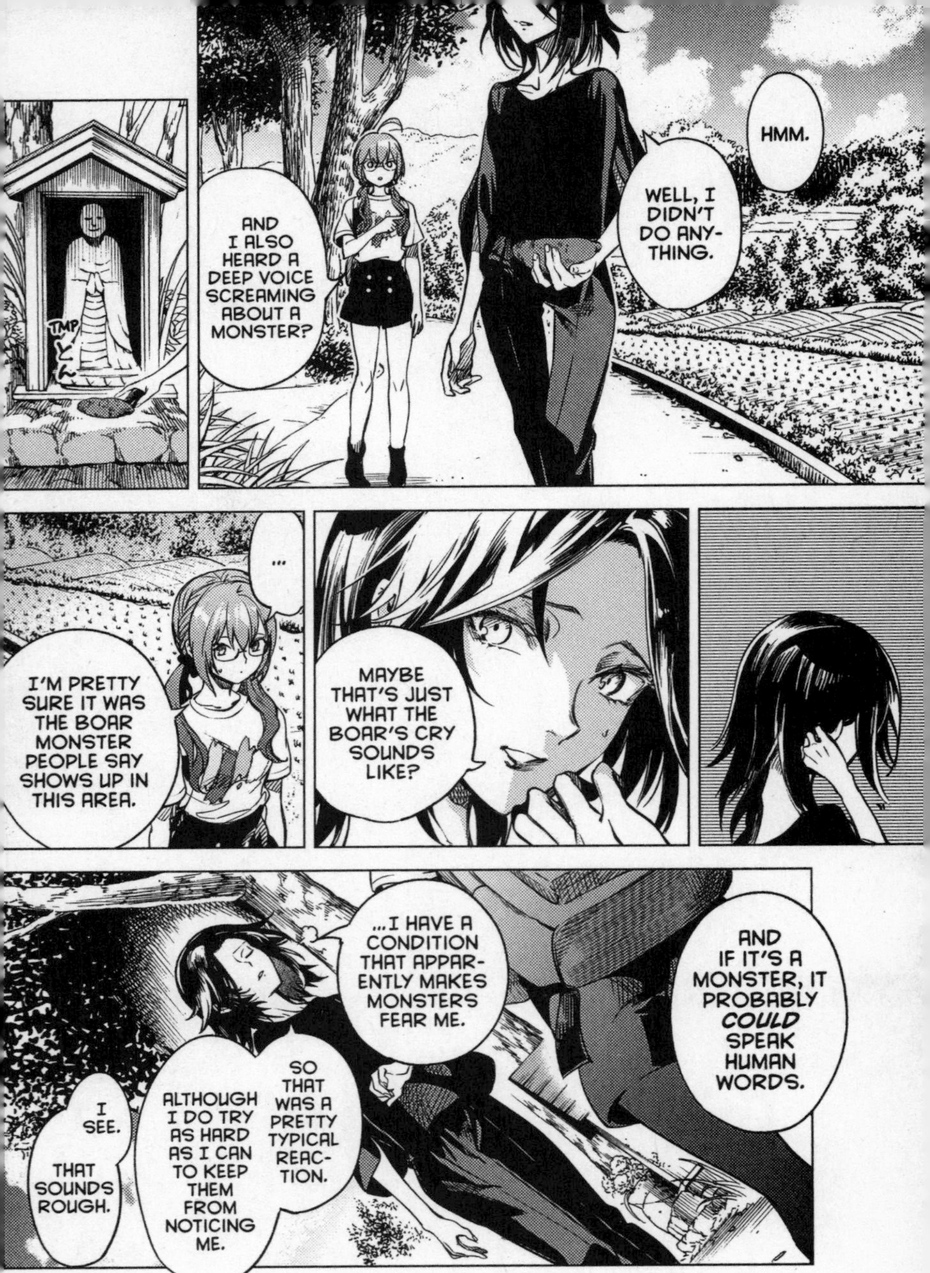
HMM.
WELL, I DIDN'T DO ANYTHING.
AND I ALSO HEARD A DEEP VOICE SCREAMING ABOUT A MONSTER?
TMP とん
MAYBE THAT'S JUST WHAT THE BOAR'S CRY SOUNDS LIKE?
...
I'M PRETTY SURE IT WAS THE BOAR MONSTER PEOPLE SAY SHOWS UP IN THIS AREA.
AND IF IT'S A MONSTER, IT PROBABLY *COULD* SPEAK HUMAN WORDS.
...I HAVE A CONDITION THAT APPARENTLY MAKES MONSTERS FEAR ME.
SO THAT WAS A PRETTY TYPICAL REACTION.
ALTHOUGH I DO TRY AS HARD AS I CAN TO KEEP THEM FROM NOTICING ME.
I SEE.
THAT SOUNDS ROUGH.

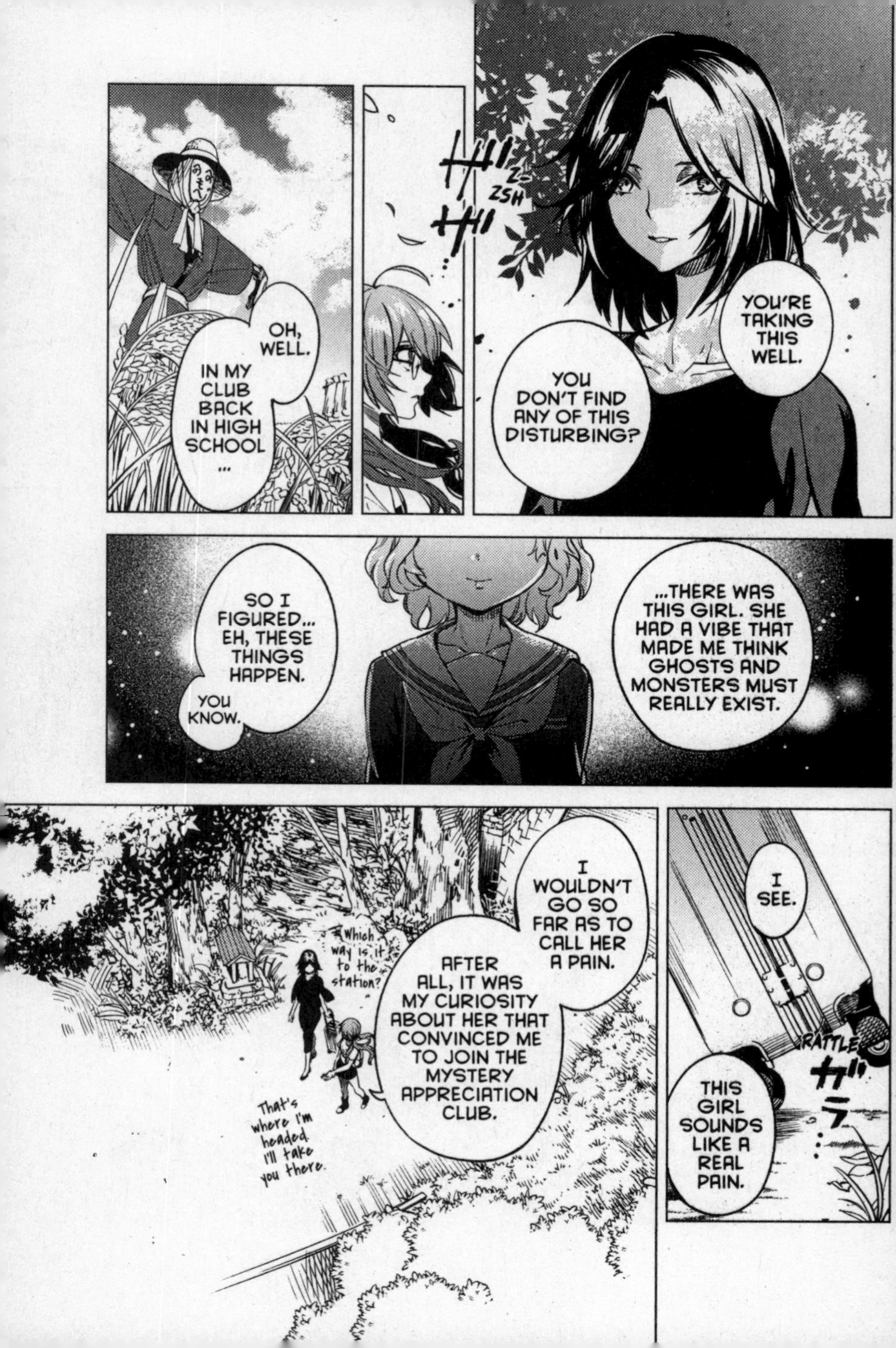
YOU'RE TAKING THIS WELL.
YOU DON'T FIND ANY OF THIS DISTURBING?
ZZSH
OH, WELL.
IN MY CLUB BACK IN HIGH SCHOOL ...
...THERE WAS THIS GIRL. SHE HAD A VIBE THAT MADE ME THINK GHOSTS AND MONSTERS MUST REALLY EXIST.
SO I FIGURED... EH, THESE THINGS HAPPEN.
YOU KNOW.
I SEE.
RATTLE
THIS GIRL SOUNDS LIKE A REAL PAIN.
I WOULDN'T GO SO FAR AS TO CALL HER A PAIN.
AFTER ALL, IT WAS MY CURIOSITY ABOUT HER THAT CONVINCED ME TO JOIN THE MYSTERY APPRECIATION CLUB.
Which way is it to the station?
That's where I'm headed. I'll take you there.

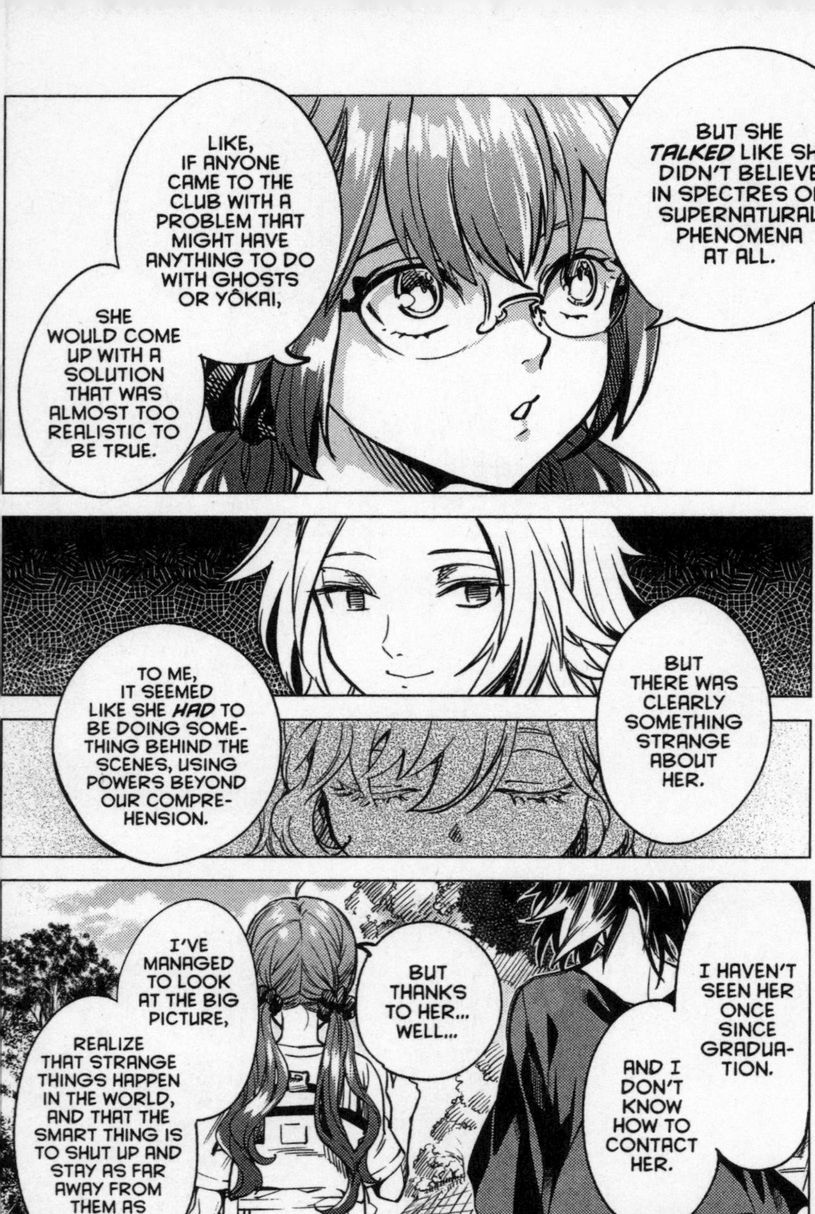
BUT SHE *TALKED* LIKE SHE DIDN'T BELIEVE IN SPECTRES OR SUPERNATURAL PHENOMENA AT ALL.
LIKE, IF ANYONE CAME TO THE CLUB WITH A PROBLEM THAT MIGHT HAVE ANYTHING TO DO WITH GHOSTS OR YÔKAI,
SHE WOULD COME UP WITH A SOLUTION THAT WAS ALMOST TOO REALISTIC TO BE TRUE.
BUT THERE WAS CLEARLY SOMETHING STRANGE ABOUT HER.
TO ME, IT SEEMED LIKE SHE *HAD* TO BE DOING SOMETHING BEHIND THE SCENES, USING POWERS BEYOND OUR COMPREHENSION.
I HAVEN'T SEEN HER ONCE SINCE GRADUATION.
AND I DON'T KNOW HOW TO CONTACT HER.
BUT THANKS TO HER... WELL...
I'VE MANAGED TO LOOK AT THE BIG PICTURE,
REALIZE THAT STRANGE THINGS HAPPEN IN THE WORLD, AND THAT THE SMART THING IS TO SHUT UP AND STAY AS FAR AWAY FROM THEM AS POSSIBLE.

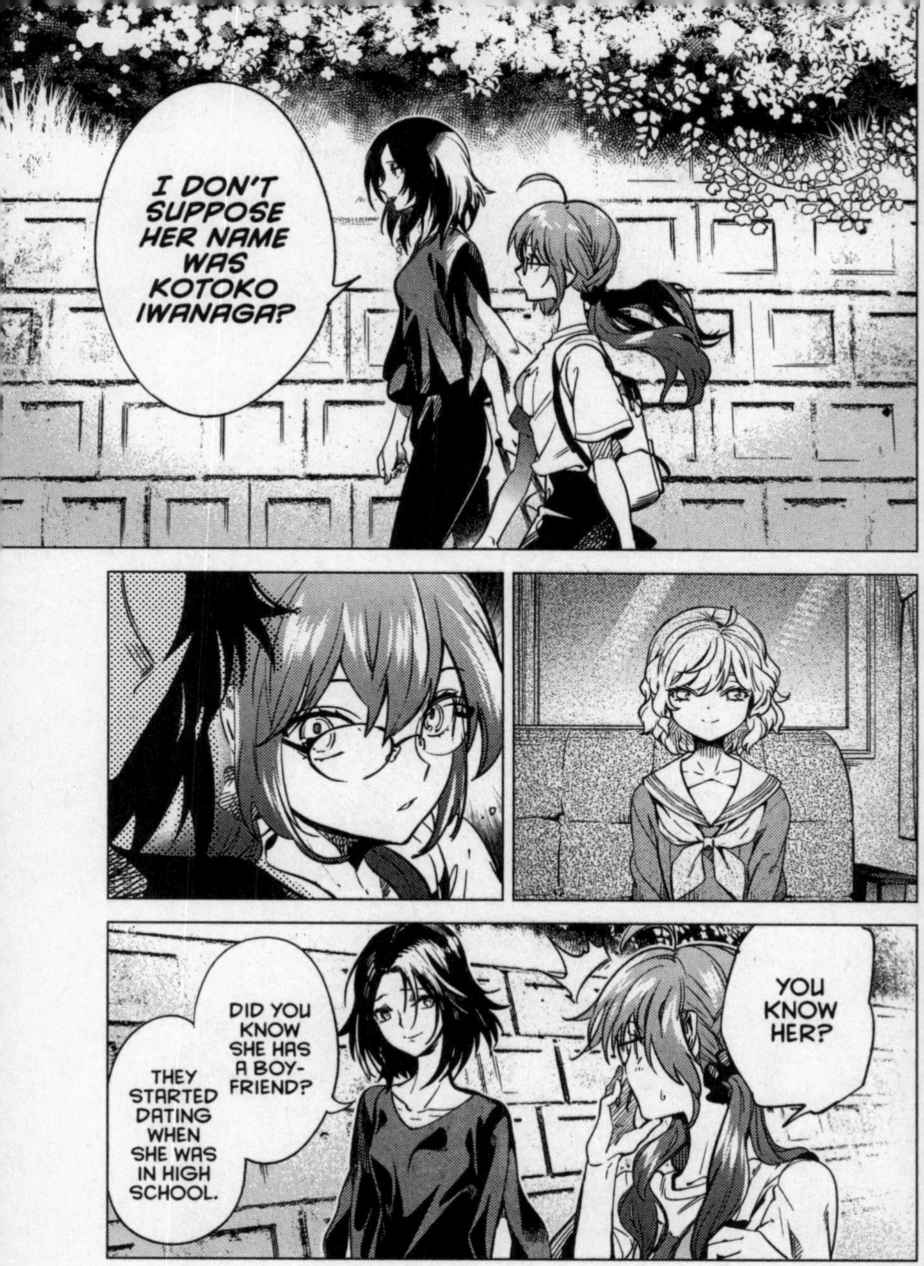
I DON'T SUPPOSE HER NAME WAS KOTOKO IWANAGA?
YOU KNOW HER?
DID YOU KNOW SHE HAS A BOY-FRIEND?
THEY STARTED DATING WHEN SHE WAS IN HIGH SCHOOL.

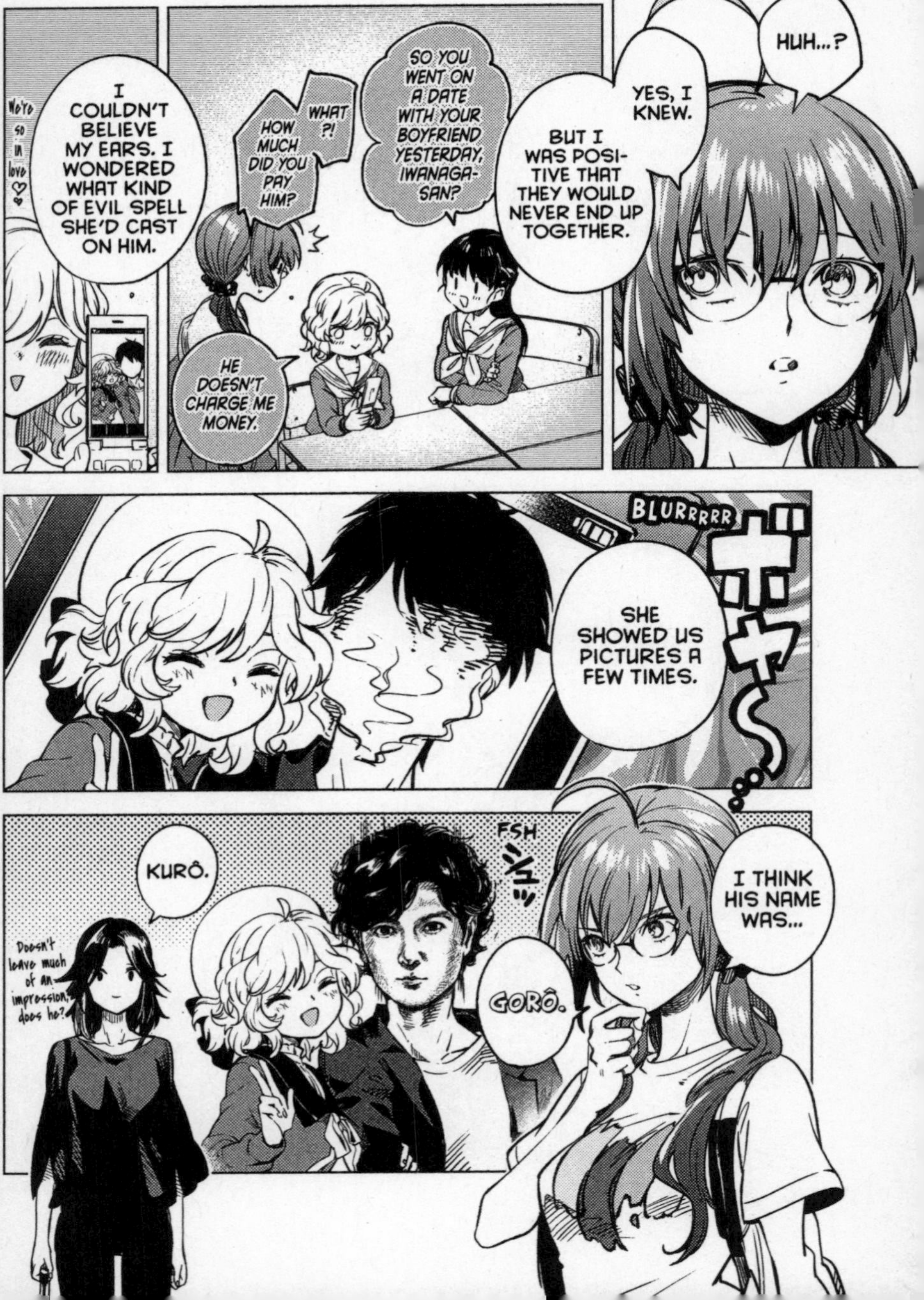
HUH...?
YES, I KNEW.
BUT I WAS POSITIVE THAT THEY WOULD NEVER END UP TOGETHER.
SO YOU WENT ON A DATE WITH YOUR BOYFRIEND YESTERDAY, IWANAGA-SAN?
WHAT?! HOW MUCH DID YOU PAY HIM?
HE DOESN'T CHARGE ME MONEY.
I COULDN'T BELIEVE MY EARS. I WONDERED WHAT KIND OF EVIL SPELL SHE'D CAST ON HIM.
We're so in love ♡
BLURRRRR
SHE SHOWED US PICTURES A FEW TIMES.
FSH
I THINK HIS NAME WAS...
GORÔ.
KURÔ.
Doesn't leave much of an impression, does he?

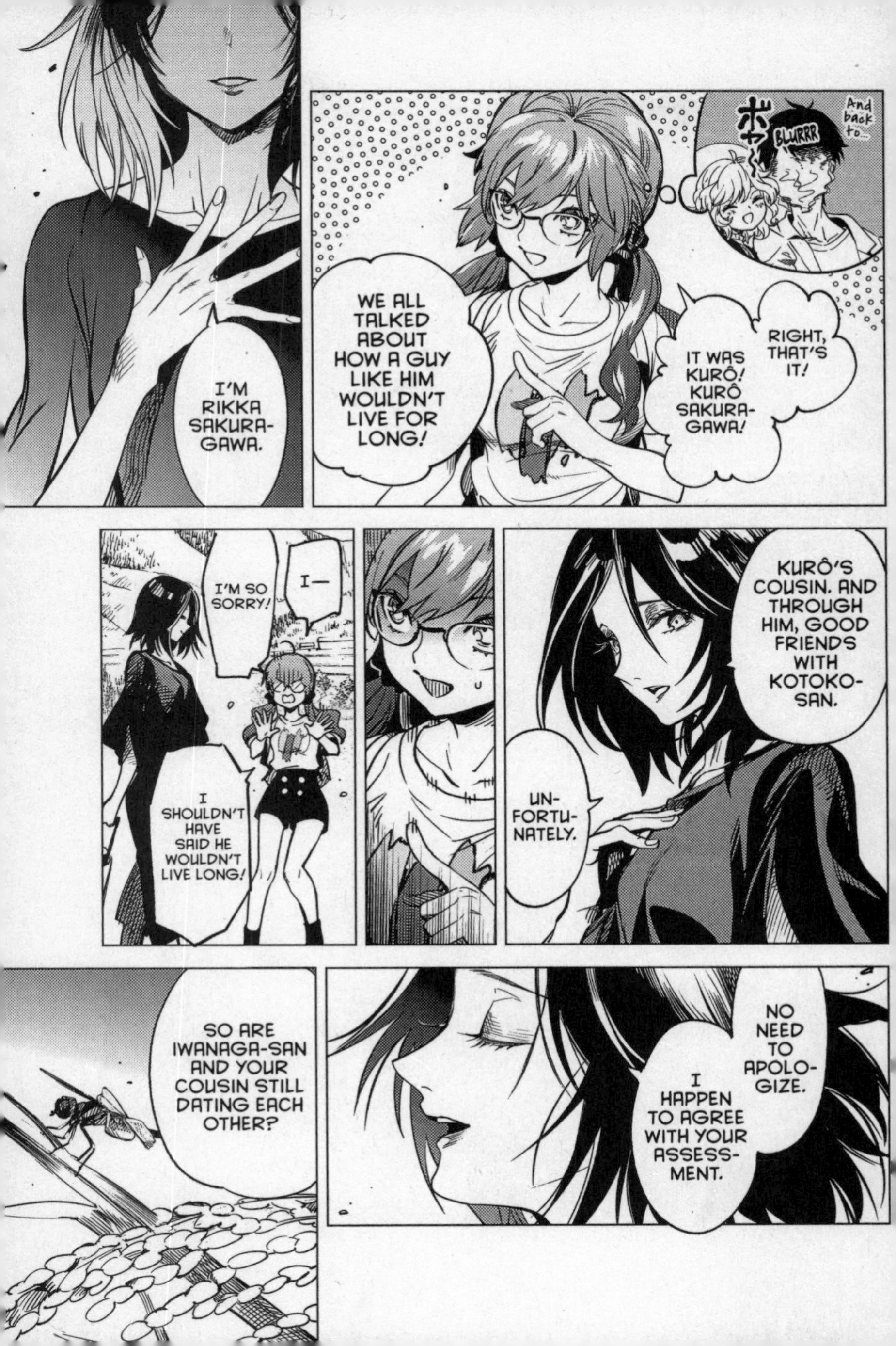
ボヤ～
BLURRR
And back to...
RIGHT, THAT'S IT!
IT WAS KURÔ! KURÔ SAKURAGAWA!
WE ALL TALKED ABOUT HOW A GUY LIKE HIM WOULDN'T LIVE FOR LONG!
I'M RIKKA SAKURAGAWA.
KURÔ'S COUSIN. AND THROUGH HIM, GOOD FRIENDS WITH KOTOKO-SAN.
UNFORTUNATELY.
I—
I'M SO SORRY!
I SHOULDN'T HAVE SAID HE WOULDN'T LIVE LONG!
NO NEED TO APOLOGIZE.
I HAPPEN TO AGREE WITH YOUR ASSESSMENT.
SO ARE IWANAGA-SAN AND YOUR COUSIN STILL DATING EACH OTHER?

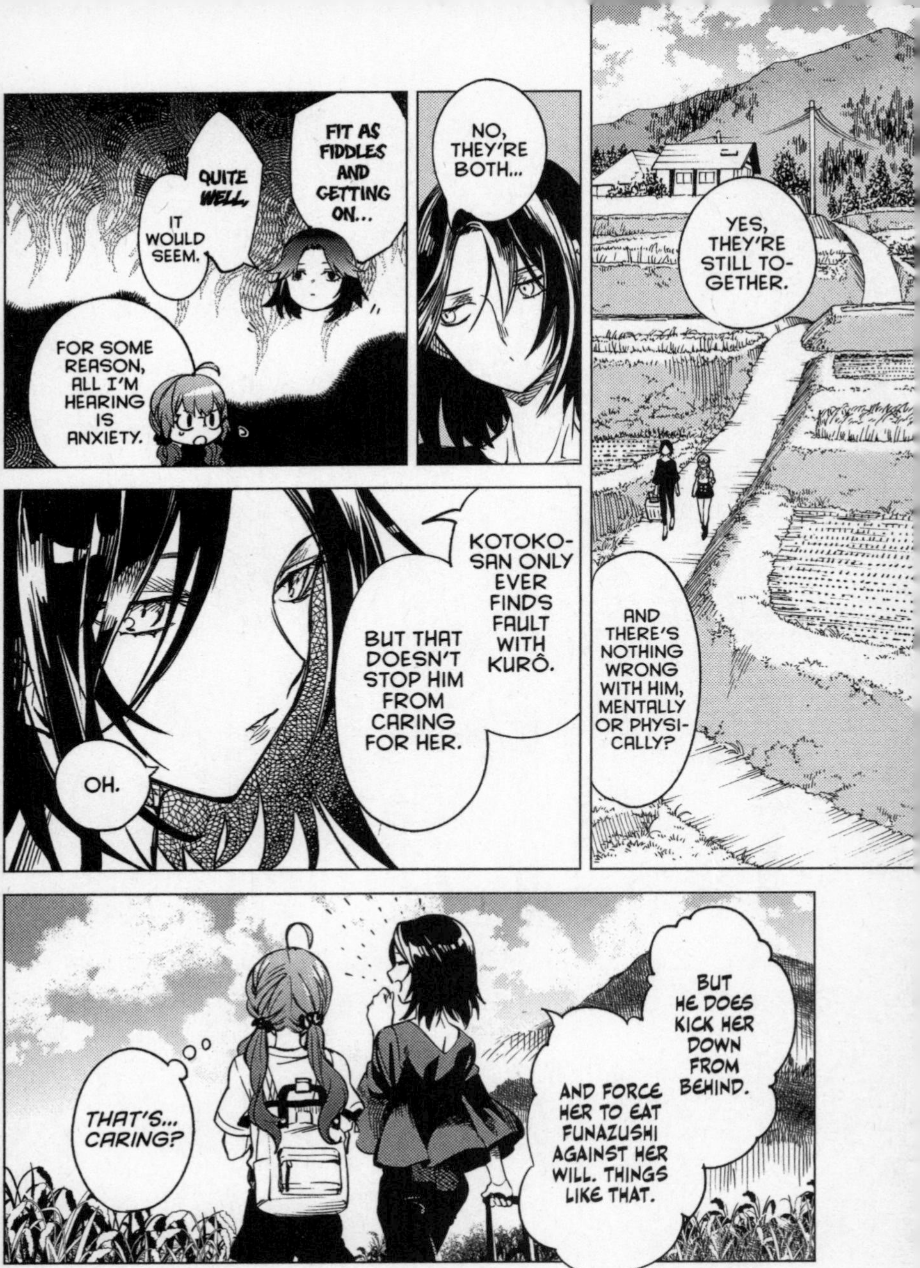

YES, THEY'RE STILL TO-GETHER.
AND THERE'S NOTHING WRONG WITH HIM, MENTALLY OR PHYSI-CALLY?
NO, THEY'RE BOTH...
FIT AS FIDDLES AND GETTING ON...
QUITE WELL, IT WOULD SEEM.
FOR SOME REASON, ALL I'M HEARING IS ANXIETY.
KOTOKO-SAN ONLY EVER FINDS FAULT WITH KURÔ.
BUT THAT DOESN'T STOP HIM FROM CARING FOR HER.
OH.
BUT HE DOES KICK HER DOWN FROM BEHIND.
AND FORCE HER TO EAT FUNAZUSHI AGAINST HER WILL. THINGS LIKE THAT.
THAT'S... CARING?

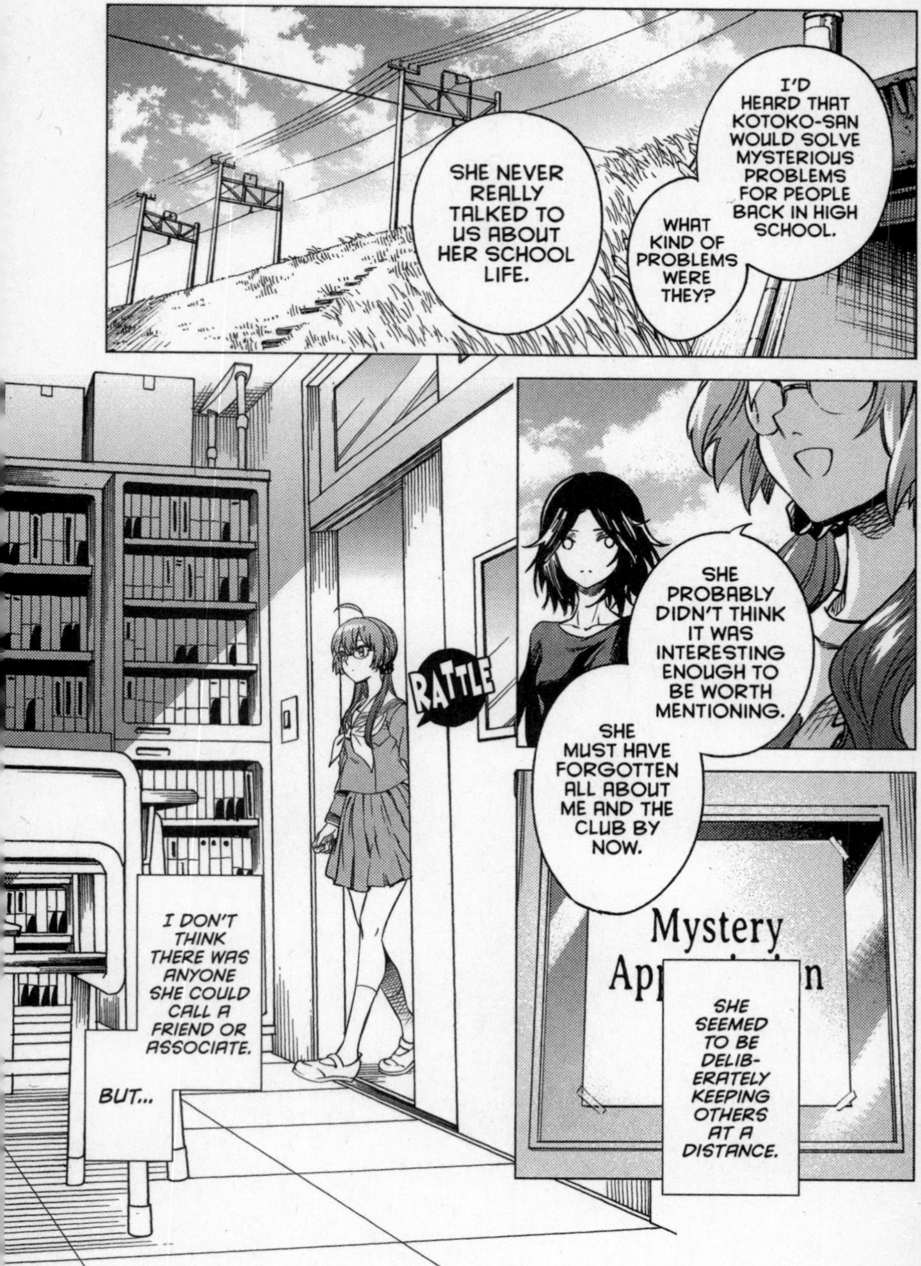
I'D HEARD THAT KOTOKO-SAN WOULD SOLVE MYSTERIOUS PROBLEMS FOR PEOPLE BACK IN HIGH SCHOOL.
WHAT KIND OF PROBLEMS WERE THEY?
SHE NEVER REALLY TALKED TO US ABOUT HER SCHOOL LIFE.
SHE PROBABLY DIDN'T THINK IT WAS INTERESTING ENOUGH TO BE WORTH MENTIONING.
SHE MUST HAVE FORGOTTEN ALL ABOUT ME AND THE CLUB BY NOW.
Mystery
SHE SEEMED TO BE DELIB-ERATELY KEEPING OTHERS AT A DISTANCE.
RATTLE
I DON'T THINK THERE WAS ANYONE SHE COULD CALL A FRIEND OR ASSOCIATE.
BUT...

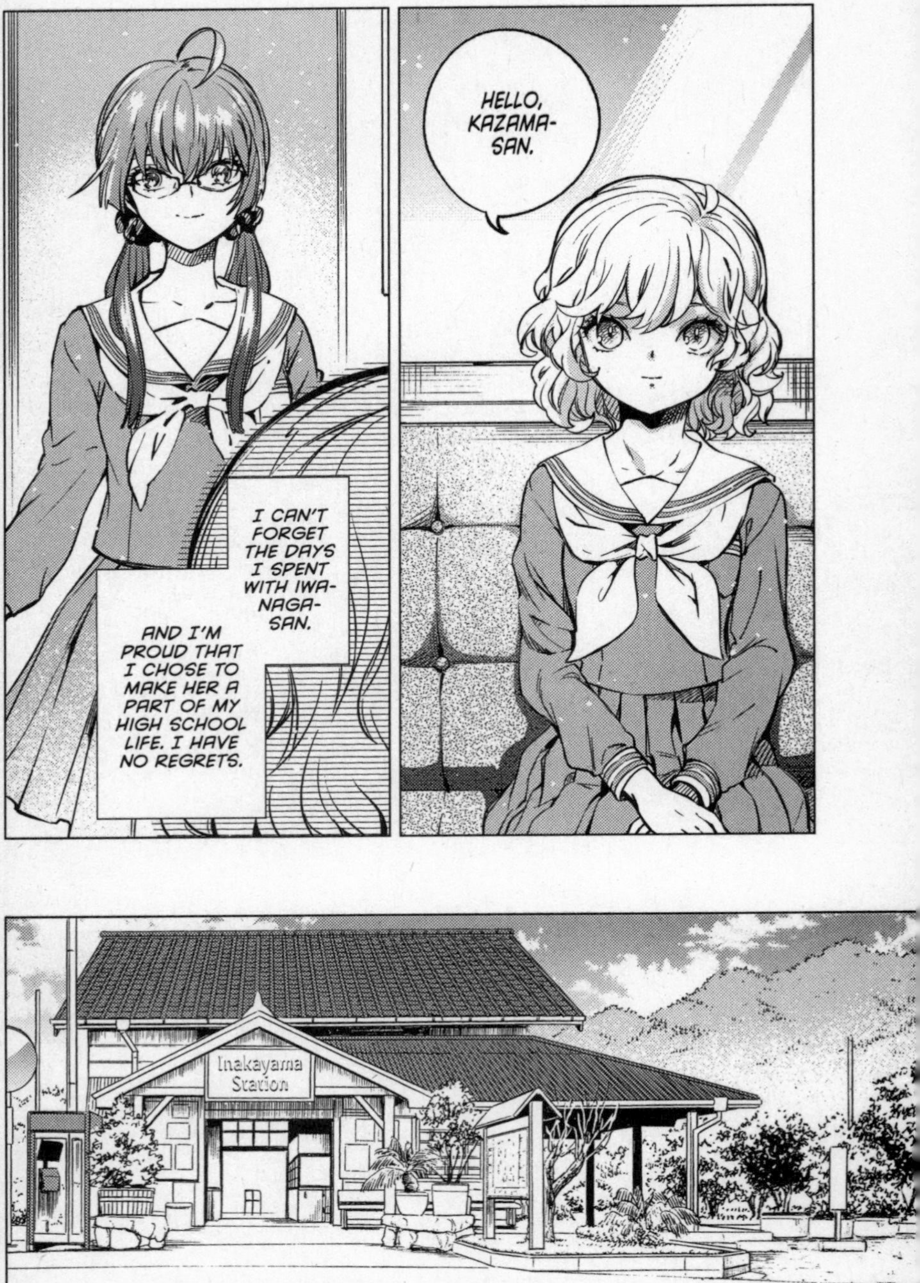
HELLO, KAZAMA-SAN.
I CAN'T FORGET THE DAYS I SPENT WITH IWA-NAGA-SAN.
AND I'M PROUD THAT I CHOSE TO MAKE HER A PART OF MY HIGH SCHOOL LIFE. I HAVE NO REGRETS.
Inakayama Station

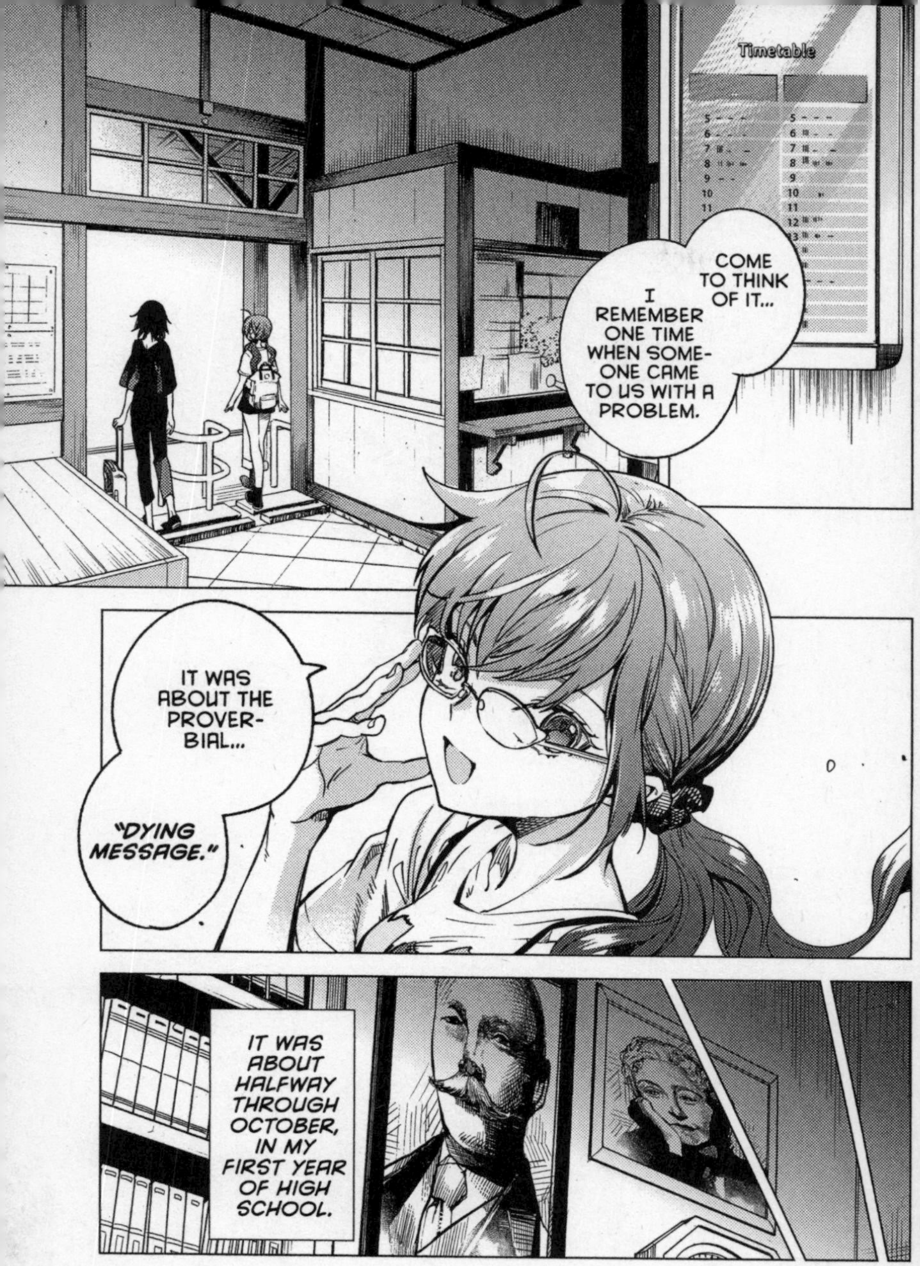
Timetable
COME TO THINK OF IT...
I REMEMBER ONE TIME WHEN SOME-ONE CAME TO US WITH A PROBLEM.
IT WAS ABOUT THE PROVER-BIAL...
“DYING MESSAGE.”
IT WAS ABOUT HALFWAY THROUGH OCTOBER, IN MY FIRST YEAR OF HIGH SCHOOL.

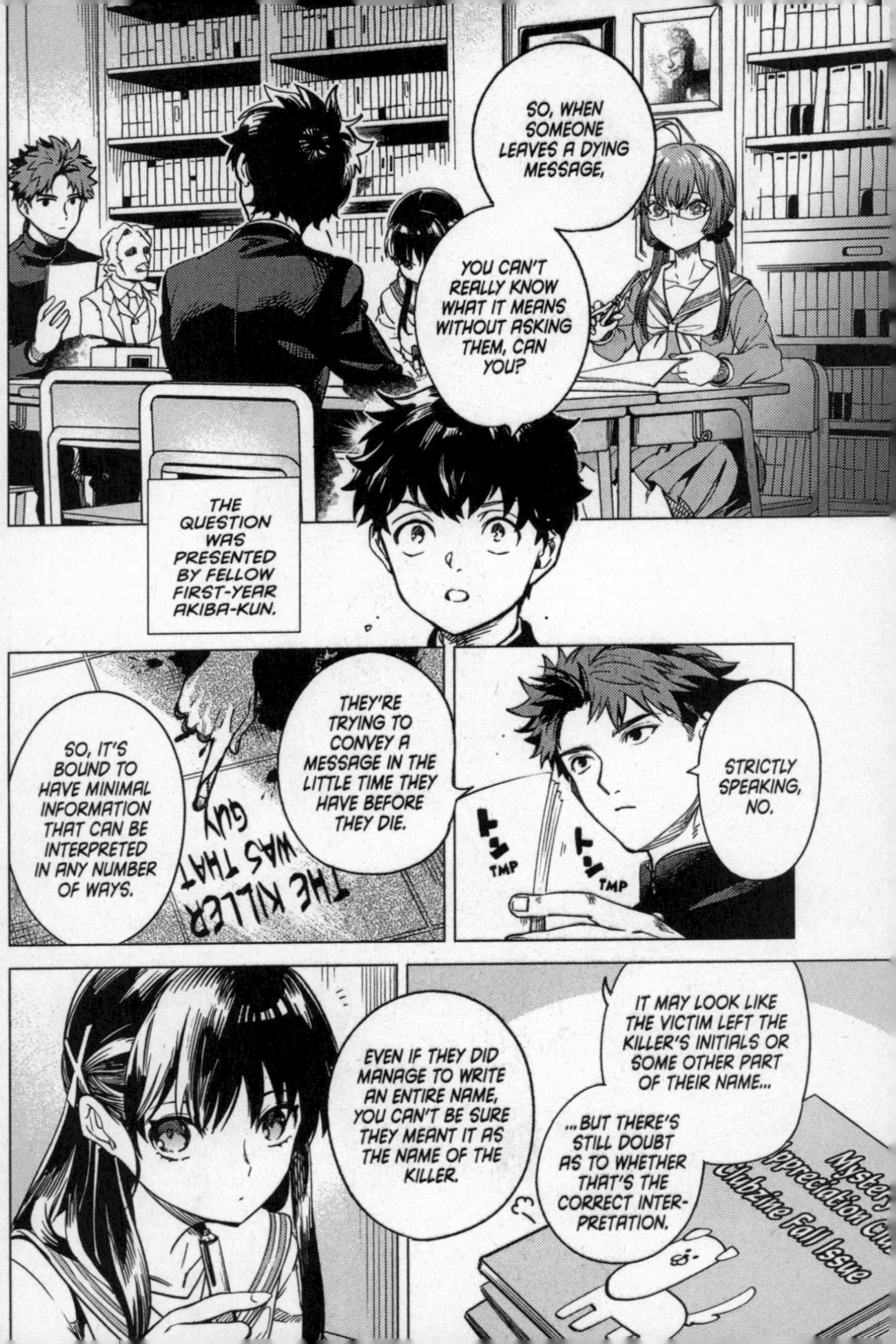
SO, WHEN SOMEONE LEAVES A DYING MESSAGE,
YOU CAN'T REALLY KNOW WHAT IT MEANS WITHOUT ASKING THEM, CAN YOU?
THE QUESTION WAS PRESENTED BY FELLOW FIRST-YEAR AKIBA-KUN.
STRICTLY SPEAKING, NO.
TMP
TMP
THEY'RE TRYING TO CONVEY A MESSAGE IN THE LITTLE TIME THEY HAVE BEFORE THEY DIE.
SO, IT'S BOUND TO HAVE MINIMAL INFORMATION THAT CAN BE INTERPRETED IN ANY NUMBER OF WAYS.
THE KILLER WAS THAT GUY
IT MAY LOOK LIKE THE VICTIM LEFT THE KILLER'S INITIALS OR SOME OTHER PART OF THEIR NAME...
...BUT THERE'S STILL DOUBT AS TO WHETHER THAT'S THE CORRECT INTER-PRETATION.
Mystery Appreciation Clu
Clubzine Fall Issue
EVEN IF THEY DID MANAGE TO WRITE AN ENTIRE NAME, YOU CAN'T BE SURE THEY MEANT IT AS THE NAME OF THE KILLER.

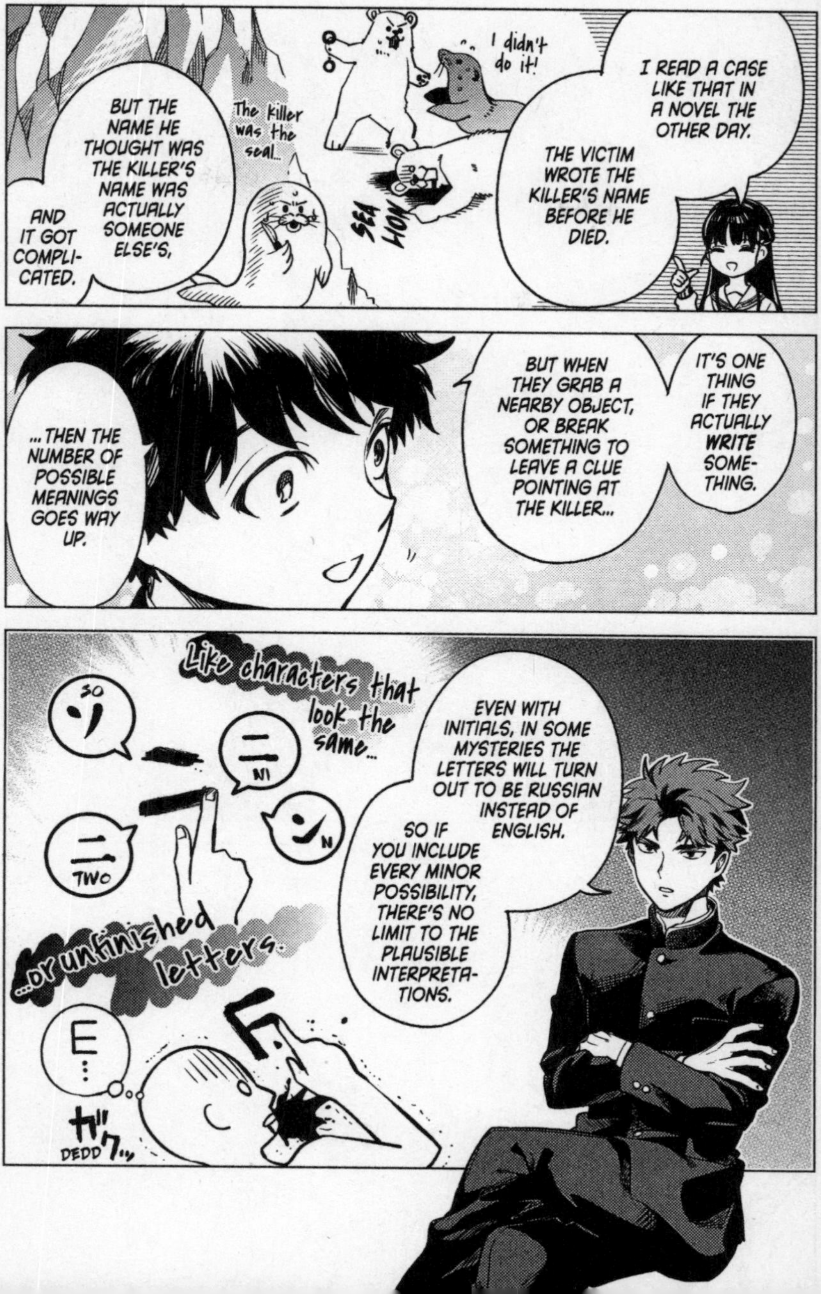
I READ A CASE LIKE THAT IN A NOVEL THE OTHER DAY.
THE VICTIM WROTE THE KILLER'S NAME BEFORE HE DIED.
I didn't do it!
SEA HOW
The killer was the seal...
BUT THE NAME HE THOUGHT WAS THE KILLER'S NAME WAS ACTUALLY SOMEONE ELSE'S,
AND IT GOT COMPLICATED.
IT'S ONE THING IF THEY ACTUALLY WRITE SOMETHING.
BUT WHEN THEY GRAB A NEARBY OBJECT, OR BREAK SOMETHING TO LEAVE A CLUE POINTING AT THE KILLER...
...THEN THE NUMBER OF POSSIBLE MEANINGS GOES WAY UP.
EVEN WITH INITIALS, IN SOME MYSTERIES THE LETTERS WILL TURN OUT TO BE RUSSIAN INSTEAD OF ENGLISH.
SO IF YOU INCLUDE EVERY MINOR POSSIBILITY, THERE'S NO LIMIT TO THE PLAUSIBLE INTERPRETATIONS.
Like characters that look the same...
ソ SO
ニ NI
ン N
二 TWO
...or unfinished letters...
E...
DEDD

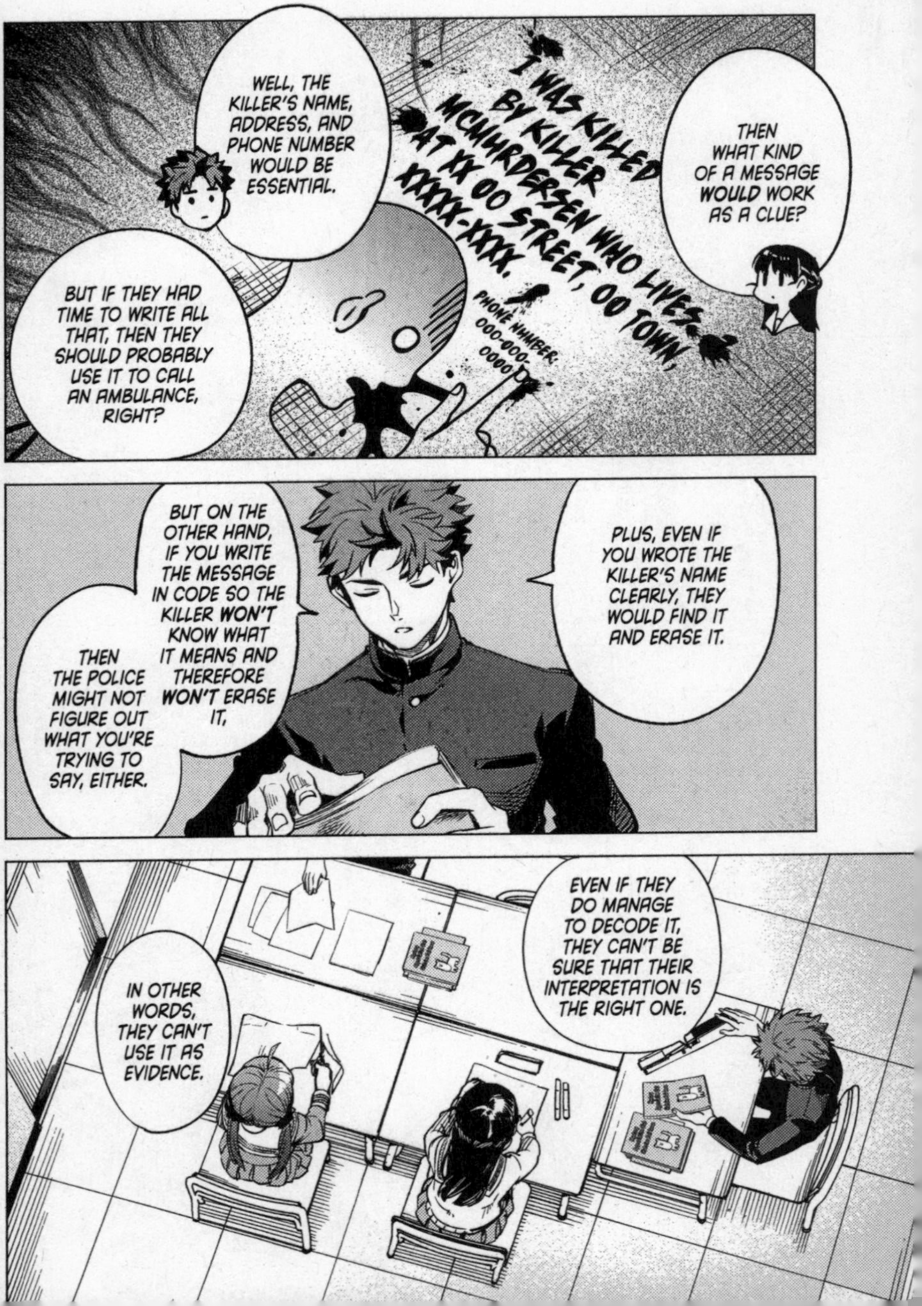
THEN WHAT KIND OF A MESSAGE WOULD WORK AS A CLUE?
I WAS KILLED BY KILLER MCMURDERSEN WHO LIVES AT XX OO STREET, OO TOWN, XXXXX-XXXX.
PHONE NUMBER: 000-000-0000
WELL, THE KILLER'S NAME, ADDRESS, AND PHONE NUMBER WOULD BE ESSENTIAL.
BUT IF THEY HAD TIME TO WRITE ALL THAT, THEN THEY SHOULD PROBABLY USE IT TO CALL AN AMBULANCE, RIGHT?
PLUS, EVEN IF YOU WROTE THE KILLER'S NAME CLEARLY, THEY WOULD FIND IT AND ERASE IT.
BUT ON THE OTHER HAND, IF YOU WRITE THE MESSAGE IN CODE SO THE KILLER WON'T KNOW WHAT IT MEANS AND THEREFORE WON'T ERASE IT,
THEN THE POLICE MIGHT NOT FIGURE OUT WHAT YOU'RE TRYING TO SAY, EITHER.
EVEN IF THEY DO MANAGE TO DECODE IT, THEY CAN'T BE SURE THAT THEIR INTERPRETATION IS THE RIGHT ONE.
IN OTHER WORDS, THEY CAN'T USE IT AS EVIDENCE.

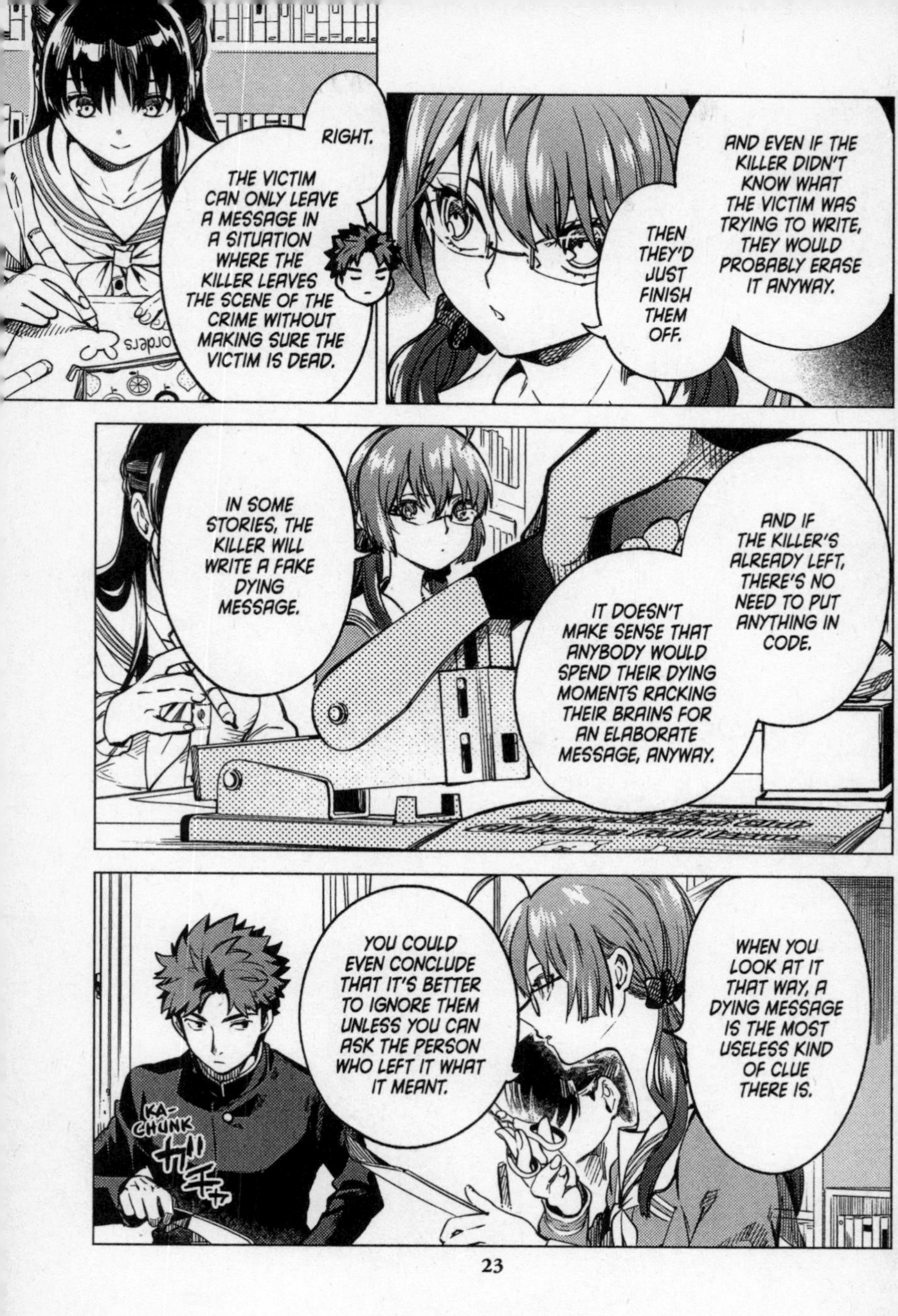
AND EVEN IF THE KILLER DIDN'T KNOW WHAT THE VICTIM WAS TRYING TO WRITE, THEY WOULD PROBABLY ERASE IT ANYWAY.
THEN THEY'D JUST FINISH THEM OFF.
RIGHT.
THE VICTIM CAN ONLY LEAVE A MESSAGE IN A SITUATION WHERE THE KILLER LEAVES THE SCENE OF THE CRIME WITHOUT MAKING SURE THE VICTIM IS DEAD.
AND IF THE KILLER'S ALREADY LEFT, THERE'S NO NEED TO PUT ANYTHING IN CODE.
IT DOESN'T MAKE SENSE THAT ANYBODY WOULD SPEND THEIR DYING MOMENTS RACKING THEIR BRAINS FOR AN ELABORATE MESSAGE, ANYWAY.
IN SOME STORIES, THE KILLER WILL WRITE A FAKE DYING MESSAGE.
WHEN YOU LOOK AT IT THAT WAY, A DYING MESSAGE IS THE MOST USELESS KIND OF CLUE THERE IS.
YOU COULD EVEN CONCLUDE THAT IT'S BETTER TO IGNORE THEM UNLESS YOU CAN ASK THE PERSON WHO LEFT IT WHAT IT MEANT.
KA-CHUNK

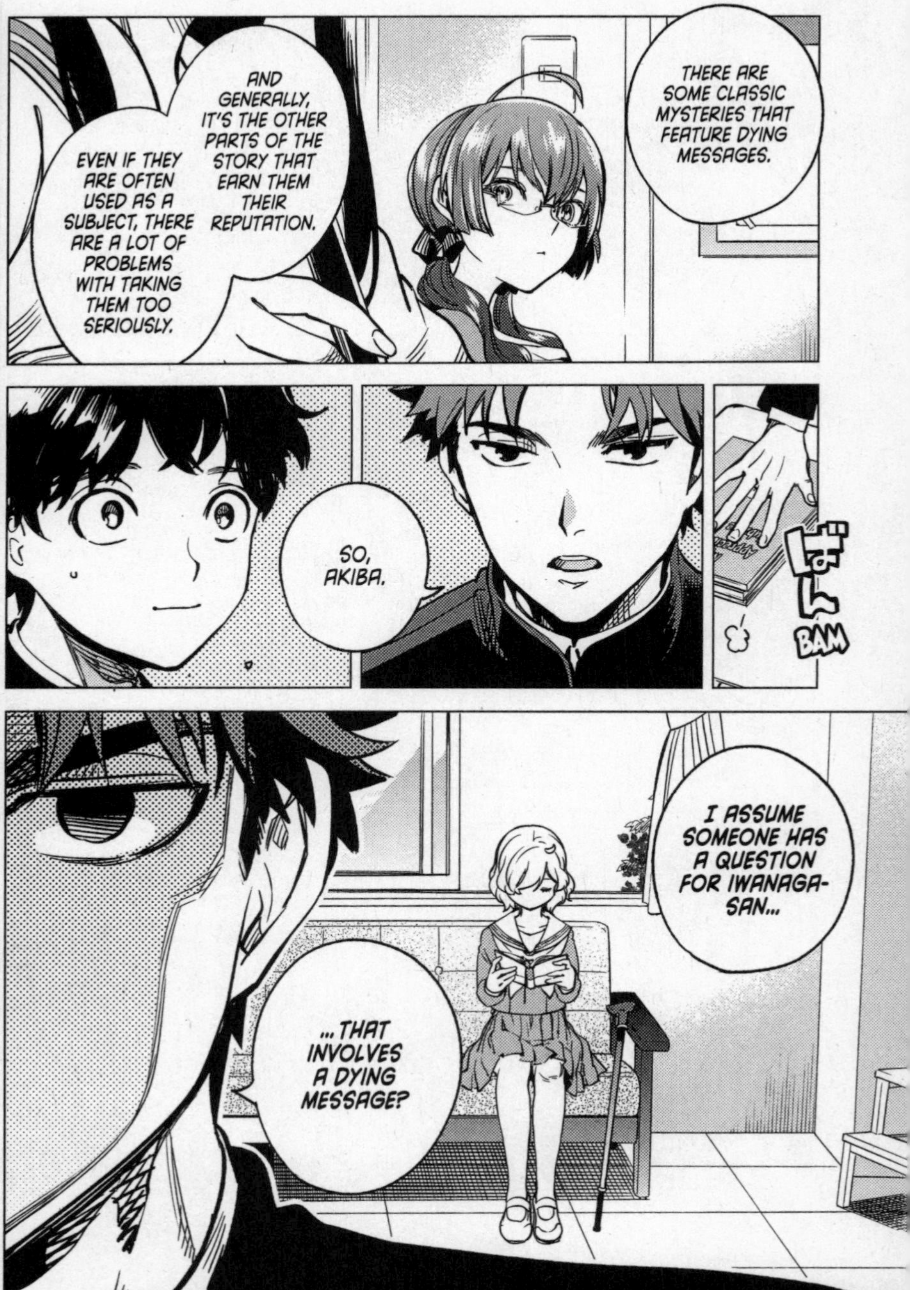
THERE ARE SOME CLASSIC MYSTERIES THAT FEATURE DYING MESSAGES.
EVEN IF THEY ARE OFTEN USED AS A SUBJECT, THERE ARE A LOT OF PROBLEMS WITH TAKING THEM TOO SERIOUSLY.
AND GENERALLY, IT'S THE OTHER PARTS OF THE STORY THAT EARN THEM THEIR REPUTATION.
ぼん
BAM
SO, AKIBA.
I ASSUME SOMEONE HAS A QUESTION FOR IWANAGA-SAN...
...THAT INVOLVES A DYING MESSAGE?

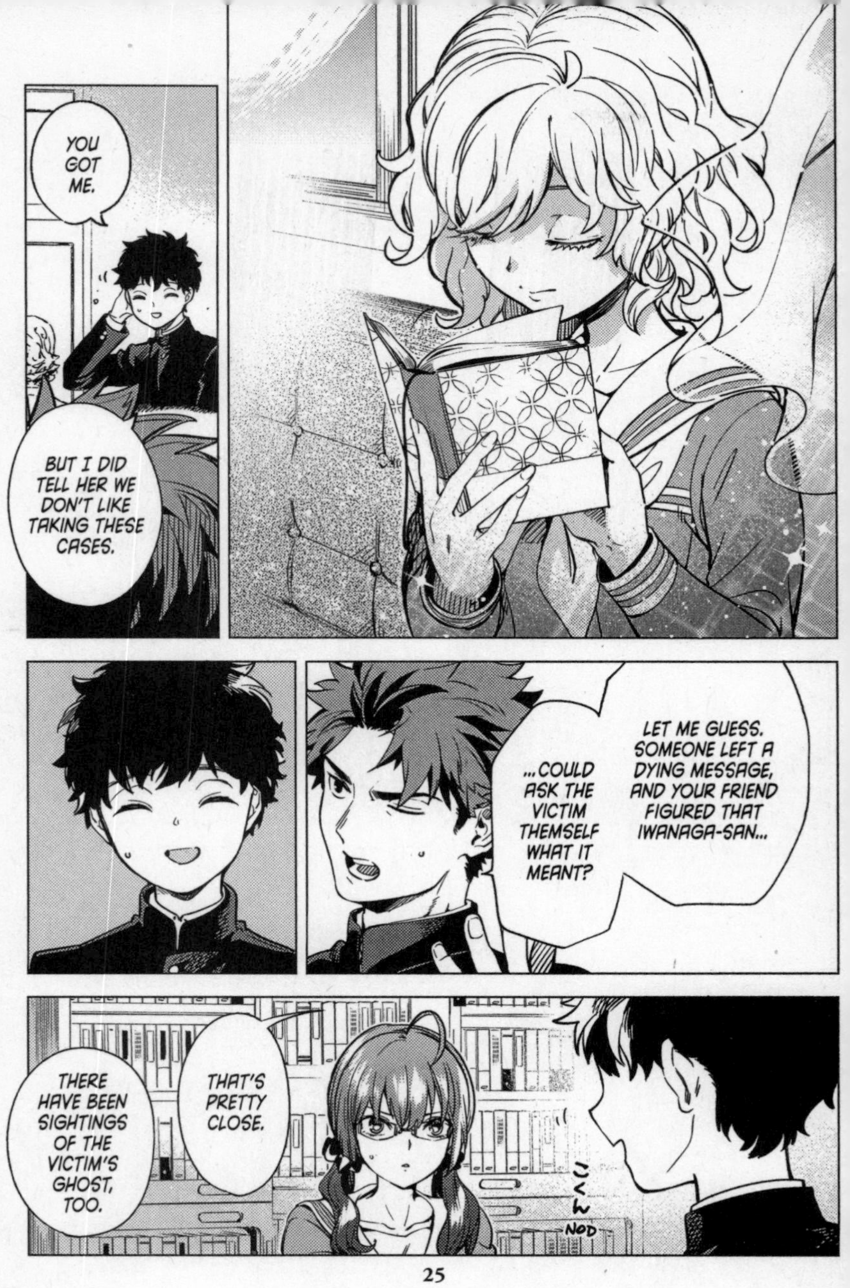
YOU GOT ME.
BUT I DID TELL HER WE DON'T LIKE TAKING THESE CASES.
LET ME GUESS. SOMEONE LEFT A DYING MESSAGE, AND YOUR FRIEND FIGURED THAT IWANAGA-SAN...
...COULD ASK THE VICTIM THEMSELF WHAT IT MEANT?
THAT'S PRETTY CLOSE.
THERE HAVE BEEN SIGHTINGS OF THE VICTIM'S GHOST, TOO.
こくん
NOD

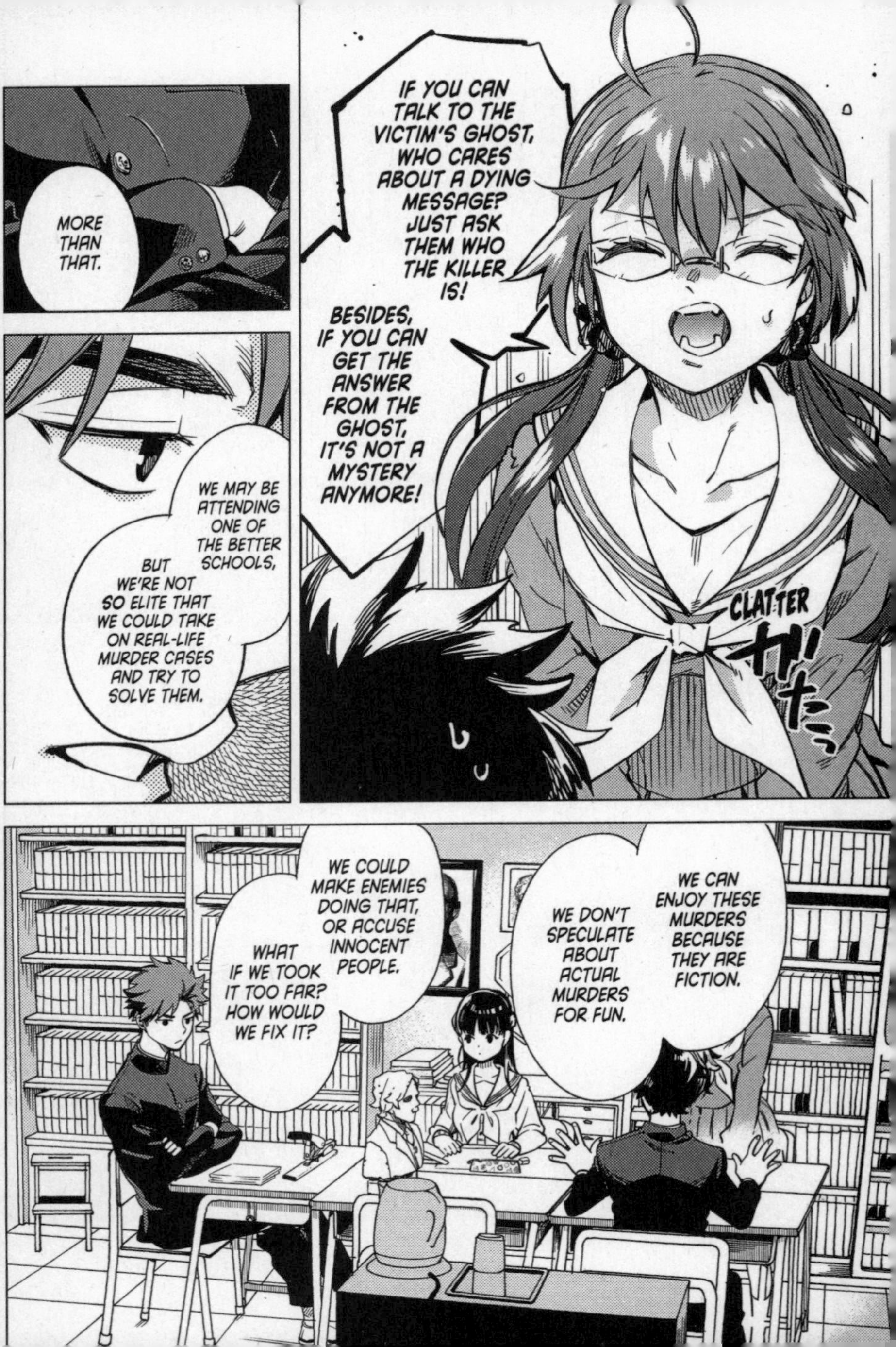
IF YOU CAN TALK TO THE VICTIM'S GHOST, WHO CARES ABOUT A DYING MESSAGE? JUST ASK THEM WHO THE KILLER IS!
BESIDES, IF YOU CAN GET THE ANSWER FROM THE GHOST, IT'S NOT A MYSTERY ANYMORE!
CLATTER
MORE THAN THAT.
WE MAY BE ATTENDING ONE OF THE BETTER SCHOOLS,
BUT WE'RE NOT SO ELITE THAT WE COULD TAKE ON REAL-LIFE MURDER CASES AND TRY TO SOLVE THEM.
WE CAN ENJOY THESE MURDERS BECAUSE THEY ARE FICTION.
WE DON'T SPECULATE ABOUT ACTUAL MURDERS FOR FUN.
WE COULD MAKE ENEMIES DOING THAT, OR ACCUSE INNOCENT PEOPLE.
WHAT IF WE TOOK IT TOO FAR? HOW WOULD WE FIX IT?

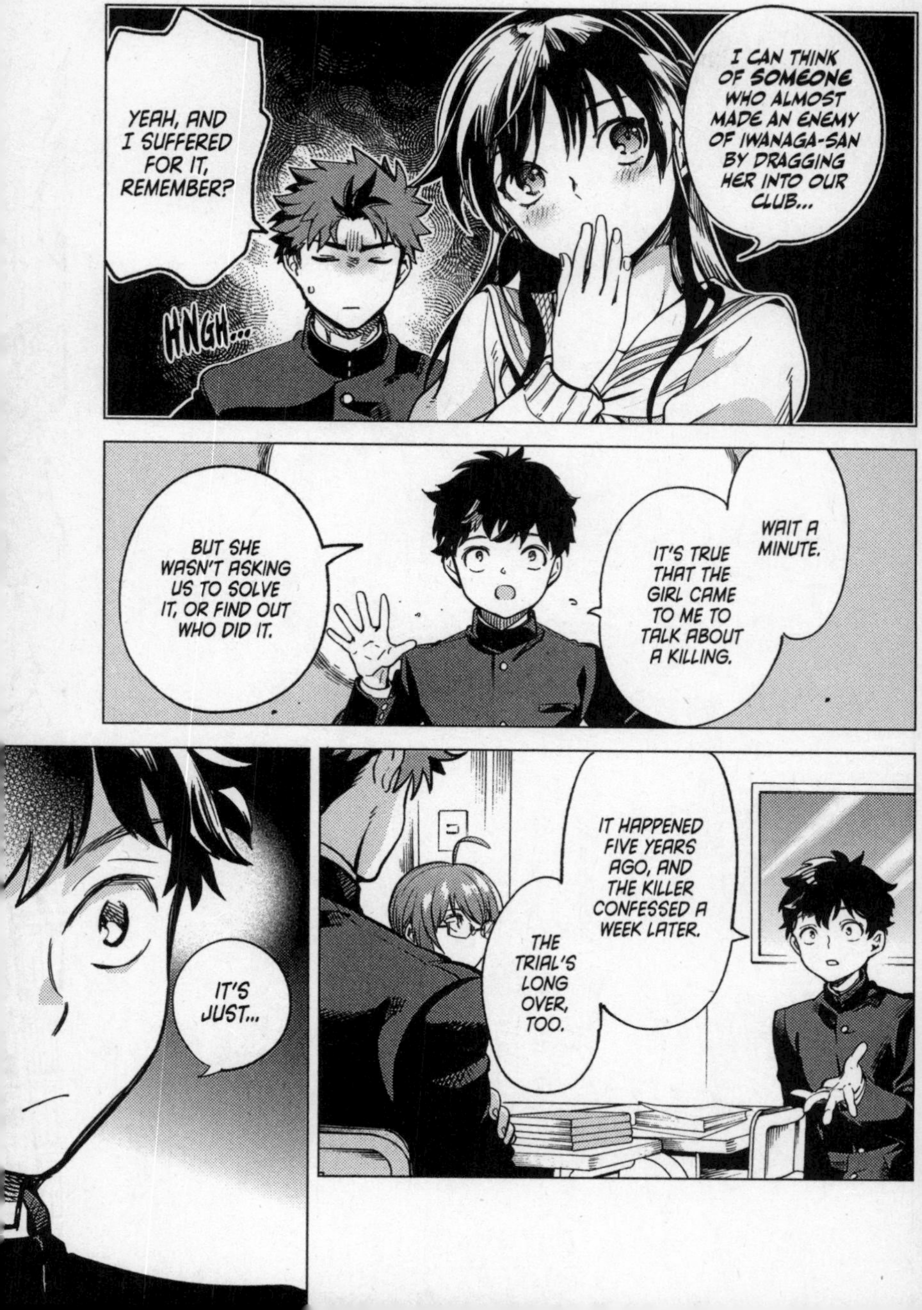
I CAN THINK OF SOMEONE WHO ALMOST MADE AN ENEMY OF IWANAGA-SAN BY DRAGGING HER INTO OUR CLUB...
YEAH, AND I SUFFERED FOR IT, REMEMBER?
HNGH...
WAIT A MINUTE.
IT'S TRUE THAT THE GIRL CAME TO ME TO TALK ABOUT A KILLING.
BUT SHE WASN'T ASKING US TO SOLVE IT, OR FIND OUT WHO DID IT.
IT HAPPENED FIVE YEARS AGO, AND THE KILLER CONFESSED A WEEK LATER.
THE TRIAL'S LONG OVER, TOO.
IT'S JUST...

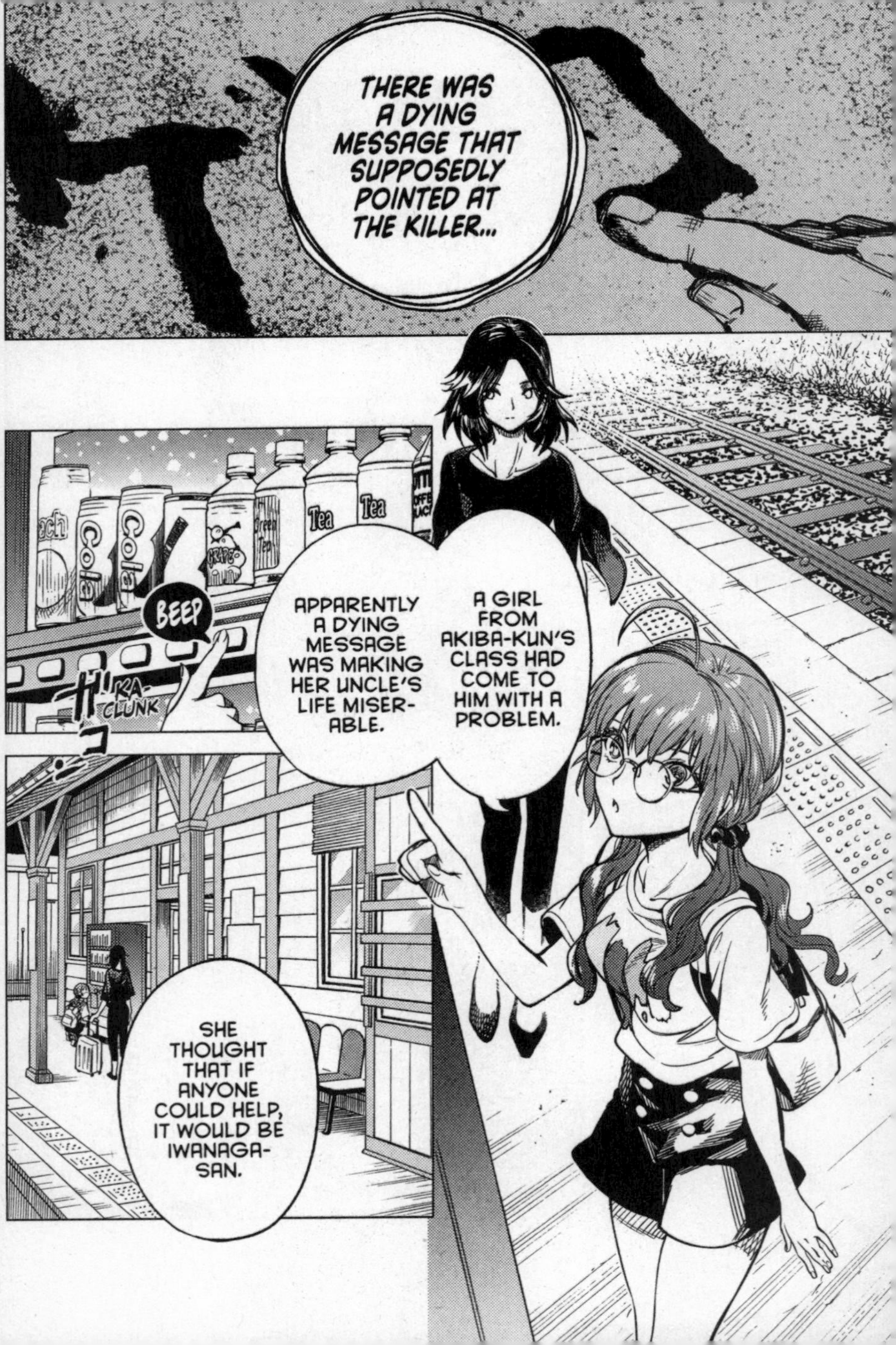
THERE WAS A DYING MESSAGE THAT SUPPOSEDLY POINTED AT THE KILLER...
A GIRL FROM AKIBA-KUN'S CLASS HAD COME TO HIM WITH A PROBLEM.
APPARENTLY A DYING MESSAGE WAS MAKING HER UNCLE'S LIFE MISER-ABLE.
SHE THOUGHT THAT IF ANYONE COULD HELP, IT WOULD BE IWANAGA-SAN.
BEEP
KA-CLUNK

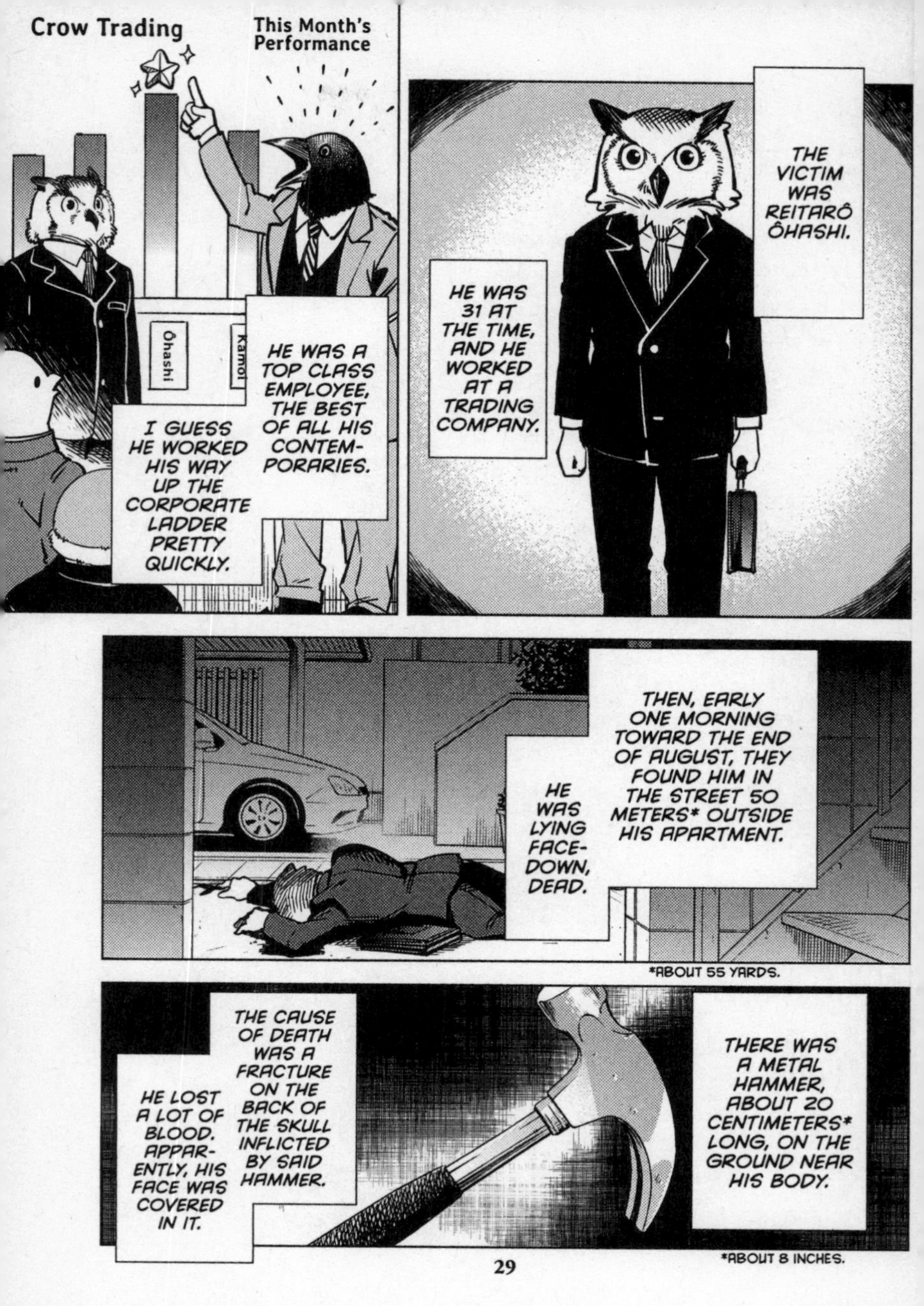
THE VICTIM WAS REITARÔ ÔHASHI.
HE WAS 31 AT THE TIME, AND HE WORKED AT A TRADING COMPANY.
Crow Trading
This Month's Performance
Ôhashi
Kamoi
HE WAS A TOP CLASS EMPLOYEE, THE BEST OF ALL HIS CONTEMPORARIES.
I GUESS HE WORKED HIS WAY UP THE CORPORATE LADDER PRETTY QUICKLY.
THEN, EARLY ONE MORNING TOWARD THE END OF AUGUST, THEY FOUND HIM IN THE STREET 50 METERS* OUTSIDE HIS APARTMENT.
HE WAS LYING FACE-DOWN, DEAD.
*ABOUT 55 YARDS.
THERE WAS A METAL HAMMER, ABOUT 20 CENTIMETERS* LONG, ON THE GROUND NEAR HIS BODY.
THE CAUSE OF DEATH WAS A FRACTURE ON THE BACK OF THE SKULL INFLICTED BY SAID HAMMER.
HE LOST A LOT OF BLOOD. APPARENTLY, HIS FACE WAS COVERED IN IT.
*ABOUT 8 INCHES.

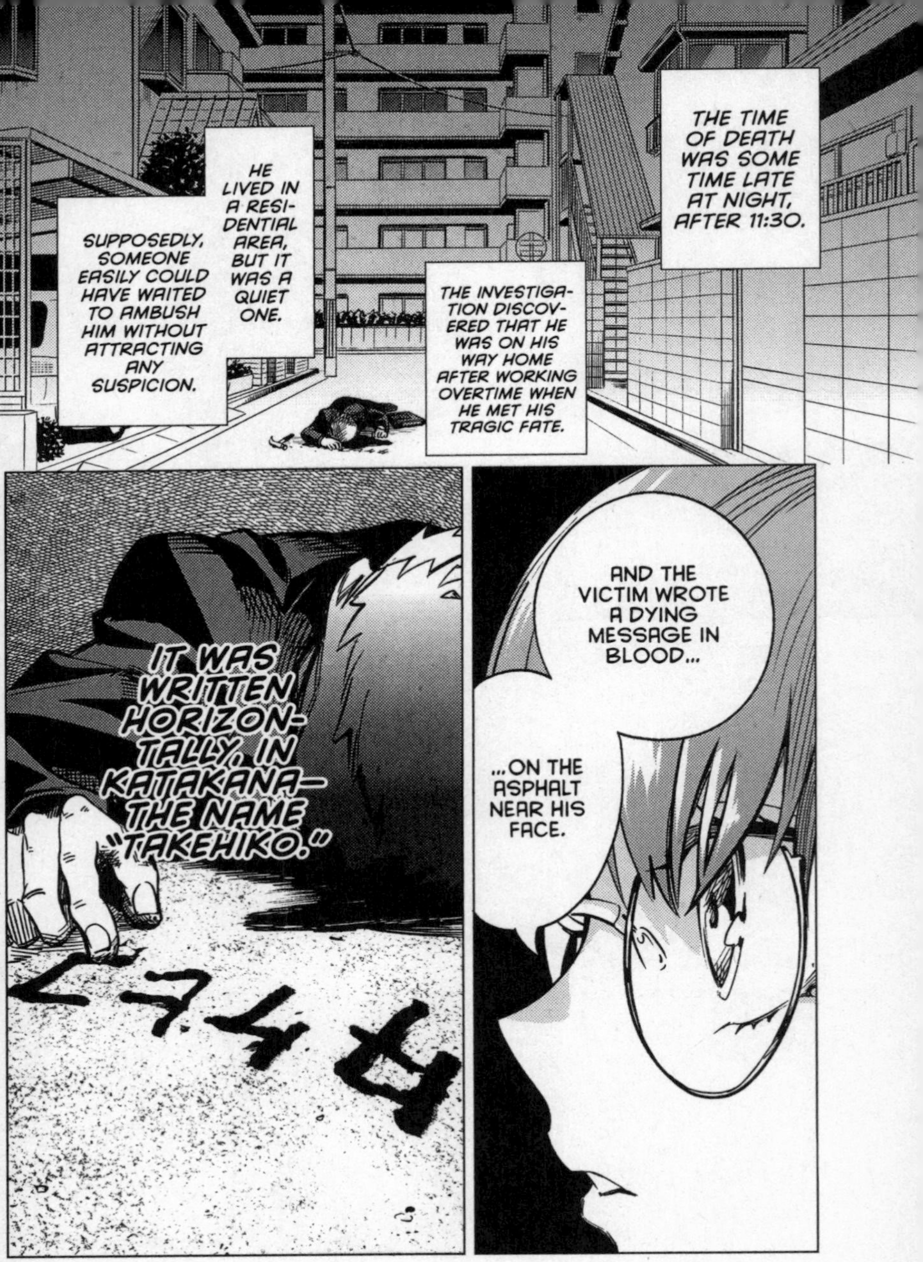
THE TIME OF DEATH WAS SOME TIME LATE AT NIGHT, AFTER 11:30.
THE INVESTIGATION DISCOVERED THAT HE WAS ON HIS WAY HOME AFTER WORKING OVERTIME WHEN HE MET HIS TRAGIC FATE.
HE LIVED IN A RESIDENTIAL AREA, BUT IT WAS A QUIET ONE.
SUPPOSEDLY, SOMEONE EASILY COULD HAVE WAITED TO AMBUSH HIM WITHOUT ATTRACTING ANY SUSPICION.
AND THE VICTIM WROTE A DYING MESSAGE IN BLOOD...
...ON THE ASPHALT NEAR HIS FACE.
IT WAS WRITTEN HORIZONTALLY, IN KATAKANA—THE NAME "TAKEHIKO."

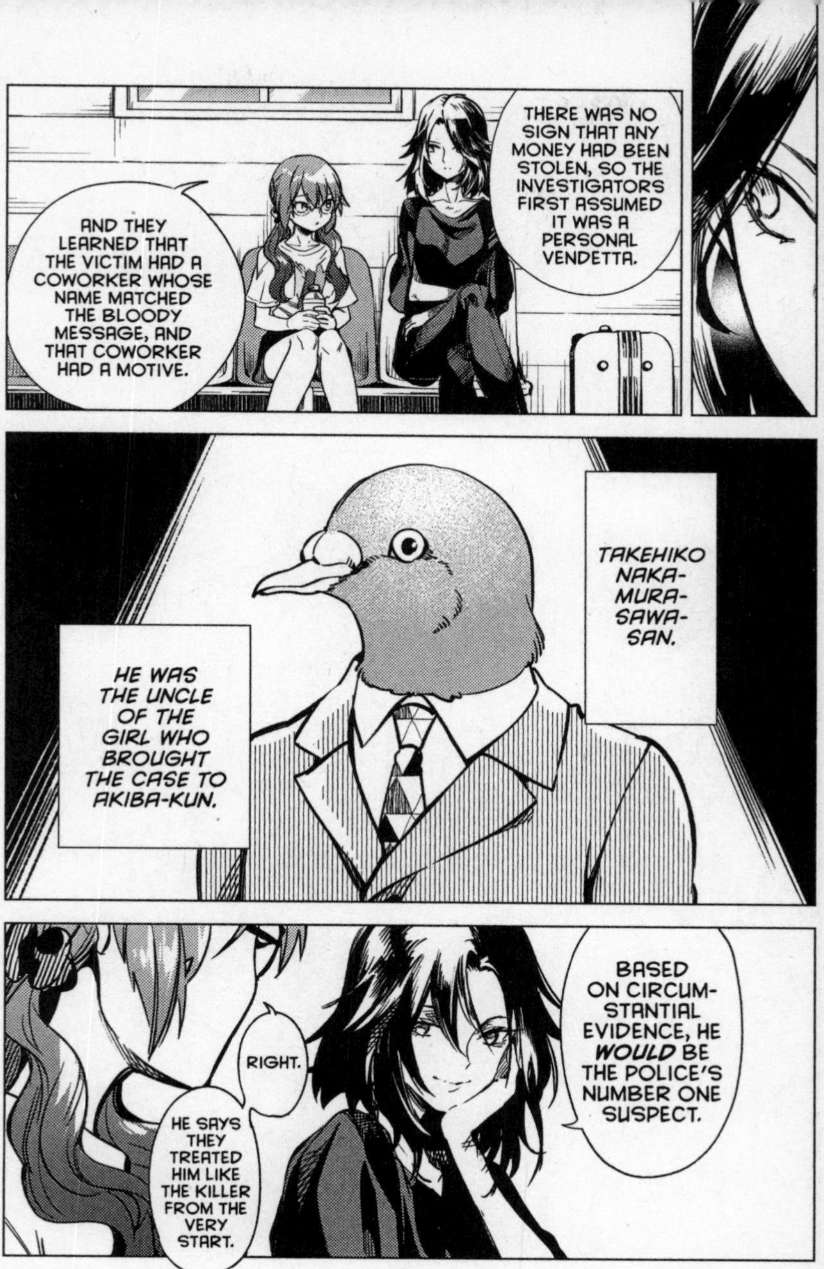
THERE WAS NO SIGN THAT ANY MONEY HAD BEEN STOLEN, SO THE INVESTIGATORS FIRST ASSUMED IT WAS A PERSONAL VENDETTA.
AND THEY LEARNED THAT THE VICTIM HAD A COWORKER WHOSE NAME MATCHED THE BLOODY MESSAGE, AND THAT COWORKER HAD A MOTIVE.
TAKEHIKO NAKAMURASAWA-SAN.
HE WAS THE UNCLE OF THE GIRL WHO BROUGHT THE CASE TO AKIBA-KUN.
BASED ON CIRCUMSTANTIAL EVIDENCE, HE ***WOULD*** BE THE POLICE'S NUMBER ONE SUSPECT.
RIGHT.
HE SAYS THEY TREATED HIM LIKE THE KILLER FROM THE VERY START.

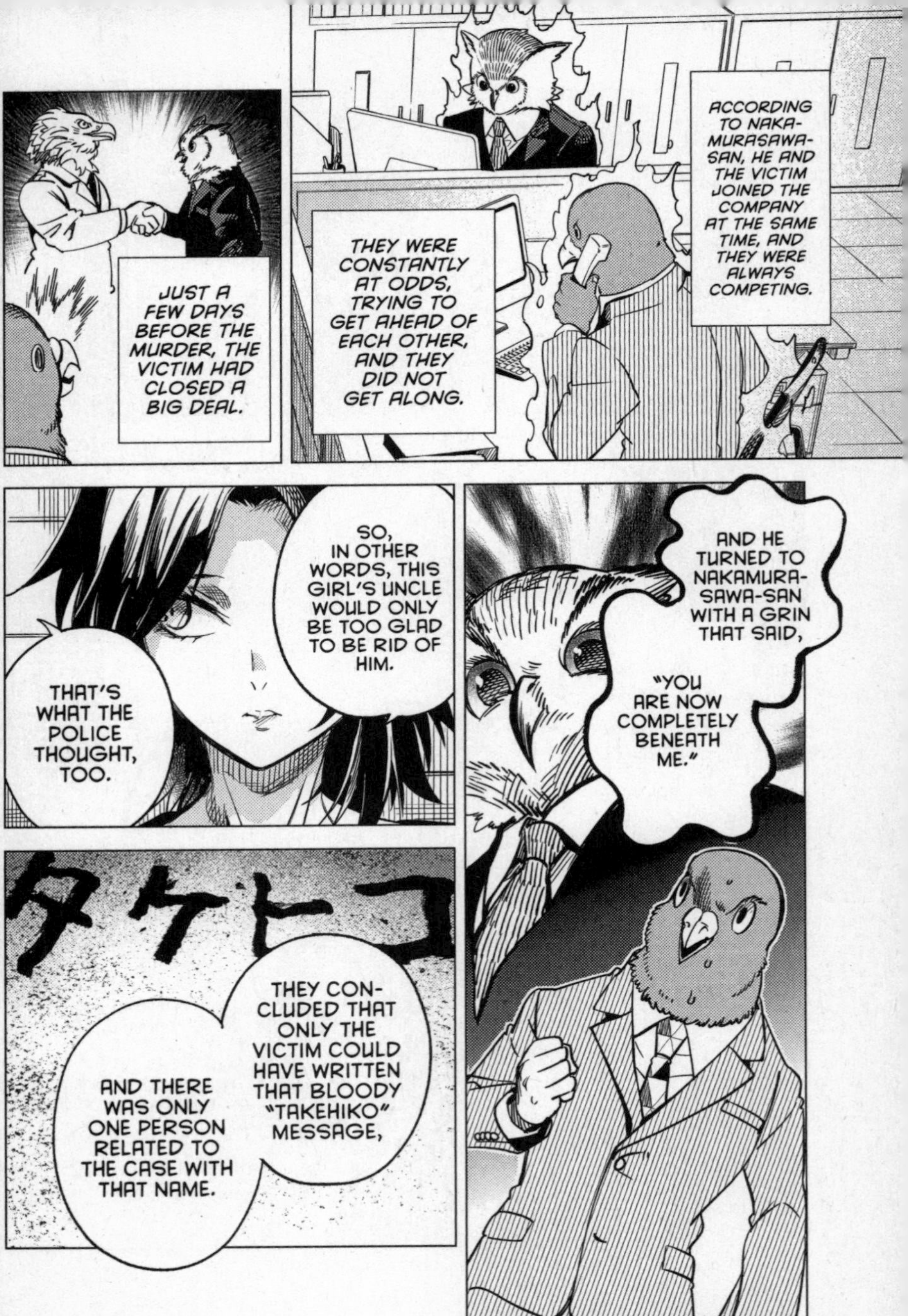
ACCORDING TO NAKAMURASAWA-SAN, HE AND THE VICTIM JOINED THE COMPANY AT THE SAME TIME, AND THEY WERE ALWAYS COMPETING.
THEY WERE CONSTANTLY AT ODDS, TRYING TO GET AHEAD OF EACH OTHER, AND THEY DID NOT GET ALONG.
JUST A FEW DAYS BEFORE THE MURDER, THE VICTIM HAD CLOSED A BIG DEAL.
AND HE TURNED TO NAKAMURASAWA-SAN WITH A GRIN THAT SAID,
"YOU ARE NOW COMPLETELY BENEATH ME."
SO, IN OTHER WORDS, THIS GIRL'S UNCLE WOULD ONLY BE TOO GLAD TO BE RID OF HIM.
THAT'S WHAT THE POLICE THOUGHT, TOO.
タケヒコ
THEY CONCLUDED THAT ONLY THE VICTIM COULD HAVE WRITTEN THAT BLOODY "TAKEHIKO" MESSAGE,
AND THERE WAS ONLY ONE PERSON RELATED TO THE CASE WITH THAT NAME.

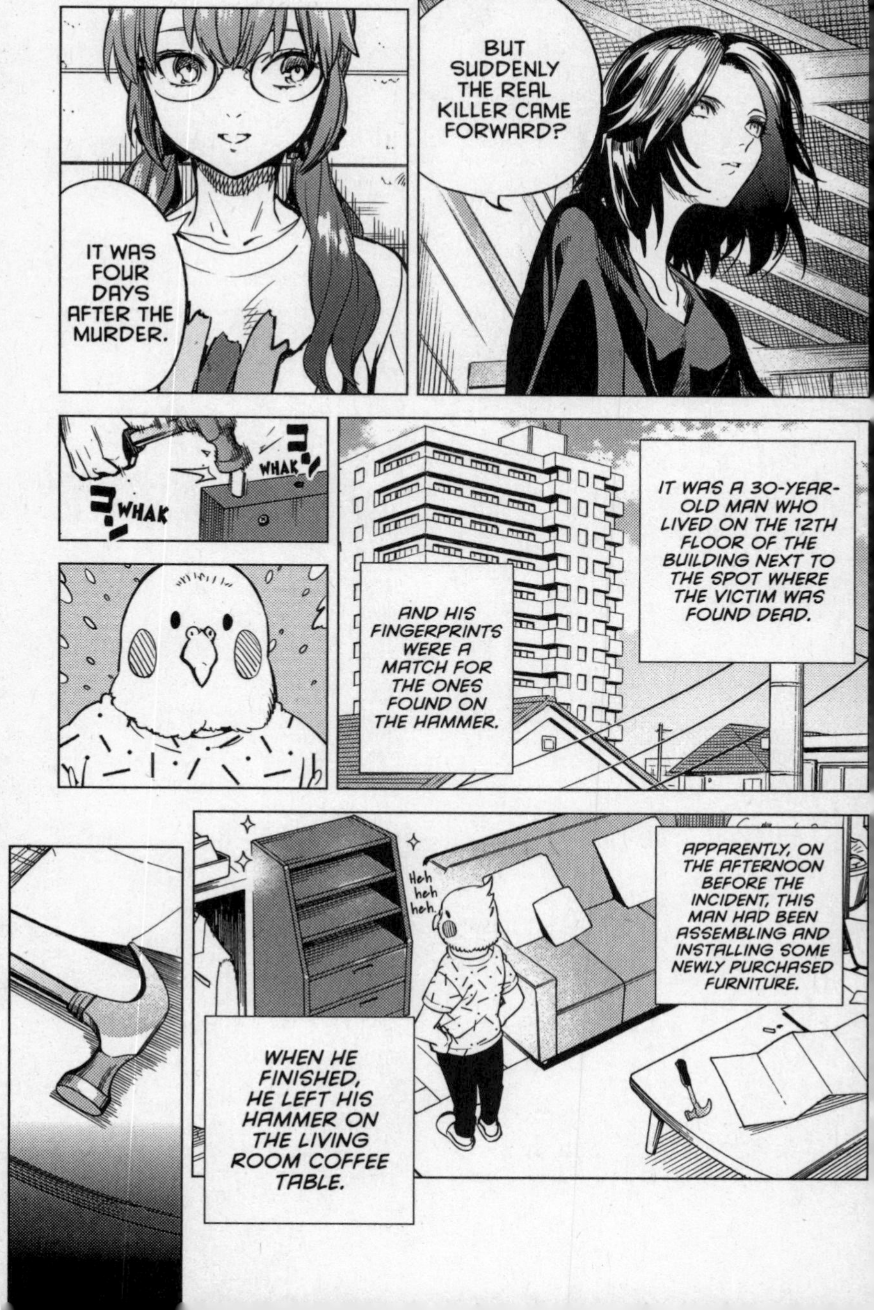
BUT SUDDENLY THE REAL KILLER CAME FORWARD?
IT WAS FOUR DAYS AFTER THE MURDER.
IT WAS A 30-YEAR-OLD MAN WHO LIVED ON THE 12TH FLOOR OF THE BUILDING NEXT TO THE SPOT WHERE THE VICTIM WAS FOUND DEAD.
AND HIS FINGERPRINTS WERE A MATCH FOR THE ONES FOUND ON THE HAMMER.
WHAK
WHAK
APPARENTLY, ON THE AFTERNOON BEFORE THE INCIDENT, THIS MAN HAD BEEN ASSEMBLING AND INSTALLING SOME NEWLY PURCHASED FURNITURE.
Heh heh heh.
WHEN HE FINISHED, HE LEFT HIS HAMMER ON THE LIVING ROOM COFFEE TABLE.

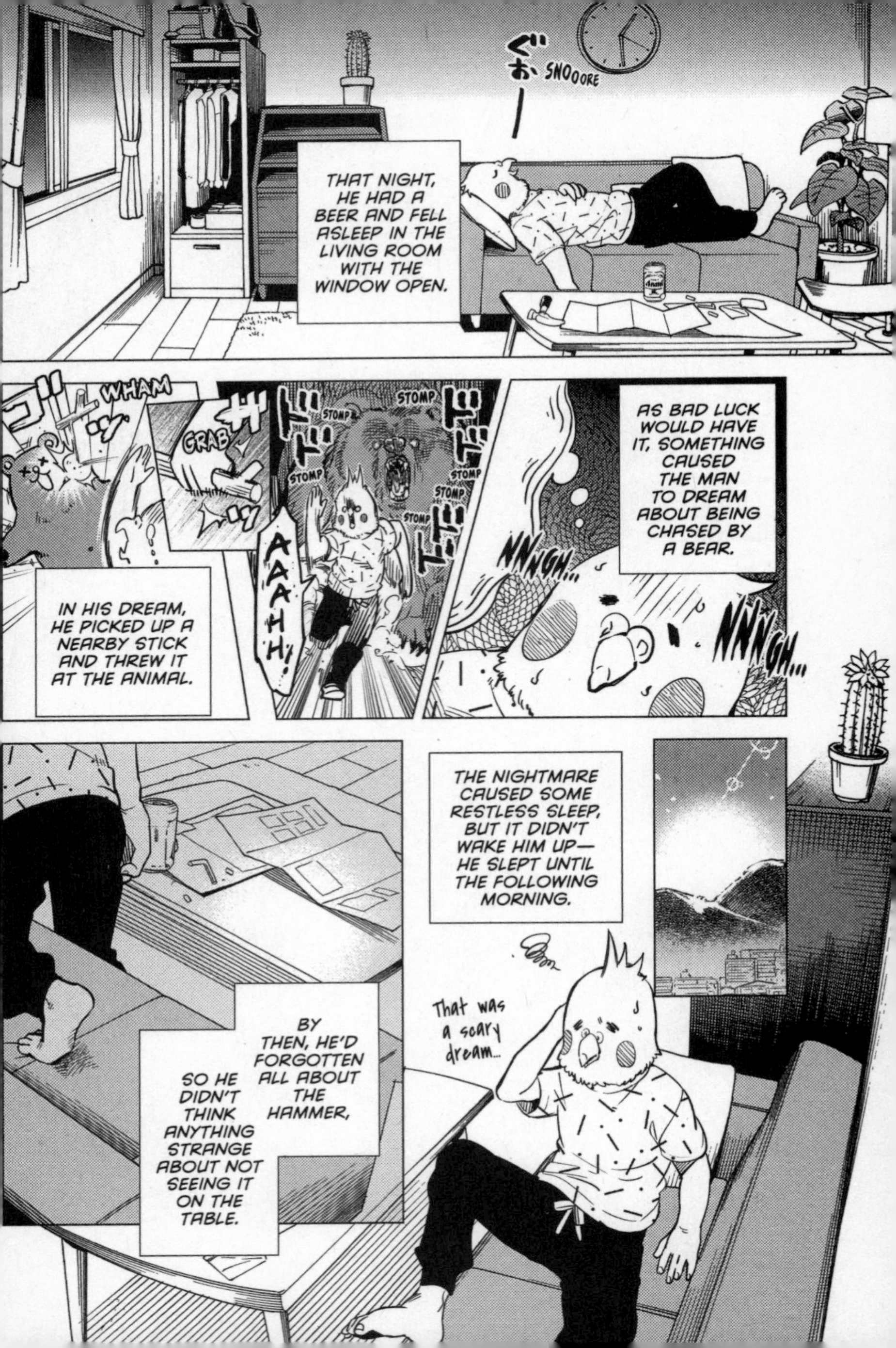
SNOOORE
THAT NIGHT, HE HAD A BEER AND FELL ASLEEP IN THE LIVING ROOM WITH THE WINDOW OPEN.
AS BAD LUCK WOULD HAVE IT, SOMETHING CAUSED THE MAN TO DREAM ABOUT BEING CHASED BY A BEAR.
NNNGH...
NNNGH...
STOMP
STOMP
STOMP
STOMP
STOMP
AAAHH!
GRAB
WHAM
IN HIS DREAM, HE PICKED UP A NEARBY STICK AND THREW IT AT THE ANIMAL.
THE NIGHTMARE CAUSED SOME RESTLESS SLEEP, BUT IT DIDN'T WAKE HIM UP—HE SLEPT UNTIL THE FOLLOWING MORNING.
That was a scary dream...
BY THEN, HE'D FORGOTTEN ALL ABOUT THE HAMMER,
SO HE DIDN'T THINK ANYTHING STRANGE ABOUT NOT SEEING IT ON THE TABLE.

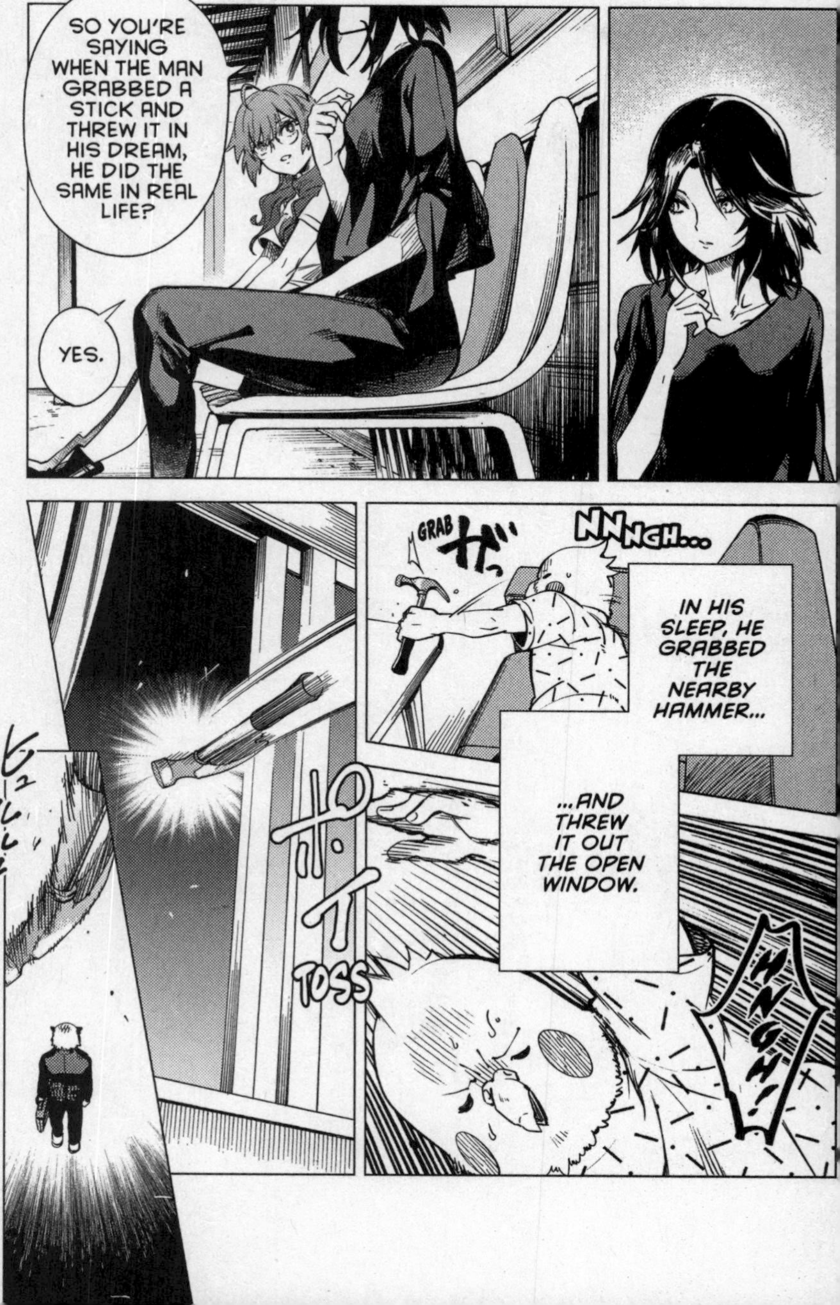
SO YOU'RE SAYING WHEN THE MAN GRABBED A STICK AND THREW IT IN HIS DREAM, HE DID THE SAME IN REAL LIFE?
YES.
GRAB
NNNGH...
IN HIS SLEEP, HE GRABBED THE NEARBY HAMMER...
...AND THREW IT OUT THE OPEN WINDOW.
HNGH!
TOSS
HISSSS

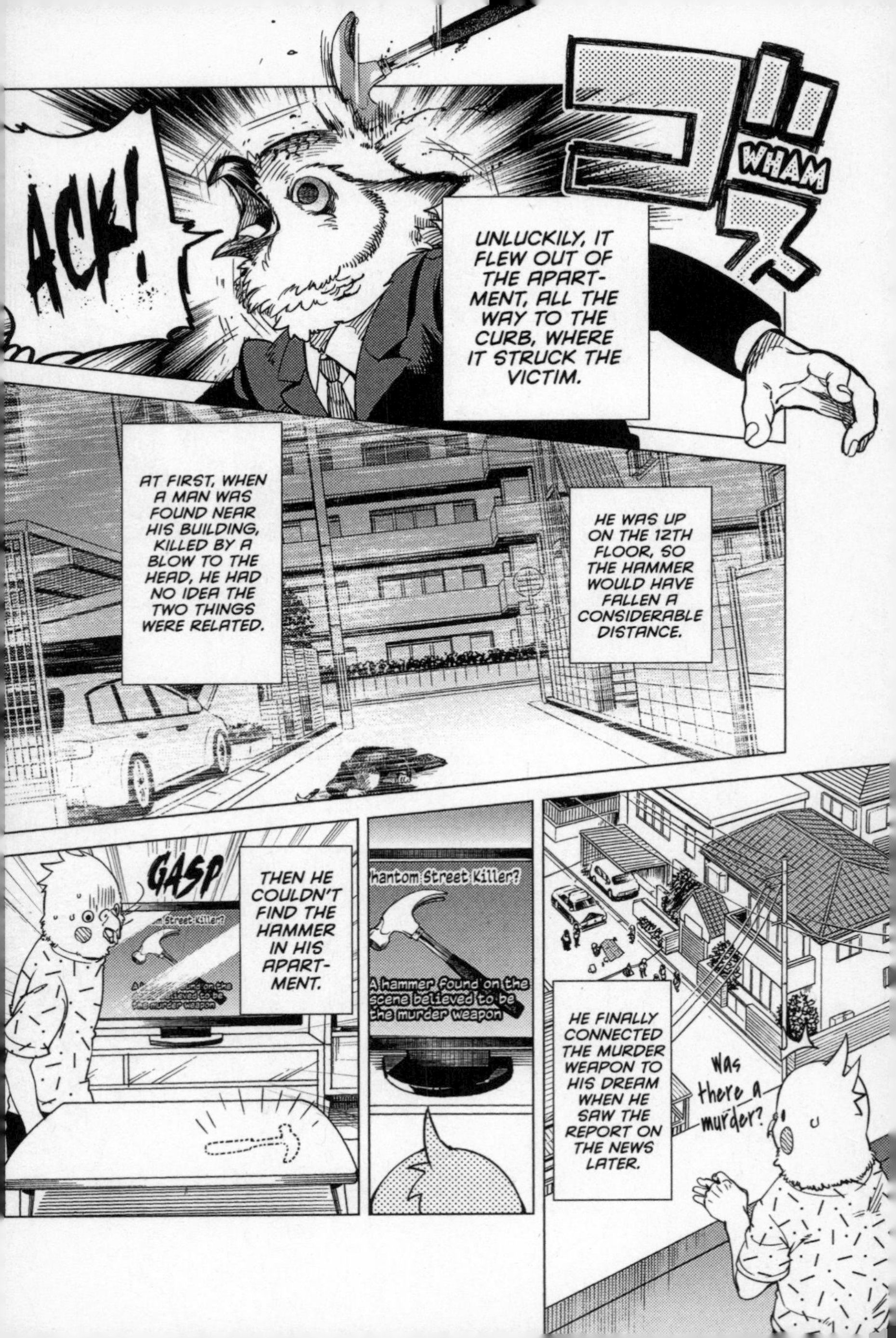
WHAM
UNLUCKILY, IT FLEW OUT OF THE APARTMENT, ALL THE WAY TO THE CURB, WHERE IT STRUCK THE VICTIM.
ACK!
AT FIRST, WHEN A MAN WAS FOUND NEAR HIS BUILDING, KILLED BY A BLOW TO THE HEAD, HE HAD NO IDEA THE TWO THINGS WERE RELATED.
HE WAS UP ON THE 12TH FLOOR, SO THE HAMMER WOULD HAVE FALLEN A CONSIDERABLE DISTANCE.
Was there a murder?
HE FINALLY CONNECTED THE MURDER WEAPON TO HIS DREAM WHEN HE SAW THE REPORT ON THE NEWS LATER.
hantom Street Killer?
A hammer found on the scene believed to be the murder weapon
THEN HE COULDN'T FIND THE HAMMER IN HIS APARTMENT.
GASP

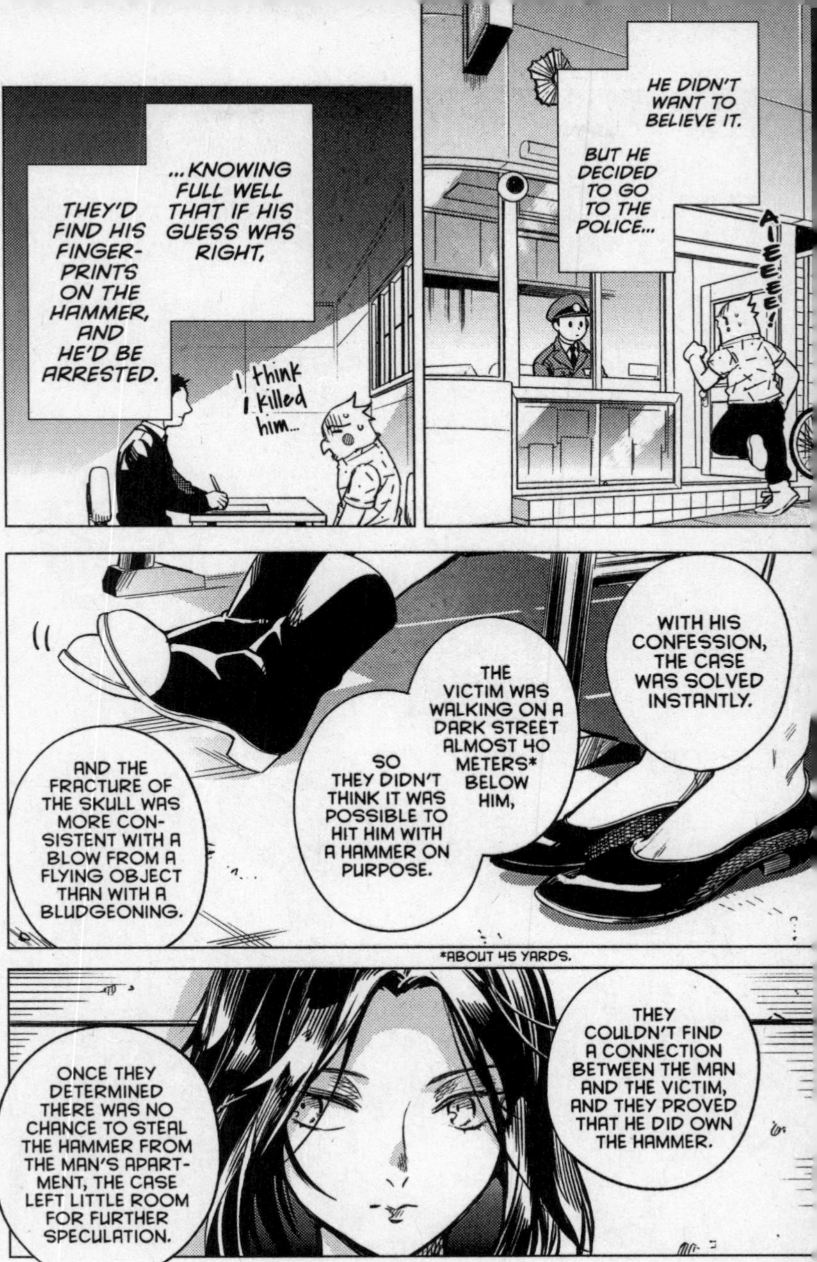
HE DIDN'T WANT TO BELIEVE IT.
BUT HE DECIDED TO GO TO THE POLICE...
AIEEEE!
...KNOWING FULL WELL THAT IF HIS GUESS WAS RIGHT,
THEY'D FIND HIS FINGER-PRINTS ON THE HAMMER, AND HE'D BE ARRESTED.
I think I killed him...
WITH HIS CONFESSION, THE CASE WAS SOLVED INSTANTLY.
THE VICTIM WAS WALKING ON A DARK STREET ALMOST 40 METERS* BELOW HIM,
SO THEY DIDN'T THINK IT WAS POSSIBLE TO HIT HIM WITH A HAMMER ON PURPOSE.
AND THE FRACTURE OF THE SKULL WAS MORE CON-SISTENT WITH A BLOW FROM A FLYING OBJECT THAN WITH A BLUDGEONING.
*ABOUT 45 YARDS.
THEY COULDN'T FIND A CONNECTION BETWEEN THE MAN AND THE VICTIM, AND THEY PROVED THAT HE DID OWN THE HAMMER.
ONCE THEY DETERMINED THERE WAS NO CHANCE TO STEAL THE HAMMER FROM THE MAN'S APART-MENT, THE CASE LEFT LITTLE ROOM FOR FURTHER SPECULATION.

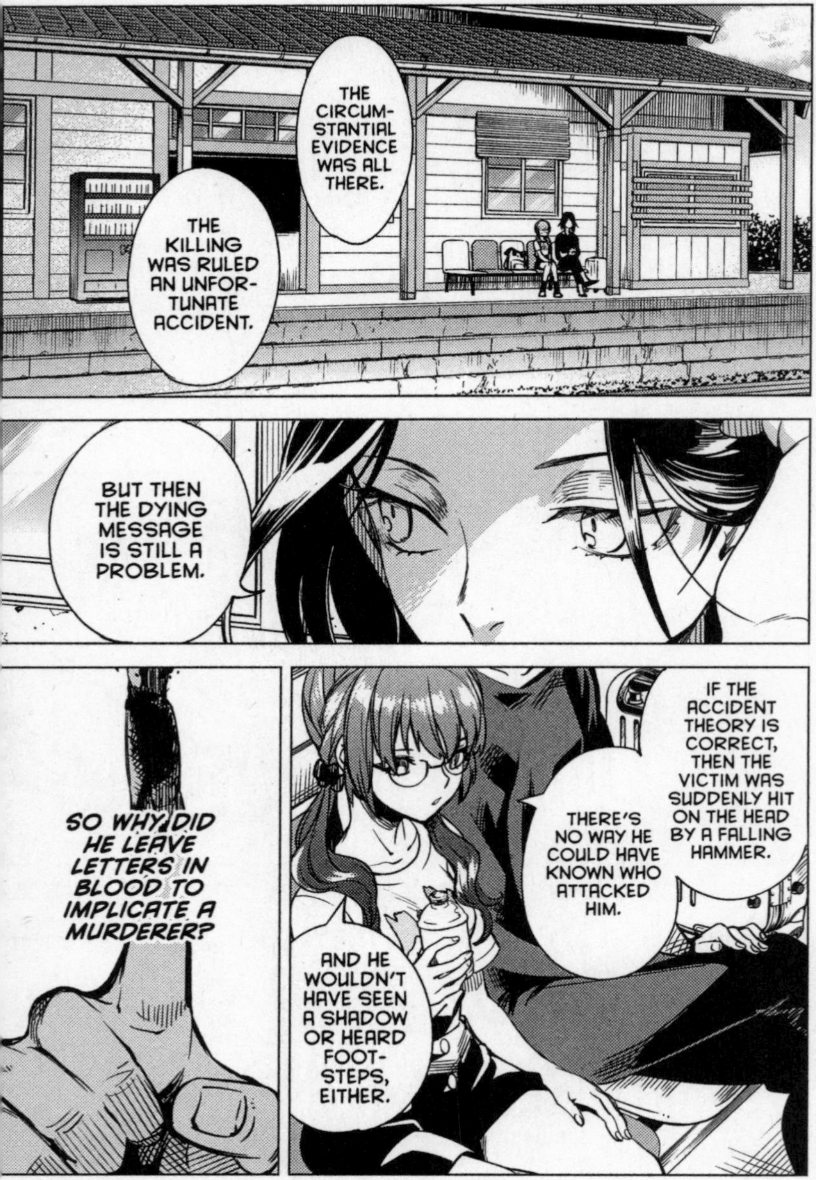
THE CIRCUMSTANTIAL EVIDENCE WAS ALL THERE.
THE KILLING WAS RULED AN UNFORTUNATE ACCIDENT.
BUT THEN THE DYING MESSAGE IS STILL A PROBLEM.
IF THE ACCIDENT THEORY IS CORRECT, THEN THE VICTIM WAS SUDDENLY HIT ON THE HEAD BY A FALLING HAMMER.
THERE'S NO WAY HE COULD HAVE KNOWN WHO ATTACKED HIM.
AND HE WOULDN'T HAVE SEEN A SHADOW OR HEARD FOOTSTEPS, EITHER.
SO WHY DID HE LEAVE LETTERS IN BLOOD TO IMPLICATE A MURDERER?

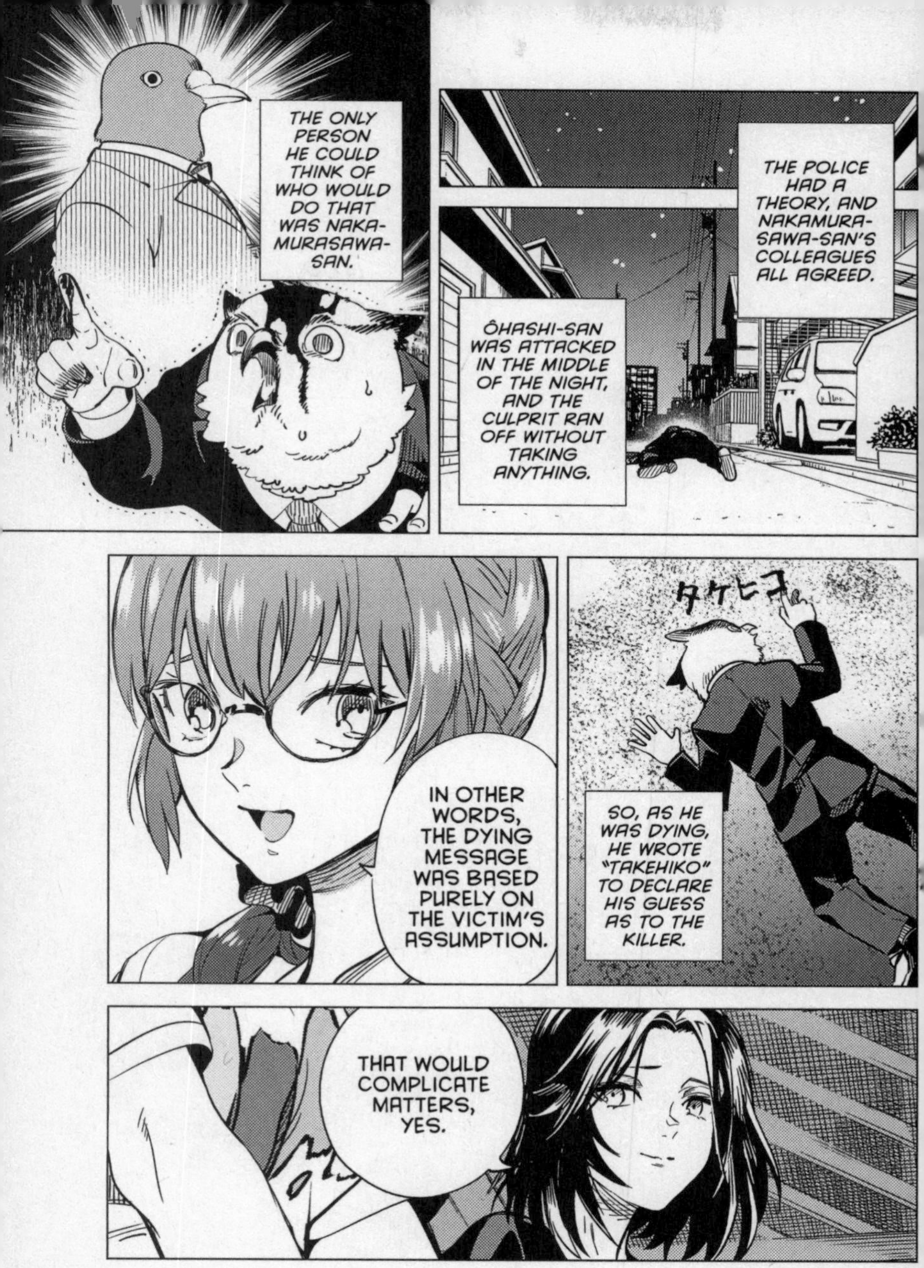
THE POLICE HAD A THEORY, AND NAKAMURA-SAWA-SAN'S COLLEAGUES ALL AGREED.
ÔHASHI-SAN WAS ATTACKED IN THE MIDDLE OF THE NIGHT, AND THE CULPRIT RAN OFF WITHOUT TAKING ANYTHING.
THE ONLY PERSON HE COULD THINK OF WHO WOULD DO THAT WAS NAKA-MURASAWA-SAN.
タケヒコ
SO, AS HE WAS DYING, HE WROTE "TAKEHIKO" TO DECLARE HIS GUESS AS TO THE KILLER.
IN OTHER WORDS, THE DYING MESSAGE WAS BASED PURELY ON THE VICTIM'S ASSUMPTION.
THAT WOULD COMPLICATE MATTERS, YES.

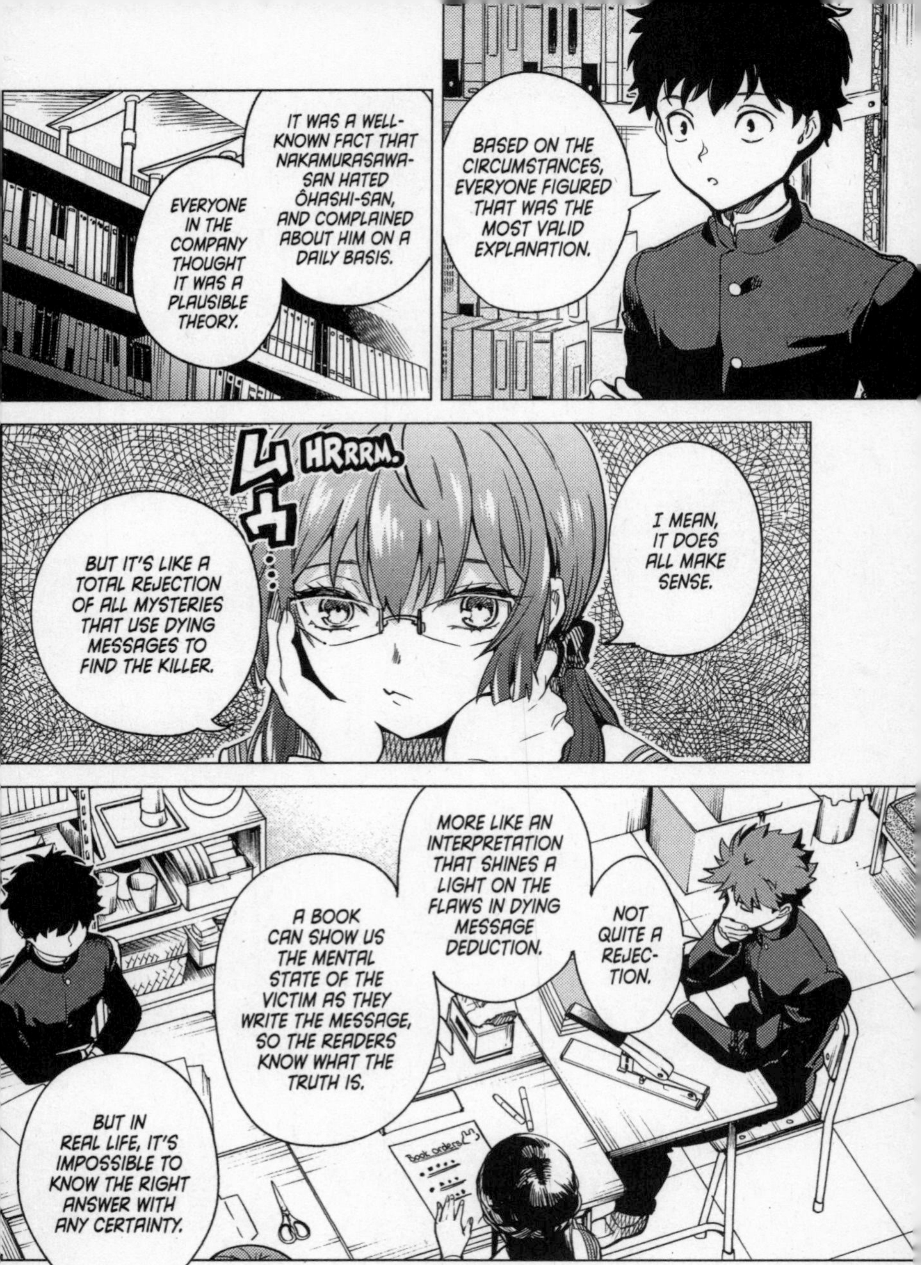
BASED ON THE CIRCUMSTANCES, EVERYONE FIGURED THAT WAS THE MOST VALID EXPLANATION.
IT WAS A WELL-KNOWN FACT THAT NAKAMURASAWA-SAN HATED ÔHASHI-SAN, AND COMPLAINED ABOUT HIM ON A DAILY BASIS.
EVERYONE IN THE COMPANY THOUGHT IT WAS A PLAUSIBLE THEORY.
I MEAN, IT DOES ALL MAKE SENSE.
HRRRM.
BUT IT'S LIKE A TOTAL REJECTION OF ALL MYSTERIES THAT USE DYING MESSAGES TO FIND THE KILLER.
NOT QUITE A REJECTION.
MORE LIKE AN INTERPRETATION THAT SHINES A LIGHT ON THE FLAWS IN DYING MESSAGE DEDUCTION.
A BOOK CAN SHOW US THE MENTAL STATE OF THE VICTIM AS THEY WRITE THE MESSAGE, SO THE READERS KNOW WHAT THE TRUTH IS.
Book orders
BUT IN REAL LIFE, IT'S IMPOSSIBLE TO KNOW THE RIGHT ANSWER WITH ANY CERTAINTY.

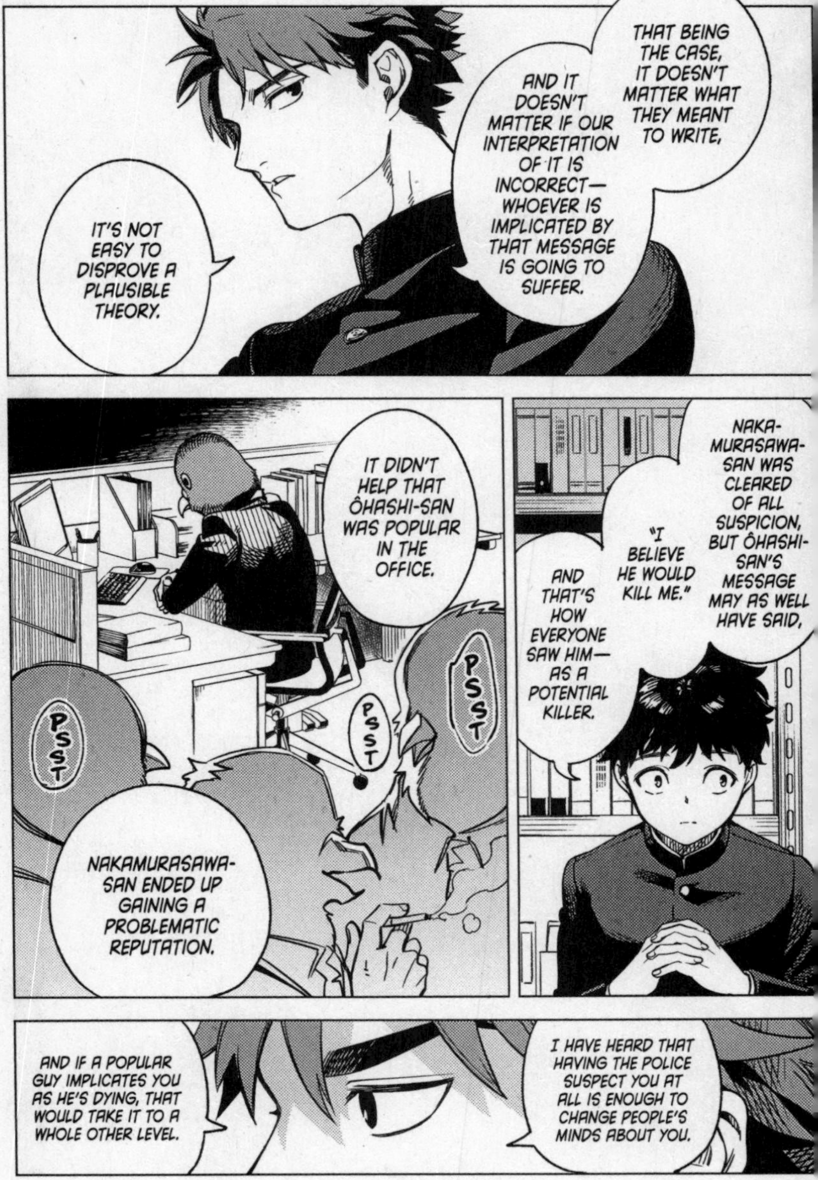
THAT BEING THE CASE, IT DOESN'T MATTER WHAT THEY MEANT TO WRITE,
AND IT DOESN'T MATTER IF OUR INTERPRETATION OF IT IS INCORRECT— WHOEVER IS IMPLICATED BY THAT MESSAGE IS GOING TO SUFFER.
IT'S NOT EASY TO DISPROVE A PLAUSIBLE THEORY.
NAKA-MURASAWA-SAN WAS CLEARED OF ALL SUSPICION, BUT ÔHASHI-SAN'S MESSAGE MAY AS WELL HAVE SAID,
“I BELIEVE HE WOULD KILL ME.”
AND THAT'S HOW EVERYONE SAW HIM— AS A POTENTIAL KILLER.
IT DIDN'T HELP THAT ÔHASHI-SAN WAS POPULAR IN THE OFFICE.
PSST
PSST
PSST
NAKAMURASAWA-SAN ENDED UP GAINING A PROBLEMATIC REPUTATION.
I HAVE HEARD THAT HAVING THE POLICE SUSPECT YOU AT ALL IS ENOUGH TO CHANGE PEOPLE'S MINDS ABOUT YOU.
AND IF A POPULAR GUY IMPLICATES YOU AS HE'S DYING, THAT WOULD TAKE IT TO A WHOLE OTHER LEVEL.

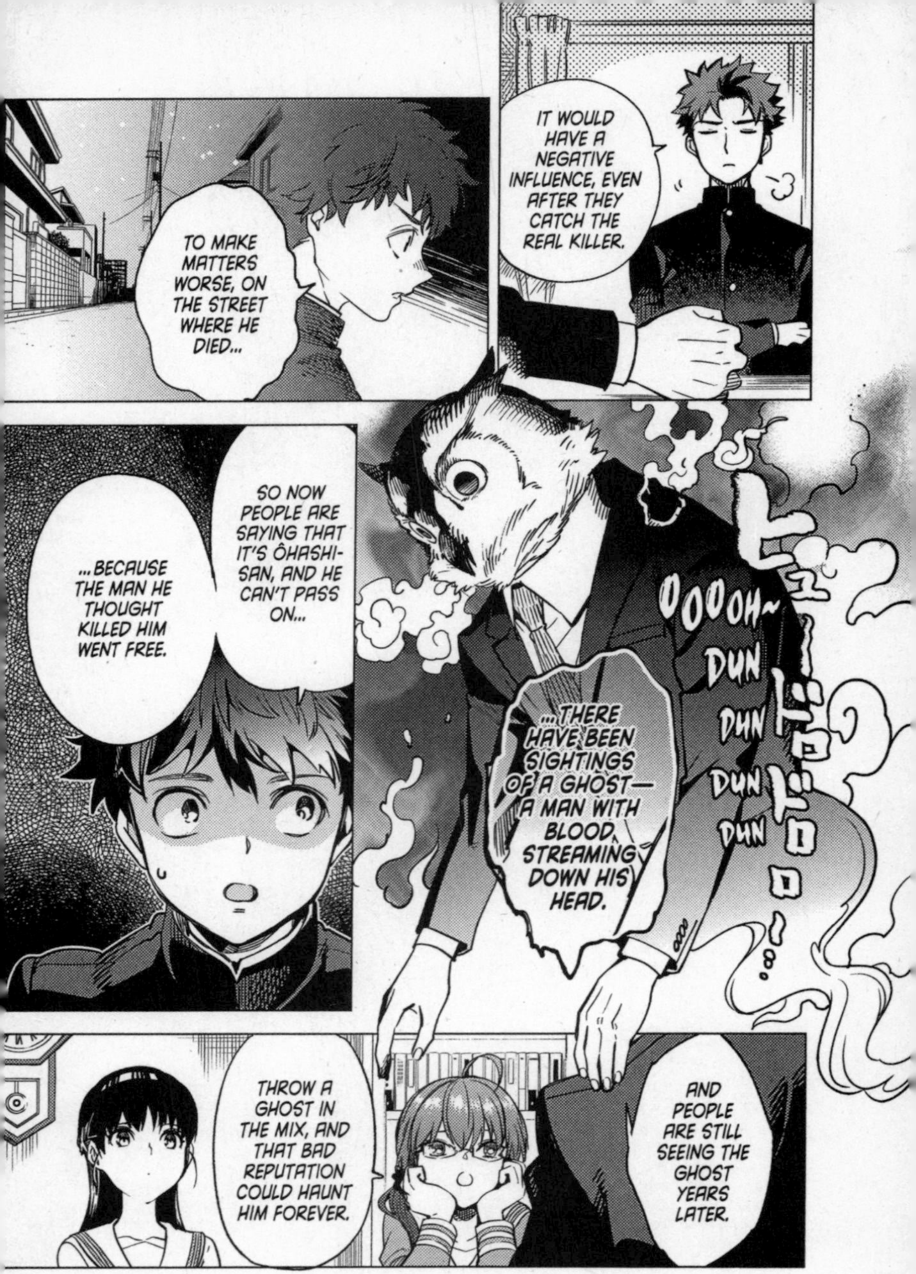
IT WOULD HAVE A NEGATIVE INFLUENCE, EVEN AFTER THEY CATCH THE REAL KILLER.
TO MAKE MATTERS WORSE, ON THE STREET WHERE HE DIED...
...THERE HAVE BEEN SIGHTINGS OF A GHOST—A MAN WITH BLOOD STREAMING DOWN HIS HEAD.
OOOOH~ DUN DUN DUN DUN
ヒュ～ドロドロ…
SO NOW PEOPLE ARE SAYING THAT IT'S ÔHASHI-SAN, AND HE CAN'T PASS ON...
...BECAUSE THE MAN HE THOUGHT KILLED HIM WENT FREE.
AND PEOPLE ARE STILL SEEING THE GHOST YEARS LATER.
THROW A GHOST IN THE MIX, AND THAT BAD REPUTATION COULD HAUNT HIM FOREVER.

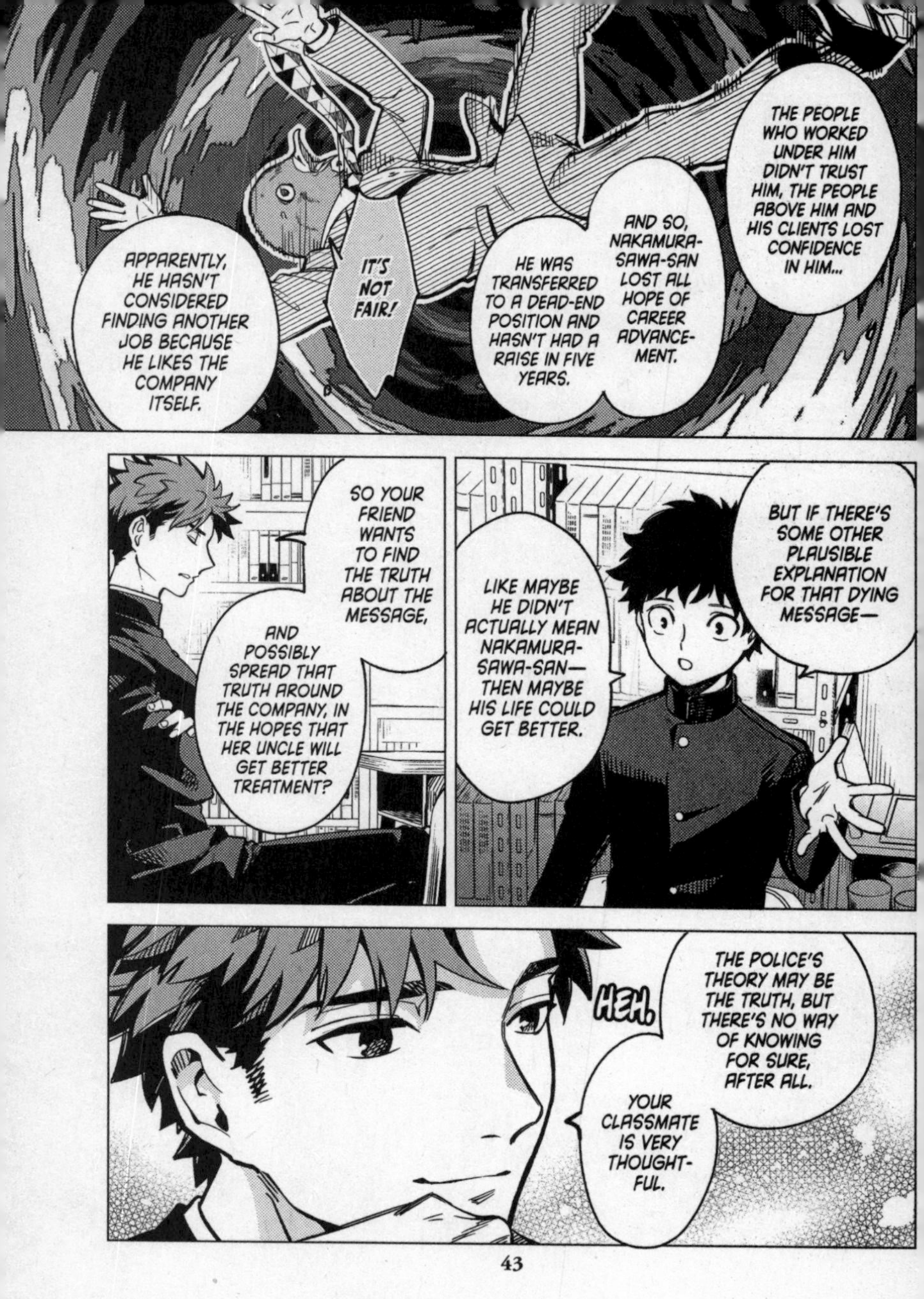
THE PEOPLE WHO WORKED UNDER HIM DIDN'T TRUST HIM, THE PEOPLE ABOVE HIM AND HIS CLIENTS LOST CONFIDENCE IN HIM...
AND SO, NAKAMURA-SAWA-SAN LOST ALL HOPE OF CAREER ADVANCE-MENT.
HE WAS TRANSFERRED TO A DEAD-END POSITION AND HASN'T HAD A RAISE IN FIVE YEARS.
IT'S NOT FAIR!
APPARENTLY, HE HASN'T CONSIDERED FINDING ANOTHER JOB BECAUSE HE LIKES THE COMPANY ITSELF.
BUT IF THERE'S SOME OTHER PLAUSIBLE EXPLANATION FOR THAT DYING MESSAGE—
LIKE MAYBE HE DIDN'T ACTUALLY MEAN NAKAMURA-SAWA-SAN—THEN MAYBE HIS LIFE COULD GET BETTER.
SO YOUR FRIEND WANTS TO FIND THE TRUTH ABOUT THE MESSAGE,
AND POSSIBLY SPREAD THAT TRUTH AROUND THE COMPANY, IN THE HOPES THAT HER UNCLE WILL GET BETTER TREATMENT?
THE POLICE'S THEORY MAY BE THE TRUTH, BUT THERE'S NO WAY OF KNOWING FOR SURE, AFTER ALL.
HEH.
YOUR CLASSMATE IS VERY THOUGHT-FUL.

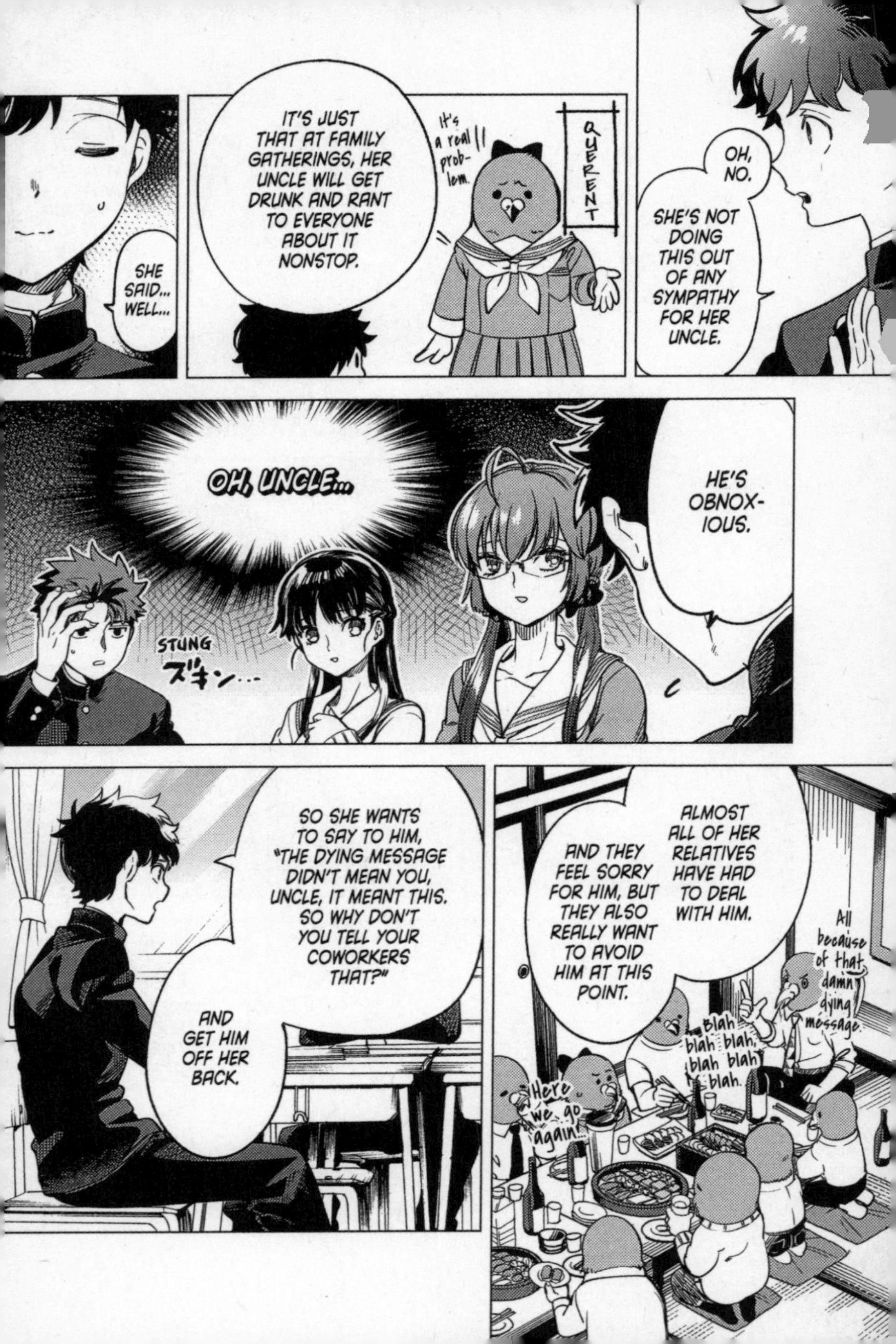
OH, NO.
SHE'S NOT DOING THIS OUT OF ANY SYMPATHY FOR HER UNCLE.
QUERENT
It's a real prob-lem.
IT'S JUST THAT AT FAMILY GATHERINGS, HER UNCLE WILL GET DRUNK AND RANT TO EVERYONE ABOUT IT NONSTOP.
SHE SAID... WELL...
HE'S OBNOXIOUS.
OH, UNCLE...
STUNG
ズキン…
ALMOST ALL OF HER RELATIVES HAVE HAD TO DEAL WITH HIM.
AND THEY FEEL SORRY FOR HIM, BUT THEY ALSO REALLY WANT TO AVOID HIM AT THIS POINT.
All because of that damn dying message.
Blah blah blah, blah blah blah.
Here we go again...
SO SHE WANTS TO SAY TO HIM, "THE DYING MESSAGE DIDN'T MEAN YOU, UNCLE, IT MEANT THIS. SO WHY DON'T YOU TELL YOUR COWORKERS THAT?"
AND GET HIM OFF HER BACK.

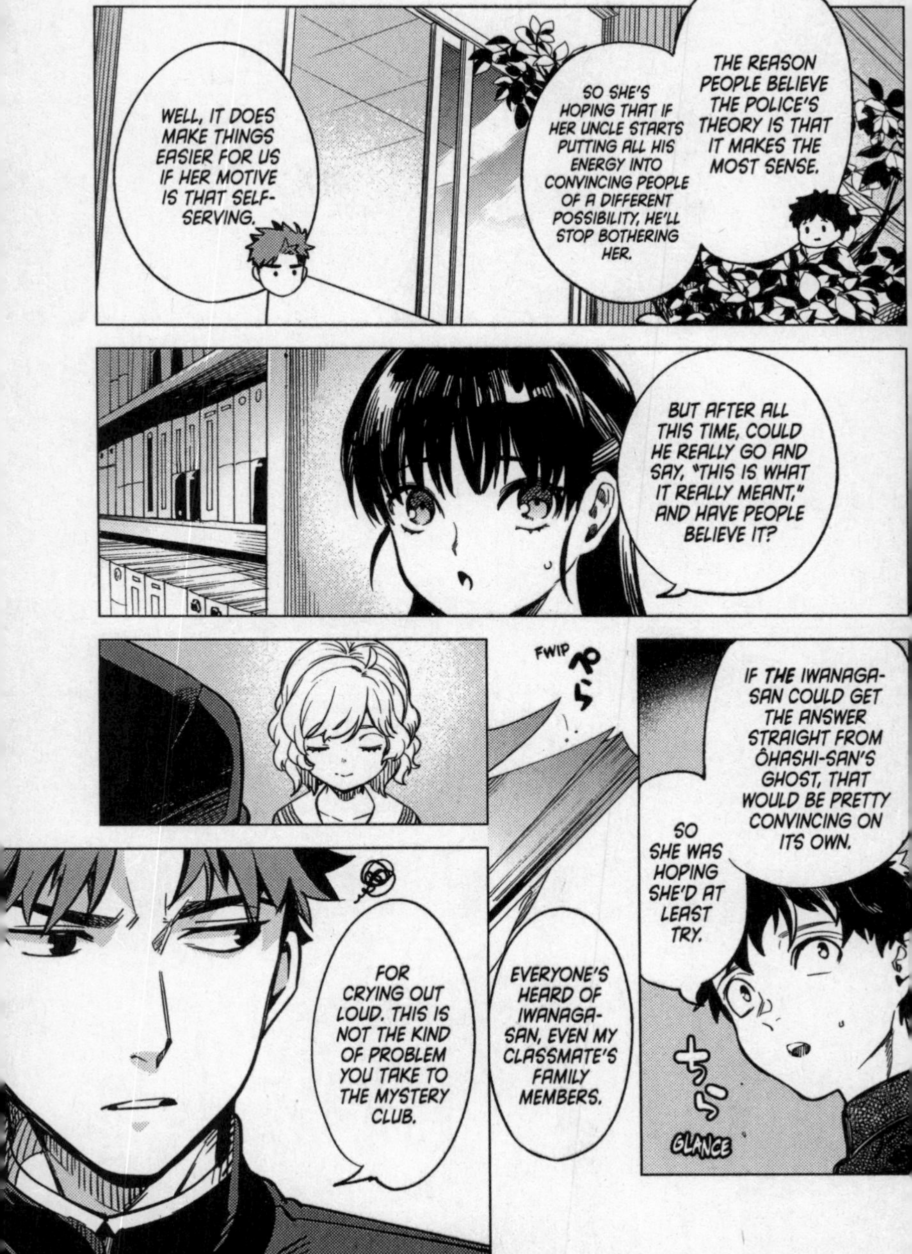
THE REASON PEOPLE BELIEVE THE POLICE'S THEORY IS THAT IT MAKES THE MOST SENSE.
SO SHE'S HOPING THAT IF HER UNCLE STARTS PUTTING ALL HIS ENERGY INTO CONVINCING PEOPLE OF A DIFFERENT POSSIBILITY, HE'LL STOP BOTHERING HER.
WELL, IT DOES MAKE THINGS EASIER FOR US IF HER MOTIVE IS THAT SELF-SERVING.
BUT AFTER ALL THIS TIME, COULD HE REALLY GO AND SAY, "THIS IS WHAT IT REALLY MEANT," AND HAVE PEOPLE BELIEVE IT?
IF THE IWANAGA-SAN COULD GET THE ANSWER STRAIGHT FROM ÔHASHI-SAN'S GHOST, THAT WOULD BE PRETTY CONVINCING ON ITS OWN.
SO SHE WAS HOPING SHE'D AT LEAST TRY.
GLANCE
FWIP
EVERYONE'S HEARD OF IWANAGA-SAN, EVEN MY CLASSMATE'S FAMILY MEMBERS.
FOR CRYING OUT LOUD. THIS IS NOT THE KIND OF PROBLEM YOU TAKE TO THE MYSTERY CLUB.

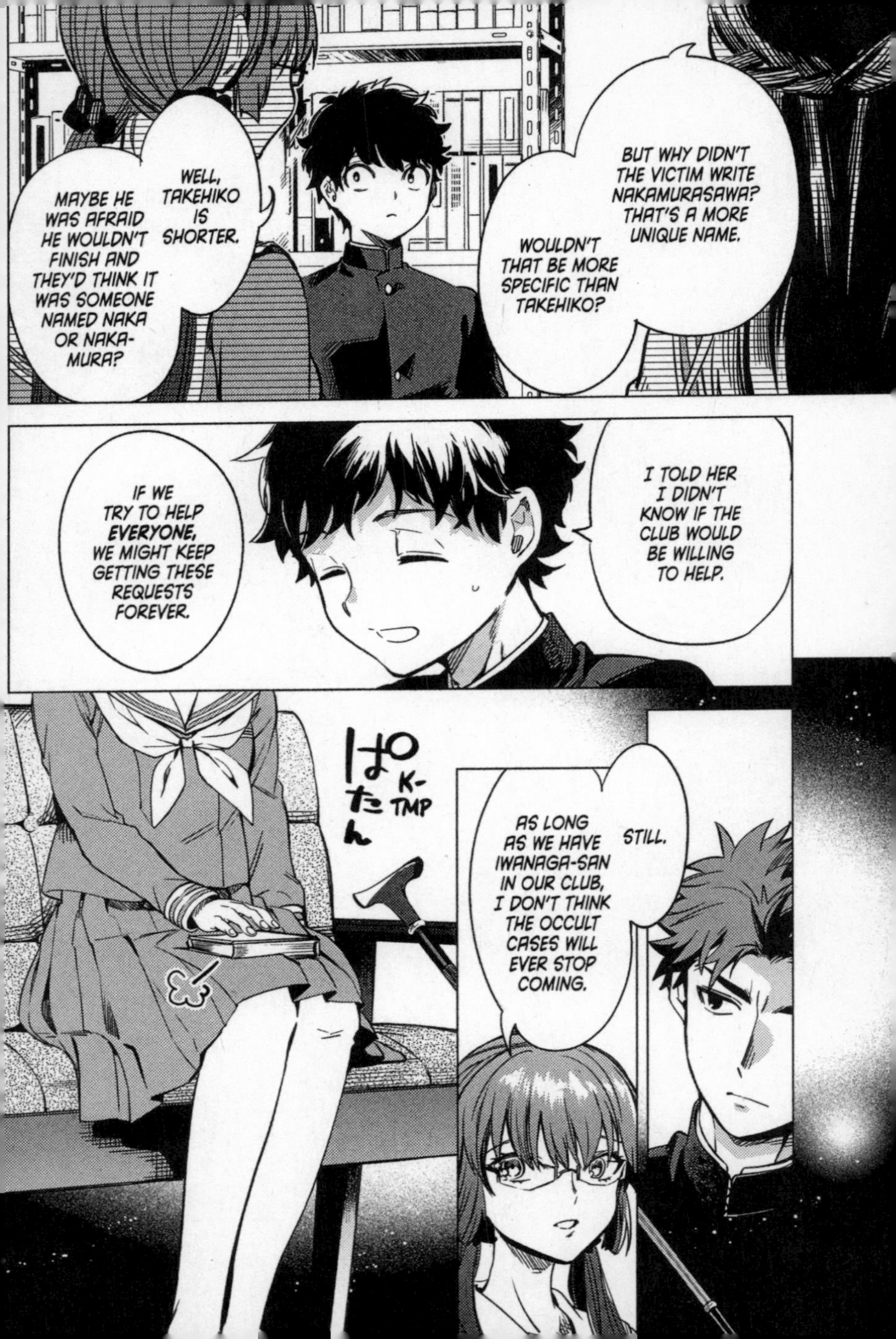
BUT WHY DIDN'T THE VICTIM WRITE NAKAMURASAWA? THAT'S A MORE UNIQUE NAME.
WOULDN'T THAT BE MORE SPECIFIC THAN TAKEHIKO?
WELL, TAKEHIKO IS SHORTER.
MAYBE HE WAS AFRAID HE WOULDN'T FINISH AND THEY'D THINK IT WAS SOMEONE NAMED NAKA OR NAKA-MURA?
I TOLD HER I DIDN'T KNOW IF THE CLUB WOULD BE WILLING TO HELP.
IF WE TRY TO HELP EVERYONE, WE MIGHT KEEP GETTING THESE REQUESTS FOREVER.
STILL.
AS LONG AS WE HAVE IWANAGA-SAN IN OUR CLUB, I DON'T THINK THE OCCULT CASES WILL EVER STOP COMING.
ぱたん
K-TMP

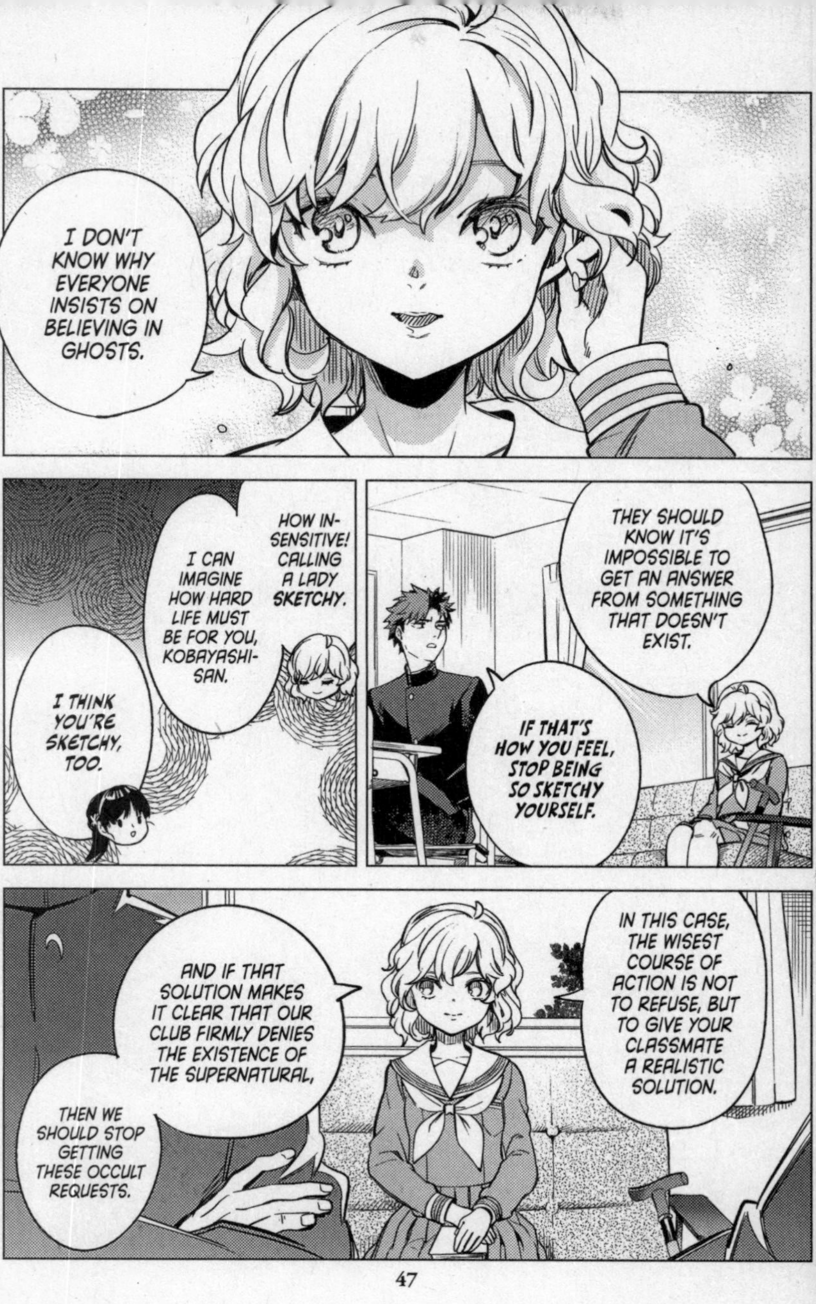
I DON'T KNOW WHY EVERYONE INSISTS ON BELIEVING IN GHOSTS.
THEY SHOULD KNOW IT'S IMPOSSIBLE TO GET AN ANSWER FROM SOMETHING THAT DOESN'T EXIST.
IF THAT'S HOW YOU FEEL, STOP BEING SO SKETCHY YOURSELF.
HOW IN-SENSITIVE! CALLING A LADY SKETCHY.
I CAN IMAGINE HOW HARD LIFE MUST BE FOR YOU, KOBAYASHI-SAN.
I THINK YOU'RE SKETCHY, TOO.
IN THIS CASE, THE WISEST COURSE OF ACTION IS NOT TO REFUSE, BUT TO GIVE YOUR CLASSMATE A REALISTIC SOLUTION.
AND IF THAT SOLUTION MAKES IT CLEAR THAT OUR CLUB FIRMLY DENIES THE EXISTENCE OF THE SUPERNATURAL,
THEN WE SHOULD STOP GETTING THESE OCCULT REQUESTS.

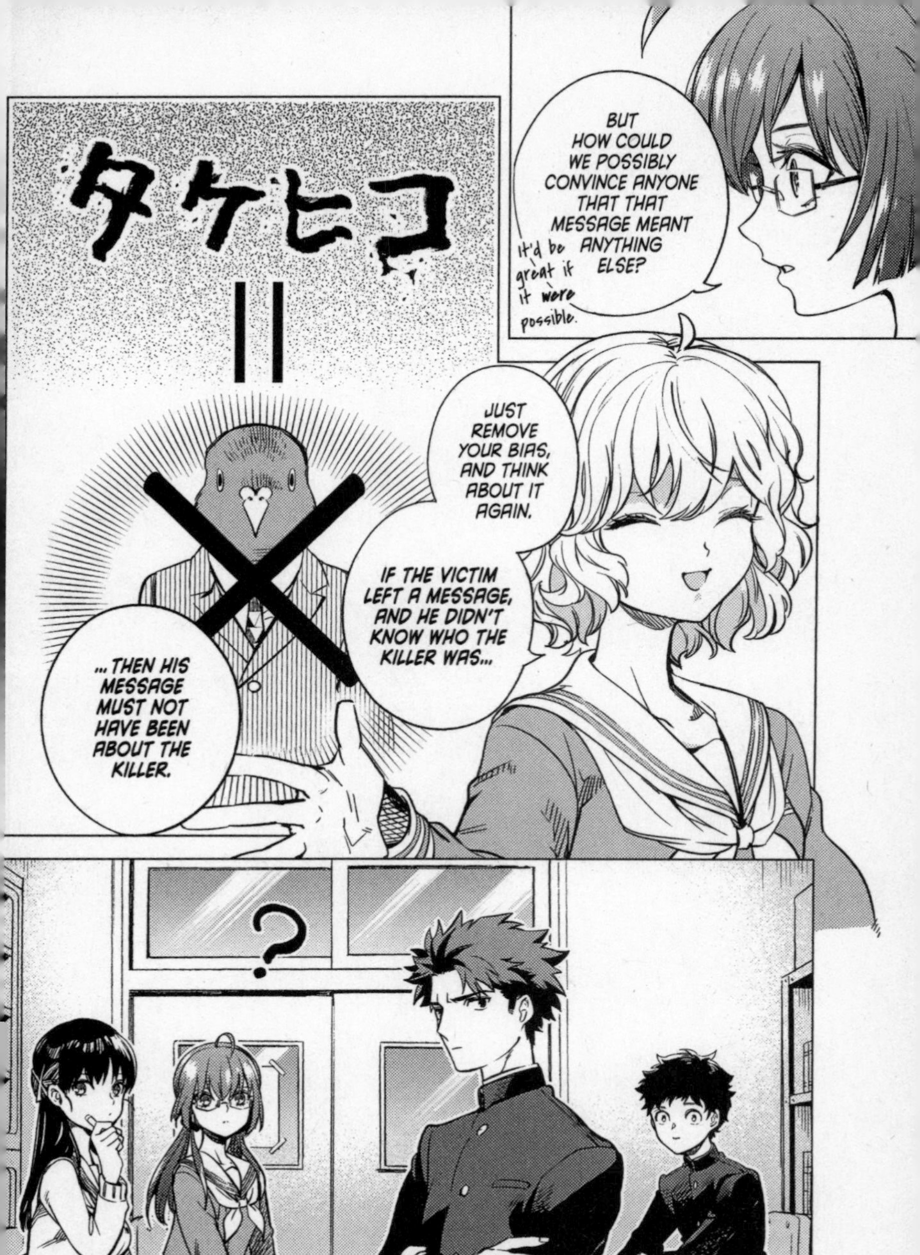
BUT HOW COULD WE POSSIBLY CONVINCE ANYONE THAT THAT MESSAGE MEANT ANYTHING ELSE?
It'd be great if it were possible.
JUST REMOVE YOUR BIAS, AND THINK ABOUT IT AGAIN.
IF THE VICTIM LEFT A MESSAGE, AND HE DIDN'T KNOW WHO THE KILLER WAS...
タケヒコ
...THEN HIS MESSAGE MUST NOT HAVE BEEN ABOUT THE KILLER.
?

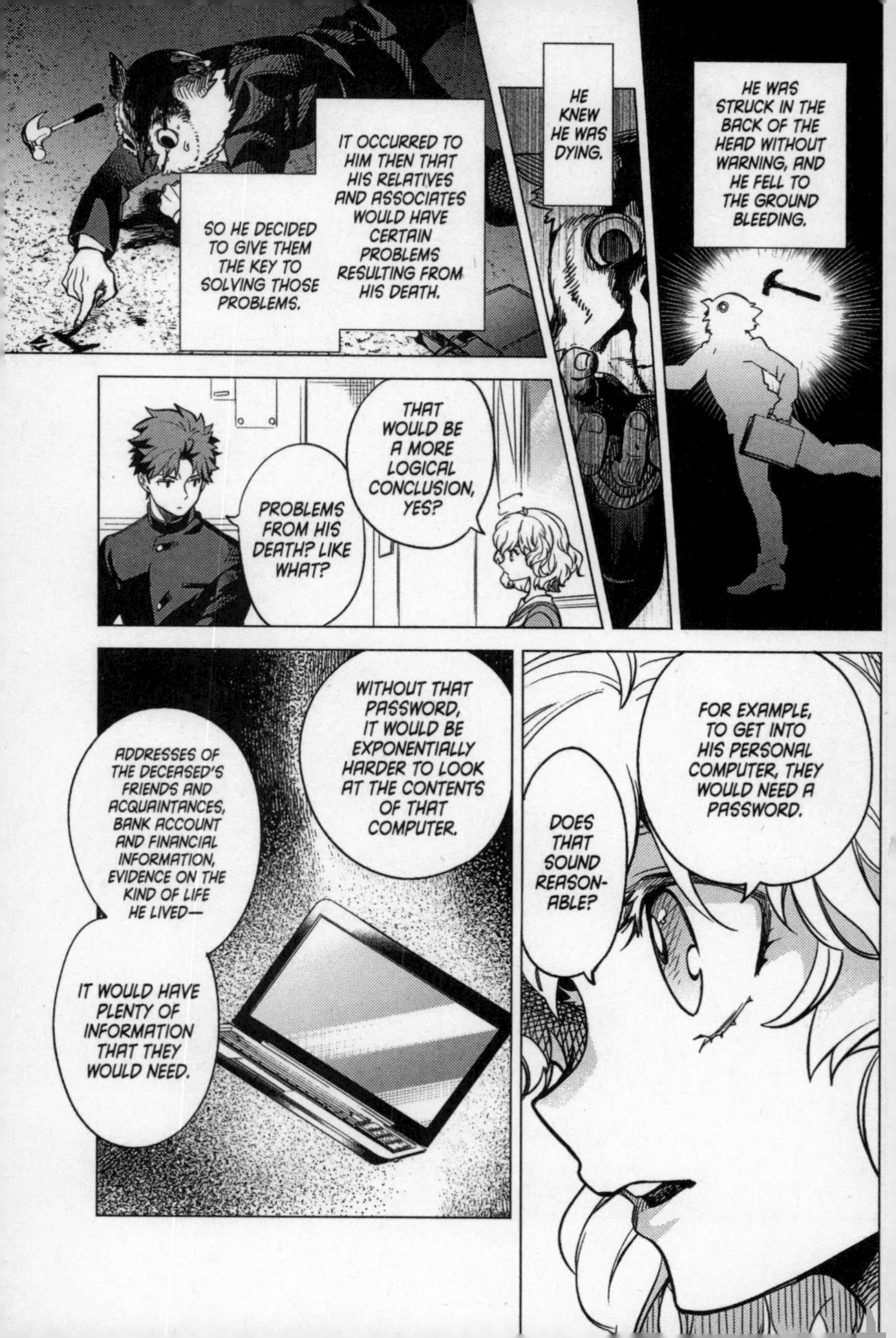
HE WAS STRUCK IN THE BACK OF THE HEAD WITHOUT WARNING, AND HE FELL TO THE GROUND BLEEDING.
HE KNEW HE WAS DYING.
IT OCCURRED TO HIM THEN THAT HIS RELATIVES AND ASSOCIATES WOULD HAVE CERTAIN PROBLEMS RESULTING FROM HIS DEATH.
SO HE DECIDED TO GIVE THEM THE KEY TO SOLVING THOSE PROBLEMS.
THAT WOULD BE A MORE LOGICAL CONCLUSION, YES?
PROBLEMS FROM HIS DEATH? LIKE WHAT?
FOR EXAMPLE, TO GET INTO HIS PERSONAL COMPUTER, THEY WOULD NEED A PASSWORD.
DOES THAT SOUND REASON-ABLE?
WITHOUT THAT PASSWORD, IT WOULD BE EXPONENTIALLY HARDER TO LOOK AT THE CONTENTS OF THAT COMPUTER.
ADDRESSES OF THE DECEASED'S FRIENDS AND ACQUAINTANCES, BANK ACCOUNT AND FINANCIAL INFORMATION, EVIDENCE ON THE KIND OF LIFE HE LIVED—
IT WOULD HAVE PLENTY OF INFORMATION THAT THEY WOULD NEED.

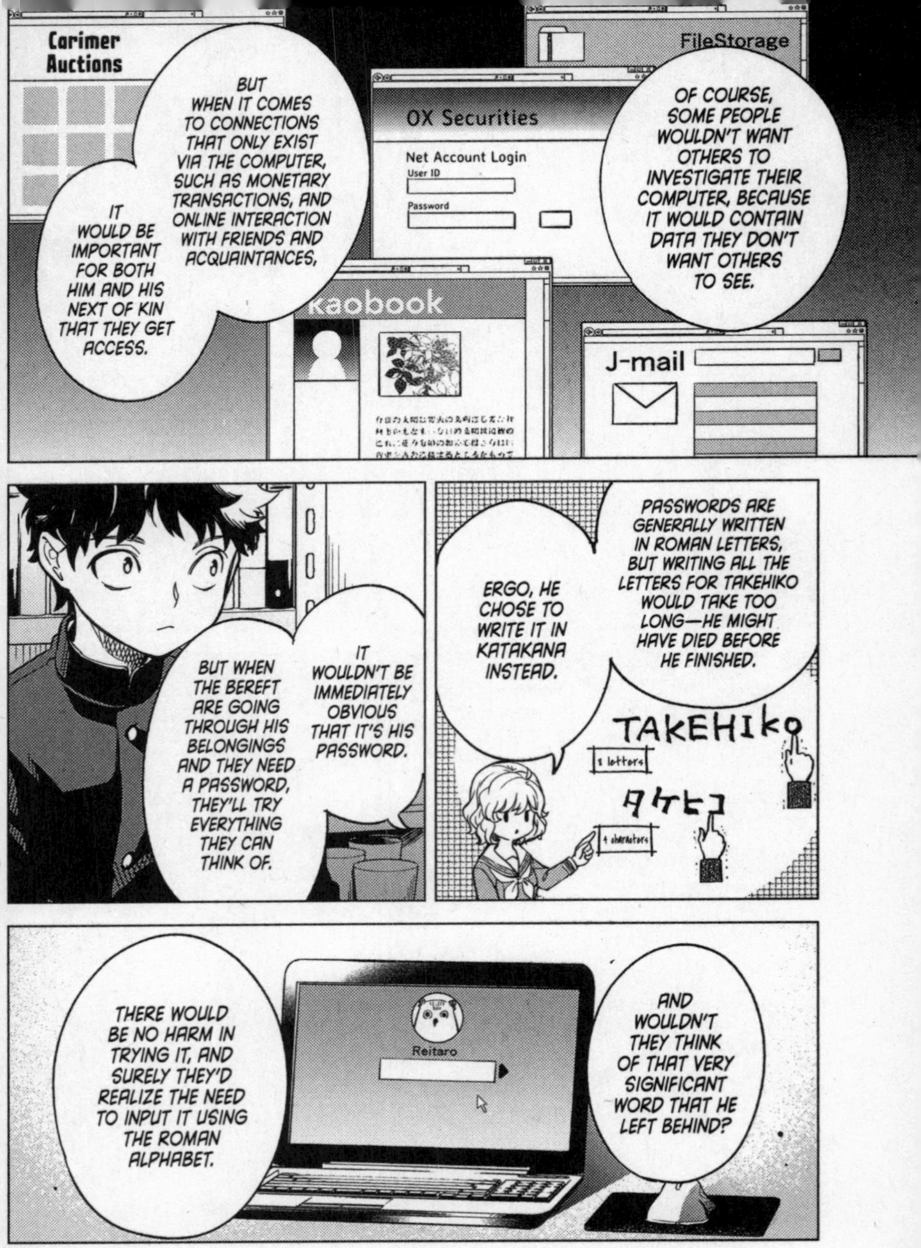
FileStorage
OX Securities
Net Account Login
User ID
Password
Carimer Auctions
OF COURSE, SOME PEOPLE WOULDN'T WANT OTHERS TO INVESTIGATE THEIR COMPUTER, BECAUSE IT WOULD CONTAIN DATA THEY DON'T WANT OTHERS TO SEE.
BUT WHEN IT COMES TO CONNECTIONS THAT ONLY EXIST VIA THE COMPUTER, SUCH AS MONETARY TRANSACTIONS, AND ONLINE INTERACTION WITH FRIENDS AND ACQUAINTANCES,
IT WOULD BE IMPORTANT FOR BOTH HIM AND HIS NEXT OF KIN THAT THEY GET ACCESS.
J-mail
kaobook
PASSWORDS ARE GENERALLY WRITTEN IN ROMAN LETTERS, BUT WRITING ALL THE LETTERS FOR TAKEHIKO WOULD TAKE TOO LONG—HE MIGHT HAVE DIED BEFORE HE FINISHED.
ERGO, HE CHOSE TO WRITE IT IN KATAKANA INSTEAD.
TAKEHIKO
8 letters
タケヒコ
4 characters
IT WOULDN'T BE IMMEDIATELY OBVIOUS THAT IT'S HIS PASSWORD.
BUT WHEN THE BEREFT ARE GOING THROUGH HIS BELONGINGS AND THEY NEED A PASSWORD, THEY'LL TRY EVERYTHING THEY CAN THINK OF.
AND WOULDN'T THEY THINK OF THAT VERY SIGNIFICANT WORD THAT HE LEFT BEHIND?
Reitaro
THERE WOULD BE NO HARM IN TRYING IT, AND SURELY THEY'D REALIZE THE NEED TO INPUT IT USING THE ROMAN ALPHABET.

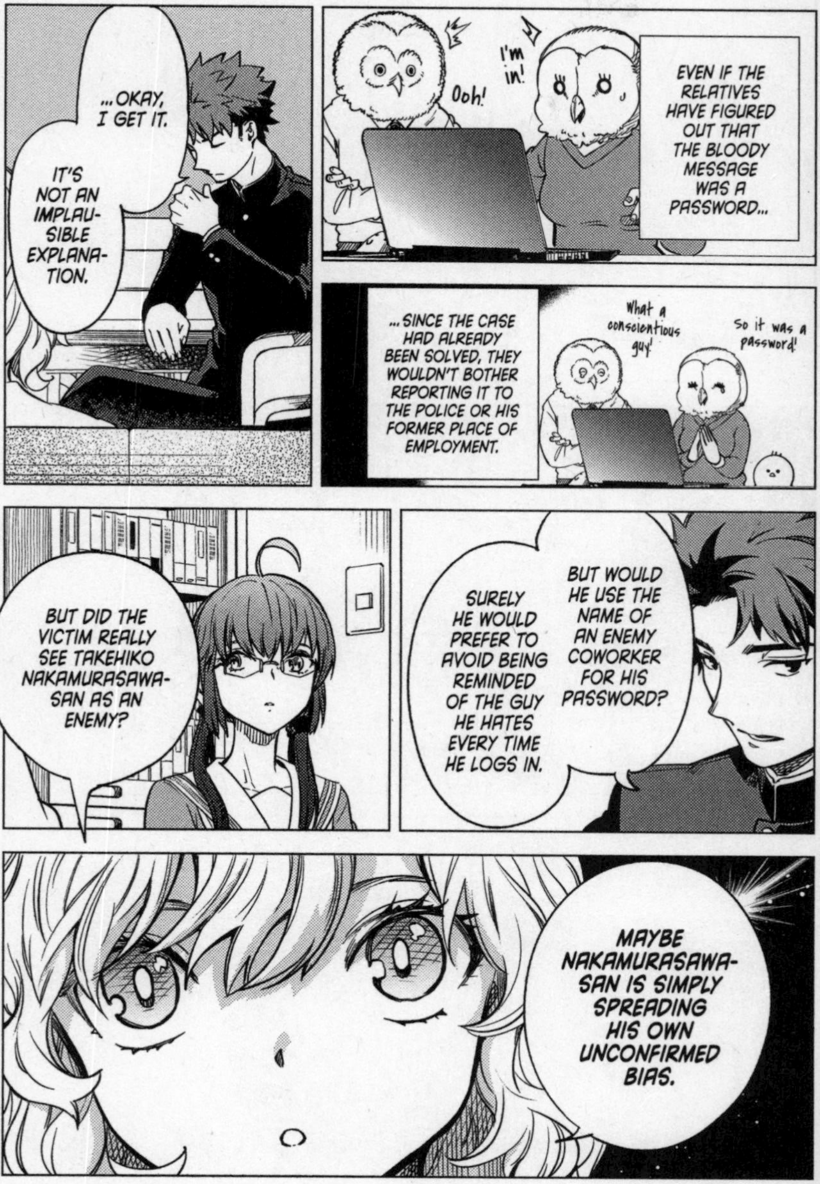
EVEN IF THE RELATIVES HAVE FIGURED OUT THAT THE BLOODY MESSAGE WAS A PASSWORD...
I'm in!
Ooh!
...SINCE THE CASE HAD ALREADY BEEN SOLVED, THEY WOULDN'T BOTHER REPORTING IT TO THE POLICE OR HIS FORMER PLACE OF EMPLOYMENT.
So it was a password!
What a conscientious guy!
...OKAY, I GET IT.
IT'S NOT AN IMPLAUSIBLE EXPLANATION.
BUT WOULD HE USE THE NAME OF AN ENEMY COWORKER FOR HIS PASSWORD?
SURELY HE WOULD PREFER TO AVOID BEING REMINDED OF THE GUY HE HATES EVERY TIME HE LOGS IN.
BUT DID THE VICTIM REALLY SEE TAKEHIKO NAKAMURASAWA-SAN AS AN ENEMY?
MAYBE NAKAMURASAWA-SAN IS SIMPLY SPREADING HIS OWN UNCONFIRMED BIAS.

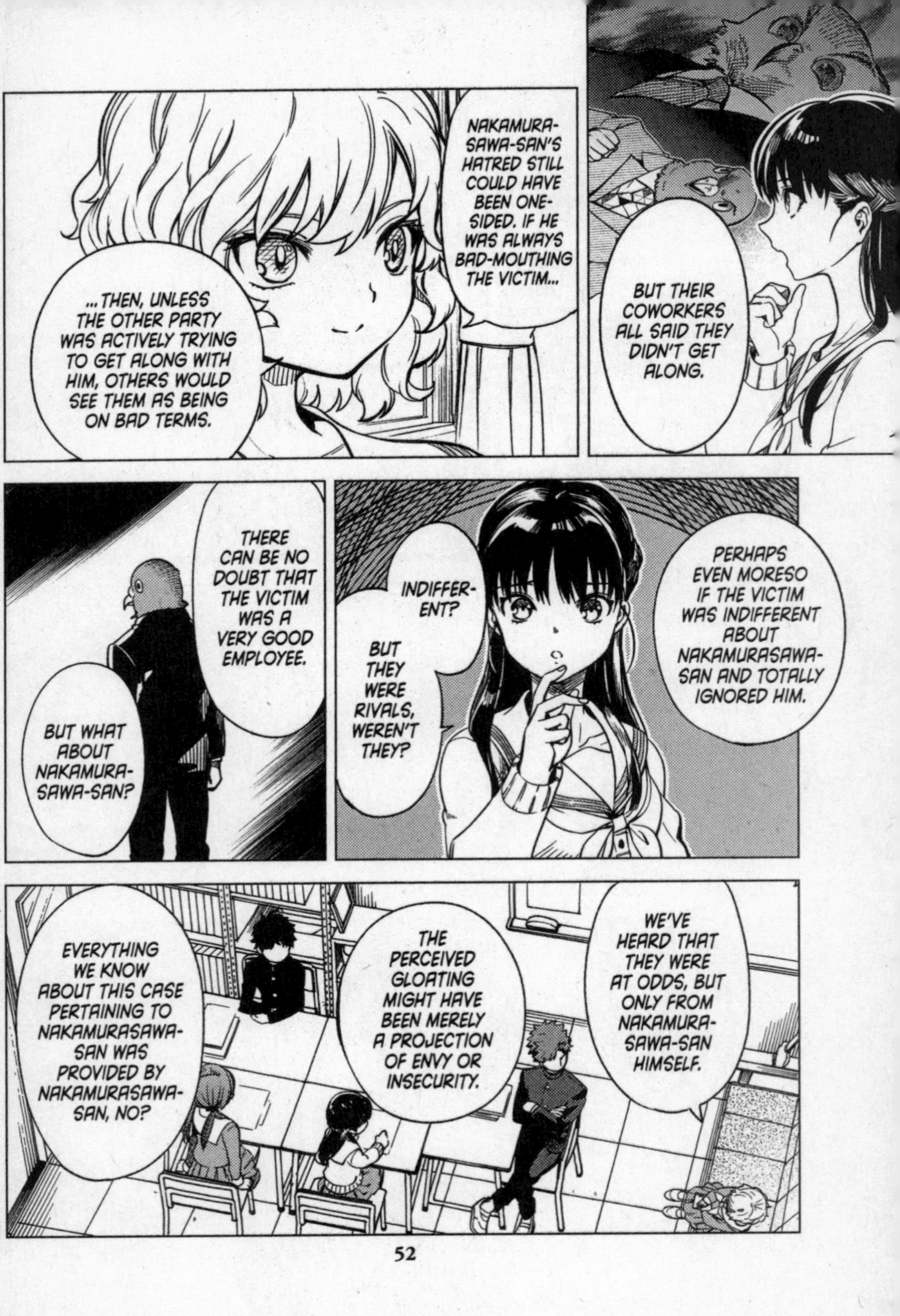
BUT THEIR COWORKERS ALL SAID THEY DIDN'T GET ALONG.
NAKAMURA-SAWA-SAN'S HATRED STILL COULD HAVE BEEN ONE-SIDED. IF HE WAS ALWAYS BAD-MOUTHING THE VICTIM...
...THEN, UNLESS THE OTHER PARTY WAS ACTIVELY TRYING TO GET ALONG WITH HIM, OTHERS WOULD SEE THEM AS BEING ON BAD TERMS.
PERHAPS EVEN MORESO IF THE VICTIM WAS INDIFFERENT ABOUT NAKAMURASAWA-SAN AND TOTALLY IGNORED HIM.
INDIFFER-ENT?
BUT THEY WERE RIVALS, WEREN'T THEY?
THERE CAN BE NO DOUBT THAT THE VICTIM WAS A VERY GOOD EMPLOYEE.
BUT WHAT ABOUT NAKAMURA-SAWA-SAN?
WE'VE HEARD THAT THEY WERE AT ODDS, BUT ONLY FROM NAKAMURA-SAWA-SAN HIMSELF.
THE PERCEIVED GLOATING MIGHT HAVE BEEN MERELY A PROJECTION OF ENVY OR INSECURITY.
EVERYTHING WE KNOW ABOUT THIS CASE PERTAINING TO NAKAMURASAWA-SAN WAS PROVIDED BY NAKAMURASAWA-SAN, NO?

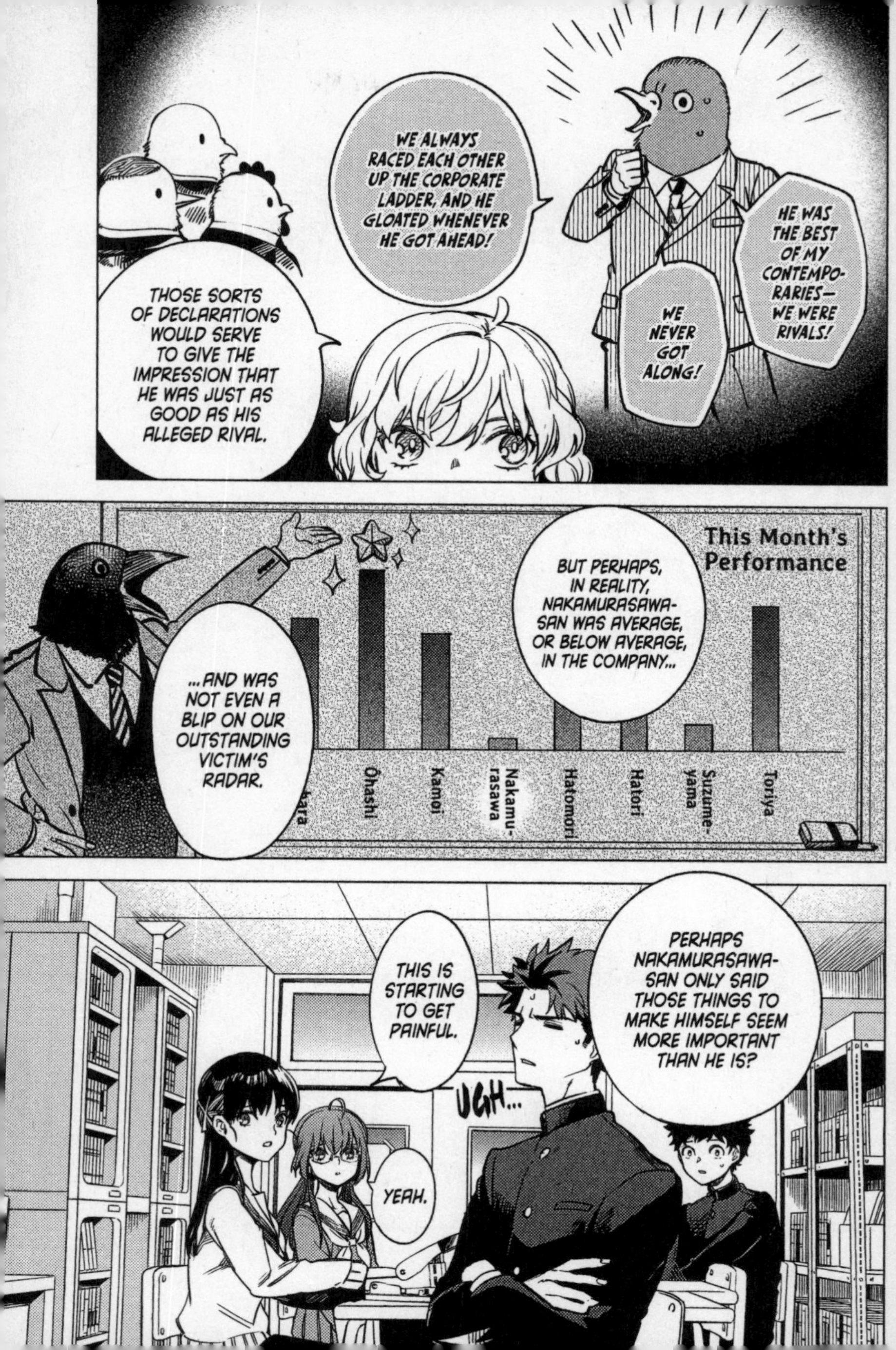
HE WAS THE BEST OF MY CONTEMPO-RARIES— WE WERE RIVALS!
WE NEVER GOT ALONG!
WE ALWAYS RACED EACH OTHER UP THE CORPORATE LADDER, AND HE GLOATED WHENEVER HE GOT AHEAD!
THOSE SORTS OF DECLARATIONS WOULD SERVE TO GIVE THE IMPRESSION THAT HE WAS JUST AS GOOD AS HIS ALLEGED RIVAL.
This Month's Performance
BUT PERHAPS, IN REALITY, NAKAMURASAWA-SAN WAS AVERAGE, OR BELOW AVERAGE, IN THE COMPANY...
...AND WAS NOT EVEN A BLIP ON OUR OUTSTANDING VICTIM'S RADAR.
Ōhashi
Kamoi
Nakamu-rasawa
Hatomori
Hatori
Suzume-yama
Toriya
PERHAPS NAKAMURASAWA-SAN ONLY SAID THOSE THINGS TO MAKE HIMSELF SEEM MORE IMPORTANT THAN HE IS?
THIS IS STARTING TO GET PAINFUL.
UGH...
YEAH.

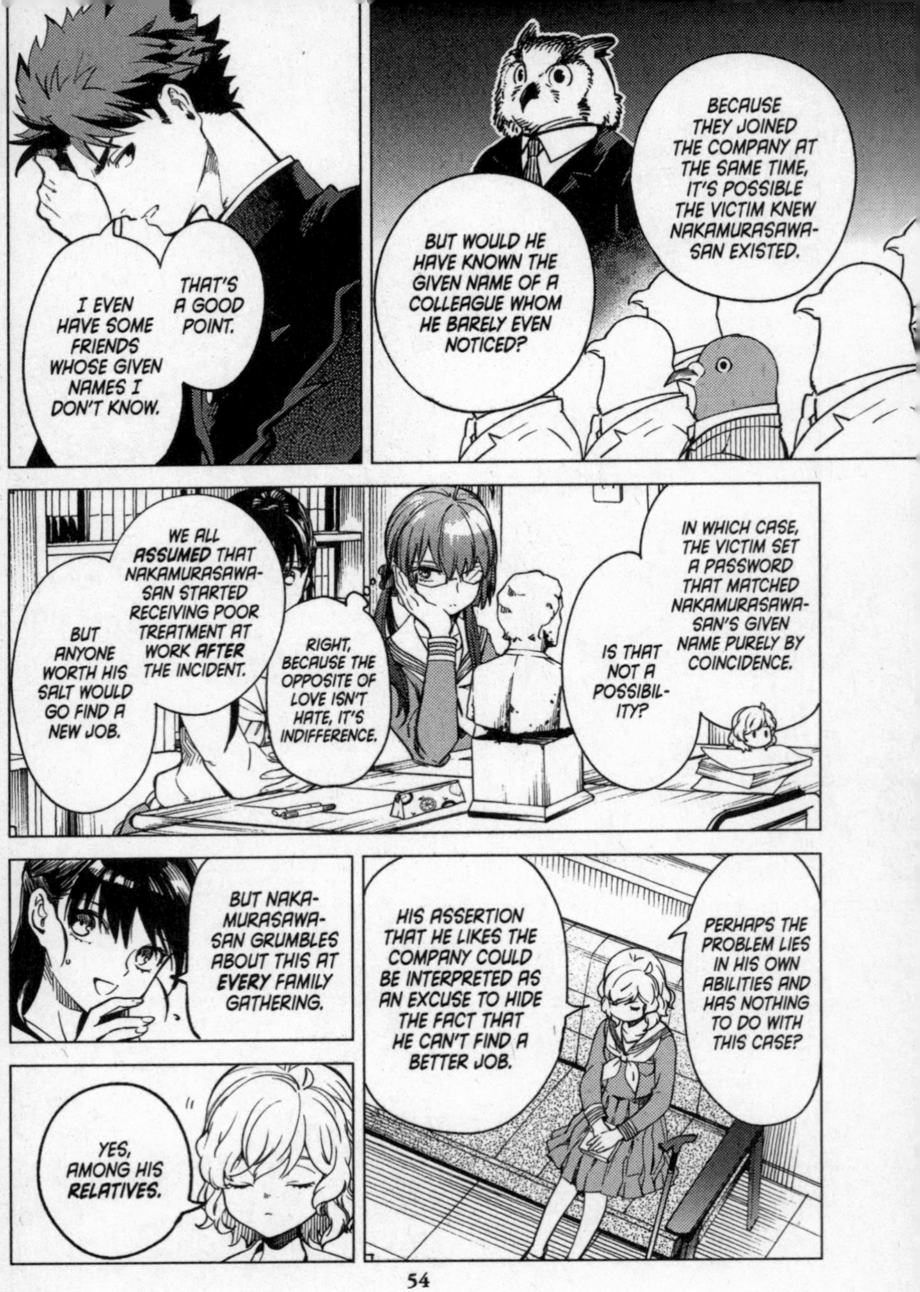
BECAUSE THEY JOINED THE COMPANY AT THE SAME TIME, IT'S POSSIBLE THE VICTIM KNEW NAKAMURASAWA-SAN EXISTED.
BUT WOULD HE HAVE KNOWN THE GIVEN NAME OF A COLLEAGUE WHOM HE BARELY EVEN NOTICED?
THAT'S A GOOD POINT.
I EVEN HAVE SOME FRIENDS WHOSE GIVEN NAMES I DON'T KNOW.
IN WHICH CASE, THE VICTIM SET A PASSWORD THAT MATCHED NAKAMURASAWA-SAN'S GIVEN NAME PURELY BY COINCIDENCE.
IS THAT NOT A POSSIBILITY?
RIGHT, BECAUSE THE OPPOSITE OF LOVE ISN'T HATE, IT'S INDIFFERENCE.
WE ALL **ASSUMED** THAT NAKAMURASAWA-SAN STARTED RECEIVING POOR TREATMENT AT WORK **AFTER** THE INCIDENT.
BUT ANYONE WORTH HIS SALT WOULD GO FIND A NEW JOB.
PERHAPS THE PROBLEM LIES IN HIS OWN ABILITIES AND HAS NOTHING TO DO WITH THIS CASE?
HIS ASSERTION THAT HE LIKES THE COMPANY COULD BE INTERPRETED AS AN EXCUSE TO HIDE THE FACT THAT HE CAN'T FIND A BETTER JOB.
BUT NAKAMURASAWA-SAN GRUMBLES ABOUT THIS AT **EVERY** FAMILY GATHERING.
YES, AMONG HIS **RELATIVES**.

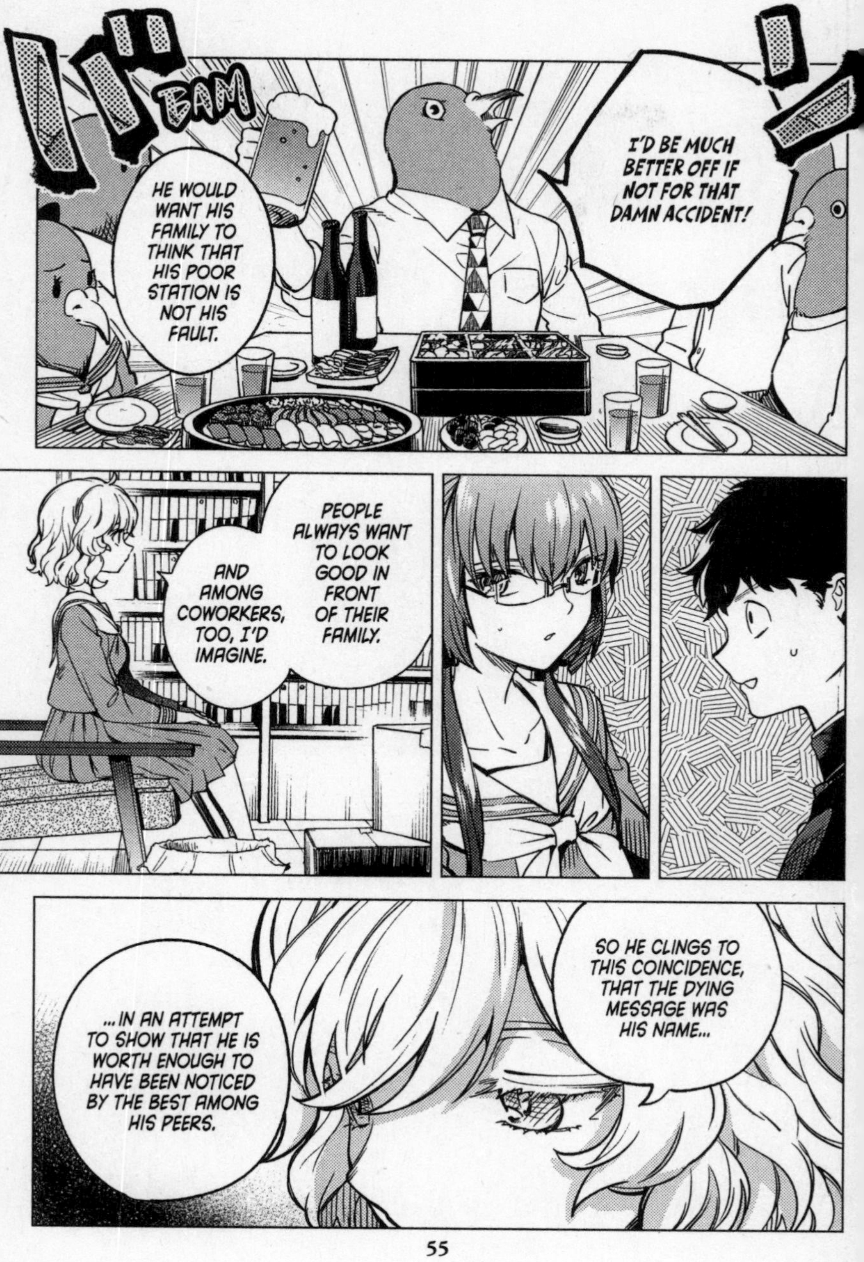
I'D BE MUCH BETTER OFF IF NOT FOR THAT DAMN ACCIDENT!
BAM
HE WOULD WANT HIS FAMILY TO THINK THAT HIS POOR STATION IS NOT HIS FAULT.
PEOPLE ALWAYS WANT TO LOOK GOOD IN FRONT OF THEIR FAMILY.
AND AMONG COWORKERS, TOO, I'D IMAGINE.
SO HE CLINGS TO THIS COINCIDENCE, THAT THE DYING MESSAGE WAS HIS NAME...
...IN AN ATTEMPT TO SHOW THAT HE IS WORTH ENOUGH TO HAVE BEEN NOTICED BY THE BEST AMONG HIS PEERS.

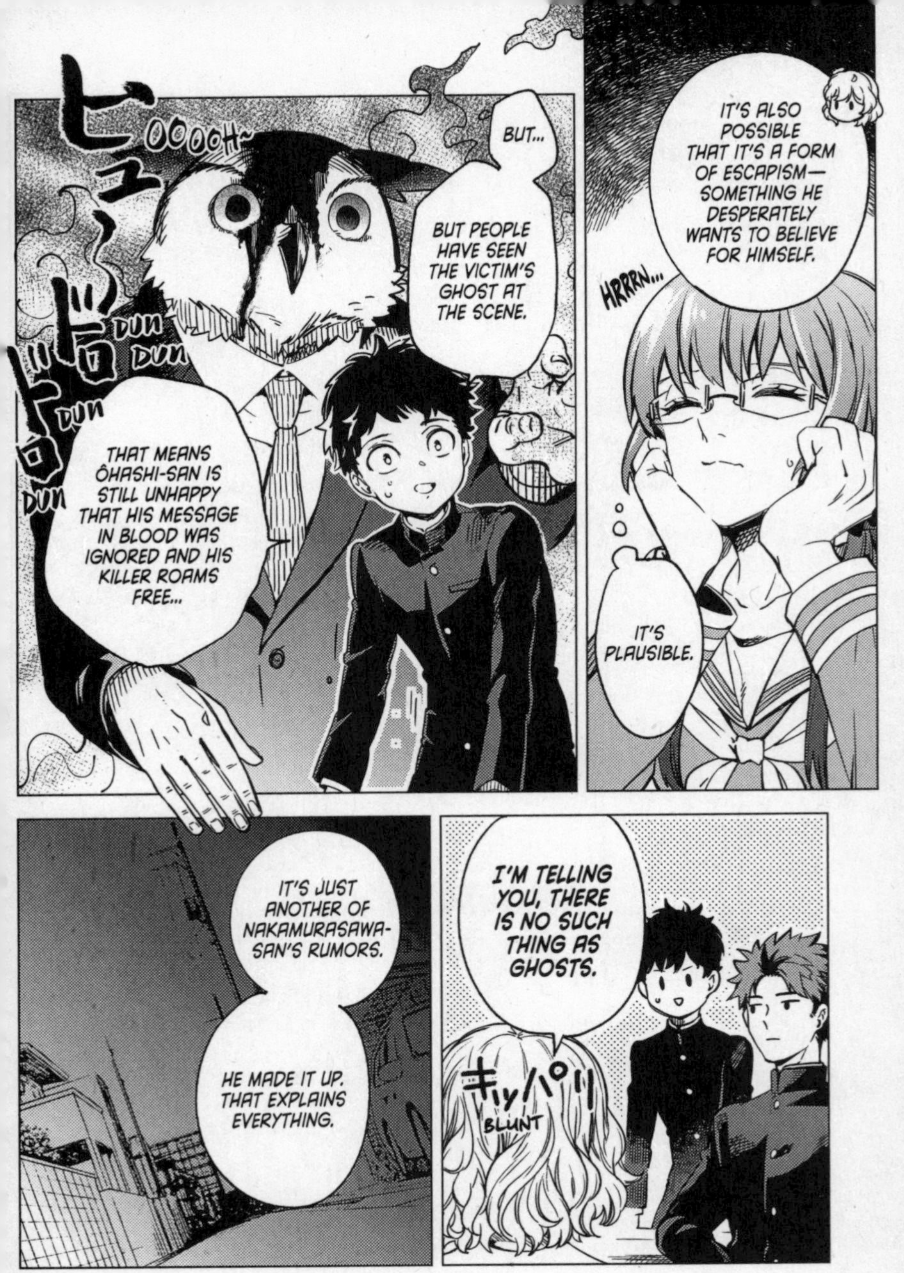

IT'S ALSO POSSIBLE THAT IT'S A FORM OF ESCAPISM—SOMETHING HE DESPERATELY WANTS TO BELIEVE FOR HIMSELF.
HRRRN...
IT'S PLAUSIBLE.
BUT...
BUT PEOPLE HAVE SEEN THE VICTIM'S GHOST AT THE SCENE.
ヒュ～～
OOOOH~
ドロドロ
DUN DUN DUN DUN
THAT MEANS ÔHASHI-SAN IS STILL UNHAPPY THAT HIS MESSAGE IN BLOOD WAS IGNORED AND HIS KILLER ROAMS FREE...
I'M TELLING YOU, THERE IS NO SUCH THING AS GHOSTS.
キッパリ
BLUNT
IT'S JUST ANOTHER OF NAKAMURASAWA-SAN'S RUMORS.
HE MADE IT UP. THAT EXPLAINS EVERYTHING.

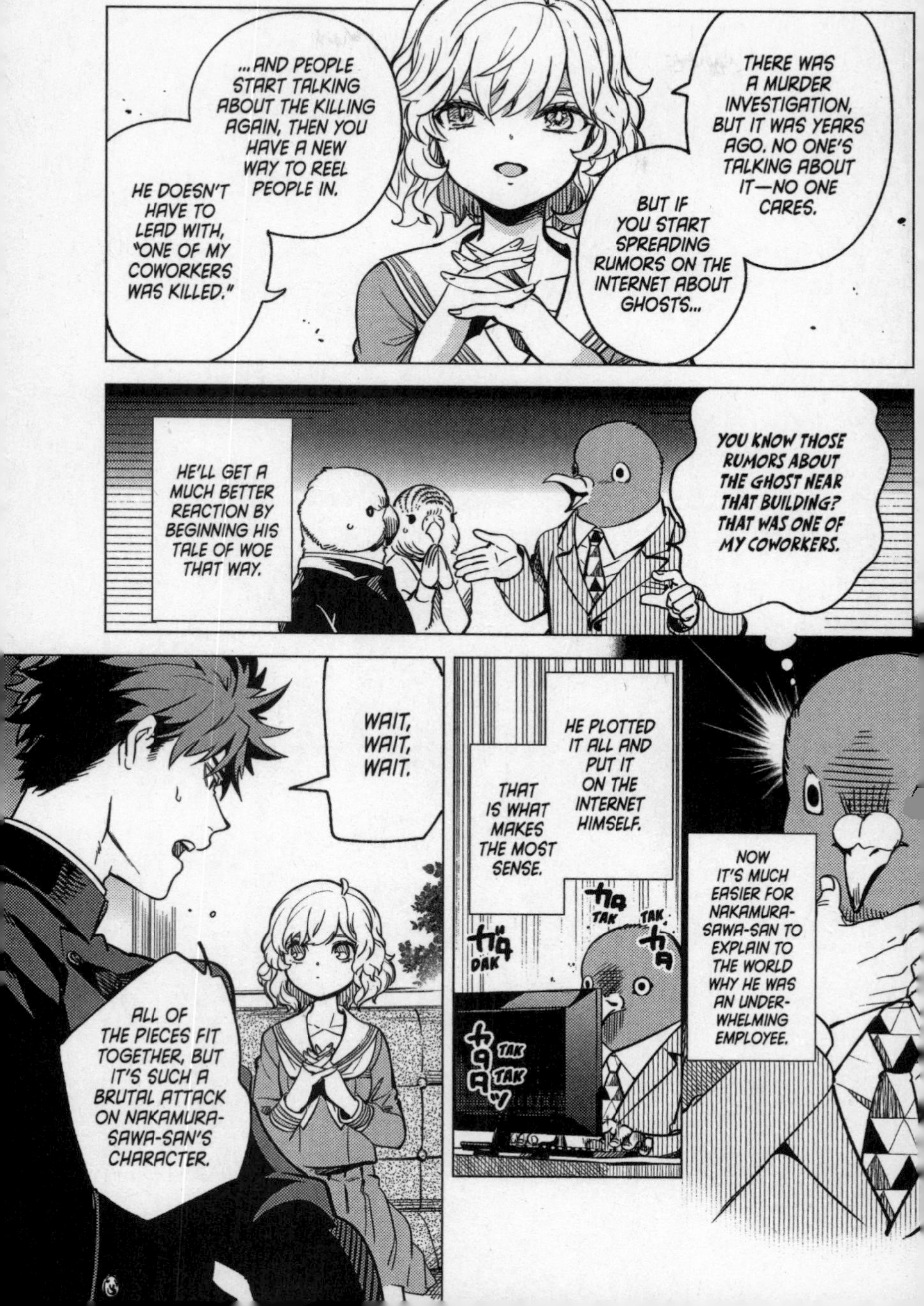
THERE WAS A MURDER INVESTIGATION, BUT IT WAS YEARS AGO. NO ONE'S TALKING ABOUT IT—NO ONE CARES.
BUT IF YOU START SPREADING RUMORS ON THE INTERNET ABOUT GHOSTS...
...AND PEOPLE START TALKING ABOUT THE KILLING AGAIN, THEN YOU HAVE A NEW WAY TO REEL PEOPLE IN.
HE DOESN'T HAVE TO LEAD WITH, "ONE OF MY COWORKERS WAS KILLED."
YOU KNOW THOSE RUMORS ABOUT THE GHOST NEAR THAT BUILDING? THAT WAS ONE OF MY COWORKERS.
HE'LL GET A MUCH BETTER REACTION BY BEGINNING HIS TALE OF WOE THAT WAY.
HE PLOTTED IT ALL AND PUT IT ON THE INTERNET HIMSELF.
THAT IS WHAT MAKES THE MOST SENSE.
TAK
TAK
DAK
TAK
TAK
NOW IT'S MUCH EASIER FOR NAKAMURA-SAWA-SAN TO EXPLAIN TO THE WORLD WHY HE WAS AN UNDER-WHELMING EMPLOYEE.
WAIT, WAIT, WAIT.
ALL OF THE PIECES FIT TOGETHER, BUT IT'S SUCH A BRUTAL ATTACK ON NAKAMURA-SAWA-SAN'S CHARACTER.

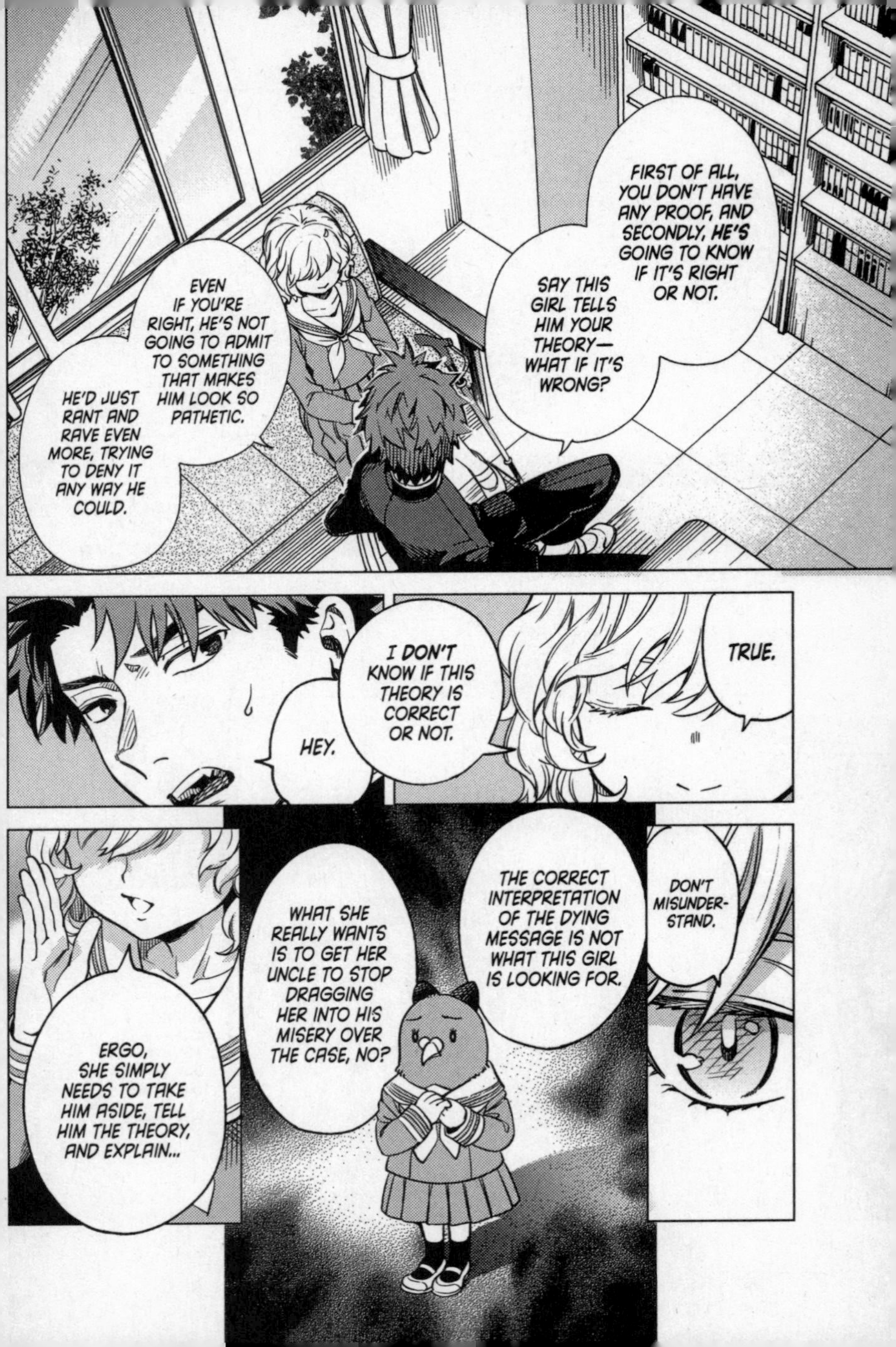
FIRST OF ALL, YOU DON'T HAVE ANY PROOF, AND SECONDLY, HE'S GOING TO KNOW IF IT'S RIGHT OR NOT.
SAY THIS GIRL TELLS HIM YOUR THEORY—WHAT IF IT'S WRONG?
EVEN IF YOU'RE RIGHT, HE'S NOT GOING TO ADMIT TO SOMETHING THAT MAKES HIM LOOK SO PATHETIC.
HE'D JUST RANT AND RAVE EVEN MORE, TRYING TO DENY IT ANY WAY HE COULD.
TRUE.
I DON'T KNOW IF THIS THEORY IS CORRECT OR NOT.
HEY.
DON'T MISUNDER-STAND.
THE CORRECT INTERPRETATION OF THE DYING MESSAGE IS NOT WHAT THIS GIRL IS LOOKING FOR.
WHAT SHE REALLY WANTS IS TO GET HER UNCLE TO STOP DRAGGING HER INTO HIS MISERY OVER THE CASE, NO?
ERGO, SHE SIMPLY NEEDS TO TAKE HIM ASIDE, TELL HIM THE THEORY, AND EXPLAIN...

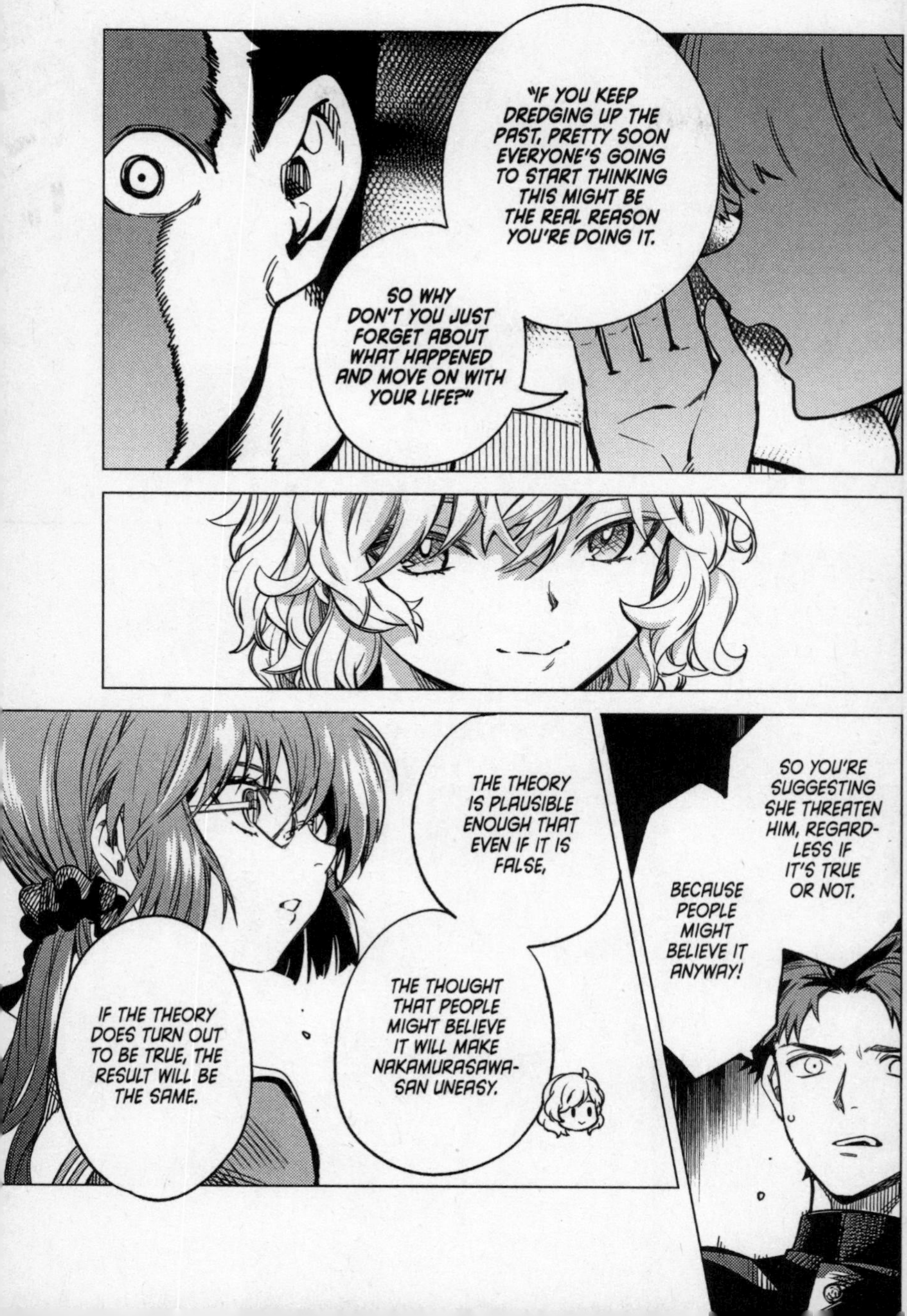
"IF YOU KEEP DREDGING UP THE PAST, PRETTY SOON EVERYONE'S GOING TO START THINKING THIS MIGHT BE THE REAL REASON YOU'RE DOING IT.
SO WHY DON'T YOU JUST FORGET ABOUT WHAT HAPPENED AND MOVE ON WITH YOUR LIFE?"
SO YOU'RE SUGGESTING SHE THREATEN HIM, REGARDLESS IF IT'S TRUE OR NOT.
BECAUSE PEOPLE MIGHT BELIEVE IT ANYWAY!
THE THEORY IS PLAUSIBLE ENOUGH THAT EVEN IF IT IS FALSE,
THE THOUGHT THAT PEOPLE MIGHT BELIEVE IT WILL MAKE NAKAMURASAWA-SAN UNEASY.
IF THE THEORY DOES TURN OUT TO BE TRUE, THE RESULT WILL BE THE SAME.

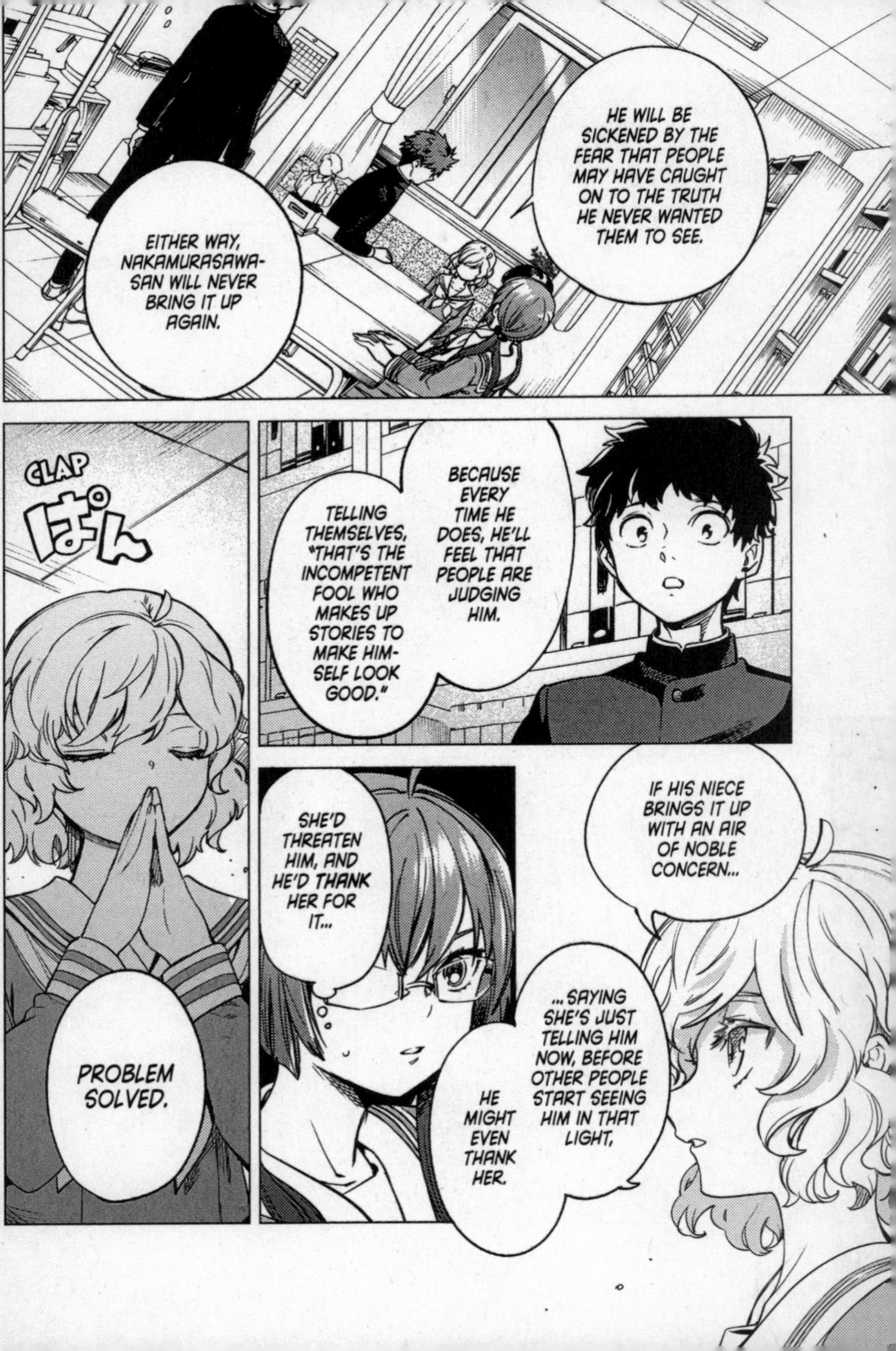
HE WILL BE SICKENED BY THE FEAR THAT PEOPLE MAY HAVE CAUGHT ON TO THE TRUTH HE NEVER WANTED THEM TO SEE.
EITHER WAY, NAKAMURASAWA-SAN WILL NEVER BRING IT UP AGAIN.
BECAUSE EVERY TIME HE DOES, HE'LL FEEL THAT PEOPLE ARE JUDGING HIM.
TELLING THEMSELVES, "THAT'S THE INCOMPETENT FOOL WHO MAKES UP STORIES TO MAKE HIM-SELF LOOK GOOD."
IF HIS NIECE BRINGS IT UP WITH AN AIR OF NOBLE CONCERN...
...SAYING SHE'S JUST TELLING HIM NOW, BEFORE OTHER PEOPLE START SEEING HIM IN THAT LIGHT,
HE MIGHT EVEN THANK HER.
SHE'D THREATEN HIM, AND HE'D THANK HER FOR IT...
CLAP
ぱん
PROBLEM SOLVED.

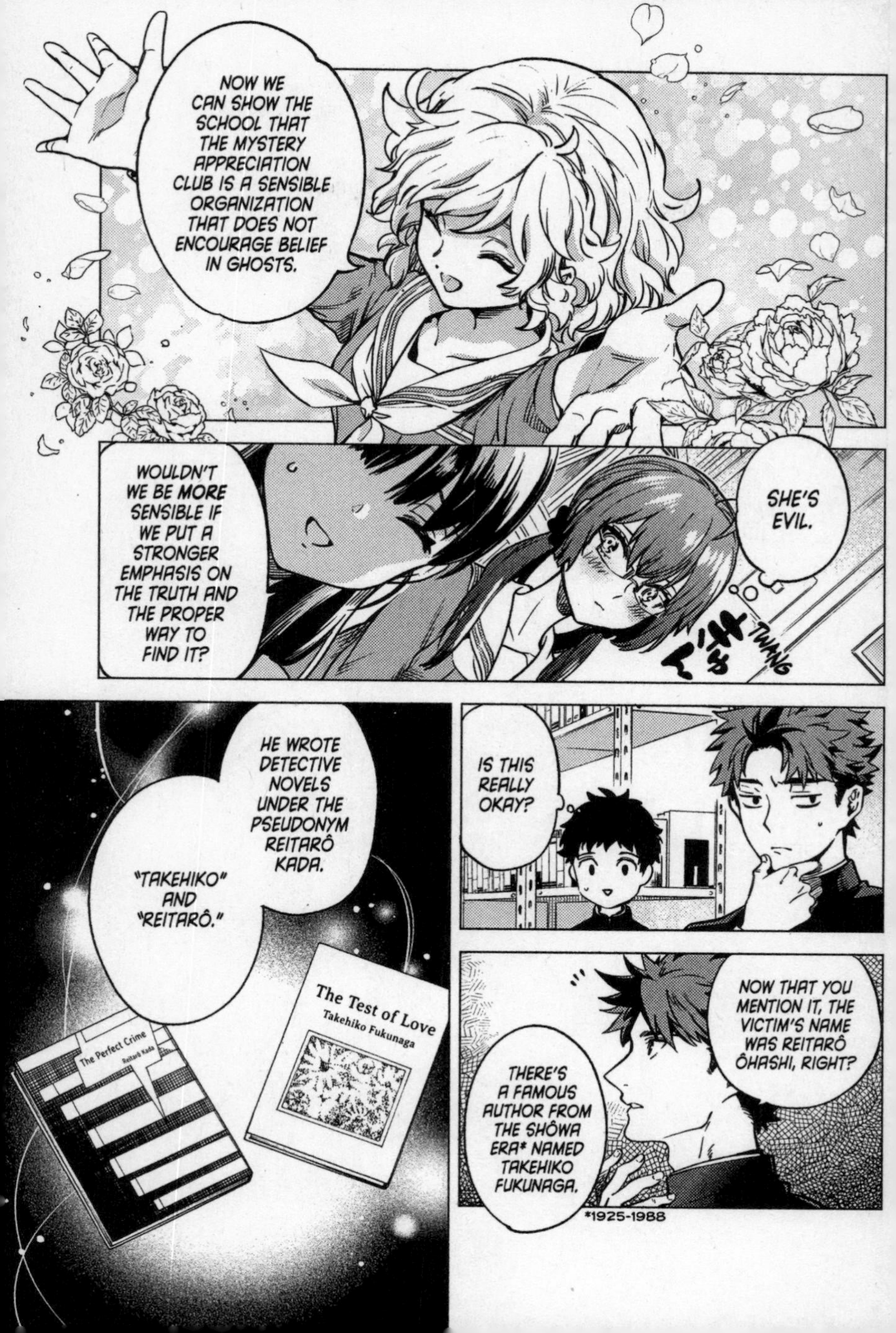
NOW WE CAN SHOW THE SCHOOL THAT THE MYSTERY APPRECIATION CLUB IS A SENSIBLE ORGANIZATION THAT DOES NOT ENCOURAGE BELIEF IN GHOSTS.
SHE'S EVIL.
TWANG
WOULDN'T WE BE MORE SENSIBLE IF WE PUT A STRONGER EMPHASIS ON THE TRUTH AND THE PROPER WAY TO FIND IT?
IS THIS REALLY OKAY?
NOW THAT YOU MENTION IT, THE VICTIM'S NAME WAS REITARÔ ÔHASHI, RIGHT?
THERE'S A FAMOUS AUTHOR FROM THE SHÔWA ERA* NAMED TAKEHIKO FUKUNAGA.
*1925-1988
HE WROTE DETECTIVE NOVELS UNDER THE PSEUDONYM REITARÔ KADA.
"TAKEHIKO" AND "REITARÔ."
The Test of Love
Takehiko Fukunaga
The Perfect Crime
Reitarô Kada

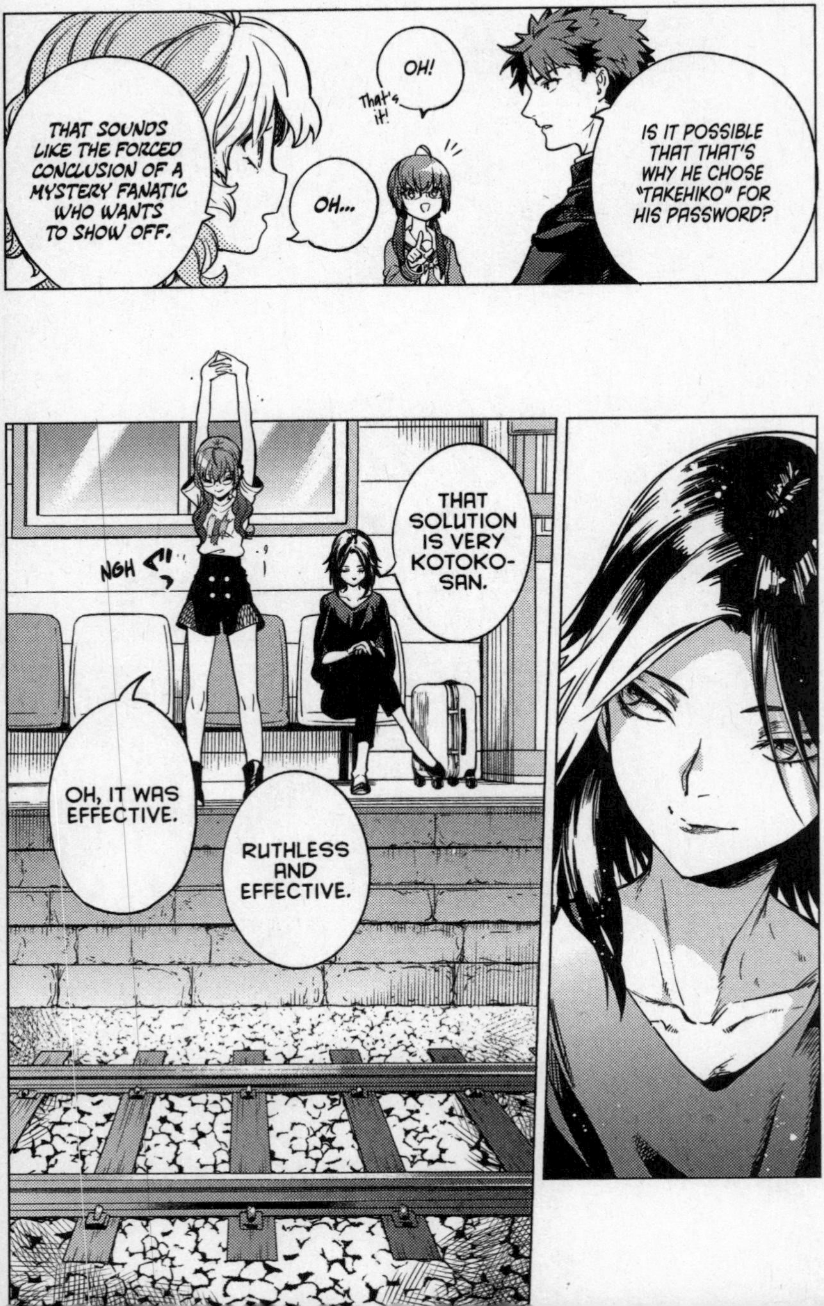
IS IT POSSIBLE THAT THAT'S WHY HE CHOSE "TAKEHIKO" FOR HIS PASSWORD?
OH!
That's it!
OH...
THAT SOUNDS LIKE THE FORCED CONCLUSION OF A MYSTERY FANATIC WHO WANTS TO SHOW OFF.
THAT SOLUTION IS VERY KOTOKO-SAN.
NGH
RUTHLESS AND EFFECTIVE.
OH, IT WAS EFFECTIVE.

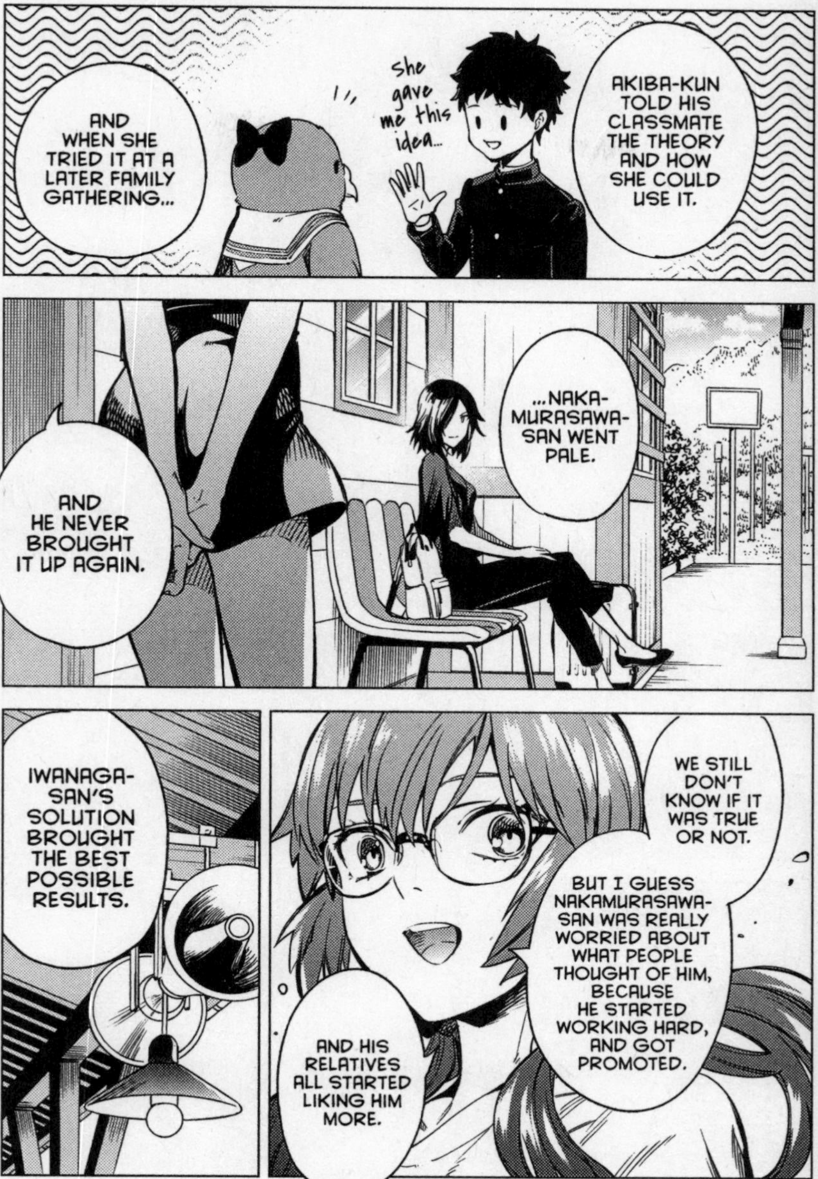
AKIBA-KUN TOLD HIS CLASSMATE THE THEORY AND HOW SHE COULD USE IT.
She gave me this idea...
AND WHEN SHE TRIED IT AT A LATER FAMILY GATHERING...
...NAKA-MURASAWA-SAN WENT PALE.
AND HE NEVER BROUGHT IT UP AGAIN.
WE STILL DON'T KNOW IF IT WAS TRUE OR NOT.
BUT I GUESS NAKAMURASAWA-SAN WAS REALLY WORRIED ABOUT WHAT PEOPLE THOUGHT OF HIM, BECAUSE HE STARTED WORKING HARD, AND GOT PROMOTED.
AND HIS RELATIVES ALL STARTED LIKING HIM MORE.
IWANAGA-SAN'S SOLUTION BROUGHT THE BEST POSSIBLE RESULTS.

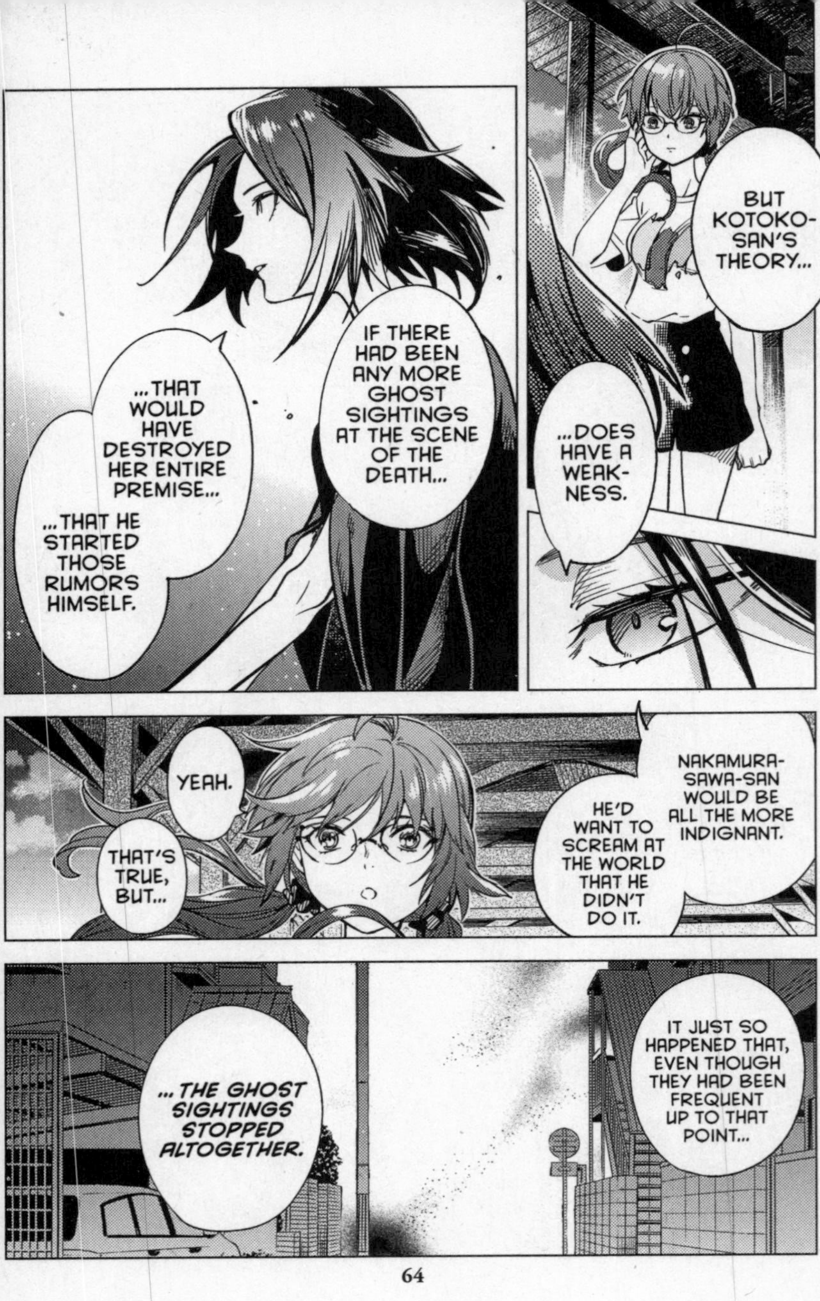
BUT KOTOKO-SAN'S THEORY...
...DOES HAVE A WEAKNESS.
IF THERE HAD BEEN ANY MORE GHOST SIGHTINGS AT THE SCENE OF THE DEATH...
...THAT WOULD HAVE DESTROYED HER ENTIRE PREMISE...
...THAT HE STARTED THOSE RUMORS HIMSELF.
NAKAMURA-SAWA-SAN WOULD BE ALL THE MORE INDIGNANT.
HE'D WANT TO SCREAM AT THE WORLD THAT HE DIDN'T DO IT.
YEAH.
THAT'S TRUE, BUT...
IT JUST SO HAPPENED THAT, EVEN THOUGH THEY HAD BEEN FREQUENT UP TO THAT POINT...
...THE GHOST SIGHTINGS STOPPED ALTOGETHER.

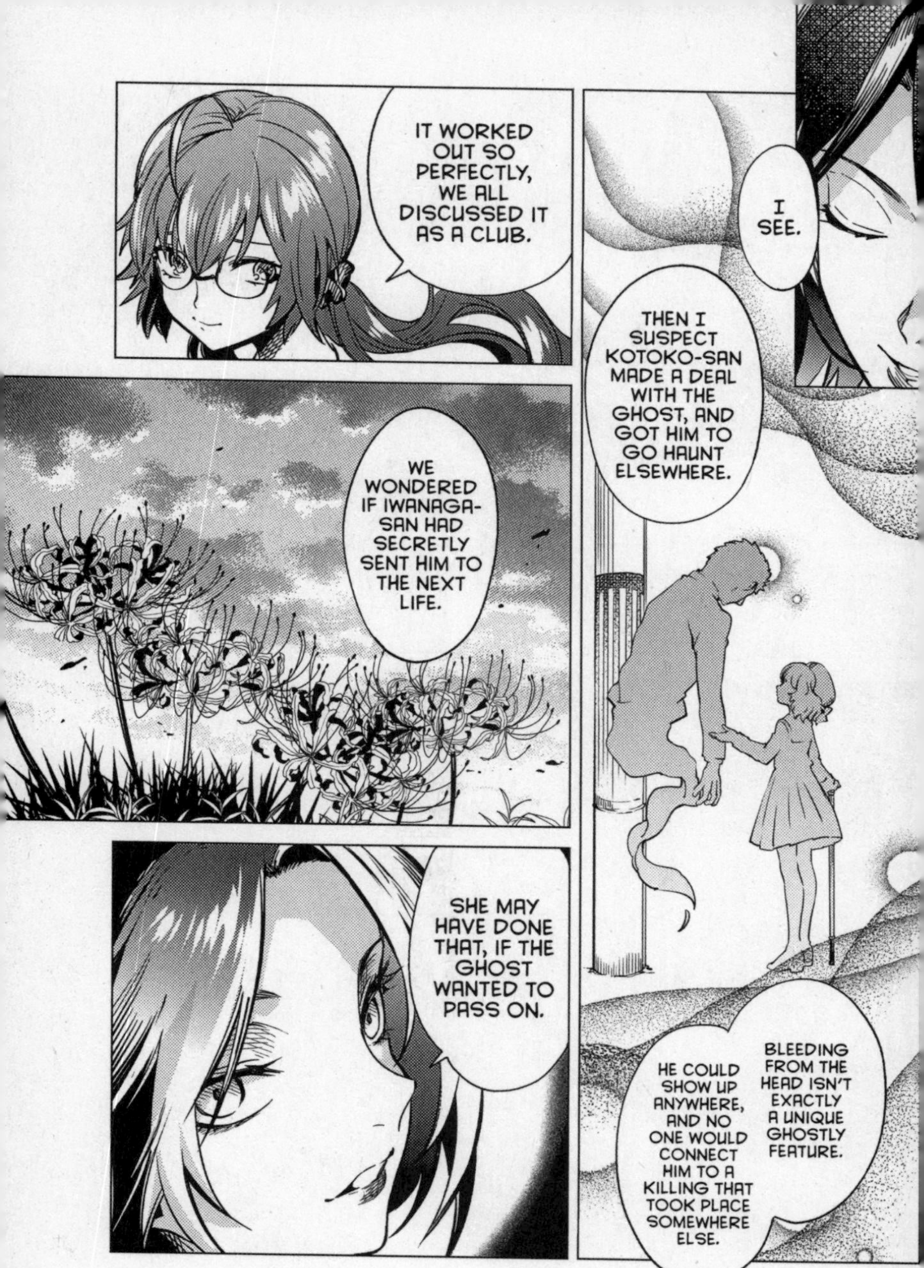
I SEE.
THEN I SUSPECT KOTOKO-SAN MADE A DEAL WITH THE GHOST, AND GOT HIM TO GO HAUNT ELSEWHERE.
BLEEDING FROM THE HEAD ISN'T EXACTLY A UNIQUE GHOSTLY FEATURE.
HE COULD SHOW UP ANYWHERE, AND NO ONE WOULD CONNECT HIM TO A KILLING THAT TOOK PLACE SOMEWHERE ELSE.
IT WORKED OUT SO PERFECTLY, WE ALL DISCUSSED IT AS A CLUB.
WE WONDERED IF IWANAGA-SAN HAD SECRETLY SENT HIM TO THE NEXT LIFE.
SHE MAY HAVE DONE THAT, IF THE GHOST WANTED TO PASS ON.

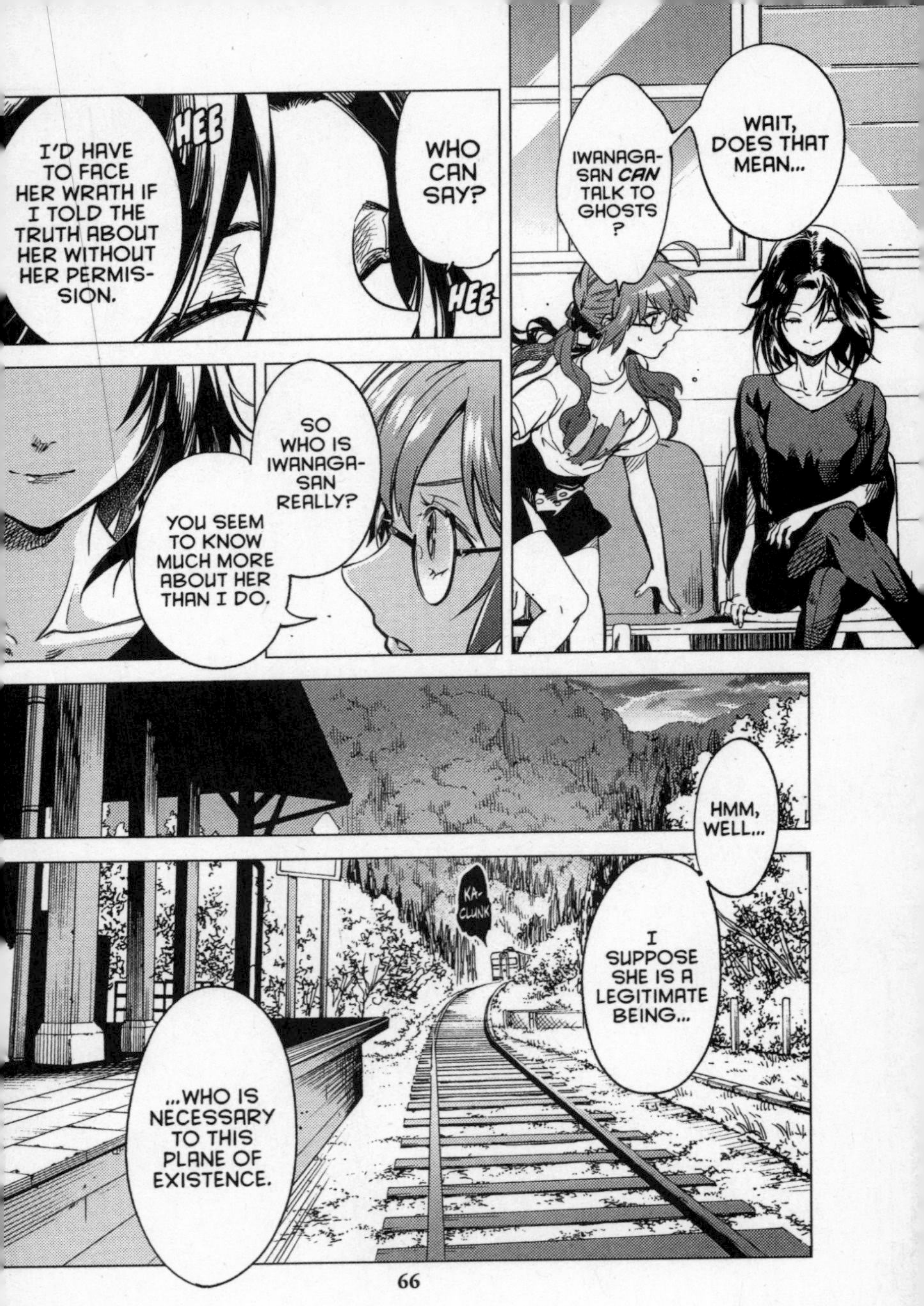
WAIT, DOES THAT MEAN...
IWANAGA-SAN *CAN* TALK TO GHOSTS?
WHO CAN SAY?
HEE
I'D HAVE TO FACE HER WRATH IF I TOLD THE TRUTH ABOUT HER WITHOUT HER PERMISSION.
HEE
SO WHO IS IWANAGA-SAN REALLY?
YOU SEEM TO KNOW MUCH MORE ABOUT HER THAN I DO.
HMM, WELL...
I SUPPOSE SHE IS A LEGITIMATE BEING...
KA-CLUNK
...WHO IS NECESSARY TO THIS PLANE OF EXISTENCE.

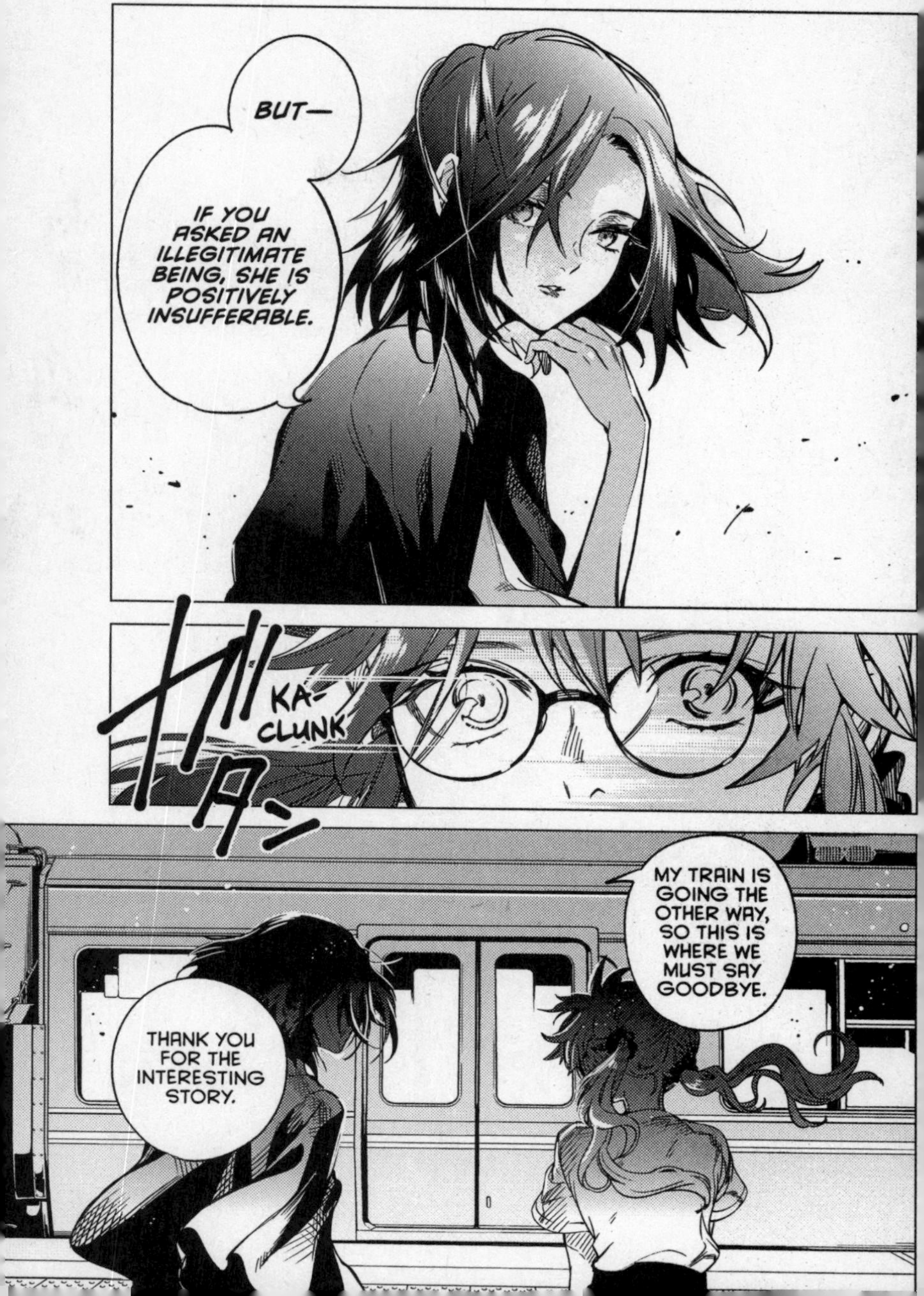
BUT—
IF YOU ASKED AN ILLEGITIMATE BEING, SHE IS POSITIVELY INSUFFERABLE.
KA-CLUNK
MY TRAIN IS GOING THE OTHER WAY, SO THIS IS WHERE WE MUST SAY GOODBYE.
THANK YOU FOR THE INTERESTING STORY.

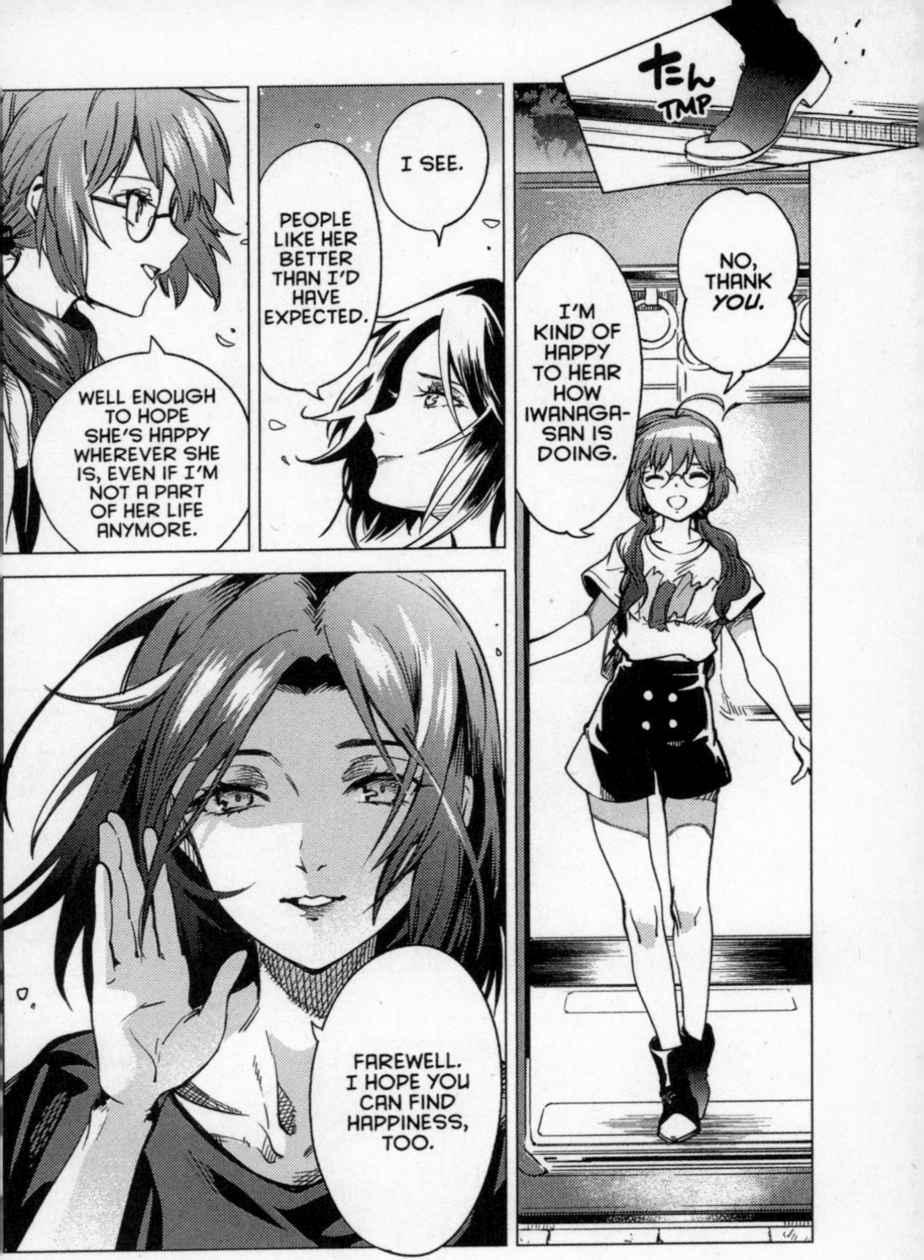
たん
TMP
NO, THANK YOU.
I'M KIND OF HAPPY TO HEAR HOW IWANAGA-SAN IS DOING.
I SEE.
PEOPLE LIKE HER BETTER THAN I'D HAVE EXPECTED.
WELL ENOUGH TO HOPE SHE'S HAPPY WHEREVER SHE IS, EVEN IF I'M NOT A PART OF HER LIFE ANYMORE.
FAREWELL. I HOPE YOU CAN FIND HAPPINESS, TOO.

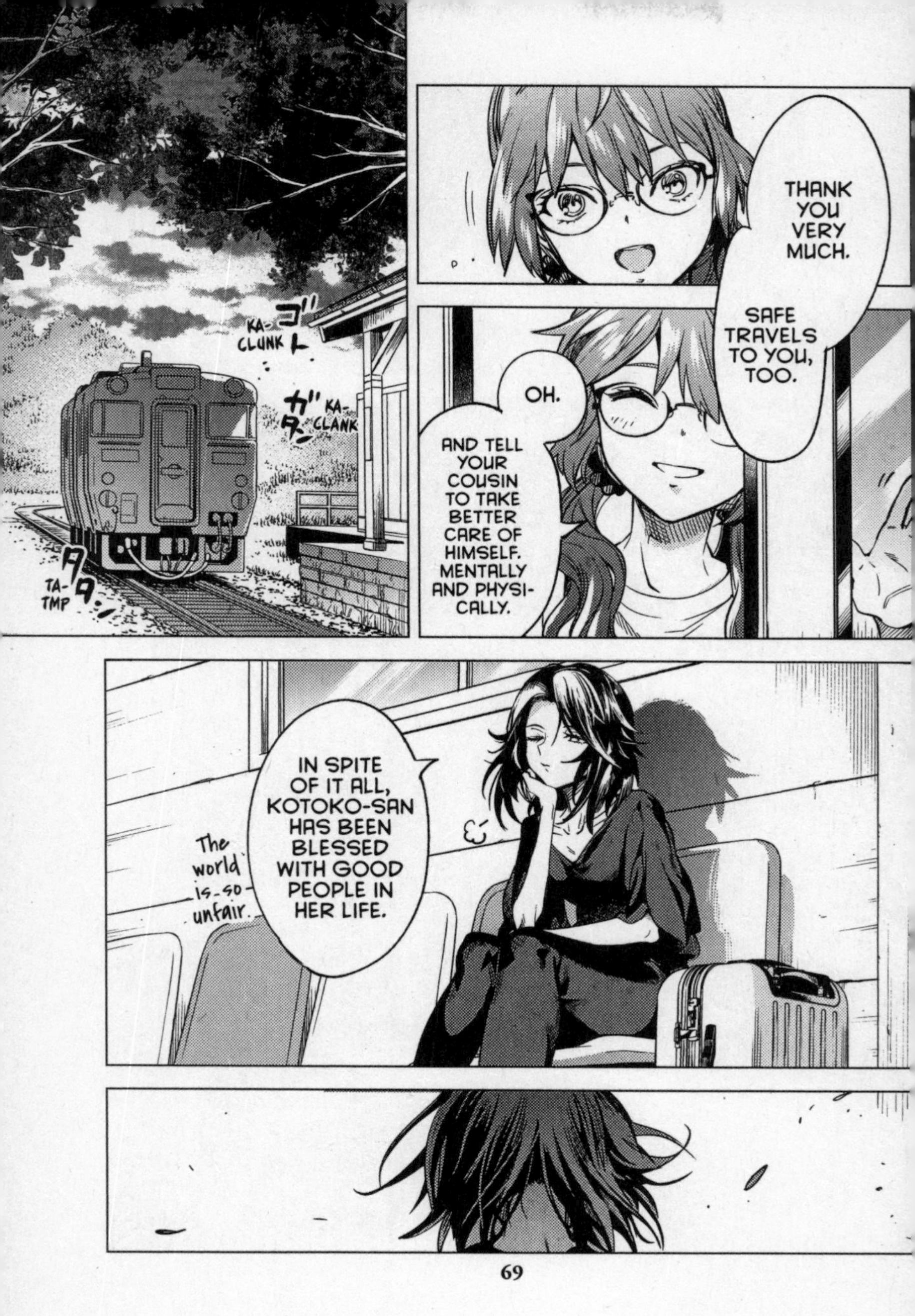
THANK YOU VERY MUCH.
SAFE TRAVELS TO YOU, TOO.
OH.
AND TELL YOUR COUSIN TO TAKE BETTER CARE OF HIMSELF. MENTALLY AND PHYSICALLY.
ゴトッ KA-CLUNK
ガタン KA-CLANK
タタ TA-TMP
IN SPITE OF IT ALL, KOTOKO-SAN HAS BEEN BLESSED WITH GOOD PEOPLE IN HER LIFE.
The world is so unfair.

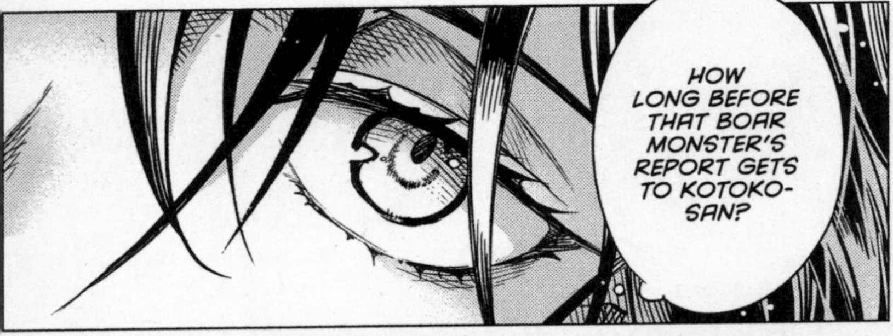
HOW LONG BEFORE THAT BOAR MONSTER'S REPORT GETS TO KOTOKO-SAN?
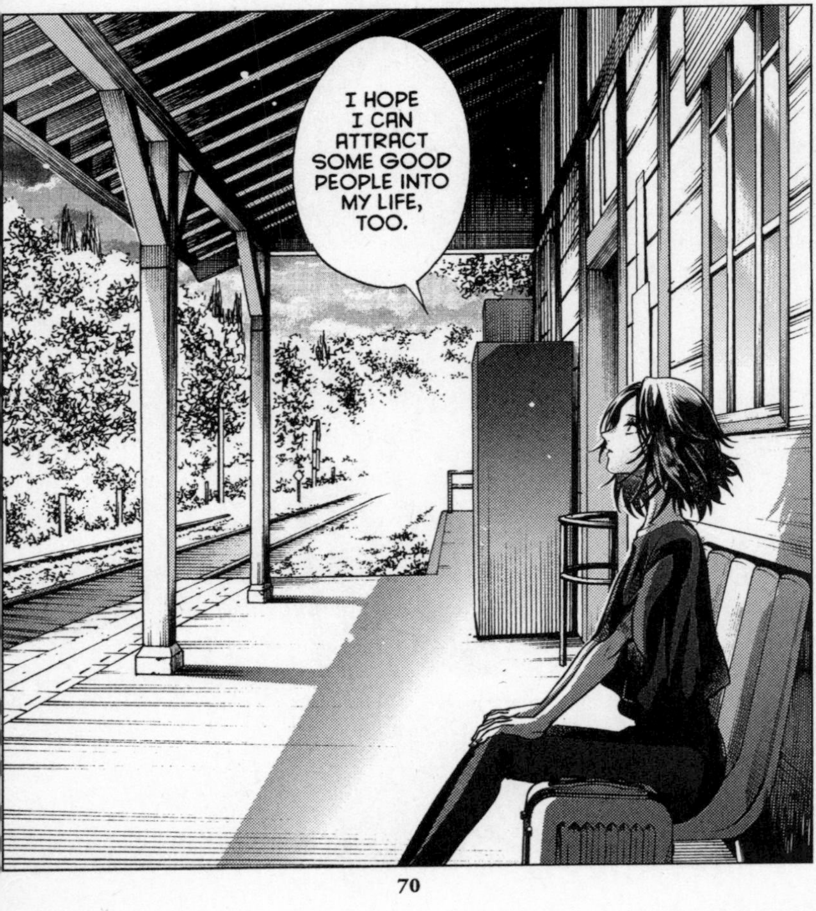
I HOPE I CAN ATTRACT SOME GOOD PEOPLE INTO MY LIFE, TOO.

IN/SPECTRE

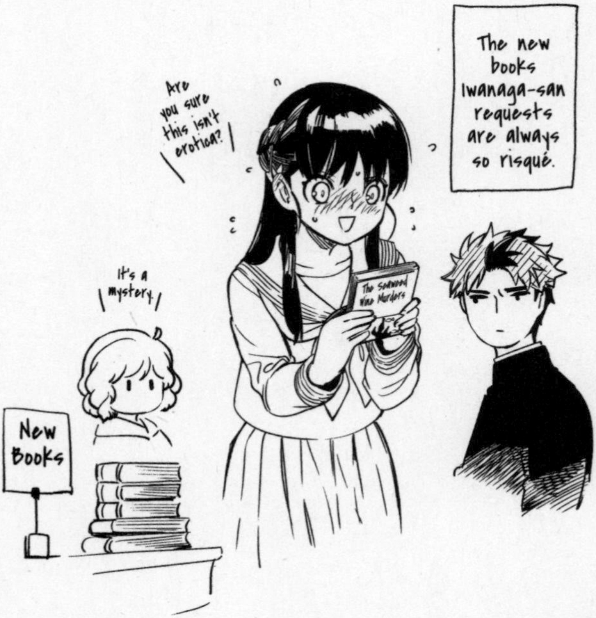
The new books Iwanaga-san requests are always so risqué.
Are you sure this isn't erotica?
The Seaweed Wine Murders
It's a mystery.
New Books

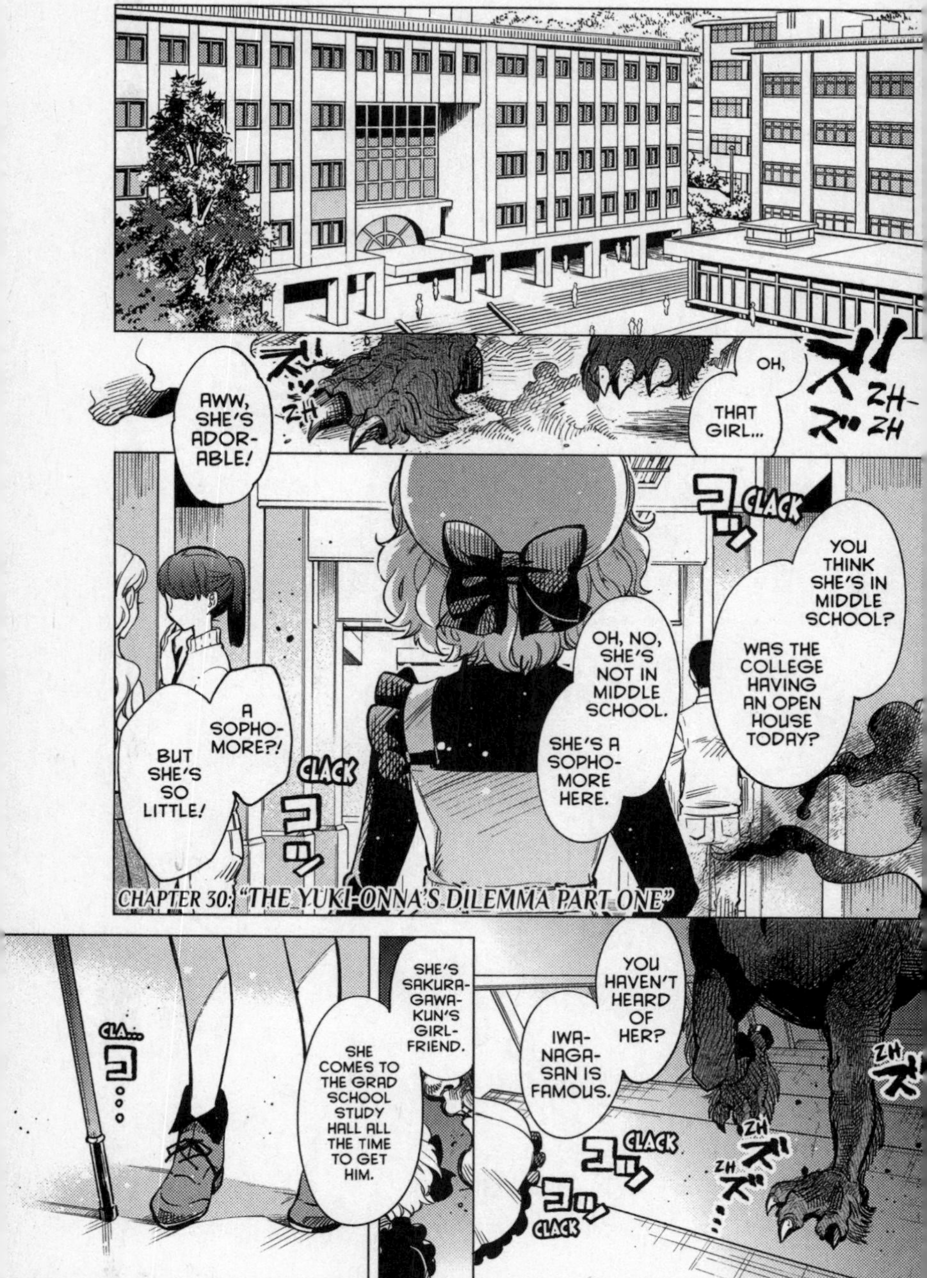
ZH-ZH
OH, THAT GIRL...
AWW, SHE'S ADORABLE!
CLACK
YOU THINK SHE'S IN MIDDLE SCHOOL?
WAS THE COLLEGE HAVING AN OPEN HOUSE TODAY?
OH, NO, SHE'S NOT IN MIDDLE SCHOOL.
SHE'S A SOPHOMORE HERE.
A SOPHOMORE?!
BUT SHE'S SO LITTLE!
CLACK
CHAPTER 30: "THE YUKI-ONNA'S DILEMMA PART ONE"
ZH
YOU HAVEN'T HEARD OF HER?
IWANAGA-SAN IS FAMOUS.
SHE'S SAKURAGAWA-KUN'S GIRLFRIEND.
SHE COMES TO THE GRAD SCHOOL STUDY HALL ALL THE TIME TO GET HIM.
ZH ZH
CLACK
CLACK
CLA...

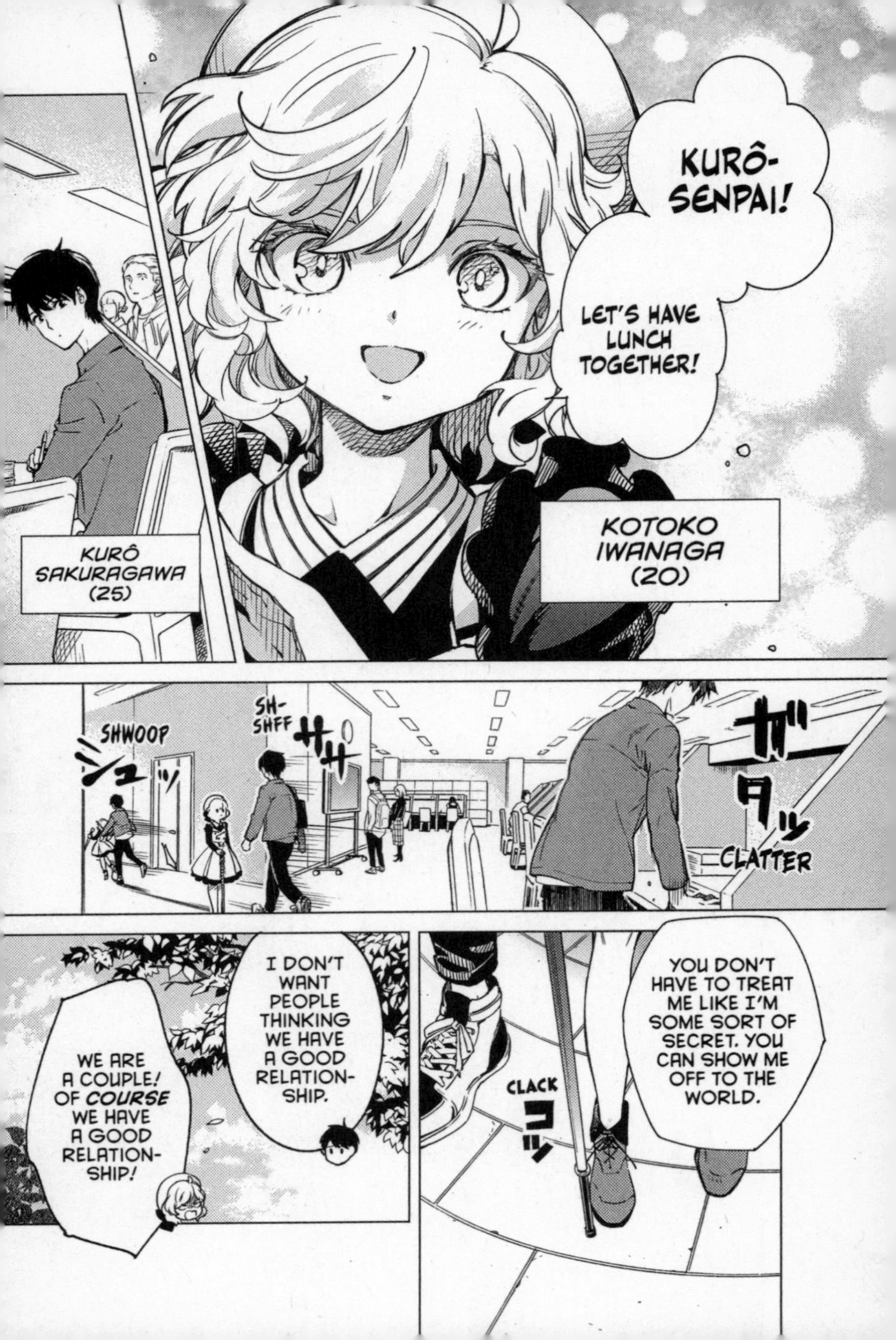
KURÔ-SENPAI!
LET'S HAVE LUNCH TOGETHER!
KOTOKO IWANAGA (20)
KURÔ SAKURAGAWA (25)
ガタッ
CLATTER
SH-SHFF
ササ
SHWOOP
シュッ
YOU DON'T HAVE TO TREAT ME LIKE I'M SOME SORT OF SECRET. YOU CAN SHOW ME OFF TO THE WORLD.
CLACK
コツ
I DON'T WANT PEOPLE THINKING WE HAVE A GOOD RELATION-SHIP.
WE ARE A COUPLE! OF *COURSE* WE HAVE A GOOD RELATION-SHIP!

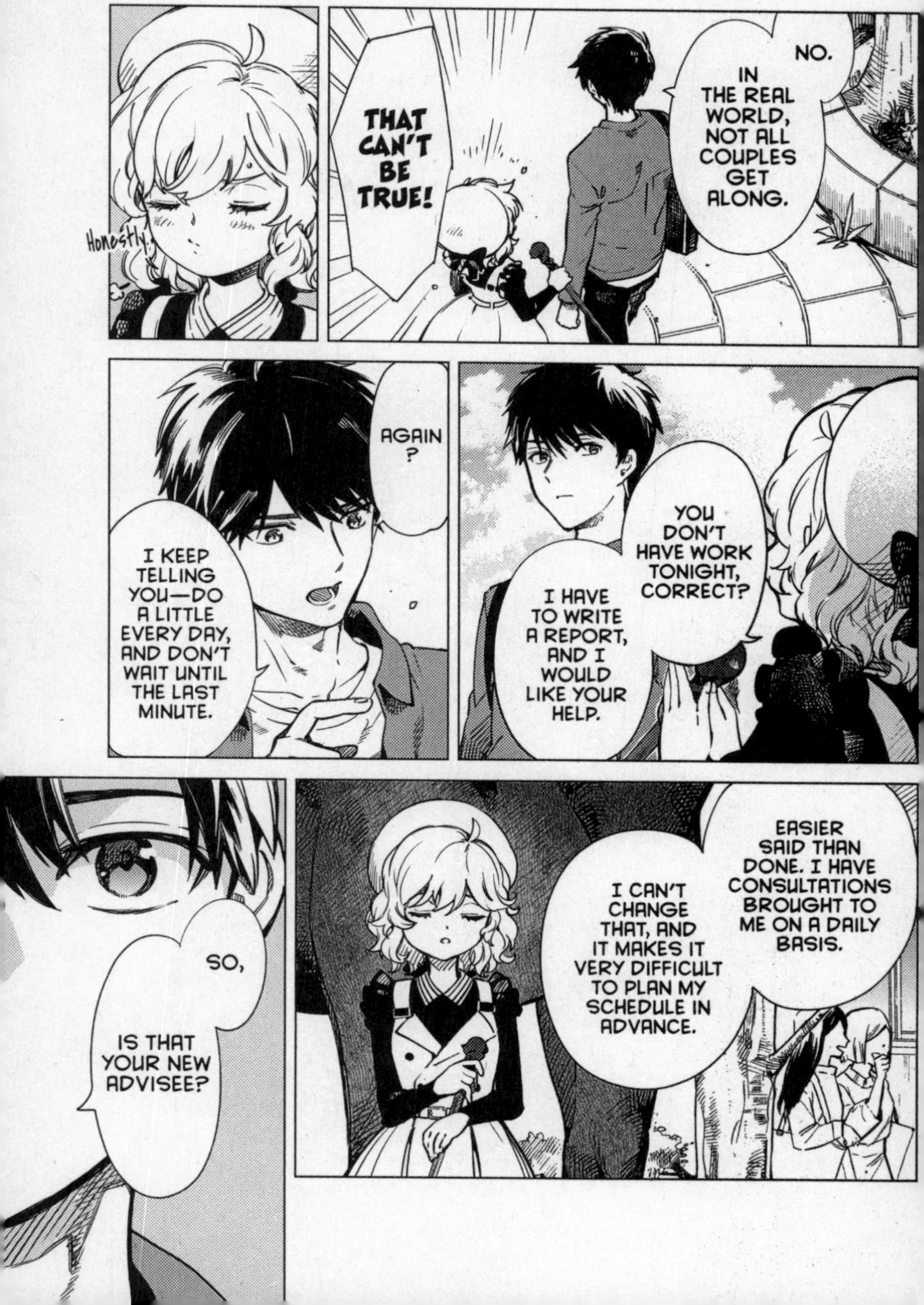
NO.
IN THE REAL WORLD, NOT ALL COUPLES GET ALONG.
THAT CAN'T BE TRUE!
Honestly.
YOU DON'T HAVE WORK TONIGHT, CORRECT?
I HAVE TO WRITE A REPORT, AND I WOULD LIKE YOUR HELP.
AGAIN?
I KEEP TELLING YOU—DO A LITTLE EVERY DAY, AND DON'T WAIT UNTIL THE LAST MINUTE.
EASIER SAID THAN DONE. I HAVE CONSULTATIONS BROUGHT TO ME ON A DAILY BASIS.
I CAN'T CHANGE THAT, AND IT MAKES IT VERY DIFFICULT TO PLAN MY SCHEDULE IN ADVANCE.
SO,
IS THAT YOUR NEW ADVISEE?

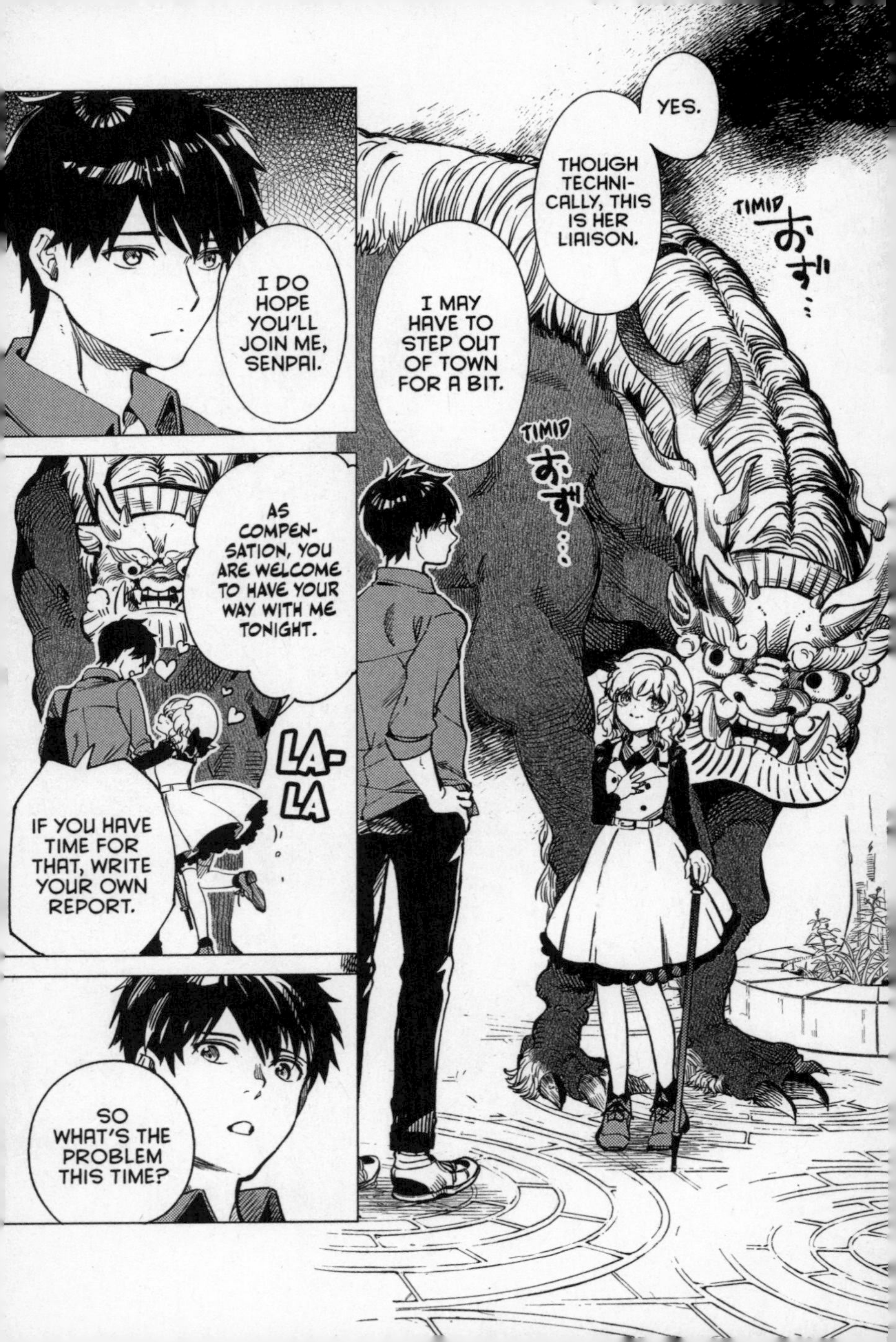
YES.
THOUGH TECHNICALLY, THIS IS HER LIAISON.
TIMID おず…
I MAY HAVE TO STEP OUT OF TOWN FOR A BIT.
TIMID おず…
I DO HOPE YOU'LL JOIN ME, SENPAI.
AS COMPENSATION, YOU ARE WELCOME TO HAVE YOUR WAY WITH ME TONIGHT.
LA-LA
IF YOU HAVE TIME FOR THAT, WRITE YOUR OWN REPORT.
SO WHAT'S THE PROBLEM THIS TIME?

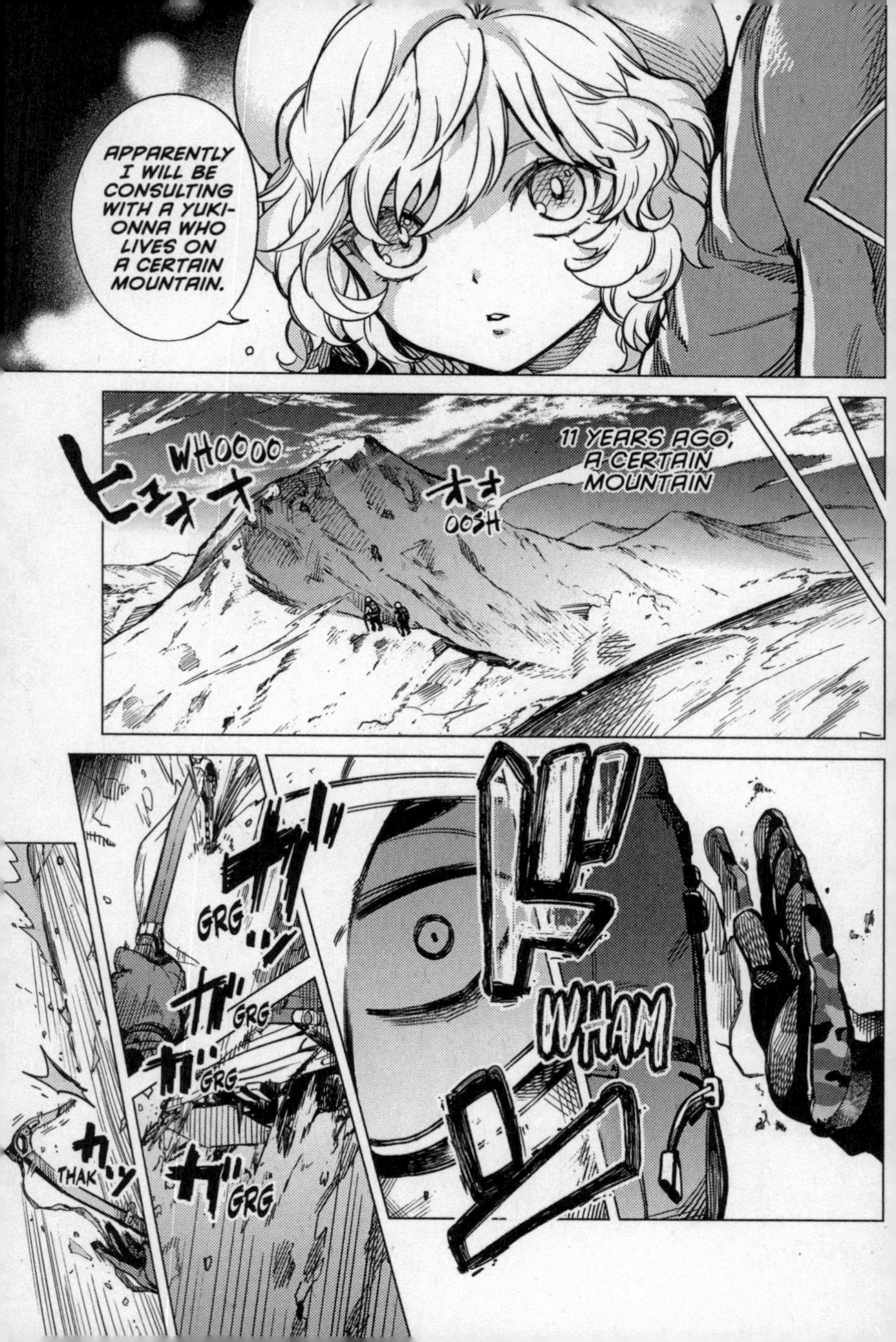
APPARENTLY I WILL BE CONSULTING WITH A YUKI-ONNA WHO LIVES ON A CERTAIN MOUNTAIN.
11 YEARS AGO, A CERTAIN MOUNTAIN
OOSH
WHOOOO
WHAM
GRG
GRG
GRG
GRG
THAK

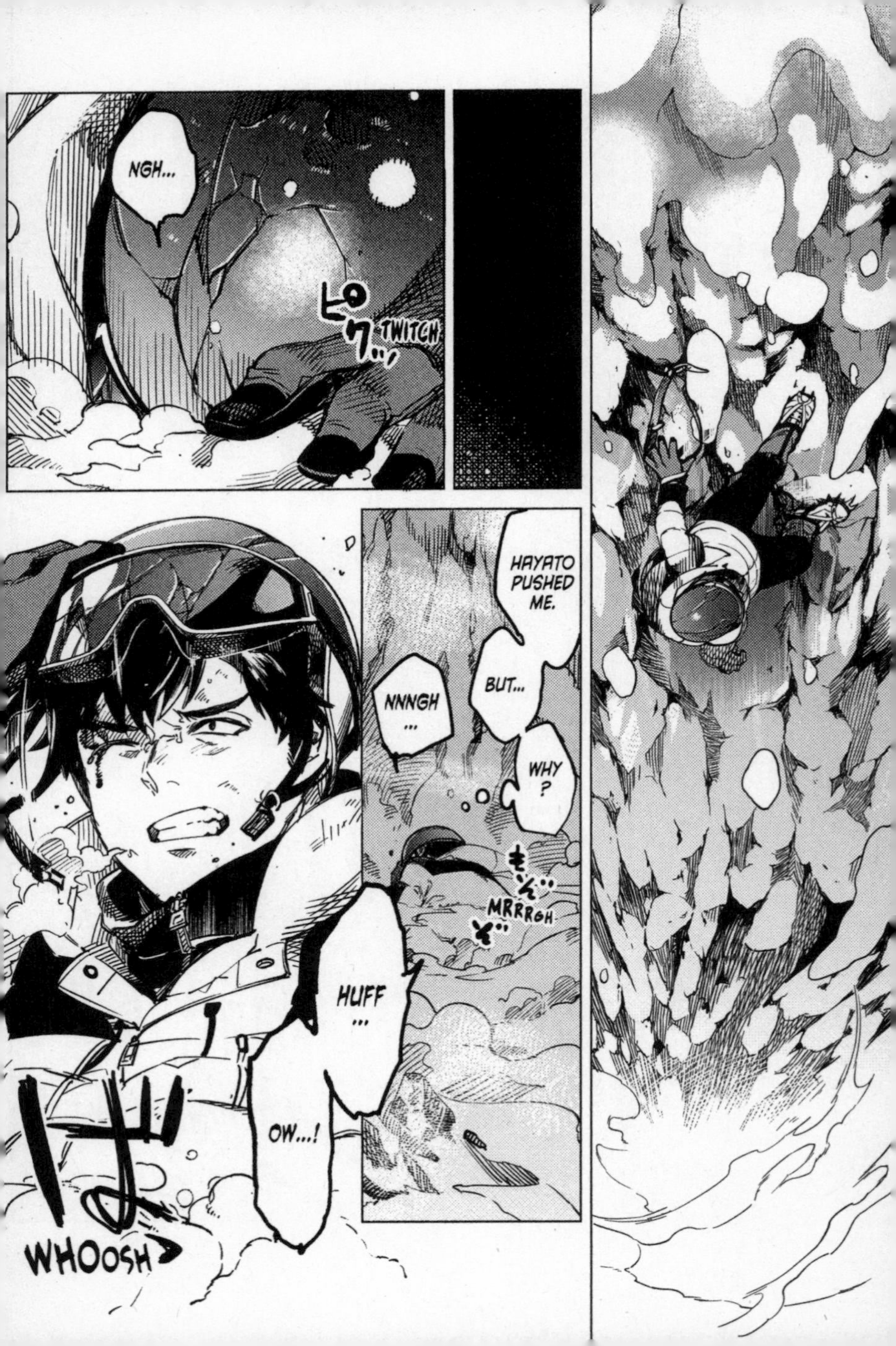
NGH...
ピク TWITCH
HAYATO PUSHED ME.
BUT...
WHY?
NNNGH...
MRRRGH
HUFF...
OW...!
WHOOSH

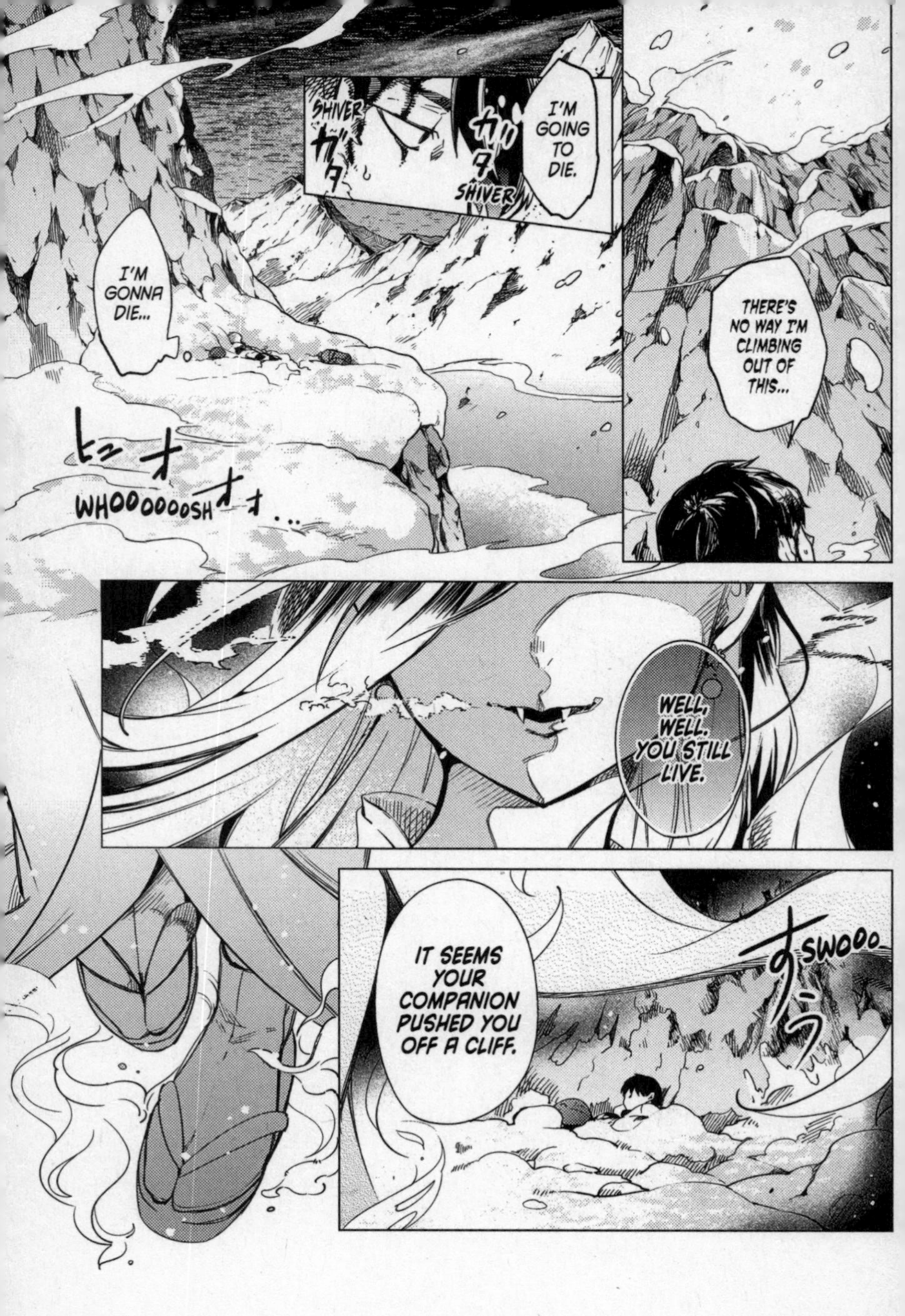

THERE'S NO WAY I'M CLIMBING OUT OF THIS...
SHIVER
I'M GOING TO DIE.
SHIVER
I'M GONNA DIE...
WHOOOOOOSH...
WELL, WELL. YOU STILL LIVE.
SWOOO
IT SEEMS YOUR COMPANION PUSHED YOU OFF A CLIFF.

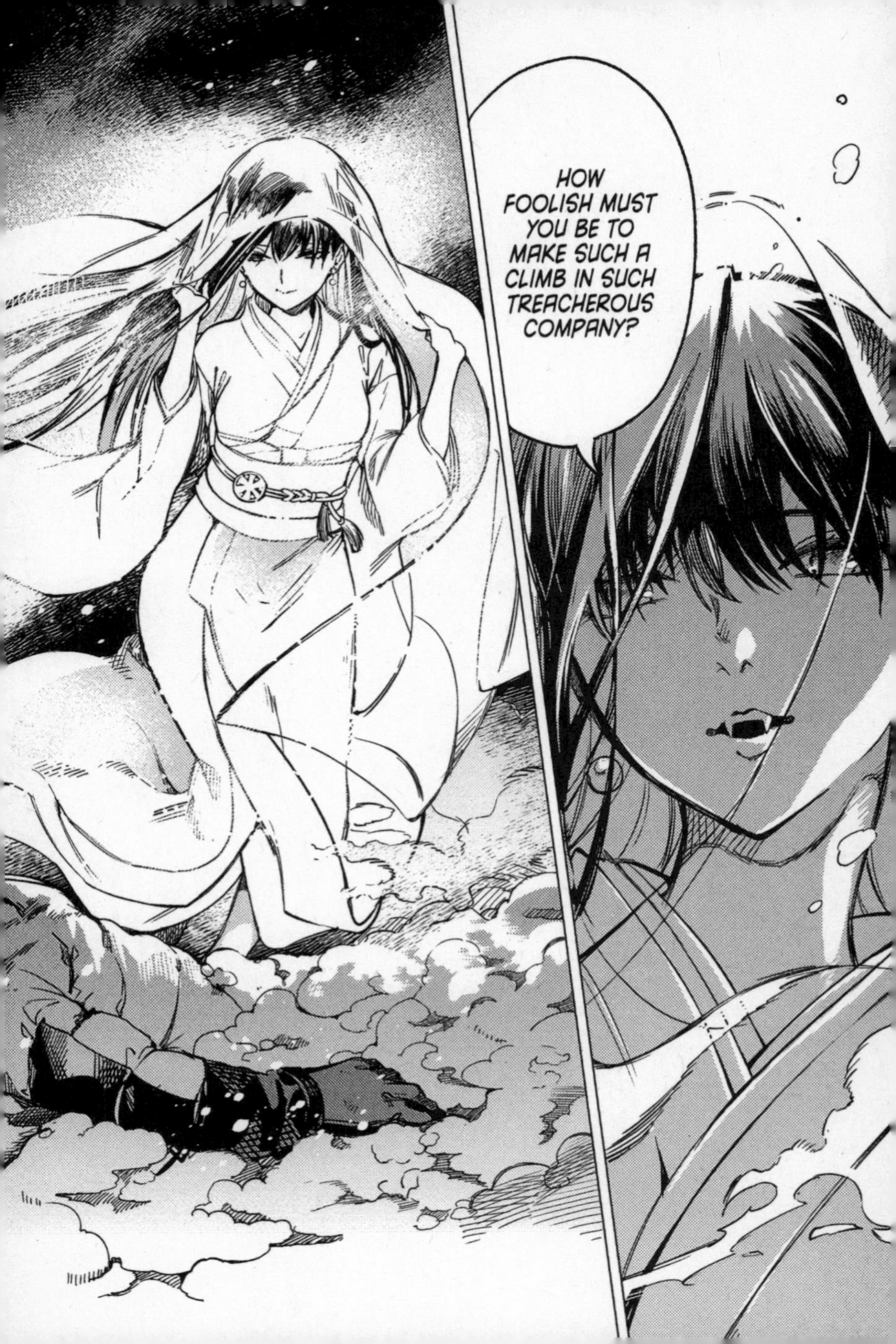
HOW FOOLISH MUST YOU BE TO MAKE SUCH A CLIMB IN SUCH TREACHEROUS COMPANY?

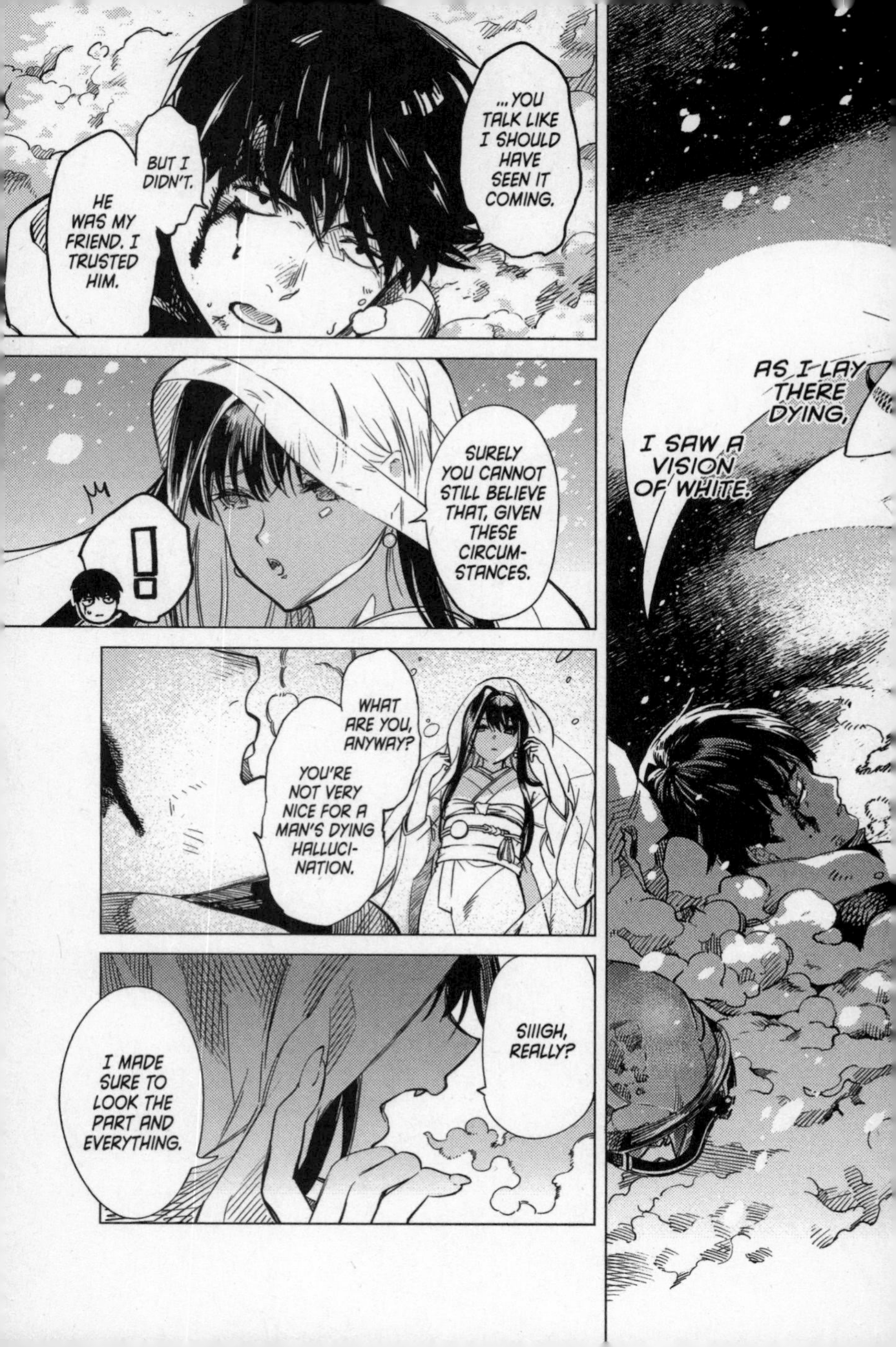
AS I LAY THERE DYING,
I SAW A VISION OF WHITE.
...YOU TALK LIKE I SHOULD HAVE SEEN IT COMING.
BUT I DIDN'T.
HE WAS MY FRIEND. I TRUSTED HIM.
SURELY YOU CANNOT STILL BELIEVE THAT, GIVEN THESE CIRCUM-STANCES.
!
WHAT ARE YOU, ANYWAY?
YOU'RE NOT VERY NICE FOR A MAN'S DYING HALLUCI-NATION.
SIIIGH, REALLY?
I MADE SURE TO LOOK THE PART AND EVERYTHING.

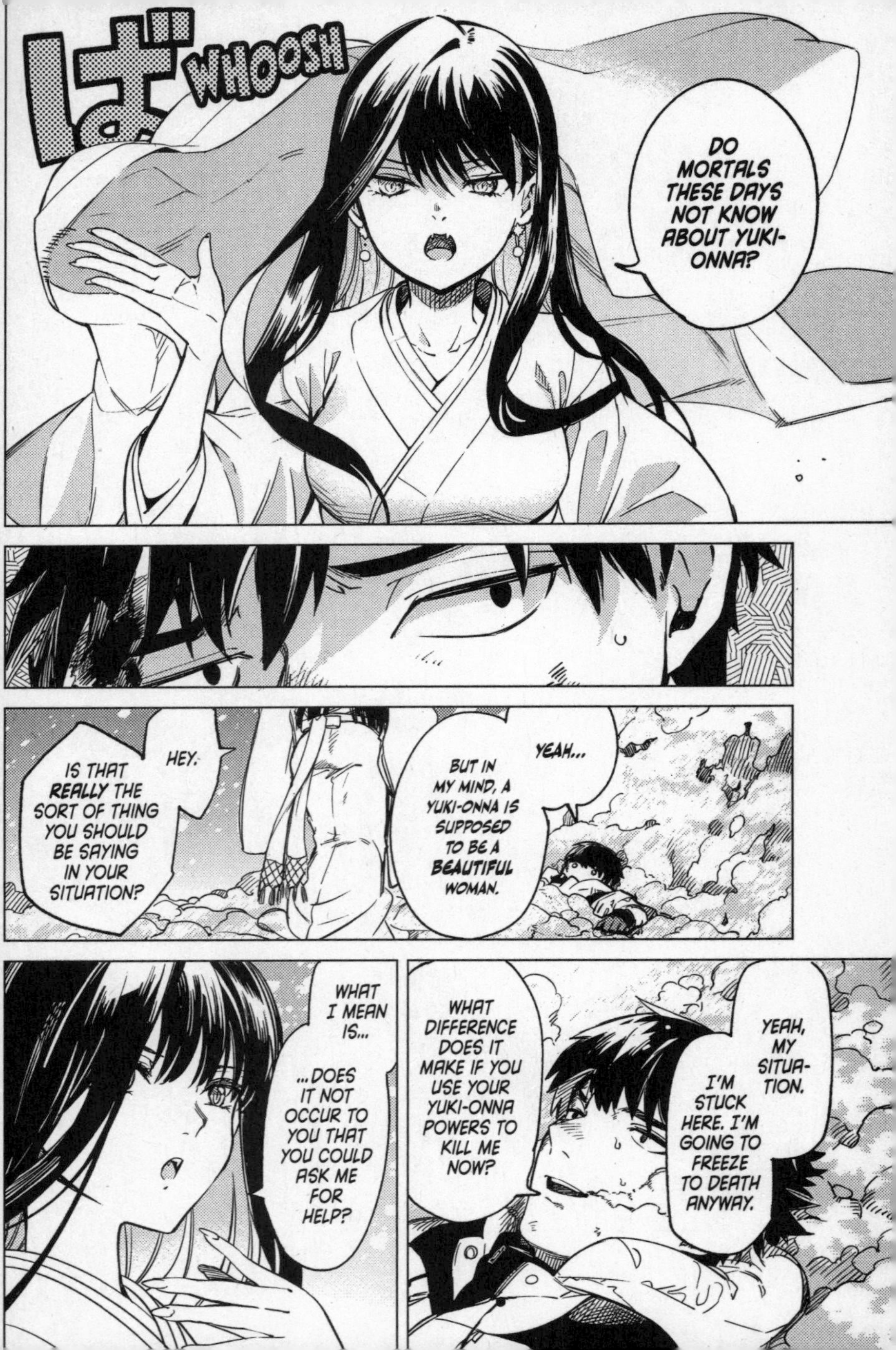
ば
WHOOSH
DO MORTALS THESE DAYS NOT KNOW ABOUT YUKI-ONNA?
YEAH...
BUT IN MY MIND, A YUKI-ONNA IS SUPPOSED TO BE A **BEAUTIFUL** WOMAN.
HEY.
IS THAT **REALLY** THE SORT OF THING YOU SHOULD BE SAYING IN YOUR SITUATION?
YEAH, MY SITUA-TION.
I'M STUCK HERE. I'M GOING TO FREEZE TO DEATH ANYWAY.
WHAT DIFFERENCE DOES IT MAKE IF YOU USE YOUR YUKI-ONNA POWERS TO KILL ME NOW?
WHAT I MEAN IS...
...DOES IT NOT OCCUR TO YOU THAT YOU COULD ASK ME FOR HELP?

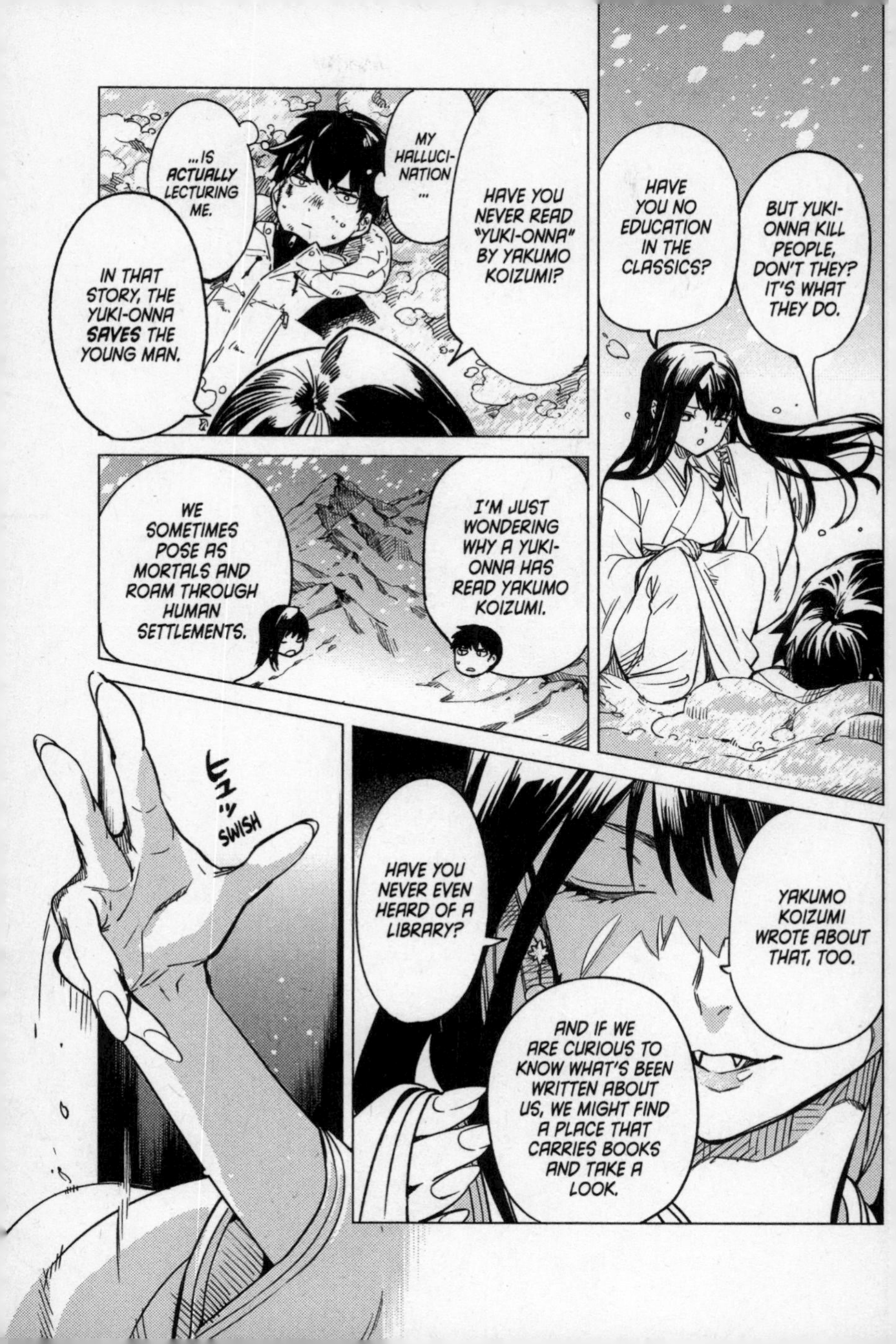
BUT YUKI-ONNA KILL PEOPLE, DON'T THEY? IT'S WHAT THEY DO.
HAVE YOU NO EDUCATION IN THE CLASSICS?
HAVE YOU NEVER READ "YUKI-ONNA" BY YAKUMO KOIZUMI?
MY HALLUCINATION...
...IS ACTUALLY LECTURING ME.
IN THAT STORY, THE YUKI-ONNA SAVES THE YOUNG MAN.
I'M JUST WONDERING WHY A YUKI-ONNA HAS READ YAKUMO KOIZUMI.
WE SOMETIMES POSE AS MORTALS AND ROAM THROUGH HUMAN SETTLEMENTS.
YAKUMO KOIZUMI WROTE ABOUT THAT, TOO.
HAVE YOU NEVER EVEN HEARD OF A LIBRARY?
AND IF WE ARE CURIOUS TO KNOW WHAT'S BEEN WRITTEN ABOUT US, WE MIGHT FIND A PLACE THAT CARRIES BOOKS AND TAKE A LOOK.
ヒュッ
SWISH

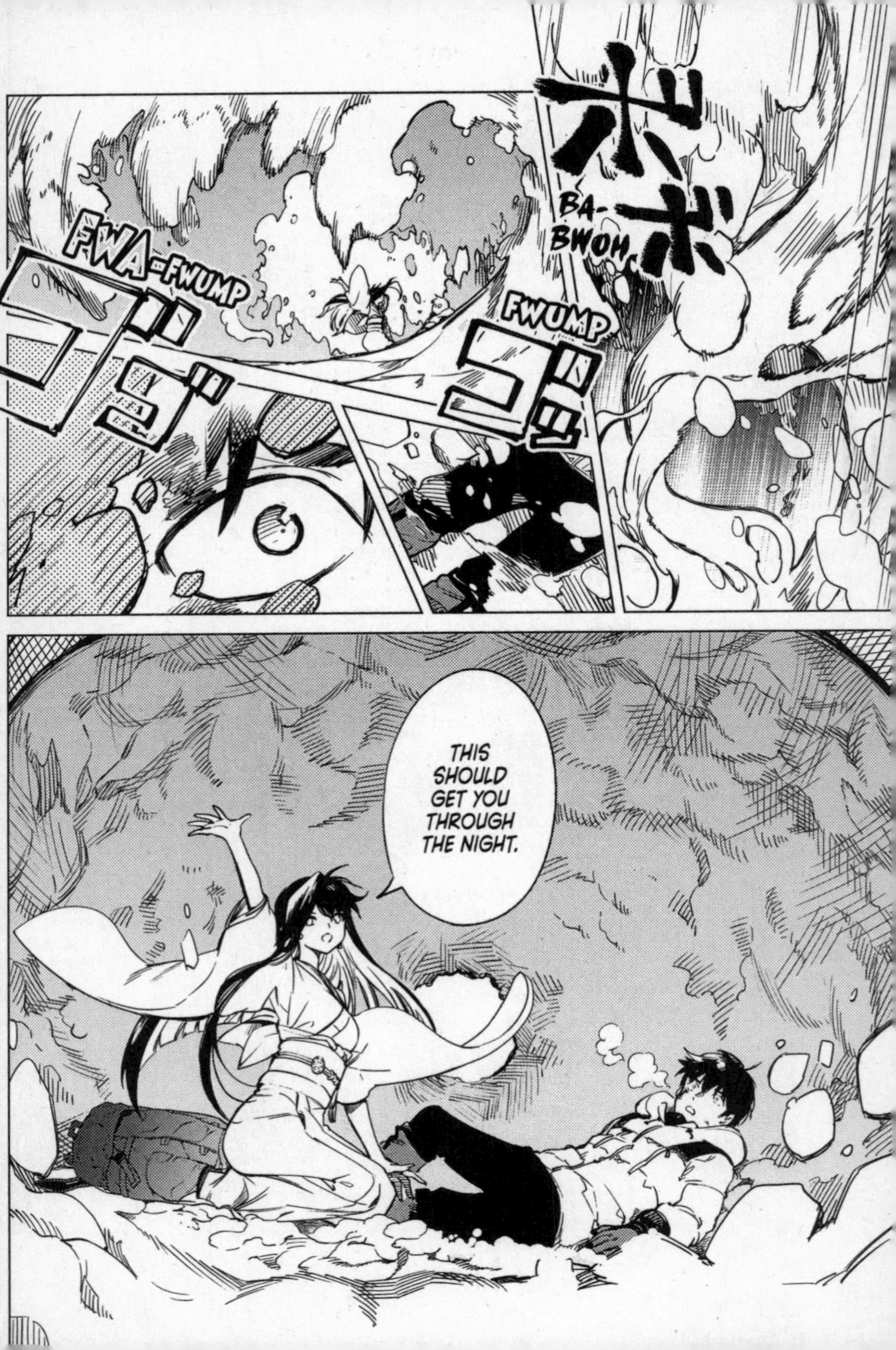

BA-BWOH
FWUMP
FWA-FWUMP
THIS SHOULD GET YOU THROUGH THE NIGHT.

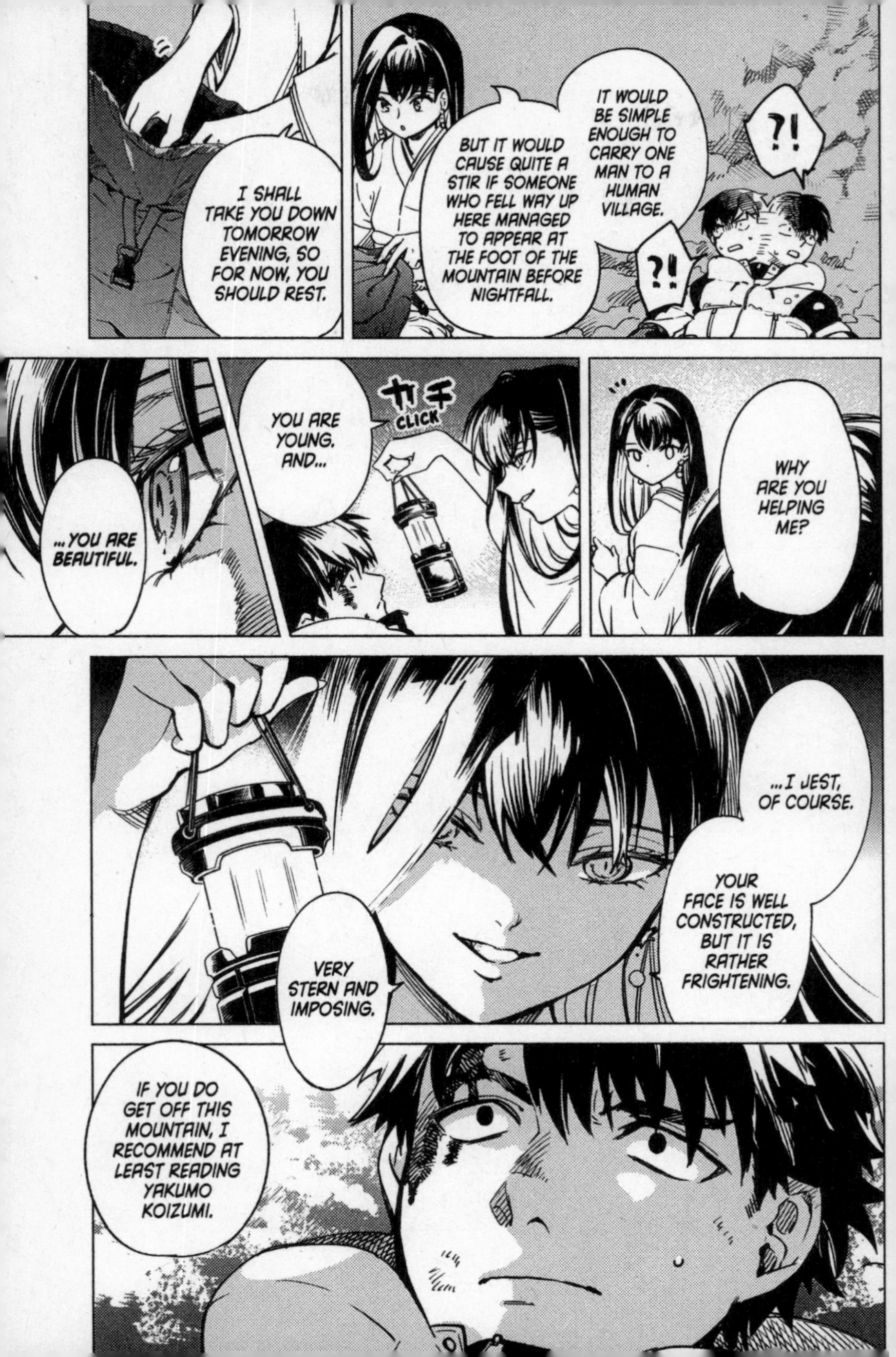
?!
?!
IT WOULD BE SIMPLE ENOUGH TO CARRY ONE MAN TO A HUMAN VILLAGE.
BUT IT WOULD CAUSE QUITE A STIR IF SOMEONE WHO FELL WAY UP HERE MANAGED TO APPEAR AT THE FOOT OF THE MOUNTAIN BEFORE NIGHTFALL.
I SHALL TAKE YOU DOWN TOMORROW EVENING, SO FOR NOW, YOU SHOULD REST.
WHY ARE YOU HELPING ME?
カチ
CLICK
YOU ARE YOUNG. AND...
...YOU ARE BEAUTIFUL.
...I JEST, OF COURSE.
YOUR FACE IS WELL CONSTRUCTED, BUT IT IS RATHER FRIGHTENING.
VERY STERN AND IMPOSING.
IF YOU DO GET OFF THIS MOUNTAIN, I RECOMMEND AT LEAST READING YAKUMO KOIZUMI.

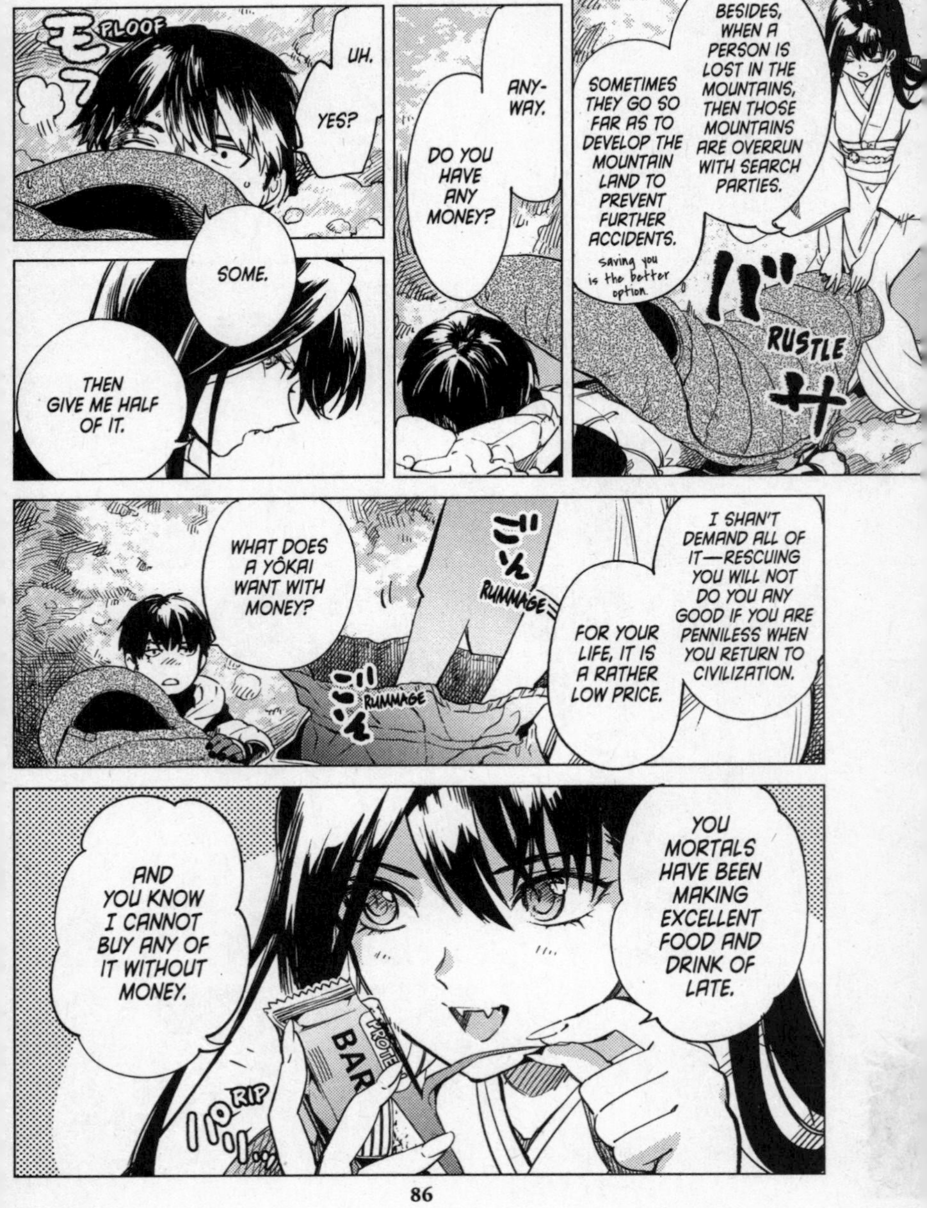
BESIDES, WHEN A PERSON IS LOST IN THE MOUNTAINS, THEN THOSE MOUNTAINS ARE OVERRUN WITH SEARCH PARTIES.
SOMETIMES THEY GO SO FAR AS TO DEVELOP THE MOUNTAIN LAND TO PREVENT FURTHER ACCIDENTS.
saving you is the better option.
RUSTLE
ANY-WAY.
DO YOU HAVE ANY MONEY?
PLOOF
UH.
YES?
SOME.
THEN GIVE ME HALF OF IT.
I SHAN'T DEMAND ALL OF IT—RESCUING YOU WILL NOT DO YOU ANY GOOD IF YOU ARE PENNILESS WHEN YOU RETURN TO CIVILIZATION.
FOR YOUR LIFE, IT IS A RATHER LOW PRICE.
RUMMAGE
RUMMAGE
WHAT DOES A YÔKAI WANT WITH MONEY?
YOU MORTALS HAVE BEEN MAKING EXCELLENT FOOD AND DRINK OF LATE.
AND YOU KNOW I CANNOT BUY ANY OF IT WITHOUT MONEY.
PROTE
BAR
RIP

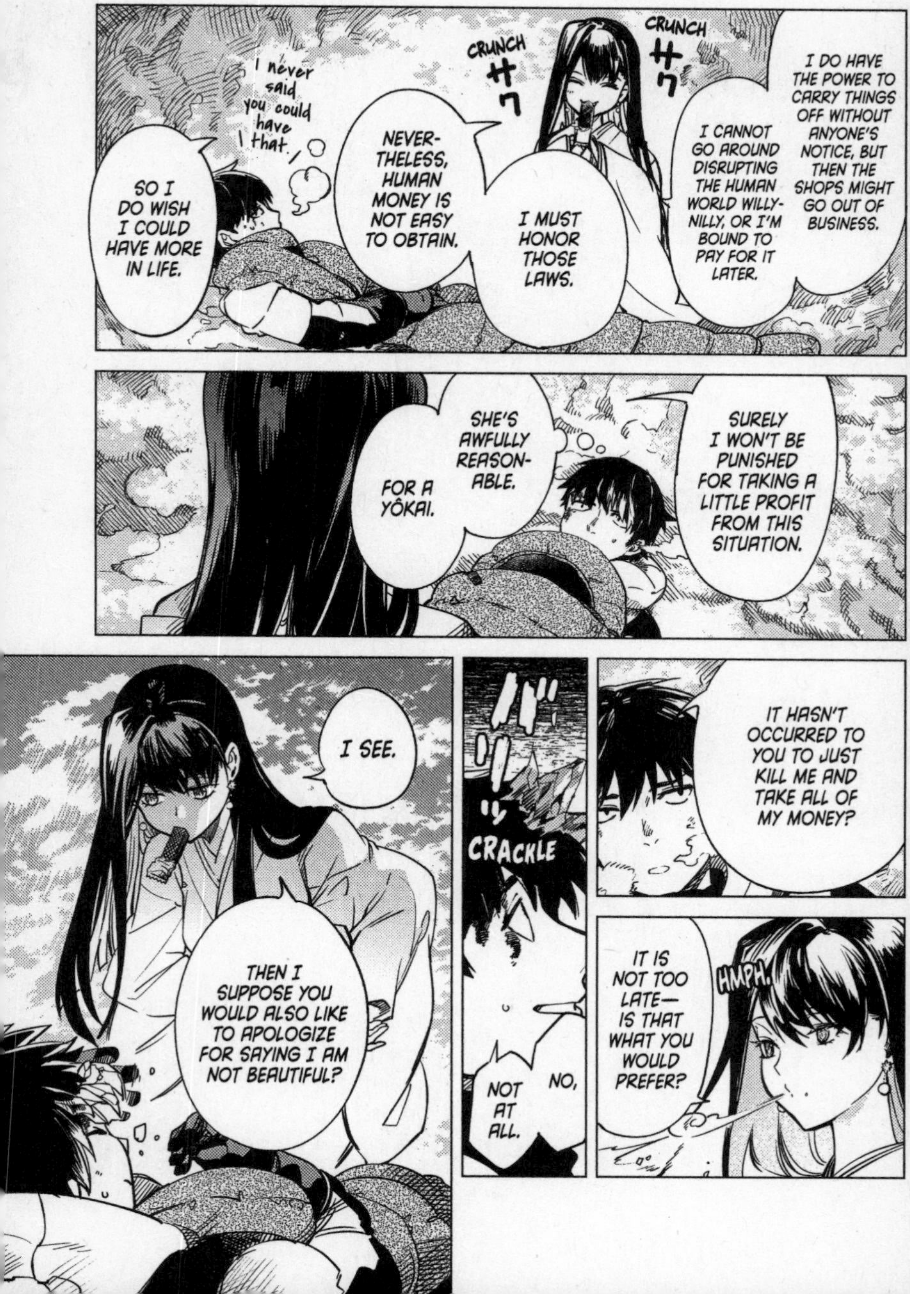
CRUNCH
I DO HAVE THE POWER TO CARRY THINGS OFF WITHOUT ANYONE'S NOTICE, BUT THEN THE SHOPS MIGHT GO OUT OF BUSINESS.
I CANNOT GO AROUND DISRUPTING THE HUMAN WORLD WILLY-NILLY, OR I'M BOUND TO PAY FOR IT LATER.
CRUNCH
I MUST HONOR THOSE LAWS.
NEVER-THELESS, HUMAN MONEY IS NOT EASY TO OBTAIN.
I never said you could have that.
SO I DO WISH I COULD HAVE MORE IN LIFE.
SURELY I WON'T BE PUNISHED FOR TAKING A LITTLE PROFIT FROM THIS SITUATION.
SHE'S AWFULLY REASON-ABLE.
FOR A YÔKAI.
IT HASN'T OCCURRED TO YOU TO JUST KILL ME AND TAKE ALL OF MY MONEY?
HMPH.
IT IS NOT TOO LATE— IS THAT WHAT YOU WOULD PREFER?
CRACKLE
NO,
NOT AT ALL.
I SEE.
THEN I SUPPOSE YOU WOULD ALSO LIKE TO APOLOGIZE FOR SAYING I AM NOT BEAUTIFUL?

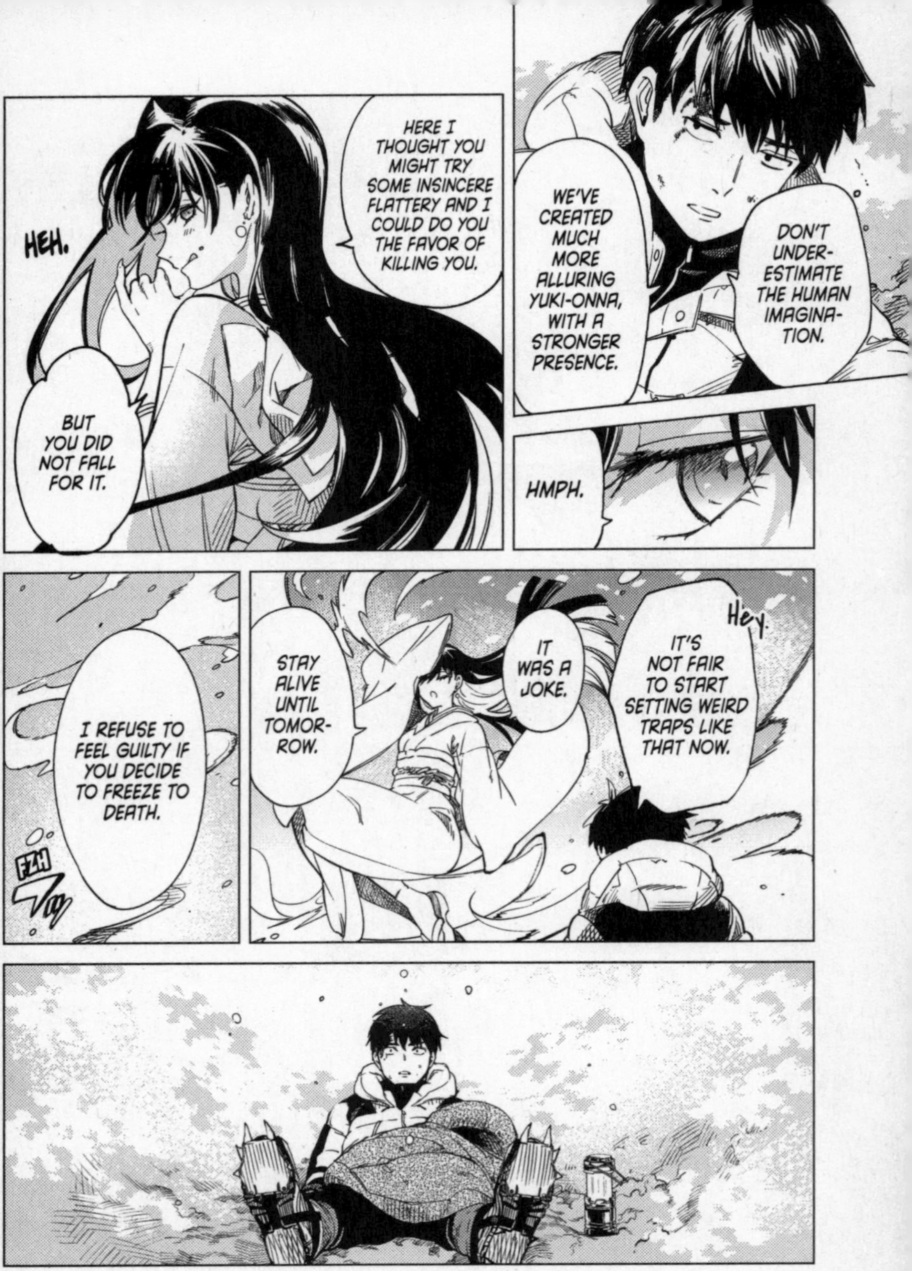
DON'T UNDER-ESTIMATE THE HUMAN IMAGINA-TION.
WE'VE CREATED MUCH MORE ALLURING YUKI-ONNA, WITH A STRONGER PRESENCE.
HMPH.
HERE I THOUGHT YOU MIGHT TRY SOME INSINCERE FLATTERY AND I COULD DO YOU THE FAVOR OF KILLING YOU.
HEH.
BUT YOU DID NOT FALL FOR IT.
Hey.
IT'S NOT FAIR TO START SETTING WEIRD TRAPS LIKE THAT NOW.
IT WAS A JOKE.
STAY ALIVE UNTIL TOMOR-ROW.
I REFUSE TO FEEL GUILTY IF YOU DECIDE TO FREEZE TO DEATH.
FZH

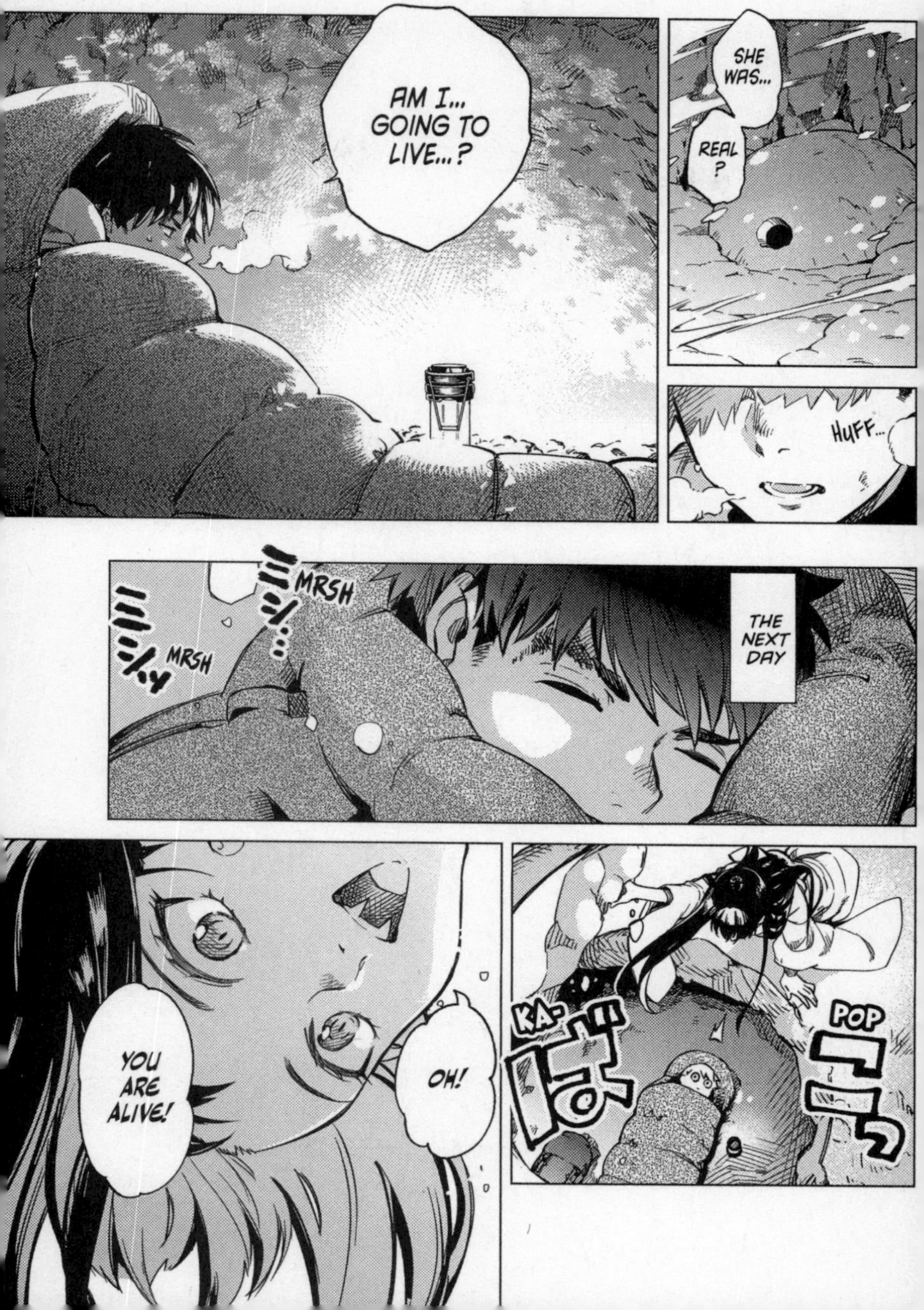
SHE WAS...
REAL ?
HUFF...
AM I... GOING TO LIVE...?
THE NEXT DAY
MRSH
MRSH
POP
KA-
OH!
YOU ARE ALIVE!

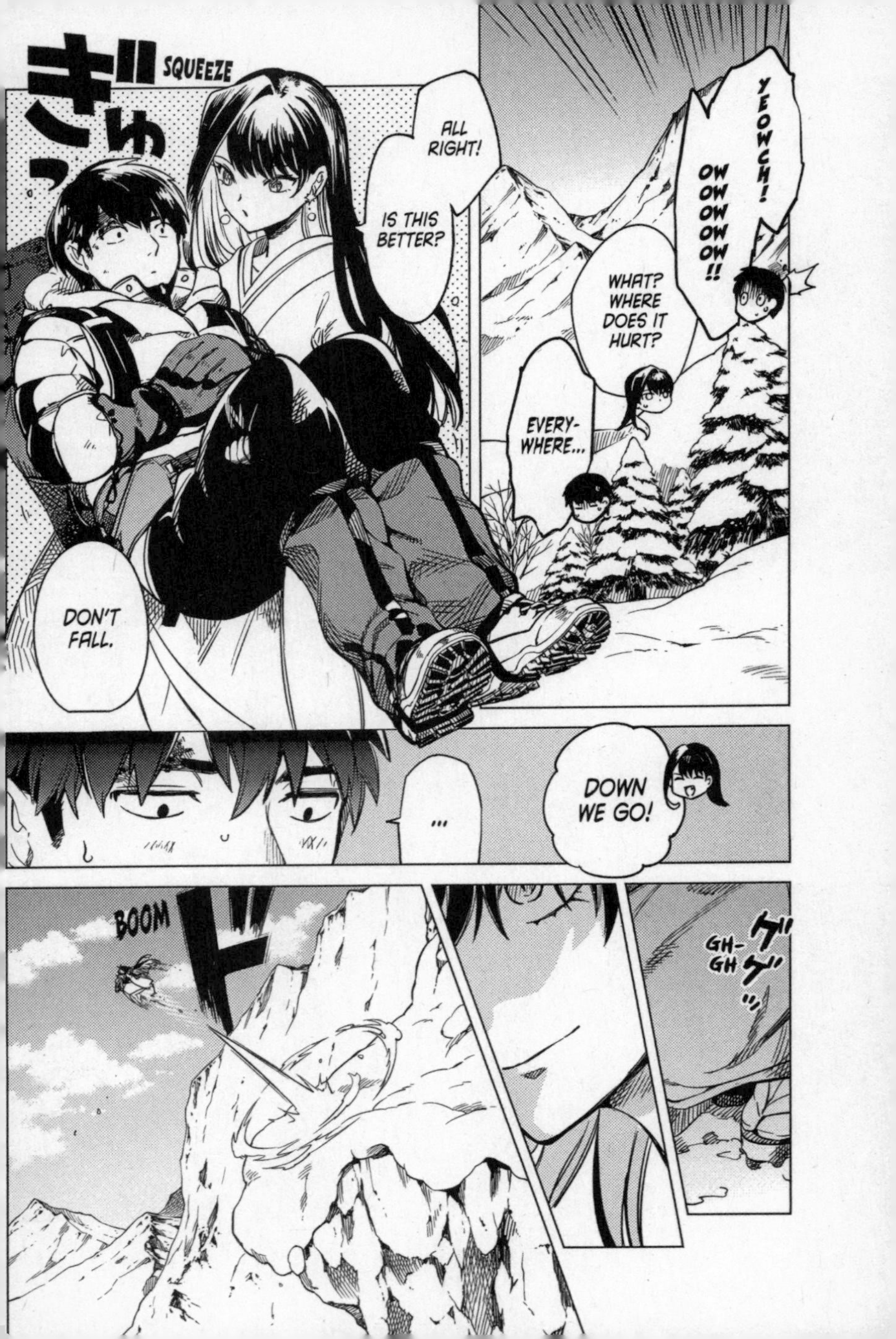
YEOWCH! OWOWOWOWOW!!
WHAT? WHERE DOES IT HURT?
EVERY-WHERE...
ぎゅっ
SQUEEZE
ALL RIGHT!
IS THIS BETTER?
DON'T FALL.
DOWN WE GO!
...
ゲゲッ
GH-GH
ド
BOOM

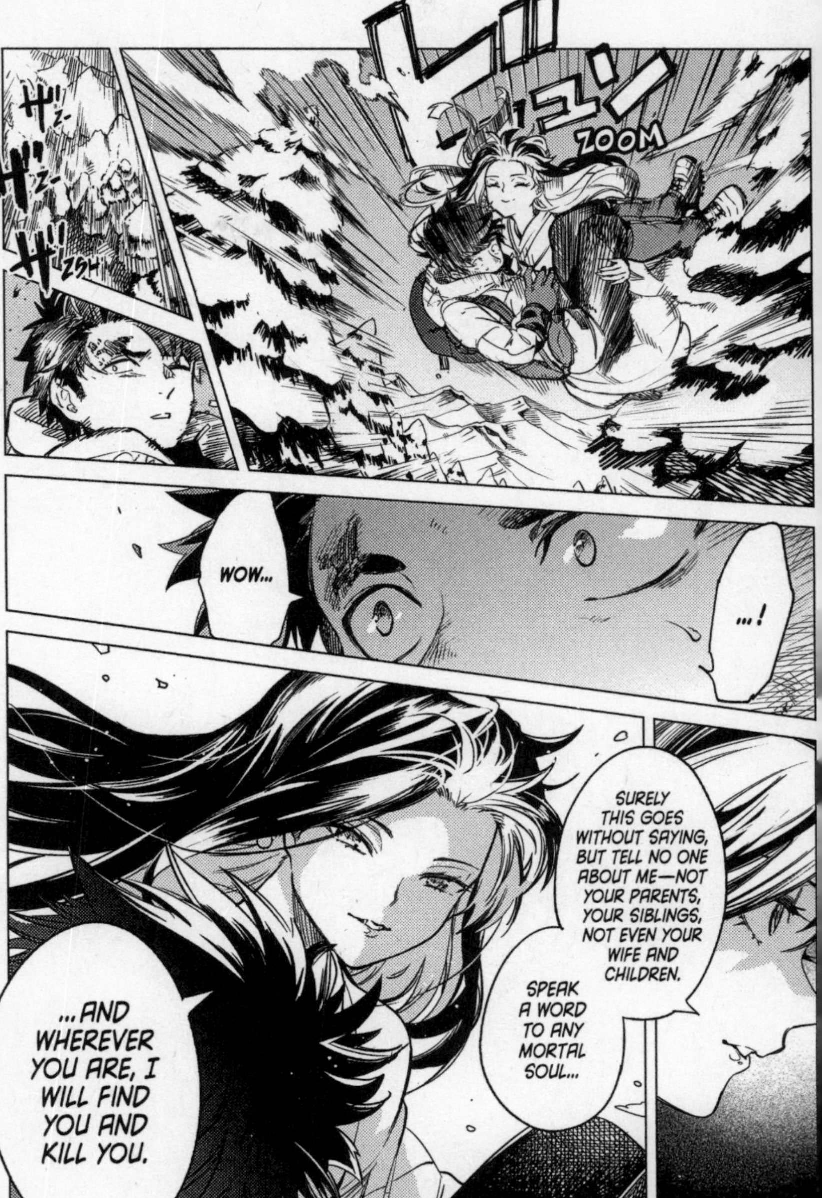
ZOOM
Z-
Z-
ZSH
WOW...
...!
SURELY THIS GOES WITHOUT SAYING, BUT TELL NO ONE ABOUT ME—NOT YOUR PARENTS, YOUR SIBLINGS, NOT EVEN YOUR WIFE AND CHILDREN.
SPEAK A WORD TO ANY MORTAL SOUL...
...AND WHEREVER YOU ARE, I WILL FIND YOU AND KILL YOU.

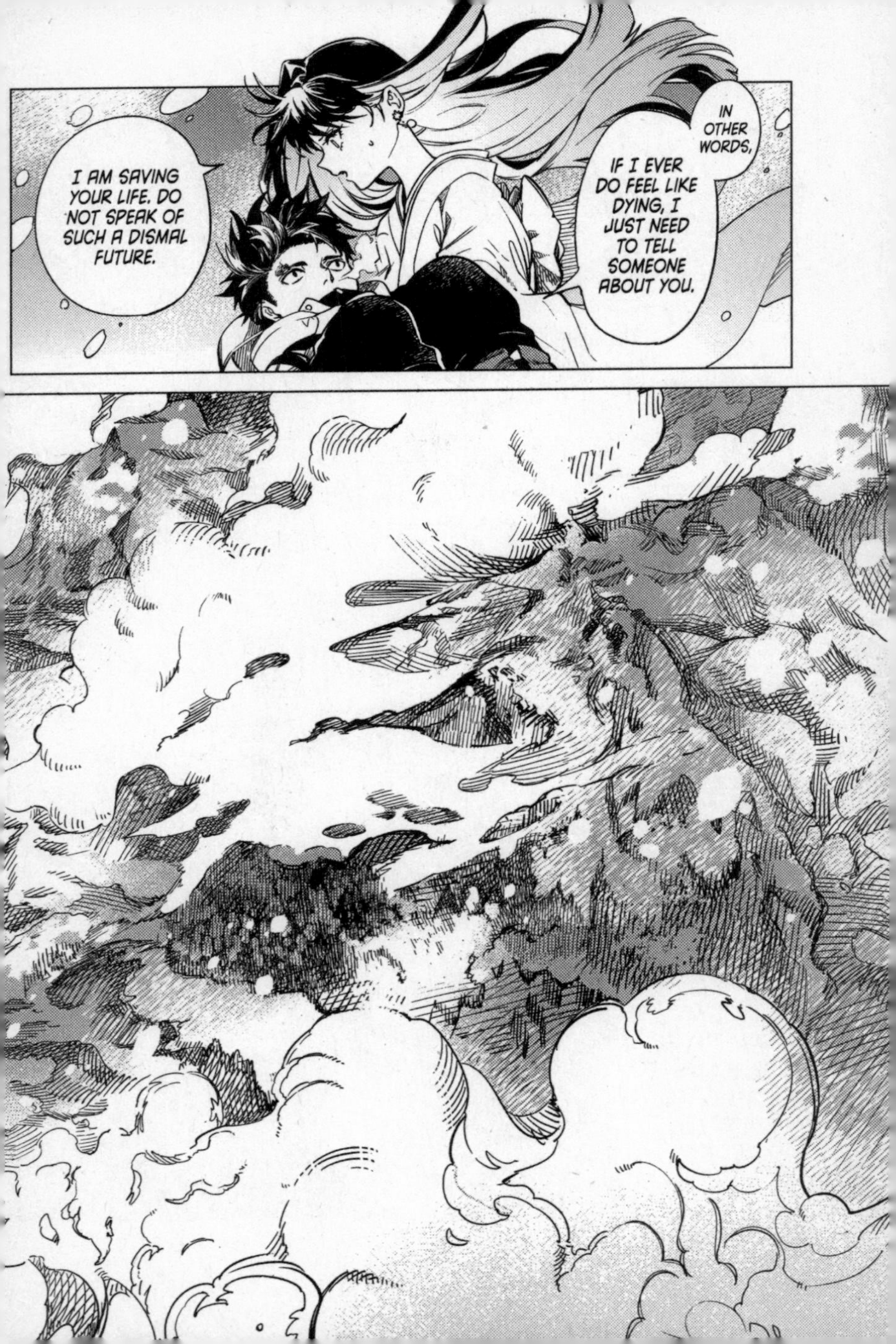
IN OTHER WORDS,
IF I EVER DO FEEL LIKE DYING, I JUST NEED TO TELL SOMEONE ABOUT YOU.
I AM SAVING YOUR LIFE. DO NOT SPEAK OF SUCH A DISMAL FUTURE.

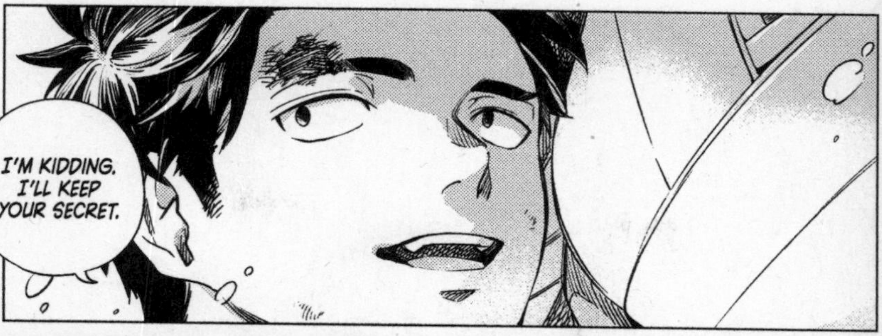
I'M KIDDING. I'LL KEEP YOUR SECRET.
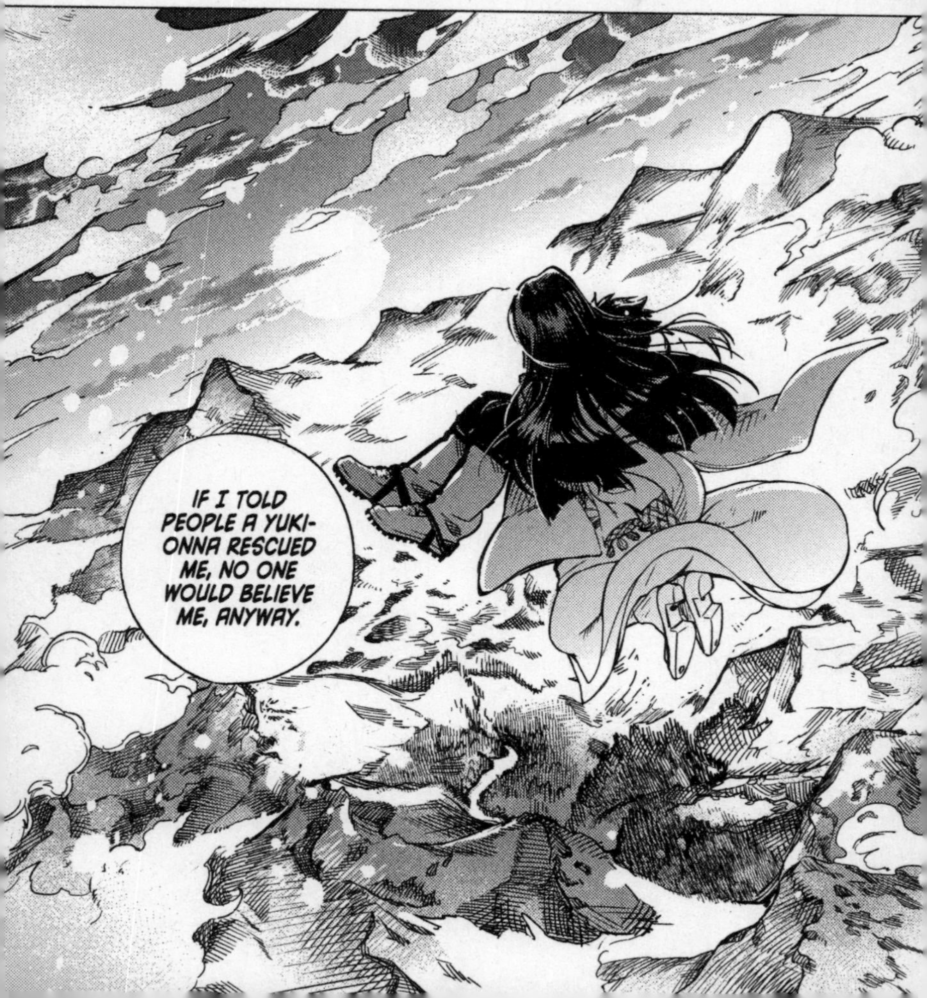
IF I TOLD PEOPLE A YUKI-ONNA RESCUED ME, NO ONE WOULD BELIEVE ME, ANYWAY.

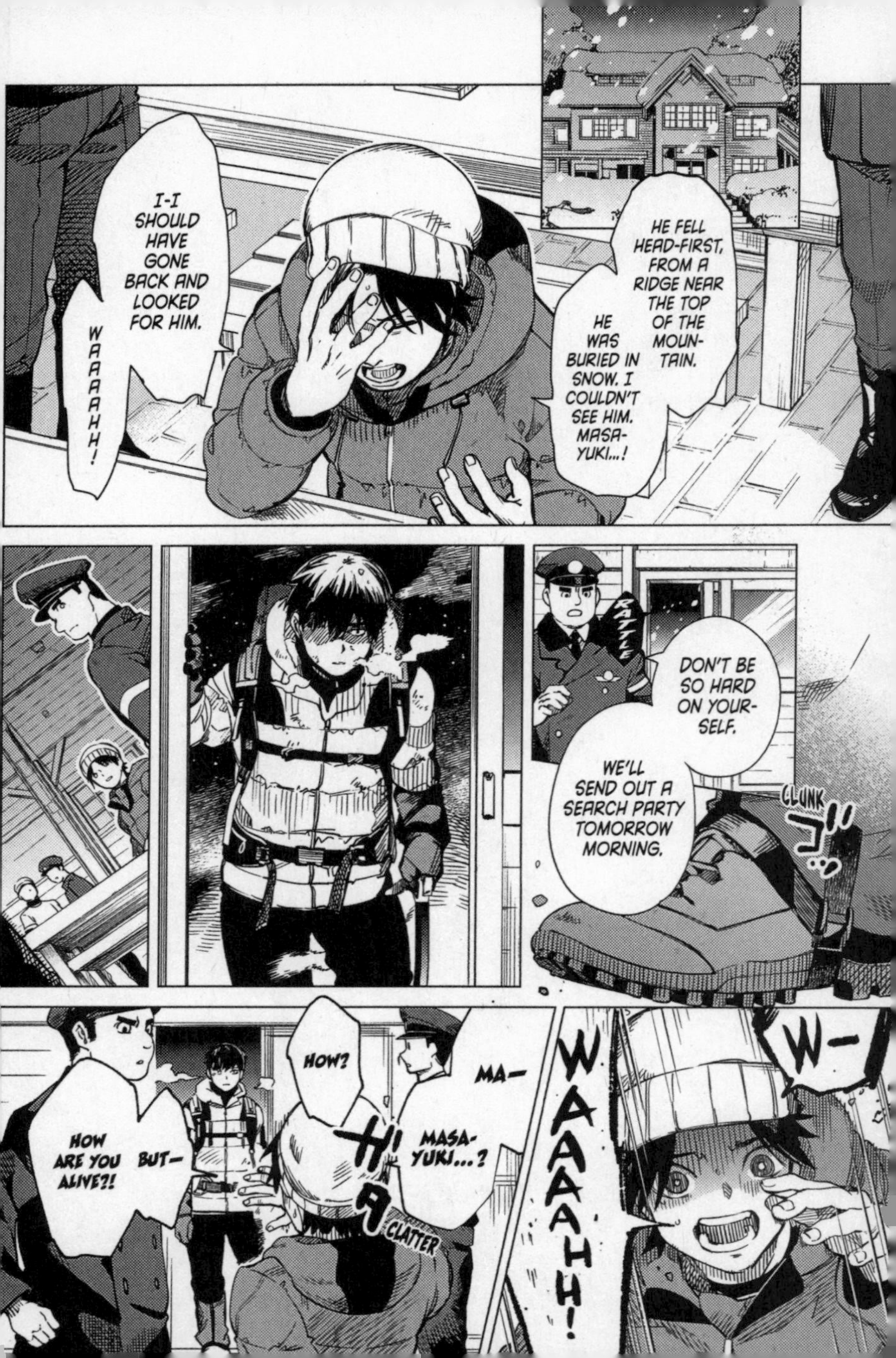
HE FELL HEAD-FIRST, FROM A RIDGE NEAR THE TOP OF THE MOUN-TAIN.
HE WAS BURIED IN SNOW. I COULDN'T SEE HIM. MASA-YUKI...!
I-I SHOULD HAVE GONE BACK AND LOOKED FOR HIM.
WAAAAAHH!
RATTLE
DON'T BE SO HARD ON YOUR-SELF.
WE'LL SEND OUT A SEARCH PARTY TOMORROW MORNING.
CLUNK
W-
WAAAAAH!
MA-
MASA-YUKI...?
HOW?
CLATTER
BUT—
HOW ARE YOU ALIVE?!

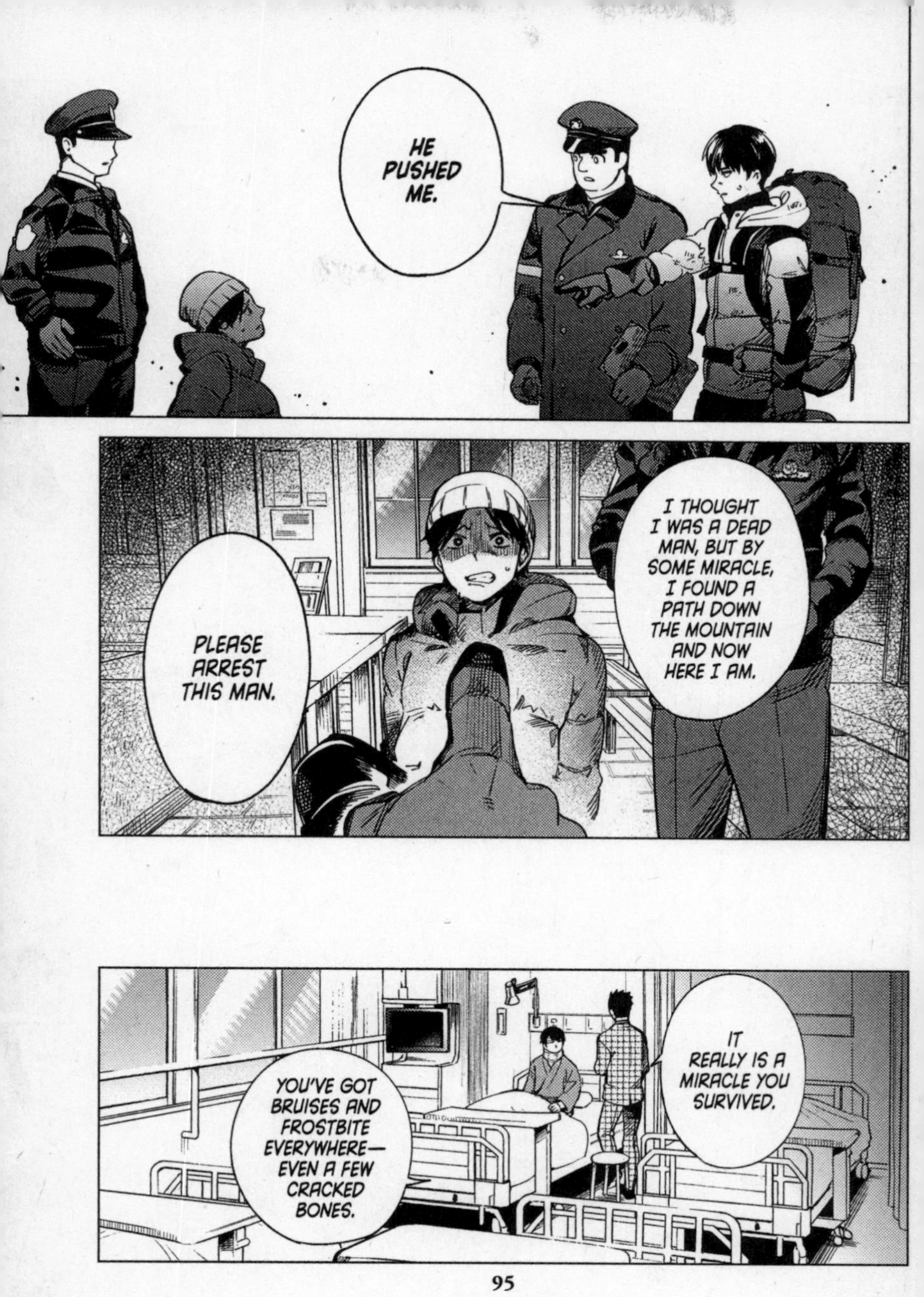
HE PUSHED ME.
I THOUGHT I WAS A DEAD MAN, BUT BY SOME MIRACLE, I FOUND A PATH DOWN THE MOUNTAIN AND NOW HERE I AM.
PLEASE ARREST THIS MAN.
IT REALLY IS A MIRACLE YOU SURVIVED.
YOU'VE GOT BRUISES AND FROSTBITE EVERYWHERE— EVEN A FEW CRACKED BONES.

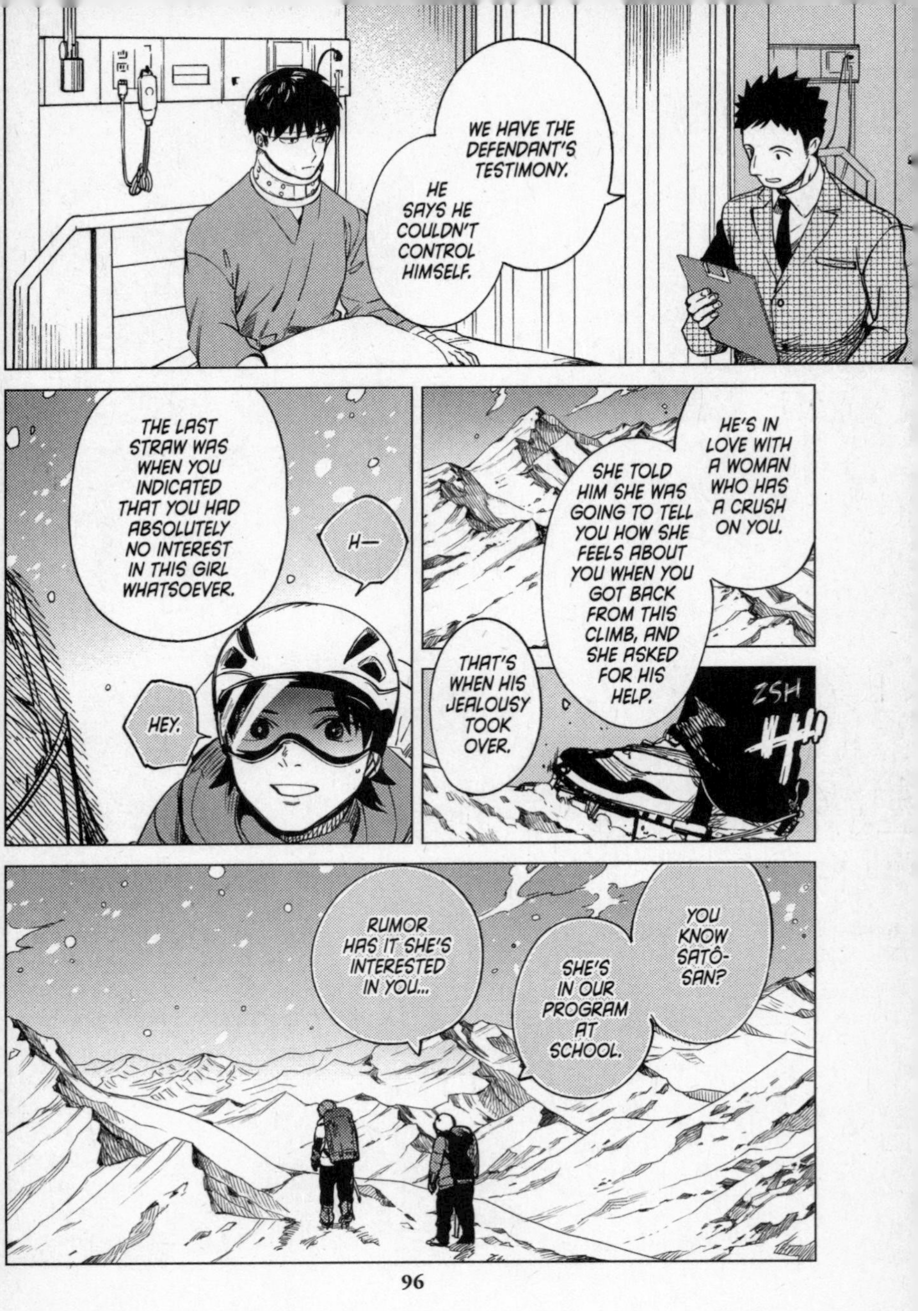
WE HAVE THE DEFENDANT'S TESTIMONY.
HE SAYS HE COULDN'T CONTROL HIMSELF.
HE'S IN LOVE WITH A WOMAN WHO HAS A CRUSH ON YOU.
SHE TOLD HIM SHE WAS GOING TO TELL YOU HOW SHE FEELS ABOUT YOU WHEN YOU GOT BACK FROM THIS CLIMB, AND SHE ASKED FOR HIS HELP.
THAT'S WHEN HIS JEALOUSY TOOK OVER.
ZSH
THE LAST STRAW WAS WHEN YOU INDICATED THAT YOU HAD ABSOLUTELY NO INTEREST IN THIS GIRL WHATSOEVER.
H—
HEY.
YOU KNOW SATÔ-SAN?
SHE'S IN OUR PROGRAM AT SCHOOL.
RUMOR HAS IT SHE'S INTERESTED IN YOU...

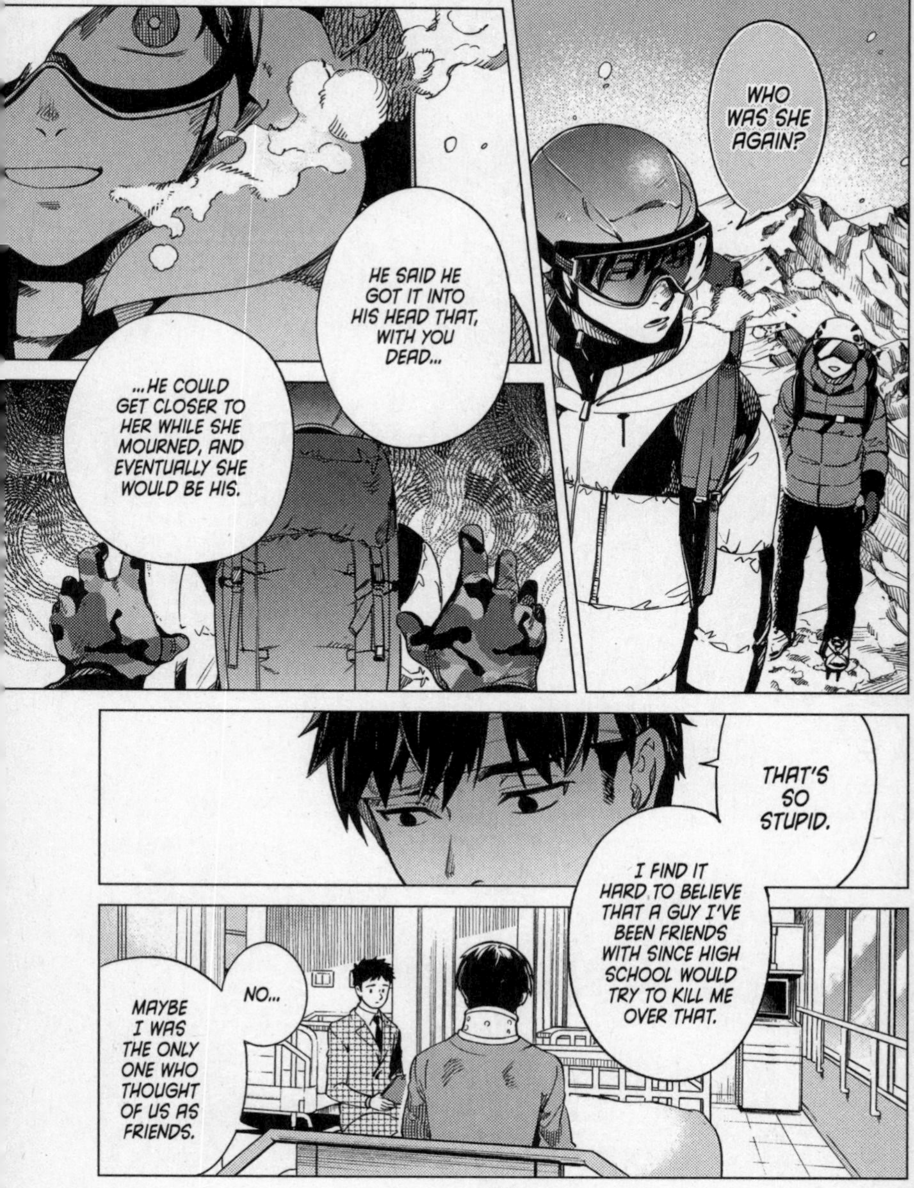
WHO WAS SHE AGAIN?
HE SAID HE GOT IT INTO HIS HEAD THAT, WITH YOU DEAD...
...HE COULD GET CLOSER TO HER WHILE SHE MOURNED, AND EVENTUALLY SHE WOULD BE HIS.
THAT'S SO STUPID.
I FIND IT HARD TO BELIEVE THAT A GUY I'VE BEEN FRIENDS WITH SINCE HIGH SCHOOL WOULD TRY TO KILL ME OVER THAT.
NO...
MAYBE I WAS THE ONLY ONE WHO THOUGHT OF US AS FRIENDS.

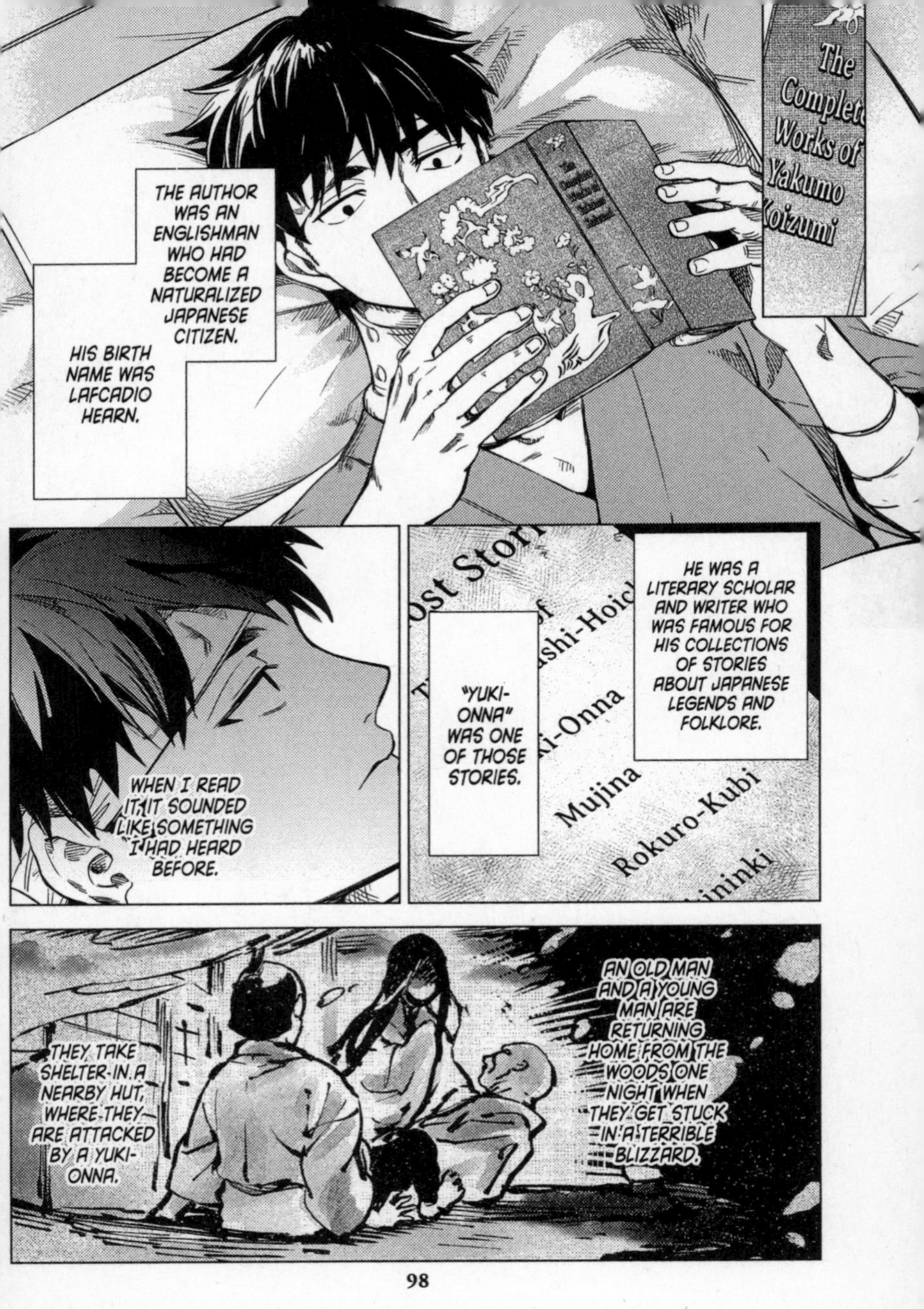
The Complet Works of Yakumo Koizumi
THE AUTHOR WAS AN ENGLISHMAN WHO HAD BECOME A NATURALIZED JAPANESE CITIZEN.
HIS BIRTH NAME WAS LAFCADIO HEARN.
HE WAS A LITERARY SCHOLAR AND WRITER WHO WAS FAMOUS FOR HIS COLLECTIONS OF STORIES ABOUT JAPANESE LEGENDS AND FOLKLORE.
"YUKI-ONNA" WAS ONE OF THOSE STORIES.
Mujina
Rokuro-Kubi
WHEN I READ IT, IT SOUNDED LIKE SOMETHING I HAD HEARD BEFORE.
AN OLD MAN AND A YOUNG MAN ARE RETURNING HOME FROM THE WOODS ONE NIGHT WHEN THEY GET STUCK IN A TERRIBLE BLIZZARD.
THEY TAKE SHELTER IN A NEARBY HUT, WHERE THEY ARE ATTACKED BY A YUKI-ONNA.

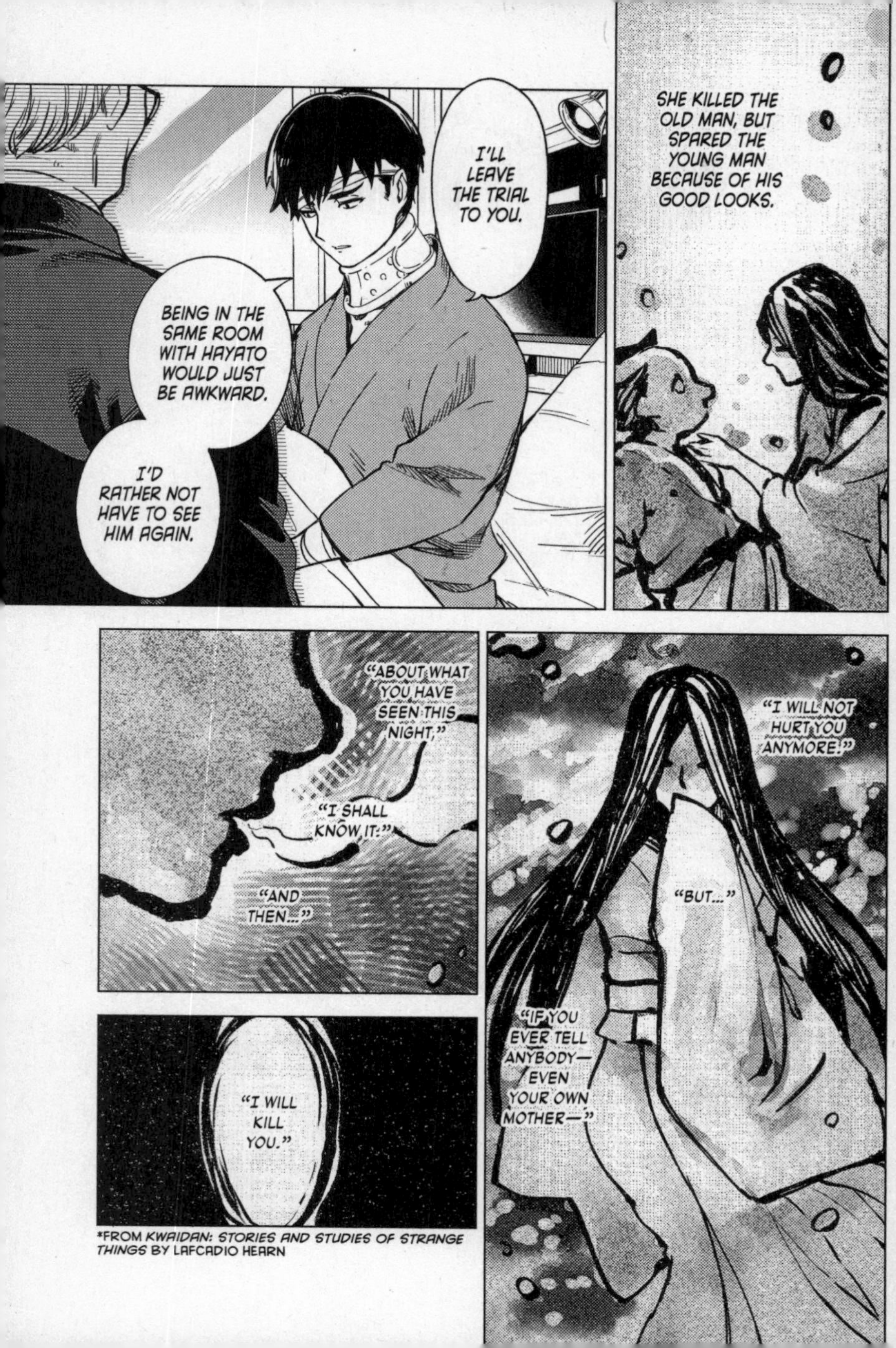
SHE KILLED THE OLD MAN, BUT SPARED THE YOUNG MAN BECAUSE OF HIS GOOD LOOKS.
I'LL LEAVE THE TRIAL TO YOU.
BEING IN THE SAME ROOM WITH HAYATO WOULD JUST BE AWKWARD.
I'D RATHER NOT HAVE TO SEE HIM AGAIN.
"I WILL NOT HURT YOU ANYMORE."
"BUT..."
"IF YOU EVER TELL ANYBODY—EVEN YOUR OWN MOTHER—"
"ABOUT WHAT YOU HAVE SEEN THIS NIGHT,"
"I SHALL KNOW IT."
"AND THEN..."
"I WILL KILL YOU."

*FROM *KWAIDAN: STORIES AND STUDIES OF STRANGE THINGS* BY LAFCADIO HEARN

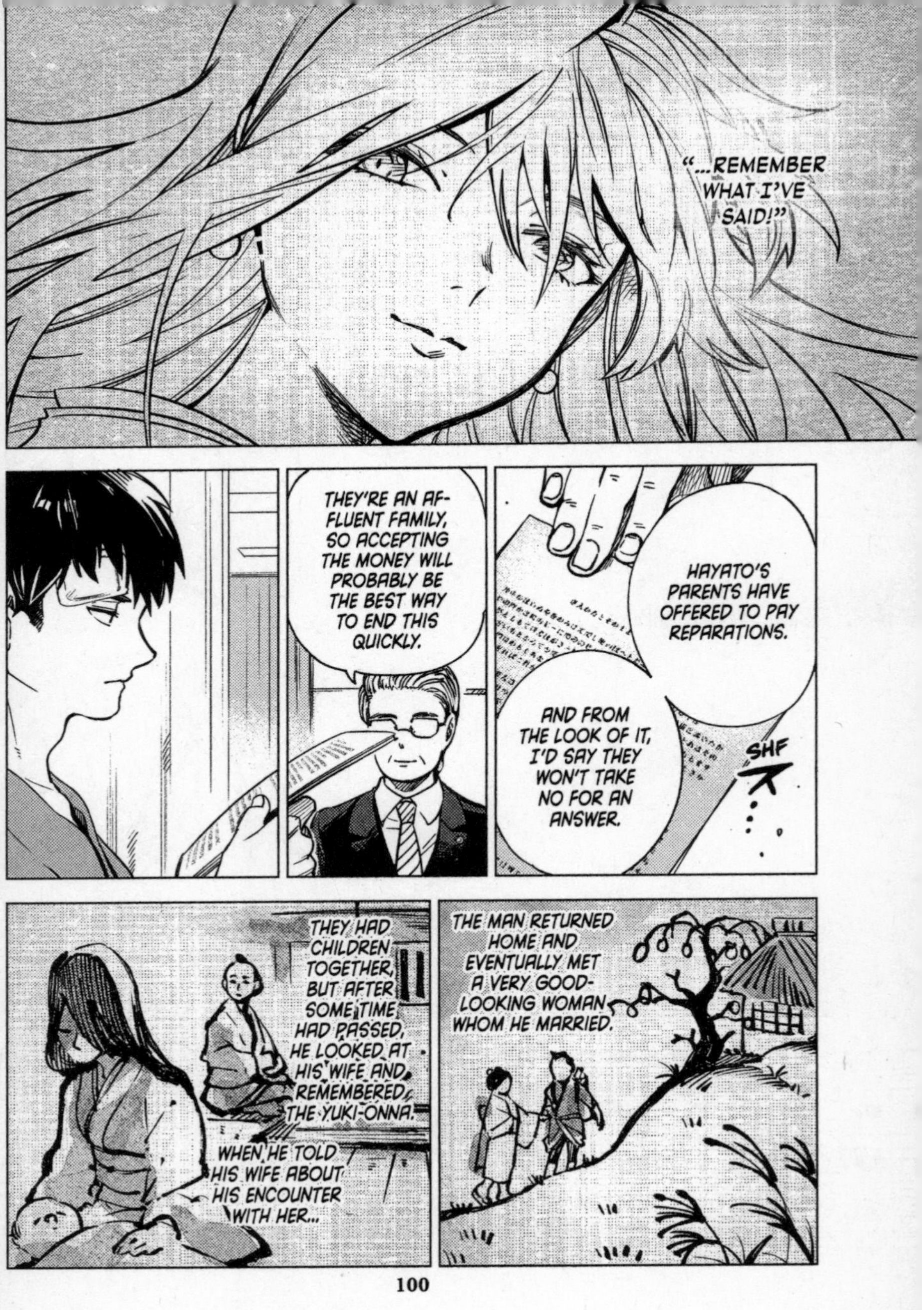
"...REMEMBER WHAT I'VE SAID!"
HAYATO'S PARENTS HAVE OFFERED TO PAY REPARATIONS.
AND FROM THE LOOK OF IT, I'D SAY THEY WON'T TAKE NO FOR AN ANSWER.
SHF
THEY'RE AN AFFLUENT FAMILY, SO ACCEPTING THE MONEY WILL PROBABLY BE THE BEST WAY TO END THIS QUICKLY.
THE MAN RETURNED HOME AND EVENTUALLY MET A VERY GOOD-LOOKING WOMAN WHOM HE MARRIED.
THEY HAD CHILDREN TOGETHER, BUT AFTER SOME TIME HAD PASSED, HE LOOKED AT HIS WIFE AND REMEMBERED THE YUKI-ONNA.
WHEN HE TOLD HIS WIFE ABOUT HIS ENCOUNTER WITH HER...

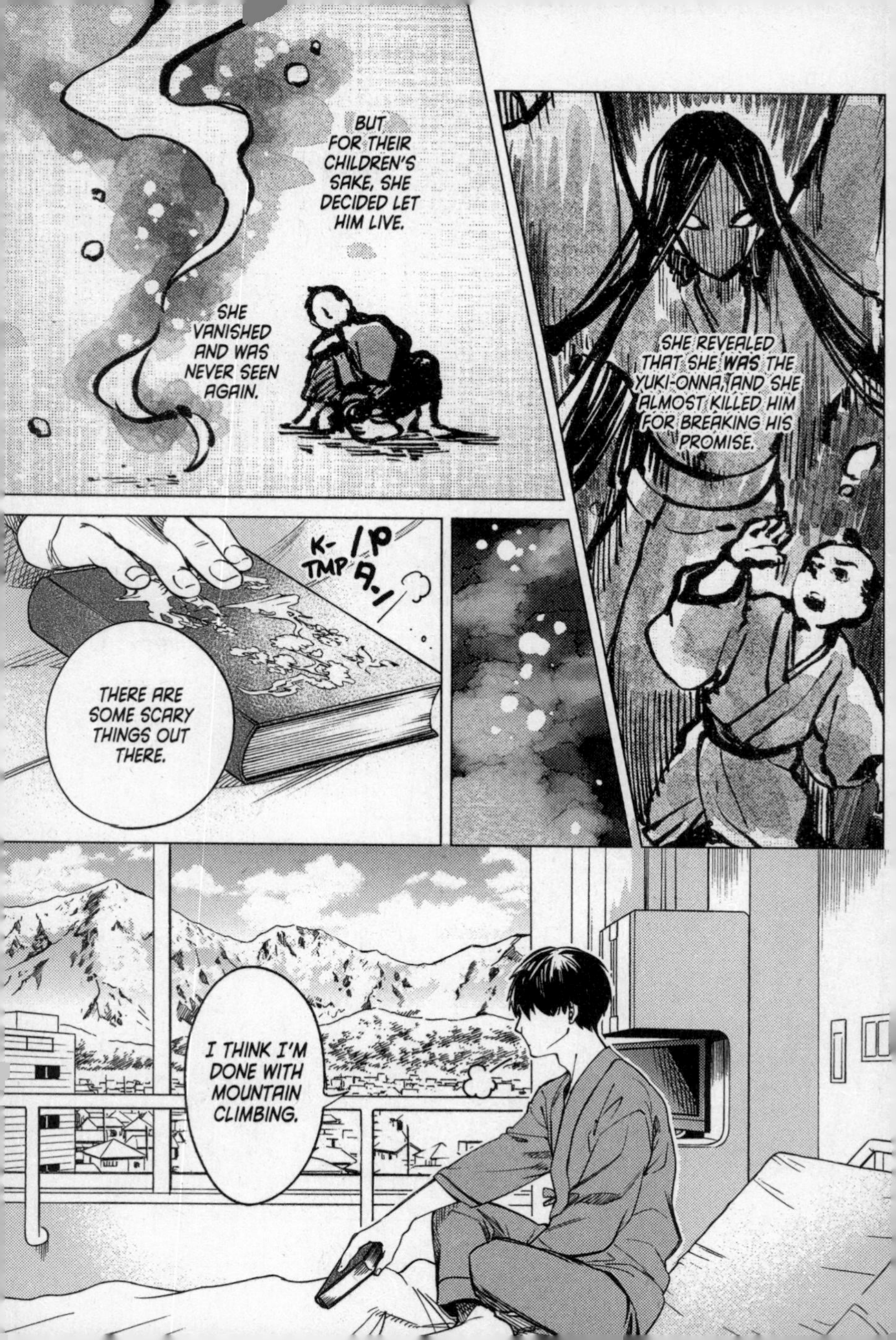
SHE REVEALED THAT SHE WAS THE YUKI-ONNA, AND SHE ALMOST KILLED HIM FOR BREAKING HIS PROMISE.
BUT FOR THEIR CHILDREN'S SAKE, SHE DECIDED LET HIM LIVE.
SHE VANISHED AND WAS NEVER SEEN AGAIN.
K-TMP
PA-
THERE ARE SOME SCARY THINGS OUT THERE.
I THINK I'M DONE WITH MOUNTAIN CLIMBING.

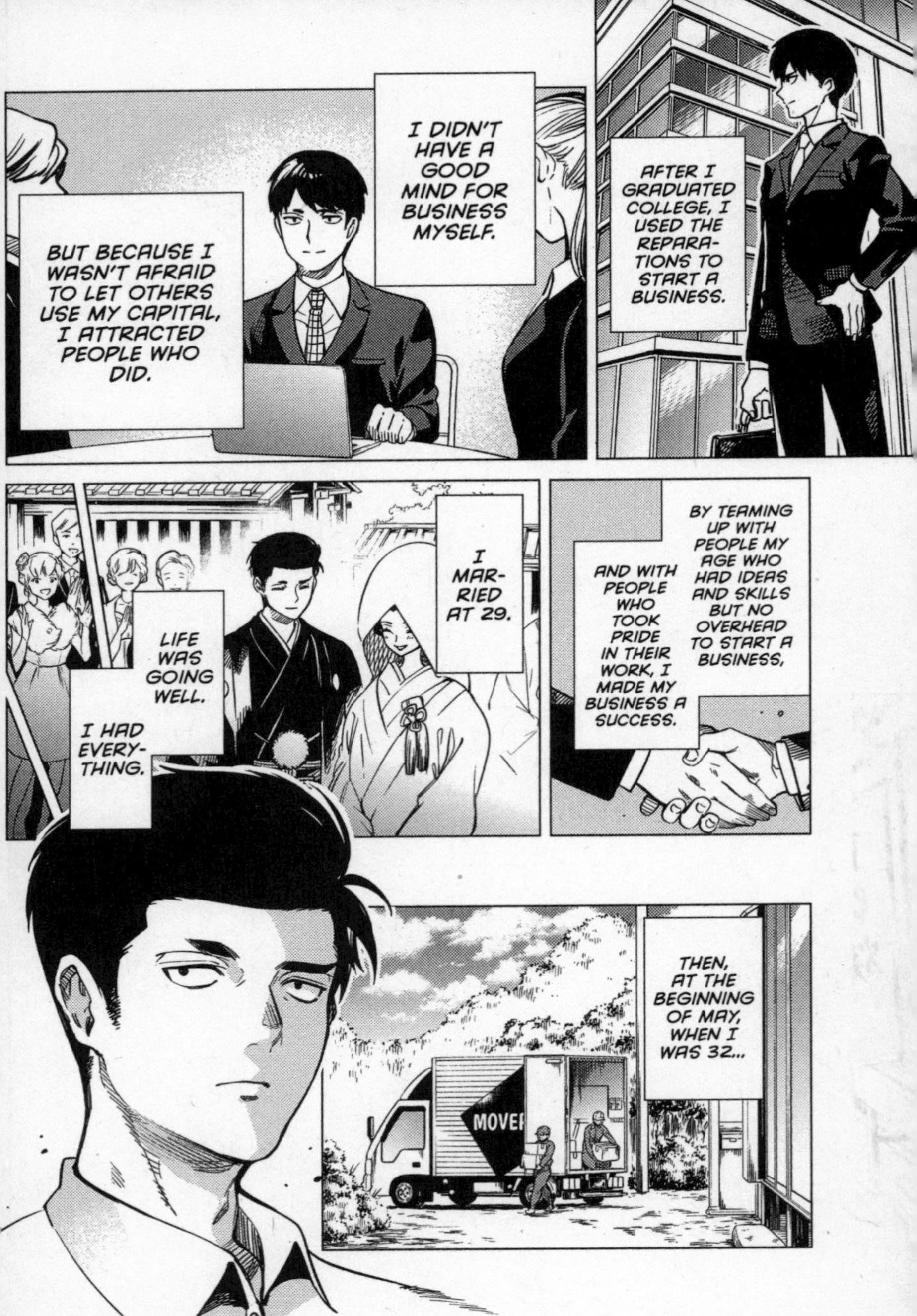
AFTER I GRADUATED COLLEGE, I USED THE REPARATIONS TO START A BUSINESS.
I DIDN'T HAVE A GOOD MIND FOR BUSINESS MYSELF.
BUT BECAUSE I WASN'T AFRAID TO LET OTHERS USE MY CAPITAL, I ATTRACTED PEOPLE WHO DID.
BY TEAMING UP WITH PEOPLE MY AGE WHO HAD IDEAS AND SKILLS BUT NO OVERHEAD TO START A BUSINESS,
AND WITH PEOPLE WHO TOOK PRIDE IN THEIR WORK, I MADE MY BUSINESS A SUCCESS.
I MARRIED AT 29.
LIFE WAS GOING WELL.
I HAD EVERYTHING.
THEN, AT THE BEGINNING OF MAY, WHEN I WAS 32...

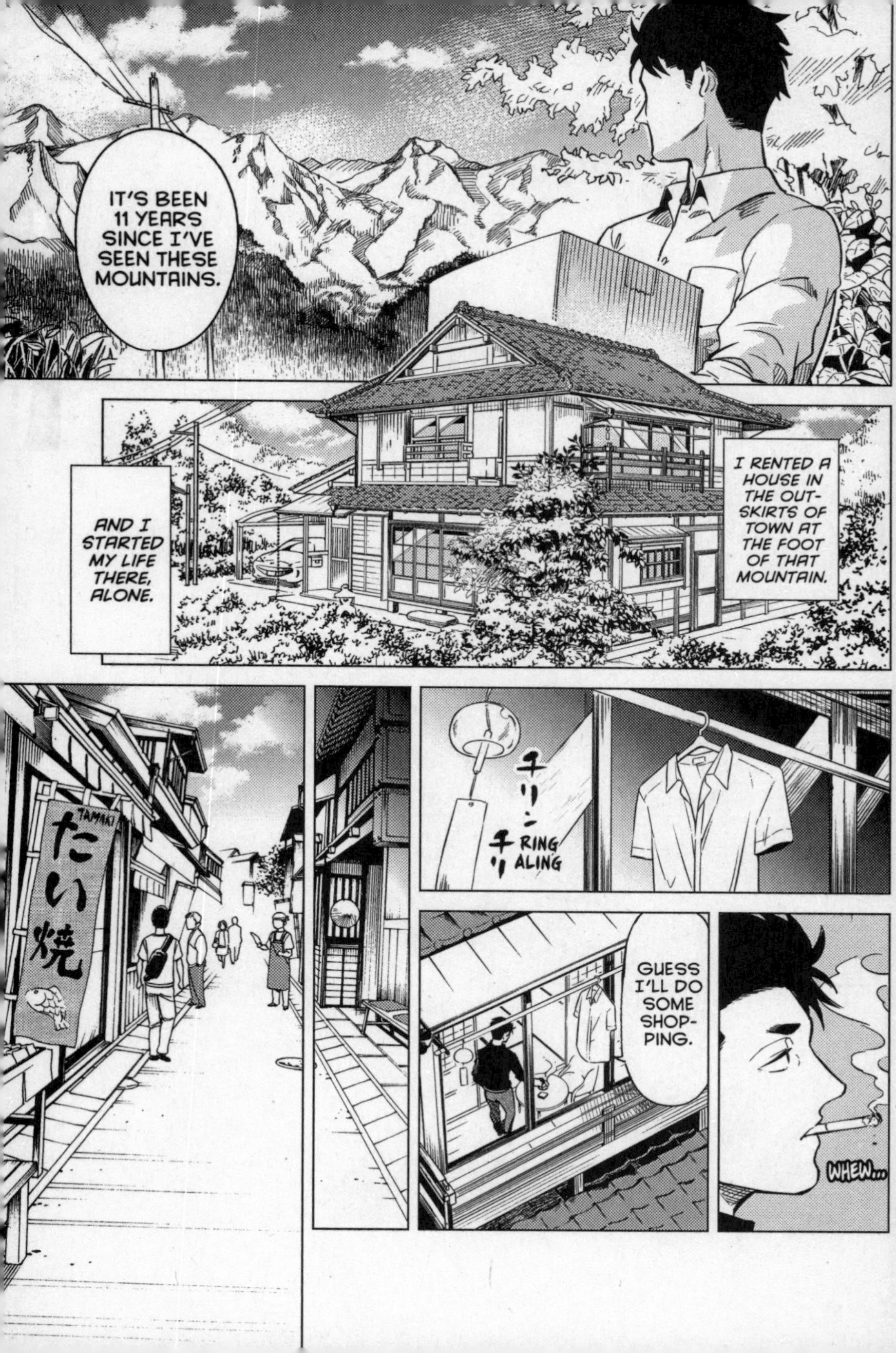
IT'S BEEN 11 YEARS SINCE I'VE SEEN THESE MOUNTAINS.
I RENTED A HOUSE IN THE OUT-SKIRTS OF TOWN AT THE FOOT OF THAT MOUNTAIN.
AND I STARTED MY LIFE THERE, ALONE.
チリン
チリ
RING ALING
WHEW...
GUESS I'LL DO SOME SHOP-PING.
TAMAKI
たい焼

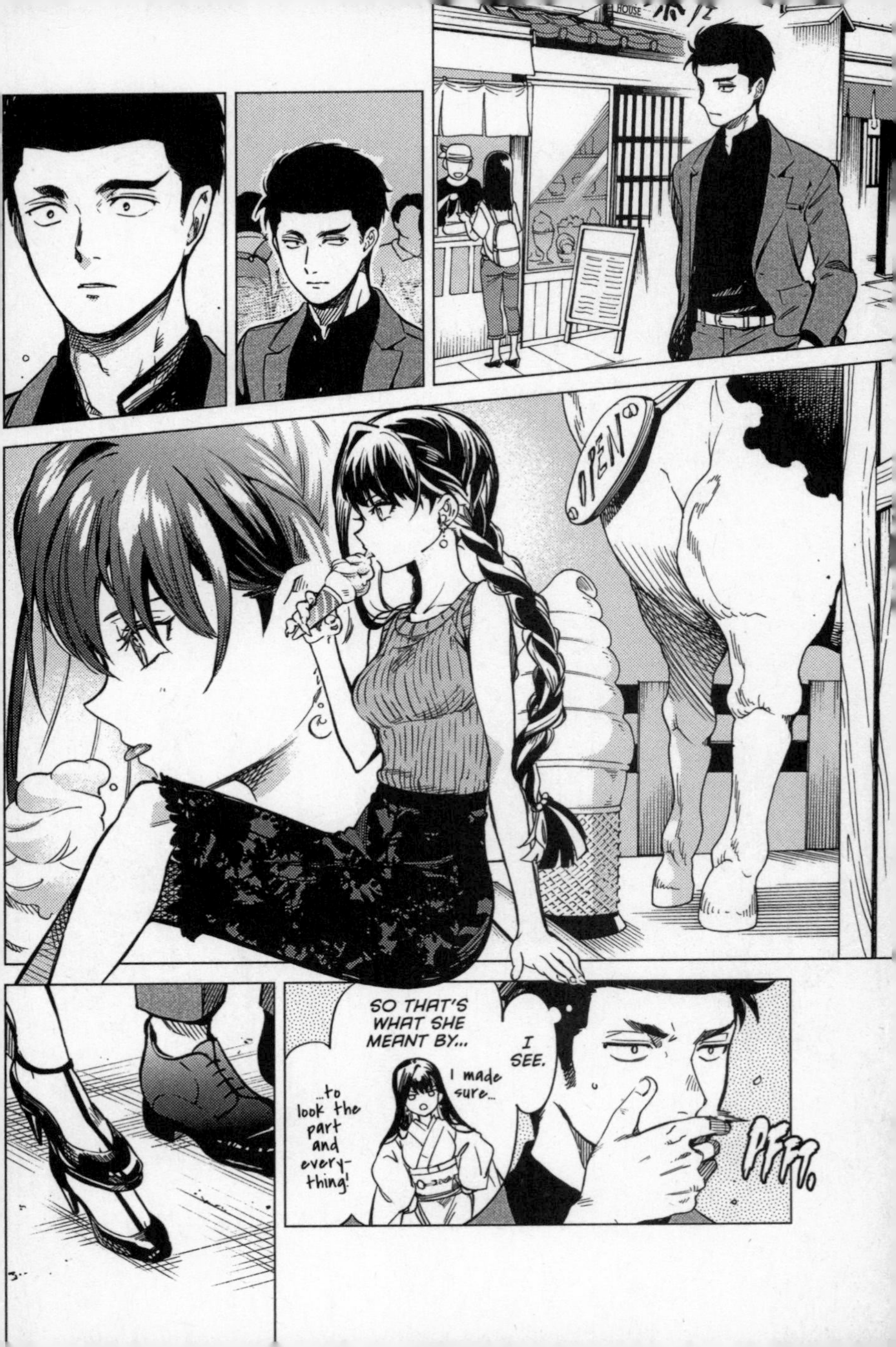
HOUSE
OPEN
I SEE.
SO THAT'S WHAT SHE MEANT BY...
I made sure...
...to look the part and every-thing!
PFFT.

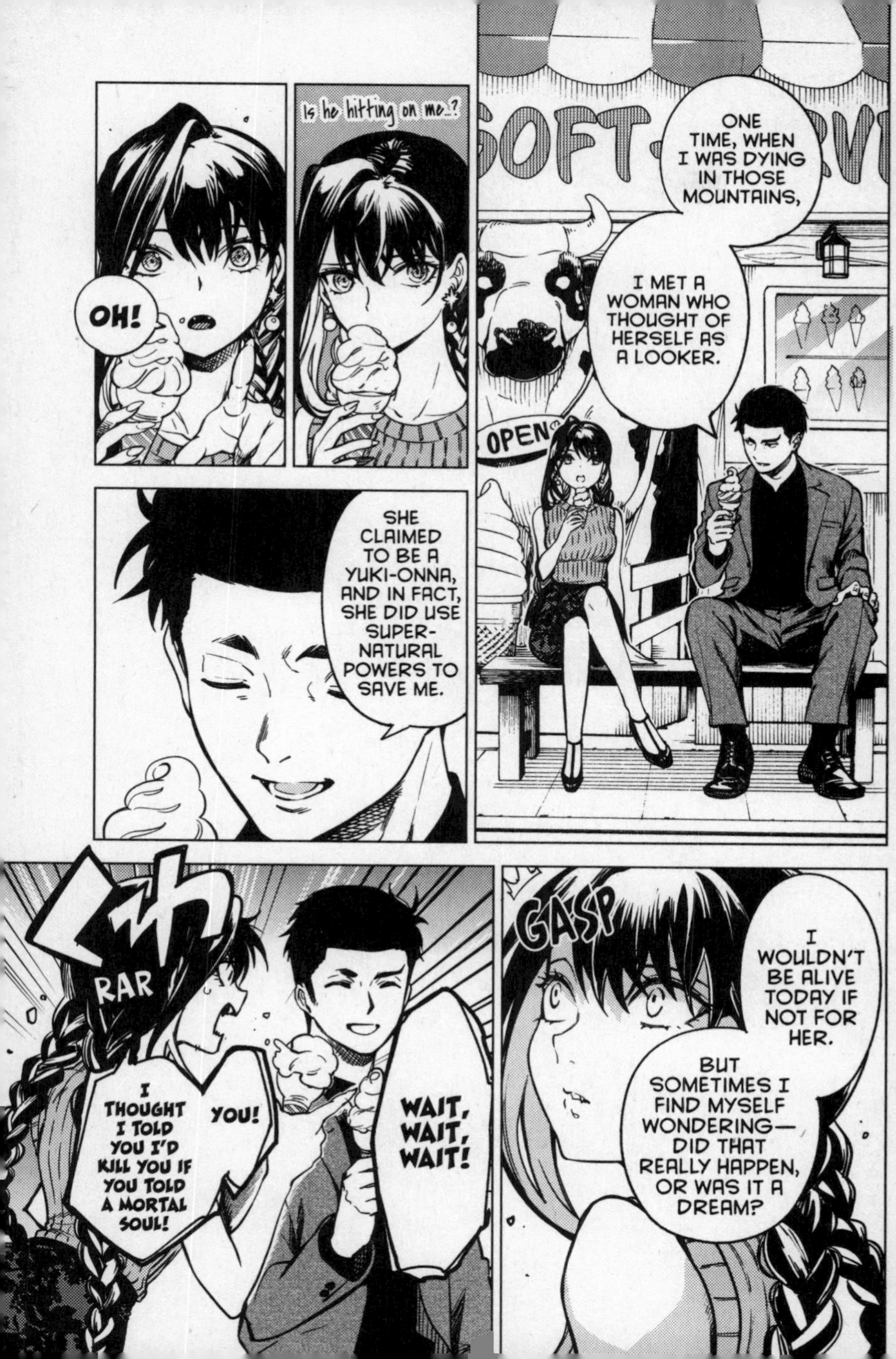
SOFT
ONE TIME, WHEN I WAS DYING IN THOSE MOUNTAINS,
I MET A WOMAN WHO THOUGHT OF HERSELF AS A LOOKER.
OPEN
Is he hitting on me..?
OH!
SHE CLAIMED TO BE A YUKI-ONNA, AND IN FACT, SHE DID USE SUPER-NATURAL POWERS TO SAVE ME.
GASP
I WOULDN'T BE ALIVE TODAY IF NOT FOR HER.
BUT SOMETIMES I FIND MYSELF WONDERING— DID THAT REALLY HAPPEN, OR WAS IT A DREAM?
RAR
YOU!
I THOUGHT I TOLD YOU I'D KILL YOU IF YOU TOLD A MORTAL SOUL!
WAIT, WAIT, WAIT!

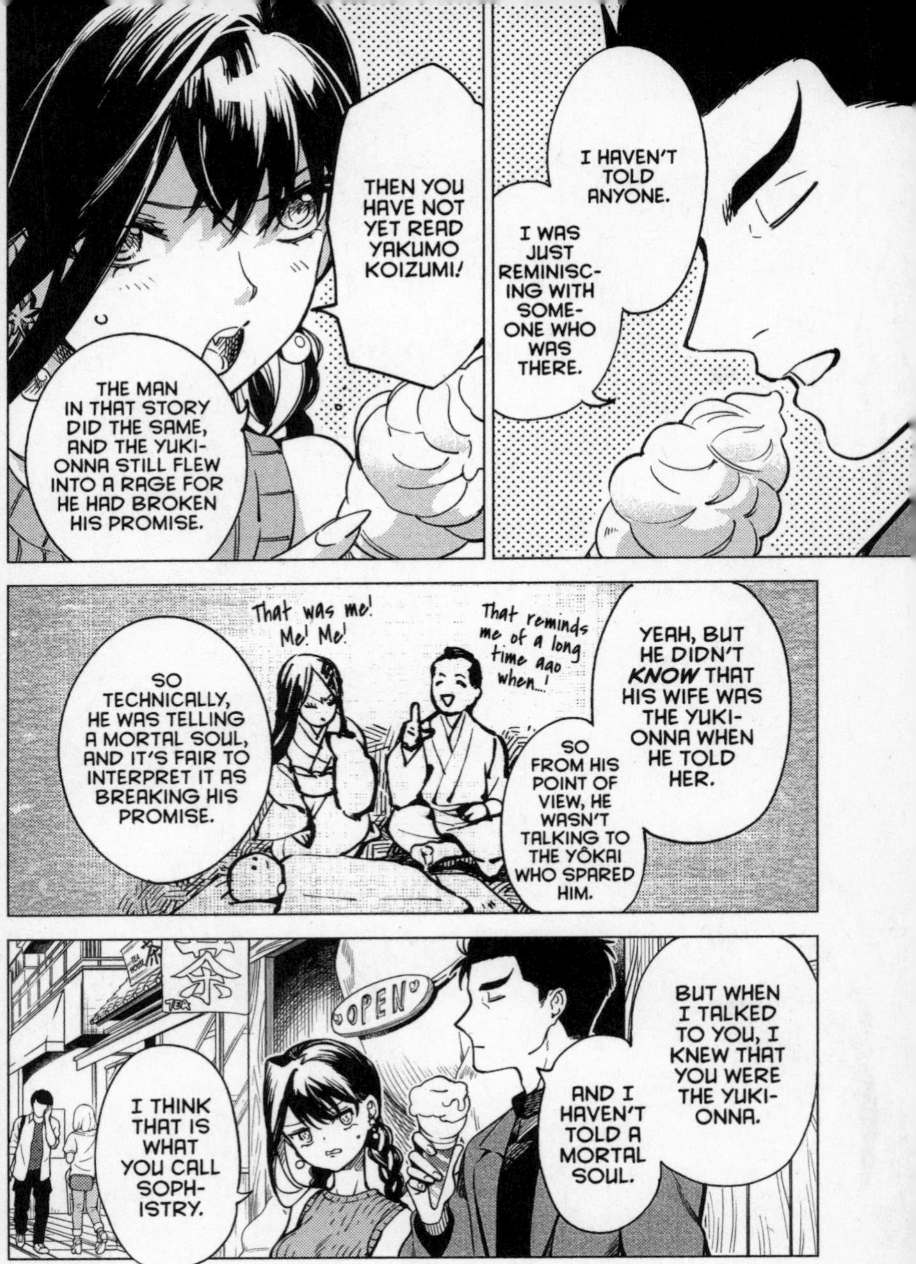
I HAVEN'T TOLD ANYONE.
I WAS JUST REMINISC-ING WITH SOME-ONE WHO WAS THERE.
THEN YOU HAVE NOT YET READ YAKUMO KOIZUMI!
THE MAN IN THAT STORY DID THE SAME, AND THE YUKI-ONNA STILL FLEW INTO A RAGE FOR HE HAD BROKEN HIS PROMISE.
YEAH, BUT HE DIDN'T *KNOW* THAT HIS WIFE WAS THE YUKI-ONNA WHEN HE TOLD HER.
SO FROM HIS POINT OF VIEW, HE WASN'T TALKING TO THE YÔKAI WHO SPARED HIM.
That reminds me of a long time ago when...!
That was me! Me! Me!
SO TECHNICALLY, HE WAS TELLING A MORTAL SOUL, AND IT'S FAIR TO INTERPRET IT AS BREAKING HIS PROMISE.
BUT WHEN I TALKED TO YOU, I KNEW THAT YOU WERE THE YUKI-ONNA.
AND I HAVEN'T TOLD A MORTAL SOUL.
OPEN
茶
TEA
I THINK THAT IS WHAT YOU CALL SOPH-ISTRY.

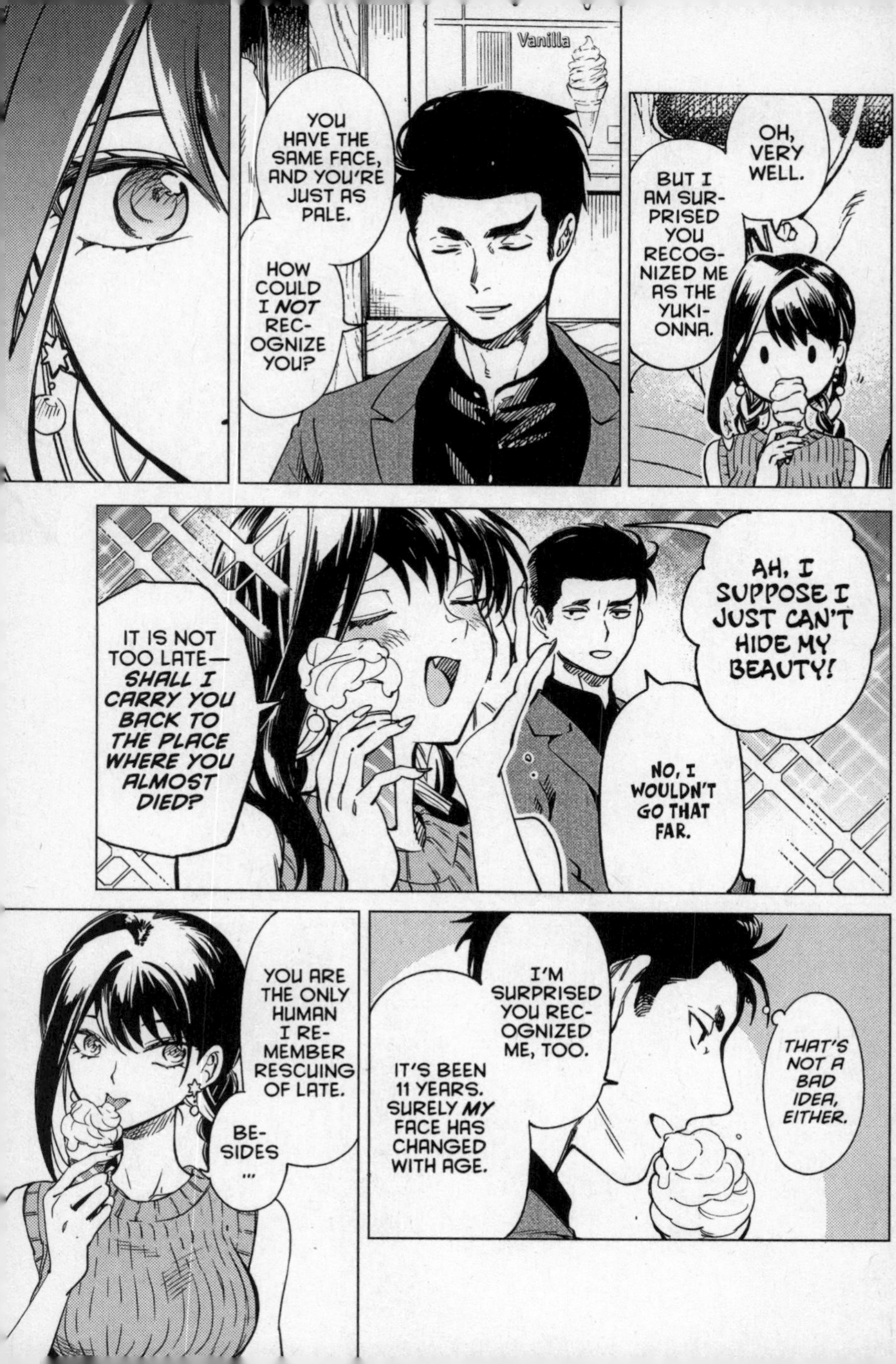
OH, VERY WELL.
BUT I AM SURPRISED YOU RECOGNIZED ME AS THE YUKI-ONNA.
Vanilla
YOU HAVE THE SAME FACE, AND YOU'RE JUST AS PALE.
HOW COULD I *NOT* RECOGNIZE YOU?
AH, I SUPPOSE I JUST CAN'T HIDE MY BEAUTY!
NO, I WOULDN'T GO THAT FAR.
IT IS NOT TOO LATE—*SHALL I CARRY YOU BACK TO THE PLACE WHERE YOU ALMOST DIED?*
THAT'S NOT A BAD IDEA, EITHER.
I'M SURPRISED YOU RECOGNIZED ME, TOO.
IT'S BEEN 11 YEARS. SURELY *MY* FACE HAS CHANGED WITH AGE.
YOU ARE THE ONLY HUMAN I REMEMBER RESCUING OF LATE.
BESIDES...

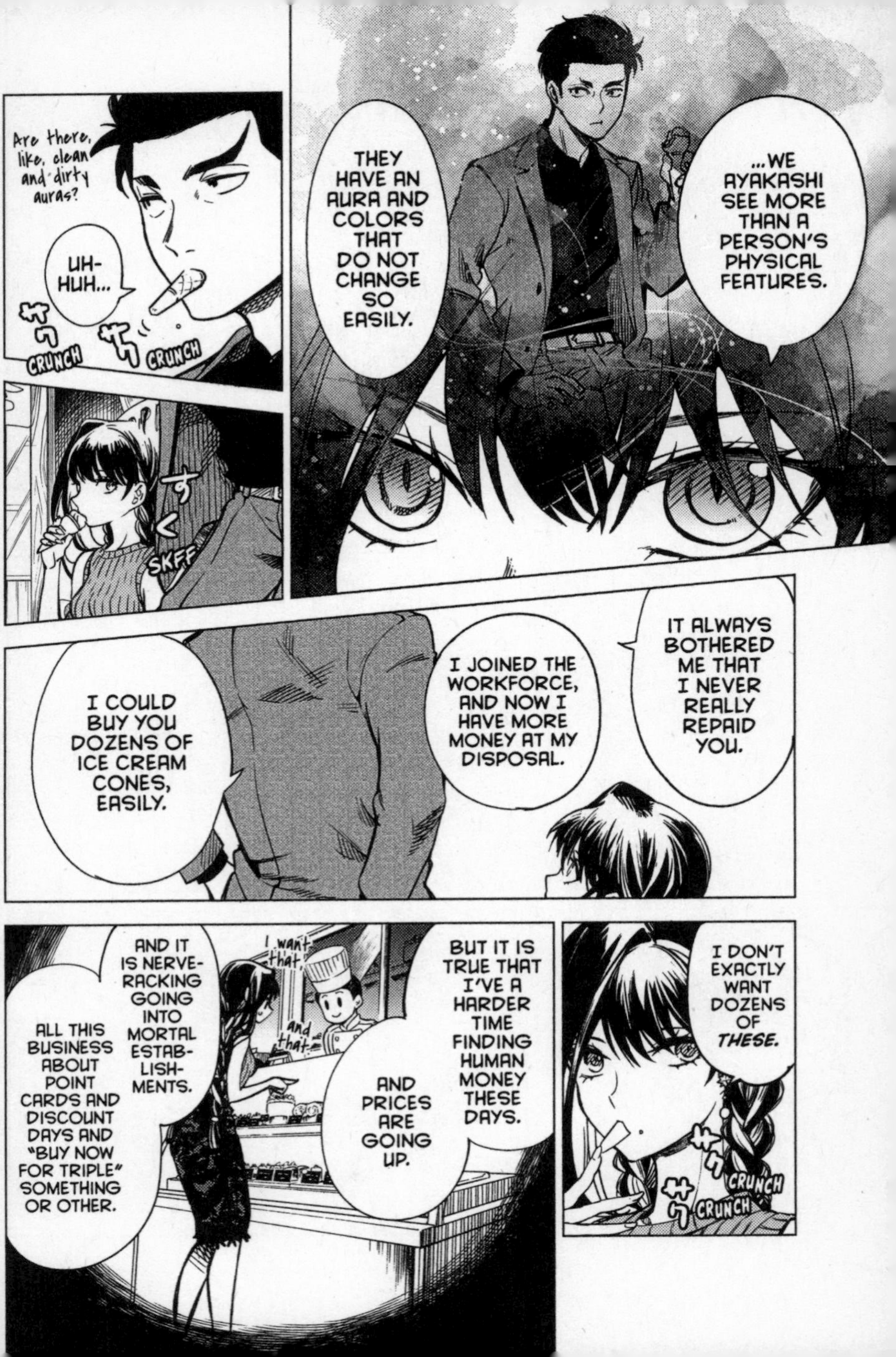
...WE AYAKASHI SEE MORE THAN A PERSON'S PHYSICAL FEATURES.
THEY HAVE AN AURA AND COLORS THAT DO NOT CHANGE SO EASILY.
Are there, like, clean and dirty auras?
UH-HUH...
CRUNCH
CRUNCH
SKFF
IT ALWAYS BOTHERED ME THAT I NEVER REALLY REPAID YOU.
I JOINED THE WORKFORCE, AND NOW I HAVE MORE MONEY AT MY DISPOSAL.
I COULD BUY YOU DOZENS OF ICE CREAM CONES, EASILY.
I DON'T EXACTLY WANT DOZENS OF *THESE.*
CRUNCH
CRUNCH
BUT IT IS TRUE THAT I'VE A HARDER TIME FINDING HUMAN MONEY THESE DAYS.
AND PRICES ARE GOING UP.
AND IT IS NERVE-RACKING GOING INTO MORTAL ESTAB-LISH-MENTS.
ALL THIS BUSINESS ABOUT POINT CARDS AND DISCOUNT DAYS AND "BUY NOW FOR TRIPLE" SOMETHING OR OTHER.
I want that,
and that.

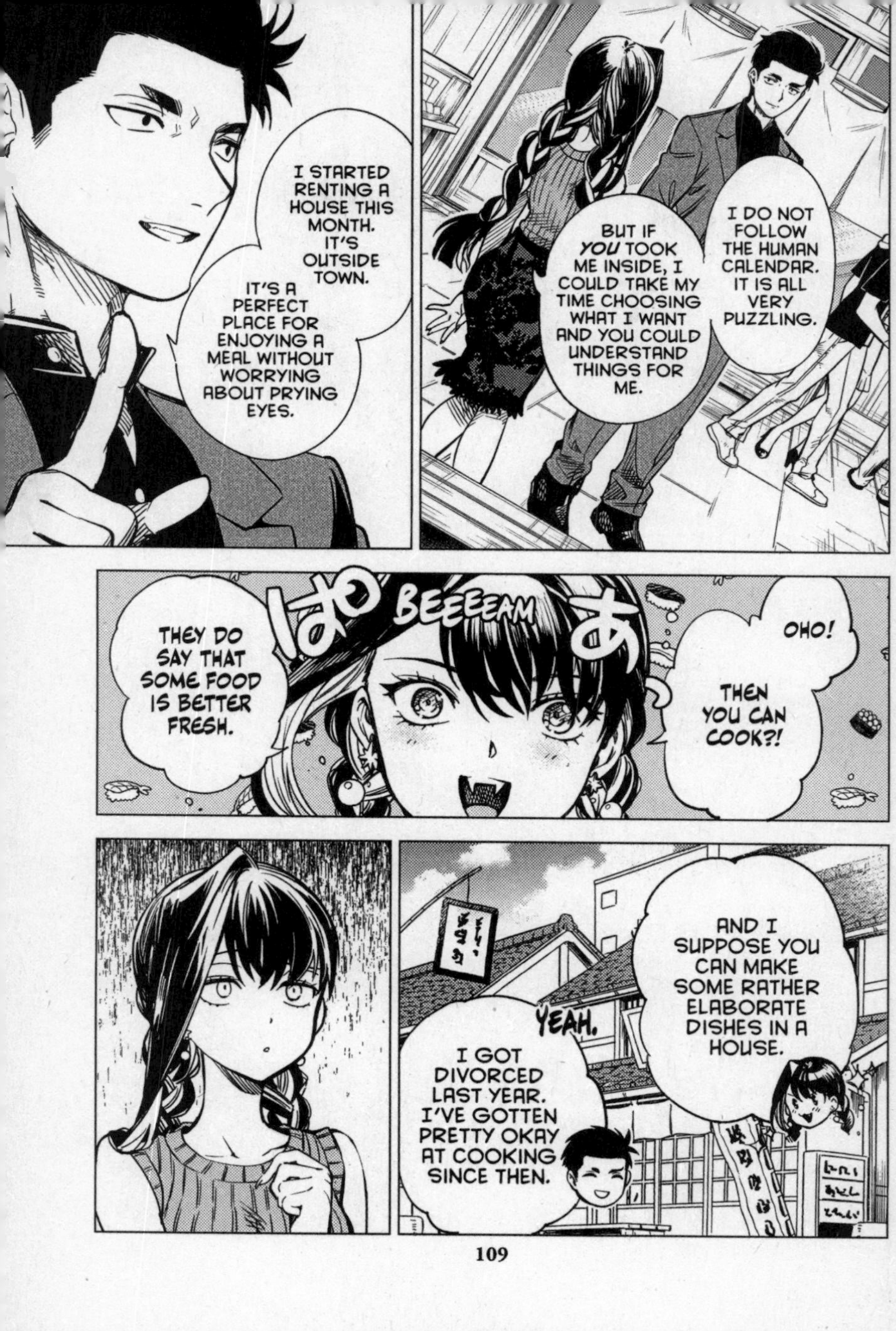
I DO NOT FOLLOW THE HUMAN CALENDAR. IT IS ALL VERY PUZZLING.
BUT IF *YOU* TOOK ME INSIDE, I COULD TAKE MY TIME CHOOSING WHAT I WANT AND YOU COULD UNDERSTAND THINGS FOR ME.
I STARTED RENTING A HOUSE THIS MONTH. IT'S OUTSIDE TOWN.
IT'S A PERFECT PLACE FOR ENJOYING A MEAL WITHOUT WORRYING ABOUT PRYING EYES.
OHO!
THEN YOU CAN COOK?!
ぱあ BEEEEAM
THEY DO SAY THAT SOME FOOD IS BETTER FRESH.
AND I SUPPOSE YOU CAN MAKE SOME RATHER ELABORATE DISHES IN A HOUSE.
YEAH.
I GOT DIVORCED LAST YEAR. I'VE GOTTEN PRETTY OKAY AT COOKING SINCE THEN.

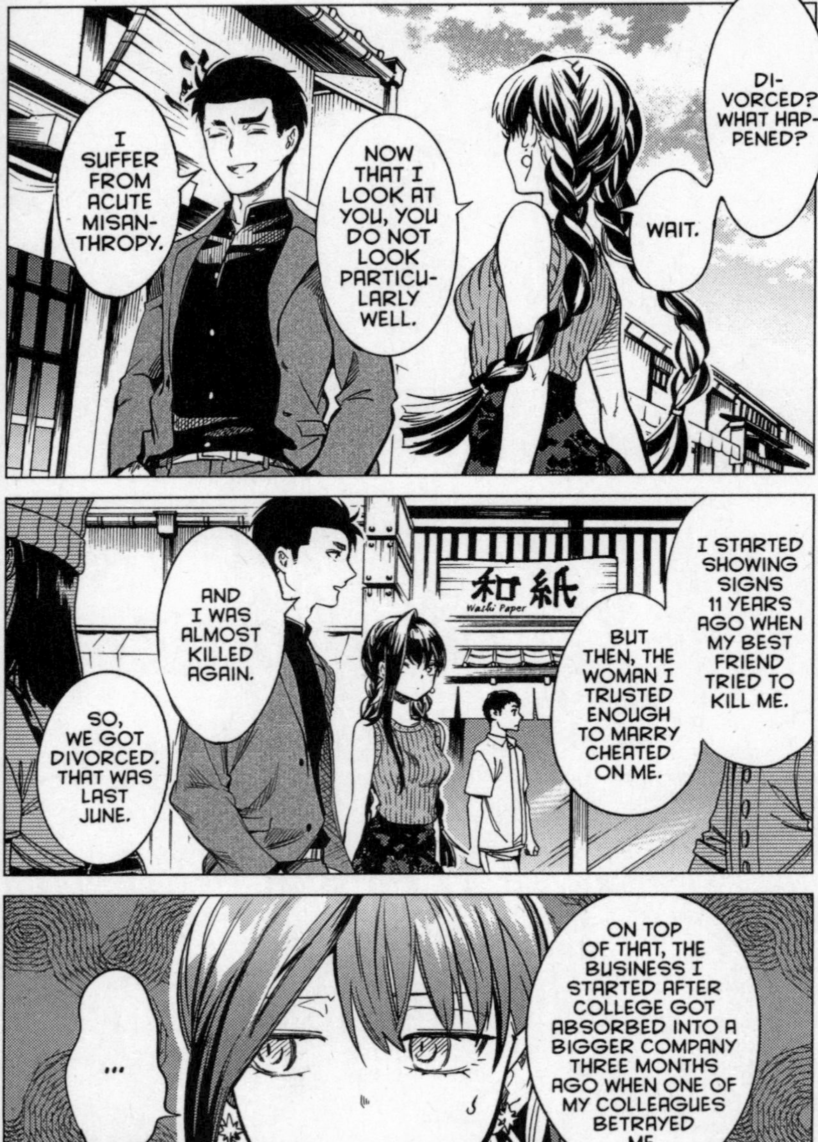
DI-VORCED? WHAT HAP-PENED?
WAIT.
NOW THAT I LOOK AT YOU, YOU DO NOT LOOK PARTICU-LARLY WELL.
I SUFFER FROM ACUTE MISAN-THROPY.
I STARTED SHOWING SIGNS 11 YEARS AGO WHEN MY BEST FRIEND TRIED TO KILL ME.
和紙
Washi Paper
BUT THEN, THE WOMAN I TRUSTED ENOUGH TO MARRY CHEATED ON ME.
AND I WAS ALMOST KILLED AGAIN.
SO, WE GOT DIVORCED. THAT WAS LAST JUNE.
ON TOP OF THAT, THE BUSINESS I STARTED AFTER COLLEGE GOT ABSORBED INTO A BIGGER COMPANY THREE MONTHS AGO WHEN ONE OF MY COLLEAGUES BETRAYED ME.
...

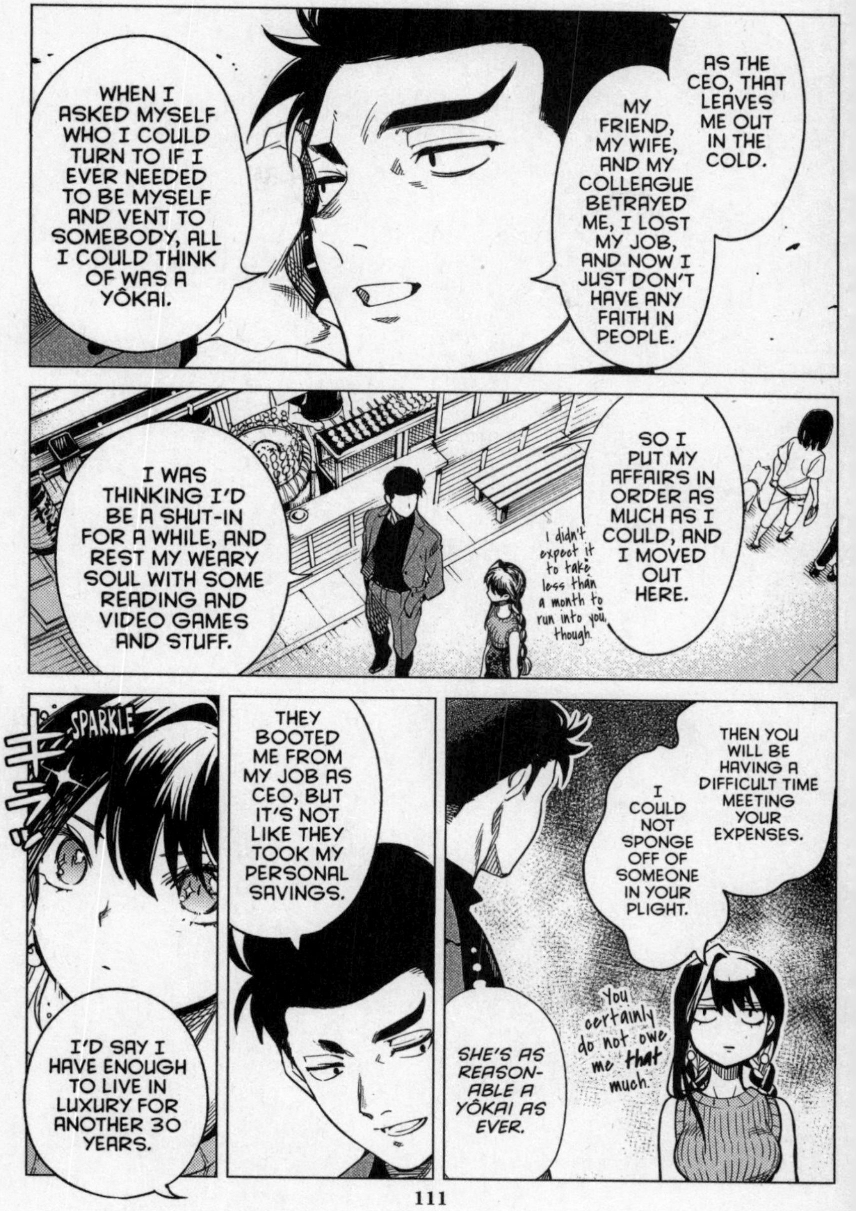
AS THE CEO, THAT LEAVES ME OUT IN THE COLD.
MY FRIEND, MY WIFE, AND MY COLLEAGUE BETRAYED ME, I LOST MY JOB, AND NOW I JUST DON'T HAVE ANY FAITH IN PEOPLE.
WHEN I ASKED MYSELF WHO I COULD TURN TO IF I EVER NEEDED TO BE MYSELF AND VENT TO SOMEBODY, ALL I COULD THINK OF WAS A YÔKAI.
SO I PUT MY AFFAIRS IN ORDER AS MUCH AS I COULD, AND I MOVED OUT HERE.
I didn't expect it to take less than a month to run into you, though.
I WAS THINKING I'D BE A SHUT-IN FOR A WHILE, AND REST MY WEARY SOUL WITH SOME READING AND VIDEO GAMES AND STUFF.
THEN YOU WILL BE HAVING A DIFFICULT TIME MEETING YOUR EXPENSES.
I COULD NOT SPONGE OFF OF SOMEONE IN YOUR PLIGHT.
You certainly do not owe me that much.
SHE'S AS REASONABLE A YÔKAI AS EVER.
THEY BOOTED ME FROM MY JOB AS CEO, BUT IT'S NOT LIKE THEY TOOK MY PERSONAL SAVINGS.
SPARKLE
I'D SAY I HAVE ENOUGH TO LIVE IN LUXURY FOR ANOTHER 30 YEARS.

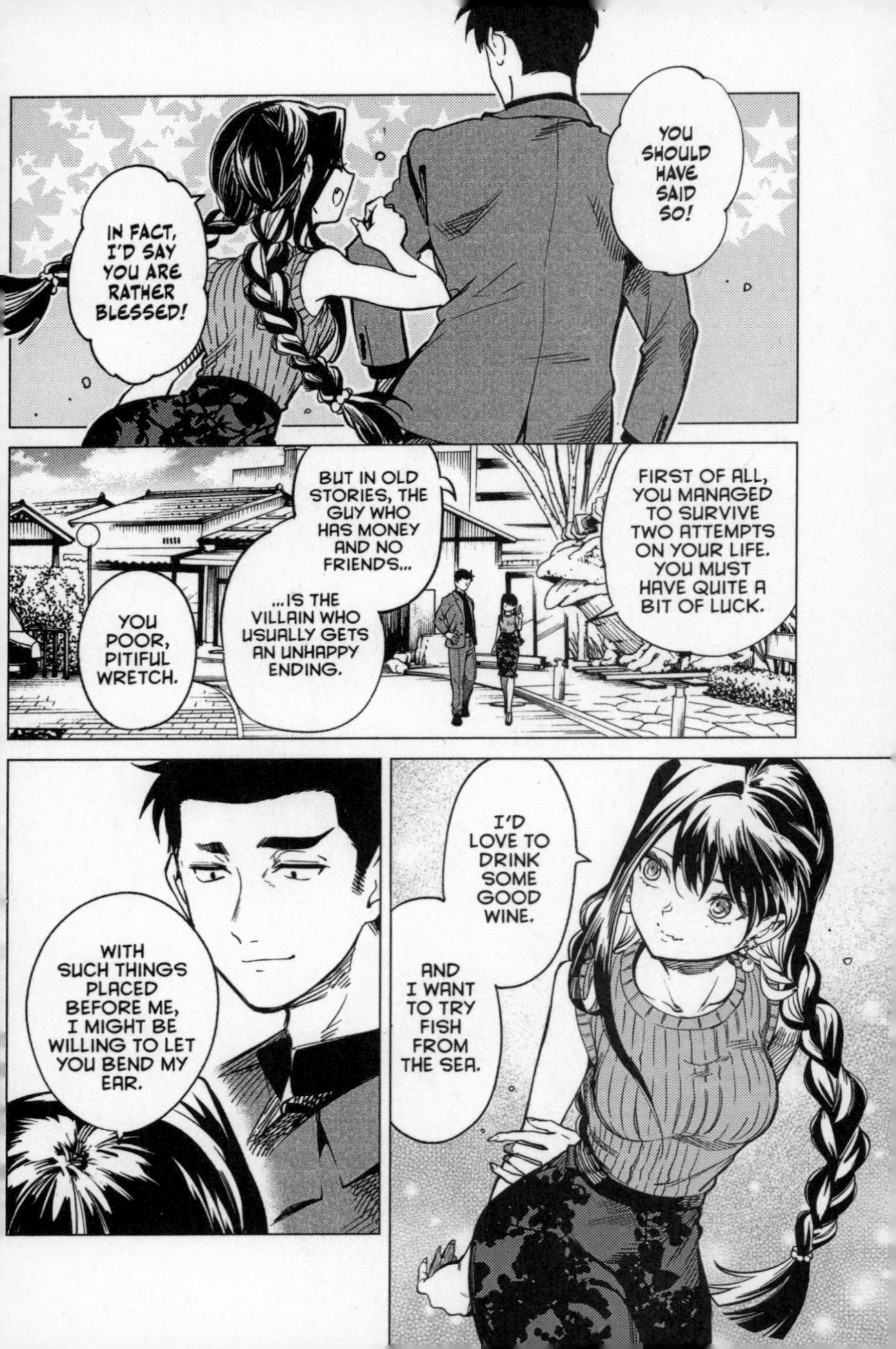
YOU SHOULD HAVE SAID SO!
IN FACT, I'D SAY YOU ARE RATHER BLESSED!
FIRST OF ALL, YOU MANAGED TO SURVIVE TWO ATTEMPTS ON YOUR LIFE. YOU MUST HAVE QUITE A BIT OF LUCK.
BUT IN OLD STORIES, THE GUY WHO HAS MONEY AND NO FRIENDS...
...IS THE VILLAIN WHO USUALLY GETS AN UNHAPPY ENDING.
YOU POOR, PITIFUL WRETCH.
I'D LOVE TO DRINK SOME GOOD WINE.
AND I WANT TO TRY FISH FROM THE SEA.
WITH SUCH THINGS PLACED BEFORE ME, I MIGHT BE WILLING TO LET YOU BEND MY EAR.

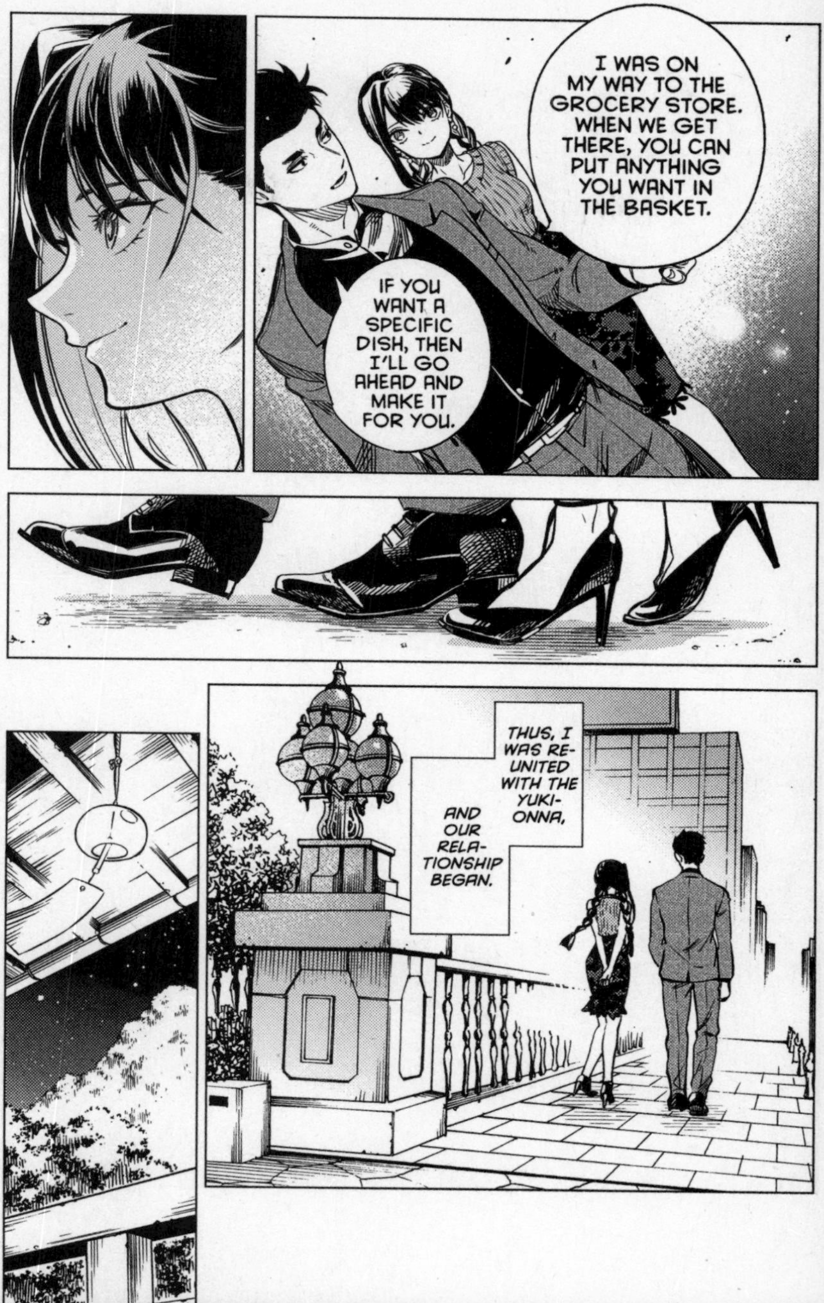
I WAS ON MY WAY TO THE GROCERY STORE. WHEN WE GET THERE, YOU CAN PUT ANYTHING YOU WANT IN THE BASKET.
IF YOU WANT A SPECIFIC DISH, THEN I'LL GO AHEAD AND MAKE IT FOR YOU.
THUS, I WAS RE-UNITED WITH THE YUKI-ONNA,
AND OUR RELA-TIONSHIP BEGAN.

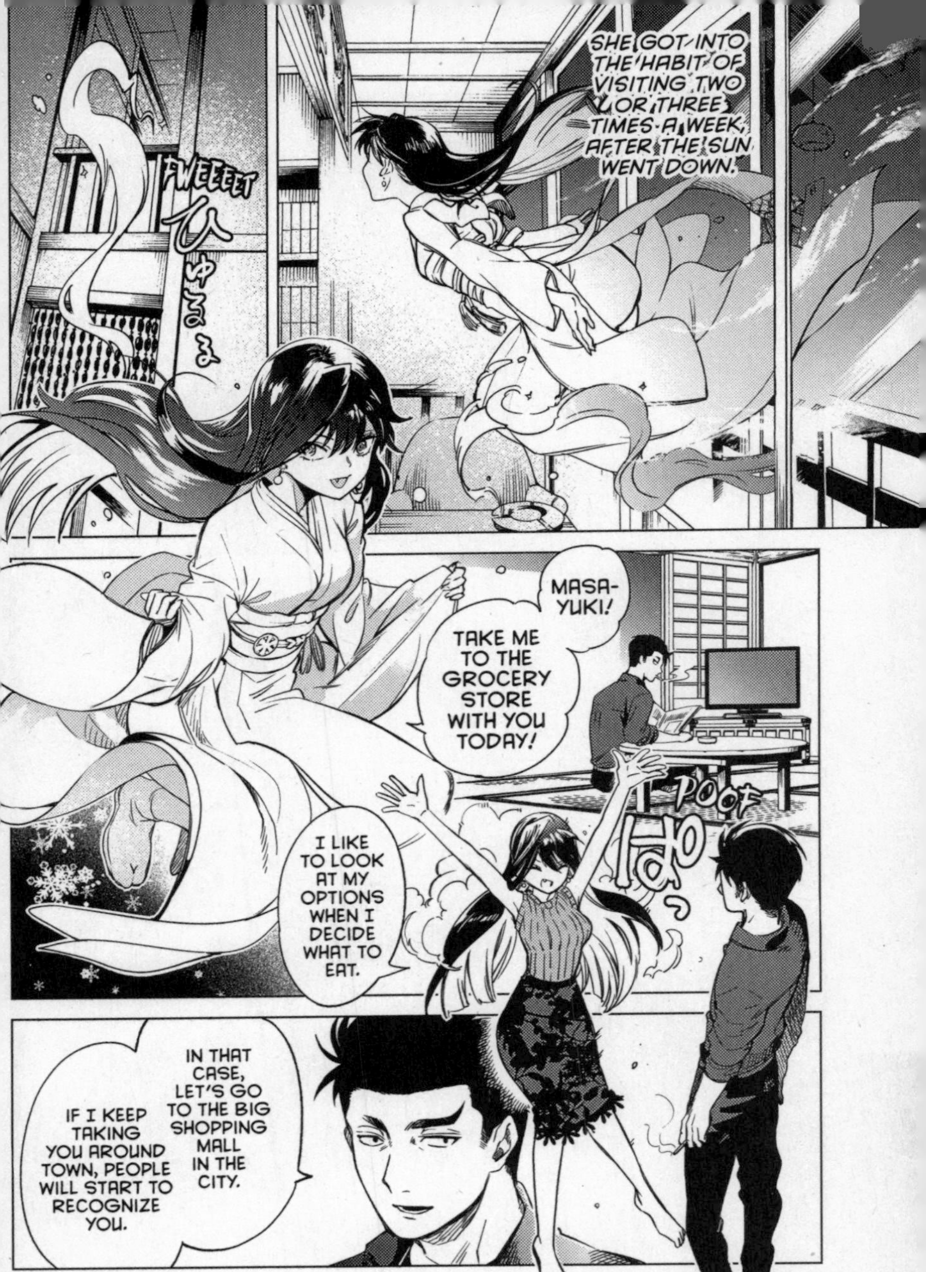
SHE GOT INTO THE HABIT OF VISITING TWO OR THREE TIMES A WEEK, AFTER THE SUN WENT DOWN.
FWEEEEET
MASA-YUKI!
TAKE ME TO THE GROCERY STORE WITH YOU TODAY!
POOF
I LIKE TO LOOK AT MY OPTIONS WHEN I DECIDE WHAT TO EAT.
IN THAT CASE, LET'S GO TO THE BIG SHOPPING MALL IN THE CITY.
IF I KEEP TAKING YOU AROUND TOWN, PEOPLE WILL START TO RECOGNIZE YOU.

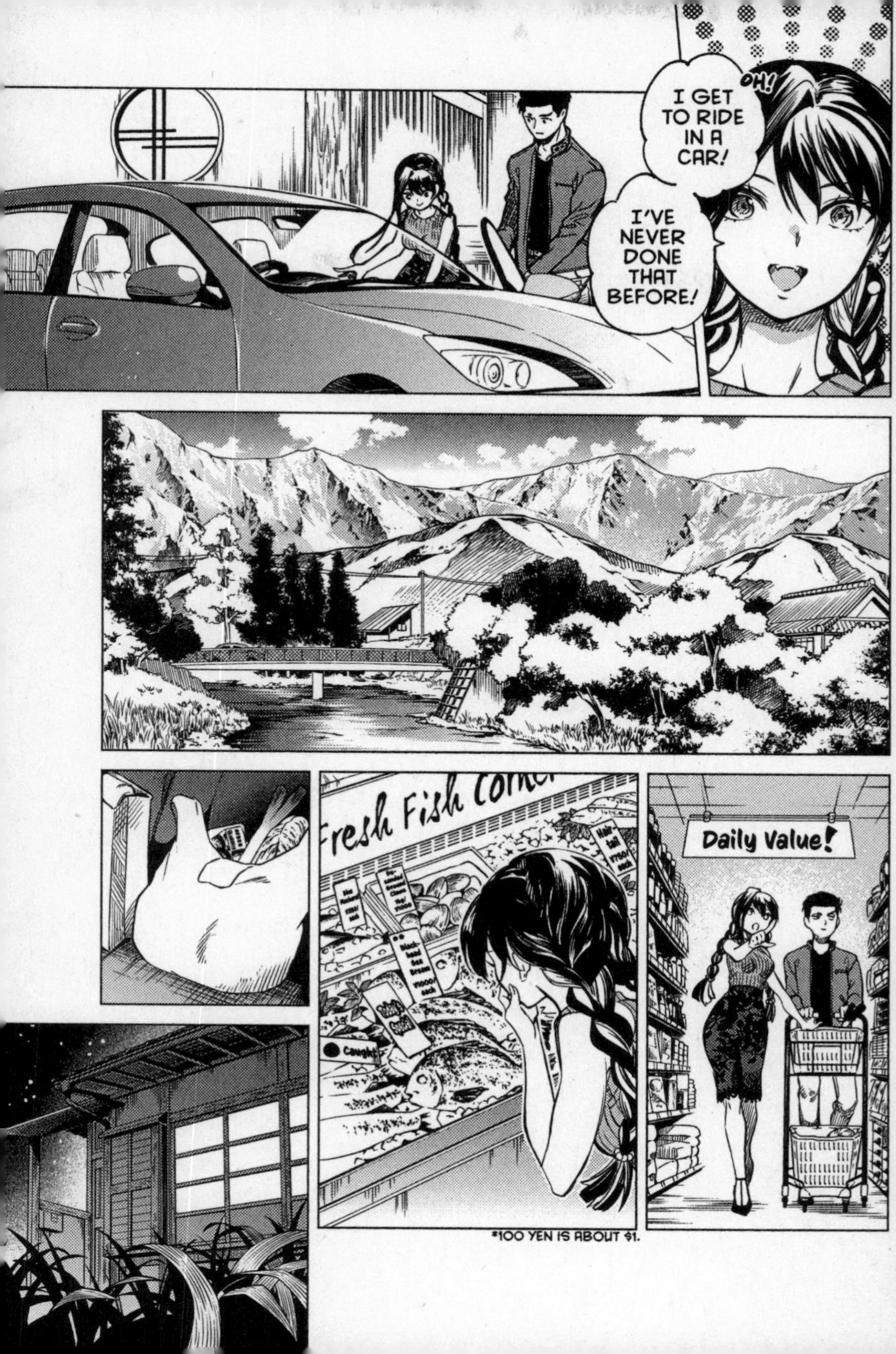
OH!
I GET TO RIDE IN A CAR!
I'VE NEVER DONE THAT BEFORE!
Daily Value!
Fresh Fish Corne
Hair-tail ¥750/ each
Black-head Sea Bream ¥1000/ each
Caught

*100 YEN IS ABOUT $1.

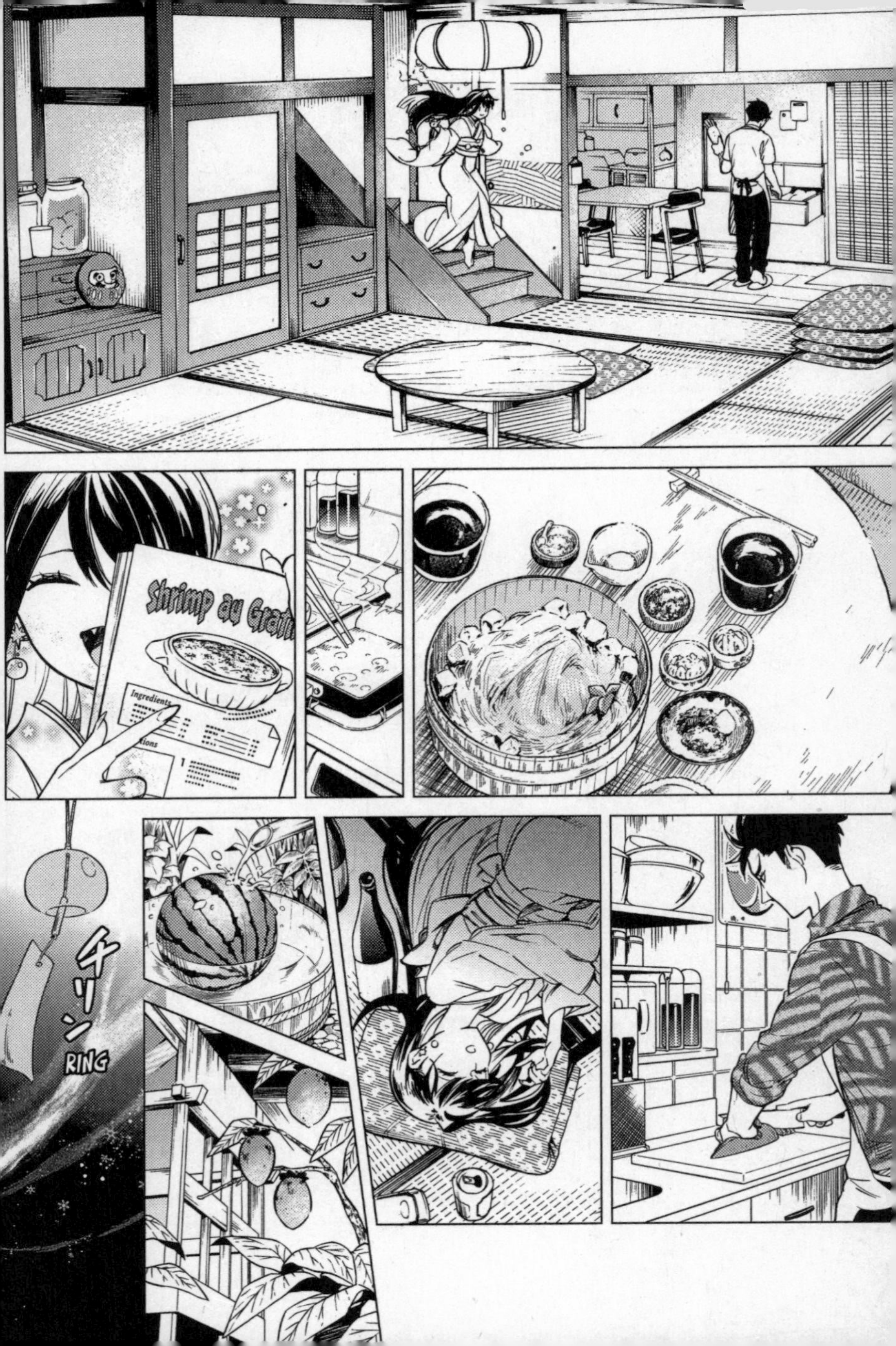
Shrimp au Grati
Ingredients
tions
チリン
RING

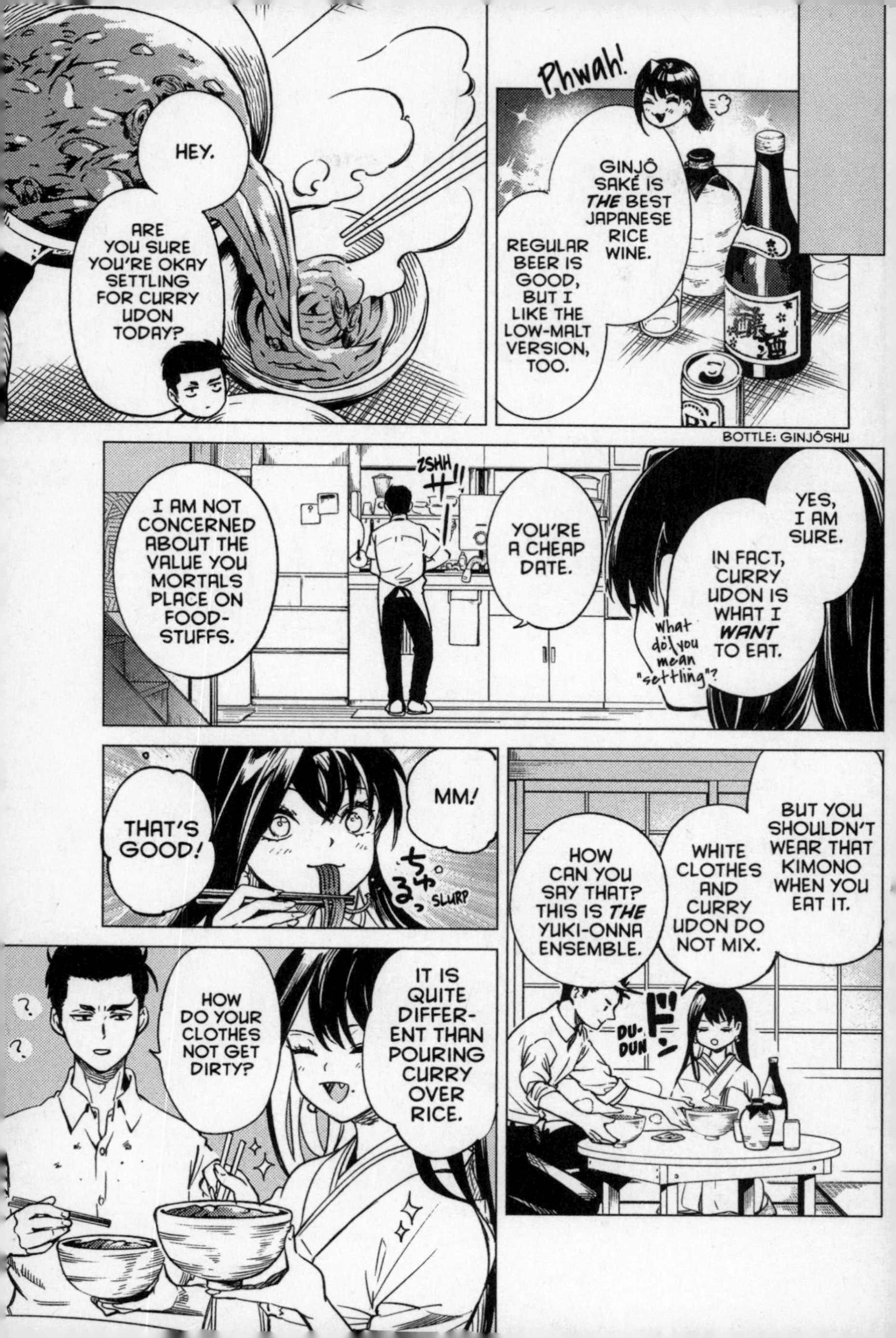
Phwah!
GINJÔ SAKÉ IS *THE* BEST JAPANESE RICE WINE.
REGULAR BEER IS GOOD, BUT I LIKE THE LOW-MALT VERSION, TOO.
BOTTLE: GINJÔSHU
HEY.
ARE YOU SURE YOU'RE OKAY SETTLING FOR CURRY UDON TODAY?
YES, I AM SURE.
IN FACT, CURRY UDON IS WHAT I *WANT* TO EAT.
What do you mean "settling"?
YOU'RE A CHEAP DATE.
ZSHH
I AM NOT CONCERNED ABOUT THE VALUE YOU MORTALS PLACE ON FOOD-STUFFS.
BUT YOU SHOULDN'T WEAR THAT KIMONO WHEN YOU EAT IT.
WHITE CLOTHES AND CURRY UDON DO NOT MIX.
HOW CAN YOU SAY THAT? THIS IS *THE* YUKI-ONNA ENSEMBLE.
DU-DUN
MM!
THAT'S GOOD!
ちゅるっ
SLURP
IT IS QUITE DIFFER-ENT THAN POURING CURRY OVER RICE.
HOW DO YOUR CLOTHES NOT GET DIRTY?

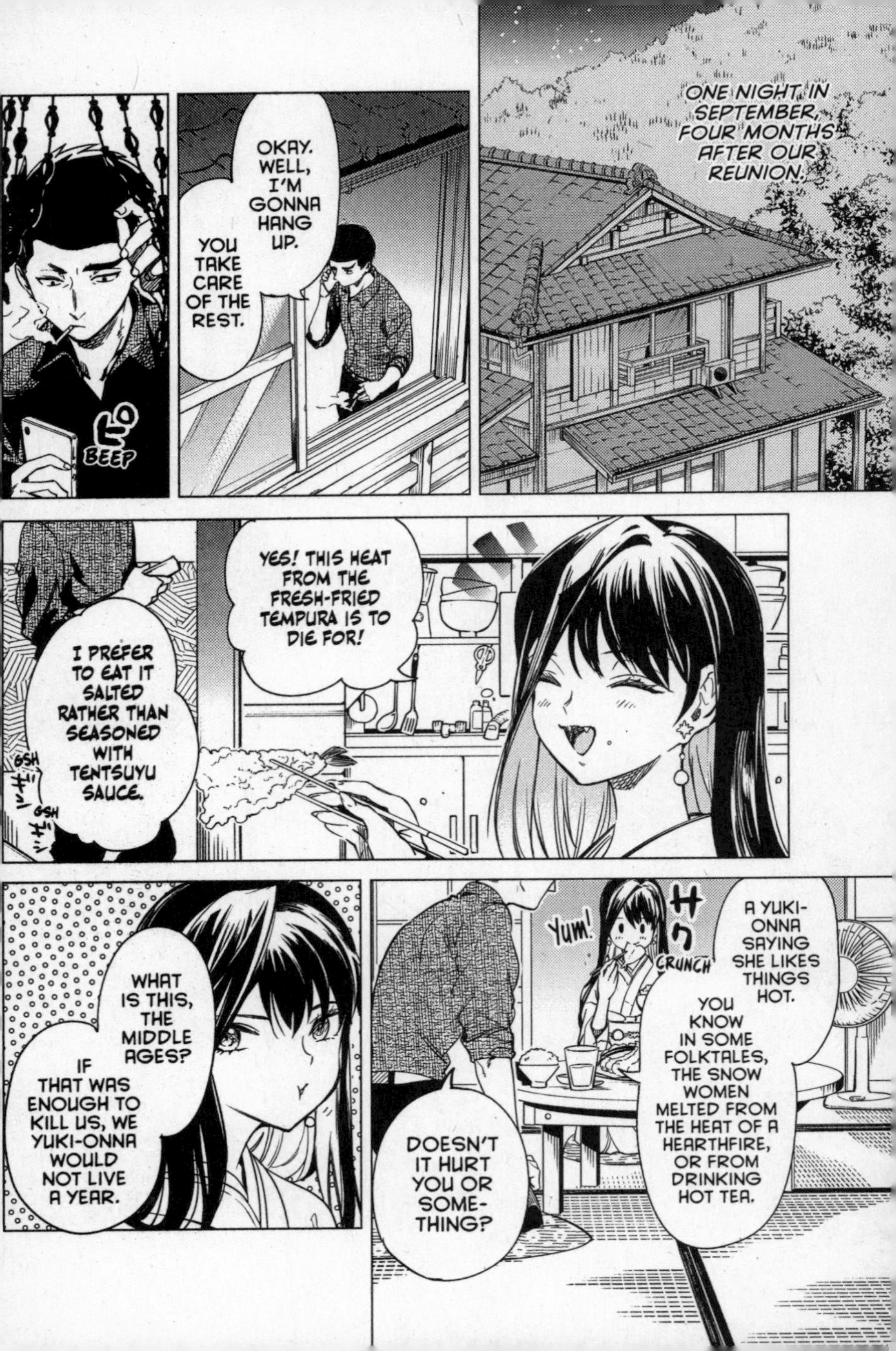
ONE NIGHT IN SEPTEMBER, FOUR MONTHS AFTER OUR REUNION.
OKAY. WELL, I'M GONNA HANG UP.
YOU TAKE CARE OF THE REST.
BEEP
YES! THIS HEAT FROM THE FRESH-FRIED TEMPURA IS TO DIE FOR!
I PREFER TO EAT IT SALTED RATHER THAN SEASONED WITH TENTSUYU SAUCE.
GSH
GSH
A YUKI-ONNA SAYING SHE LIKES THINGS HOT.
YOU KNOW IN SOME FOLKTALES, THE SNOW WOMEN MELTED FROM THE HEAT OF A HEARTHFIRE, OR FROM DRINKING HOT TEA.
サク
CRUNCH
Yum!
DOESN'T IT HURT YOU OR SOME-THING?
WHAT IS THIS, THE MIDDLE AGES?
IF THAT WAS ENOUGH TO KILL US, WE YUKI-ONNA WOULD NOT LIVE A YEAR.

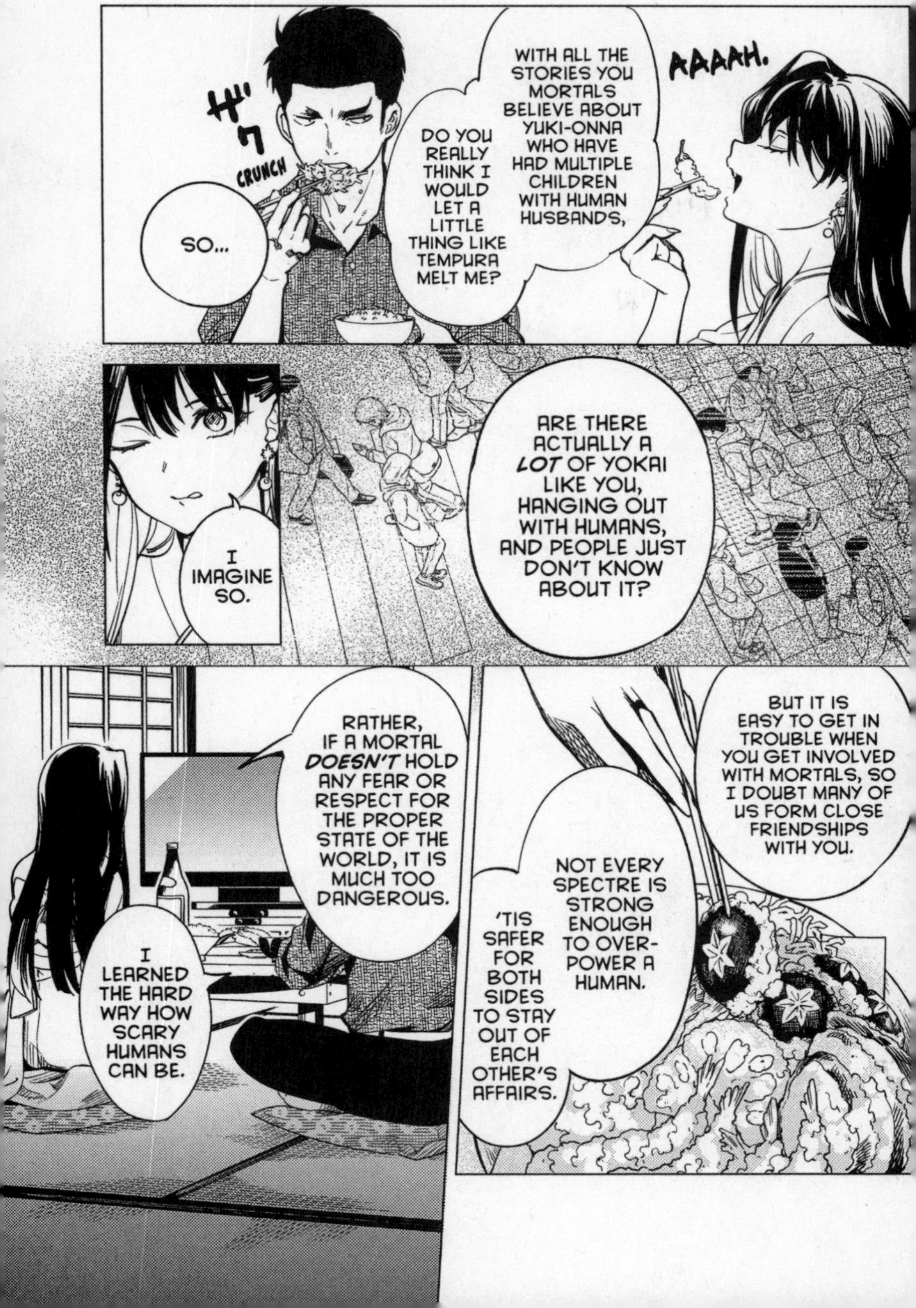
AAAAH.
WITH ALL THE STORIES YOU MORTALS BELIEVE ABOUT YUKI-ONNA WHO HAVE HAD MULTIPLE CHILDREN WITH HUMAN HUSBANDS,
DO YOU REALLY THINK I WOULD LET A LITTLE THING LIKE TEMPURA MELT ME?
ザク
CRUNCH
SO...
ARE THERE ACTUALLY A *LOT* OF YOKAI LIKE YOU, HANGING OUT WITH HUMANS, AND PEOPLE JUST DON'T KNOW ABOUT IT?
I IMAGINE SO.
BUT IT IS EASY TO GET IN TROUBLE WHEN YOU GET INVOLVED WITH MORTALS, SO I DOUBT MANY OF US FORM CLOSE FRIENDSHIPS WITH YOU.
NOT EVERY SPECTRE IS STRONG ENOUGH TO OVER-POWER A HUMAN.
'TIS SAFER FOR BOTH SIDES TO STAY OUT OF EACH OTHER'S AFFAIRS.
RATHER, IF A MORTAL ***DOESN'T*** HOLD ANY FEAR OR RESPECT FOR THE PROPER STATE OF THE WORLD, IT IS MUCH TOO DANGEROUS.
I LEARNED THE HARD WAY HOW SCARY HUMANS CAN BE.

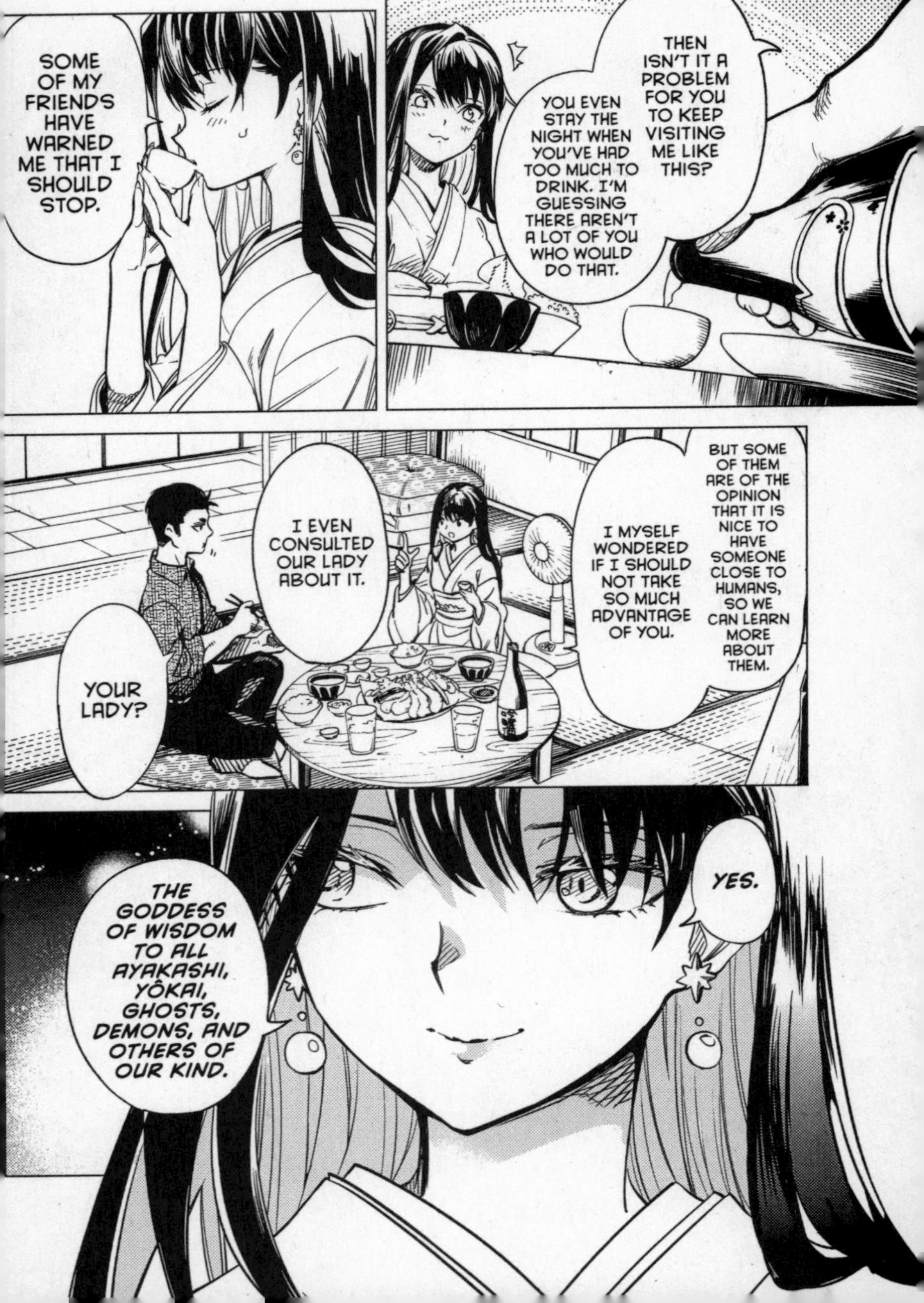
THEN ISN'T IT A PROBLEM FOR YOU TO KEEP VISITING ME LIKE THIS?
YOU EVEN STAY THE NIGHT WHEN YOU'VE HAD TOO MUCH TO DRINK. I'M GUESSING THERE AREN'T A LOT OF YOU WHO WOULD DO THAT.
SOME OF MY FRIENDS HAVE WARNED ME THAT I SHOULD STOP.
I MYSELF WONDERED IF I SHOULD NOT TAKE SO MUCH ADVANTAGE OF YOU.
BUT SOME OF THEM ARE OF THE OPINION THAT IT IS NICE TO HAVE SOMEONE CLOSE TO HUMANS, SO WE CAN LEARN MORE ABOUT THEM.
I EVEN CONSULTED OUR LADY ABOUT IT.
YOUR LADY?
YES.
THE GODDESS OF WISDOM TO ALL AYAKASHI, YÔKAI, GHOSTS, DEMONS, AND OTHERS OF OUR KIND.

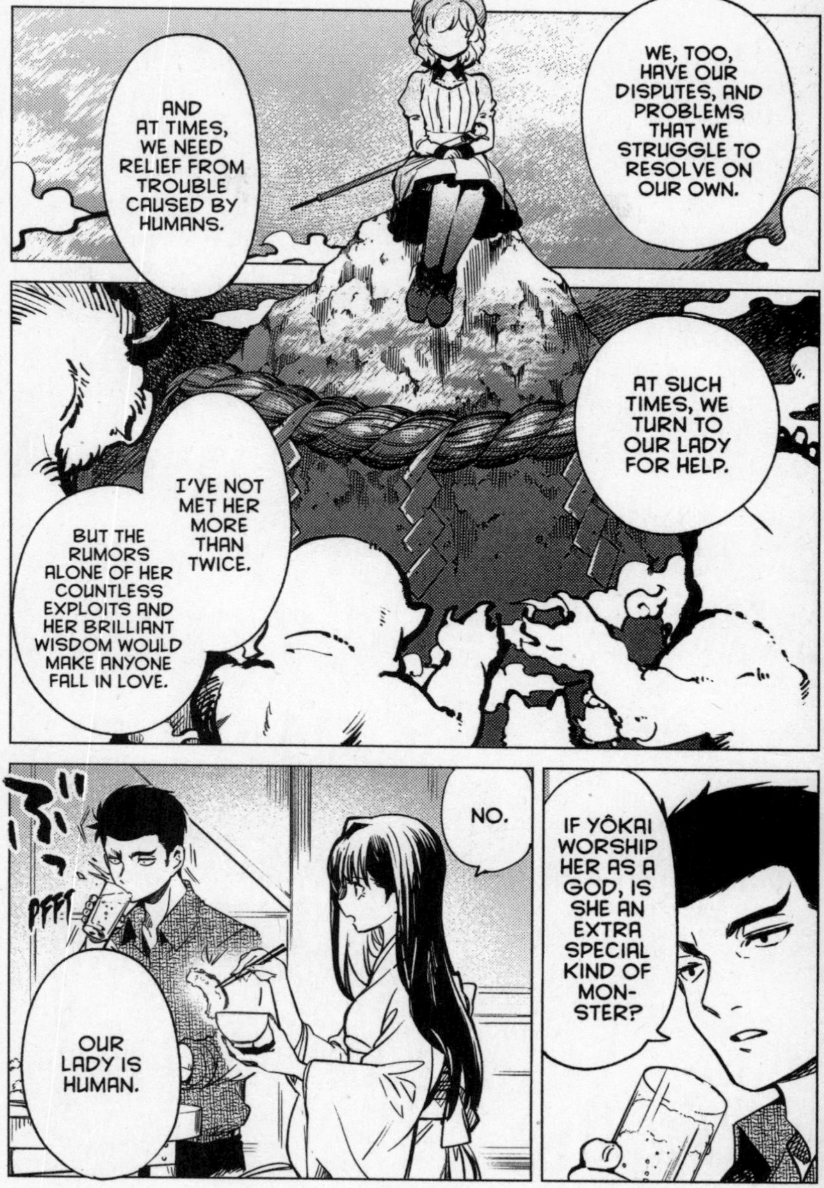
WE, TOO, HAVE OUR DISPUTES, AND PROBLEMS THAT WE STRUGGLE TO RESOLVE ON OUR OWN.
AND AT TIMES, WE NEED RELIEF FROM TROUBLE CAUSED BY HUMANS.
AT SUCH TIMES, WE TURN TO OUR LADY FOR HELP.
I'VE NOT MET HER MORE THAN TWICE.
BUT THE RUMORS ALONE OF HER COUNTLESS EXPLOITS AND HER BRILLIANT WISDOM WOULD MAKE ANYONE FALL IN LOVE.
IF YÔKAI WORSHIP HER AS A GOD, IS SHE AN EXTRA SPECIAL KIND OF MON-STER?
NO.
OUR LADY IS HUMAN.
ぶっ
PFFT

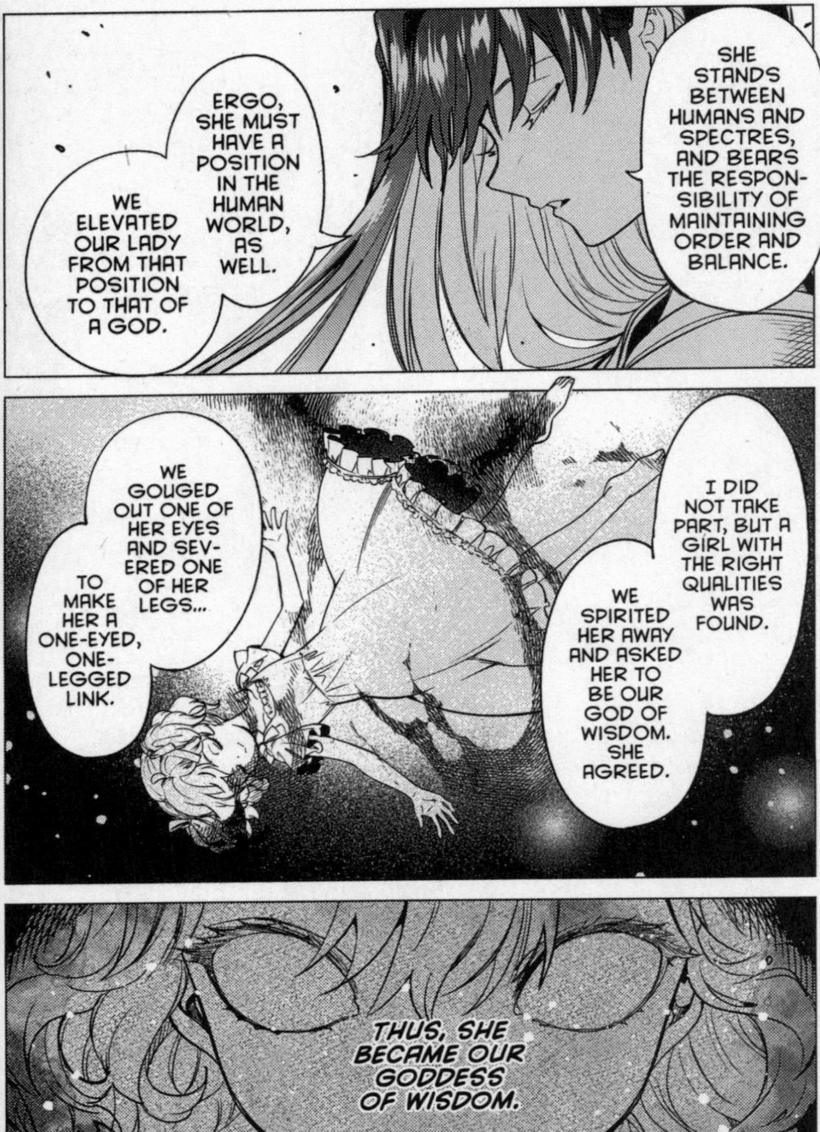
SHE STANDS BETWEEN HUMANS AND SPECTRES, AND BEARS THE RESPONSIBILITY OF MAINTAINING ORDER AND BALANCE.
ERGO, SHE MUST HAVE A POSITION IN THE HUMAN WORLD, AS WELL.
WE ELEVATED OUR LADY FROM THAT POSITION TO THAT OF A GOD.
I DID NOT TAKE PART, BUT A GIRL WITH THE RIGHT QUALITIES WAS FOUND.
WE SPIRITED HER AWAY AND ASKED HER TO BE OUR GOD OF WISDOM. SHE AGREED.
WE GOUGED OUT ONE OF HER EYES AND SEVERED ONE OF HER LEGS...
TO MAKE HER A ONE-EYED, ONE-LEGGED LINK.
THUS, SHE BECAME OUR GODDESS OF WISDOM.

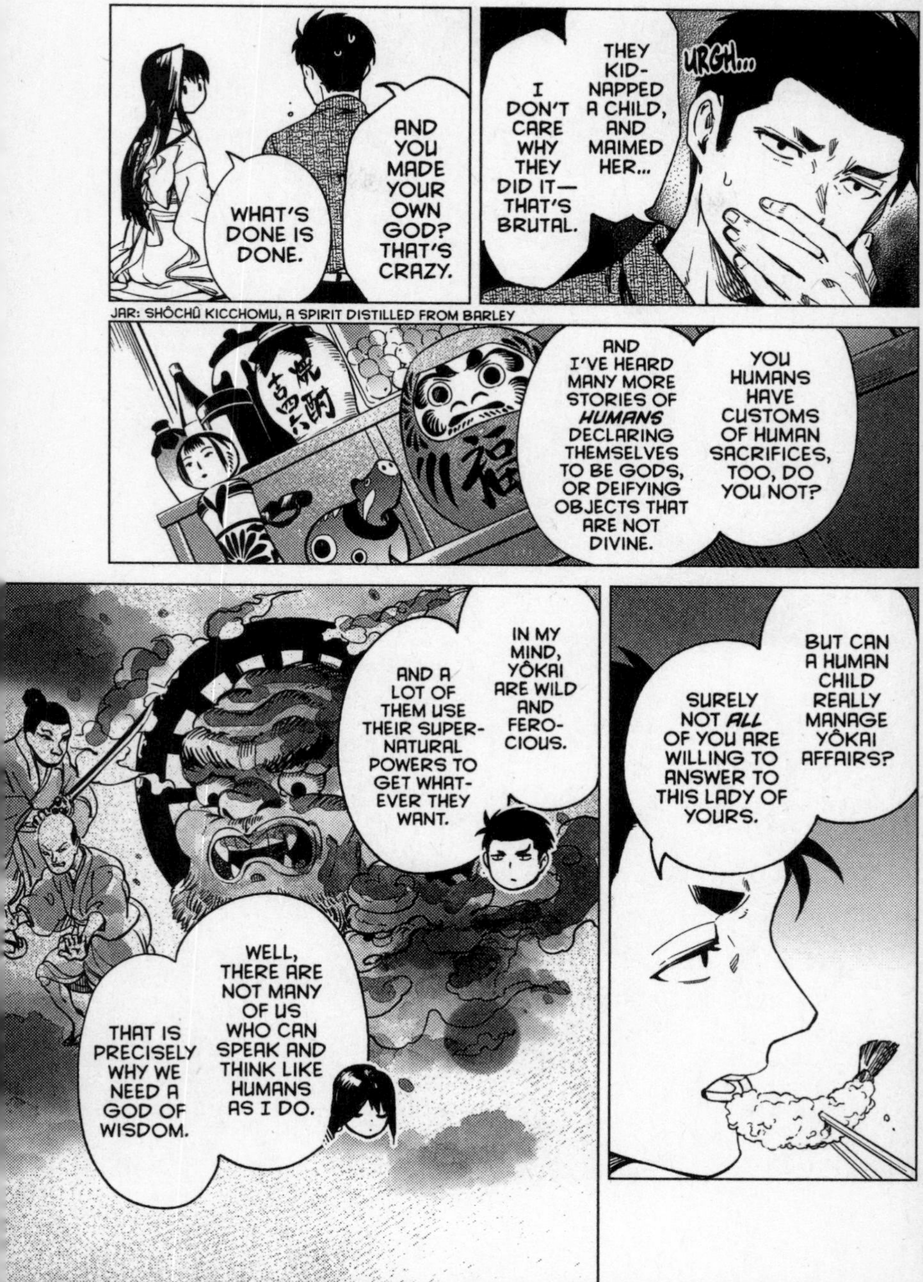
URGH...
THEY KIDNAPPED A CHILD, AND MAIMED HER...
I DON'T CARE WHY THEY DID IT—THAT'S BRUTAL.
AND YOU MADE YOUR OWN GOD? THAT'S CRAZY.
WHAT'S DONE IS DONE.
JAR: SHÔCHÛ KICCHOMU, A SPIRIT DISTILLED FROM BARLEY
YOU HUMANS HAVE CUSTOMS OF HUMAN SACRIFICES, TOO, DO YOU NOT?
AND I'VE HEARD MANY MORE STORIES OF *HUMANS* DECLARING THEMSELVES TO BE GODS, OR DEIFYING OBJECTS THAT ARE NOT DIVINE.
BUT CAN A HUMAN CHILD REALLY MANAGE YÔKAI AFFAIRS?
SURELY NOT *ALL* OF YOU ARE WILLING TO ANSWER TO THIS LADY OF YOURS.
IN MY MIND, YÔKAI ARE WILD AND FEROCIOUS.
AND A LOT OF THEM USE THEIR SUPERNATURAL POWERS TO GET WHATEVER THEY WANT.
WELL, THERE ARE NOT MANY OF US WHO CAN SPEAK AND THINK LIKE HUMANS AS I DO.
THAT IS PRECISELY WHY WE NEED A GOD OF WISDOM.

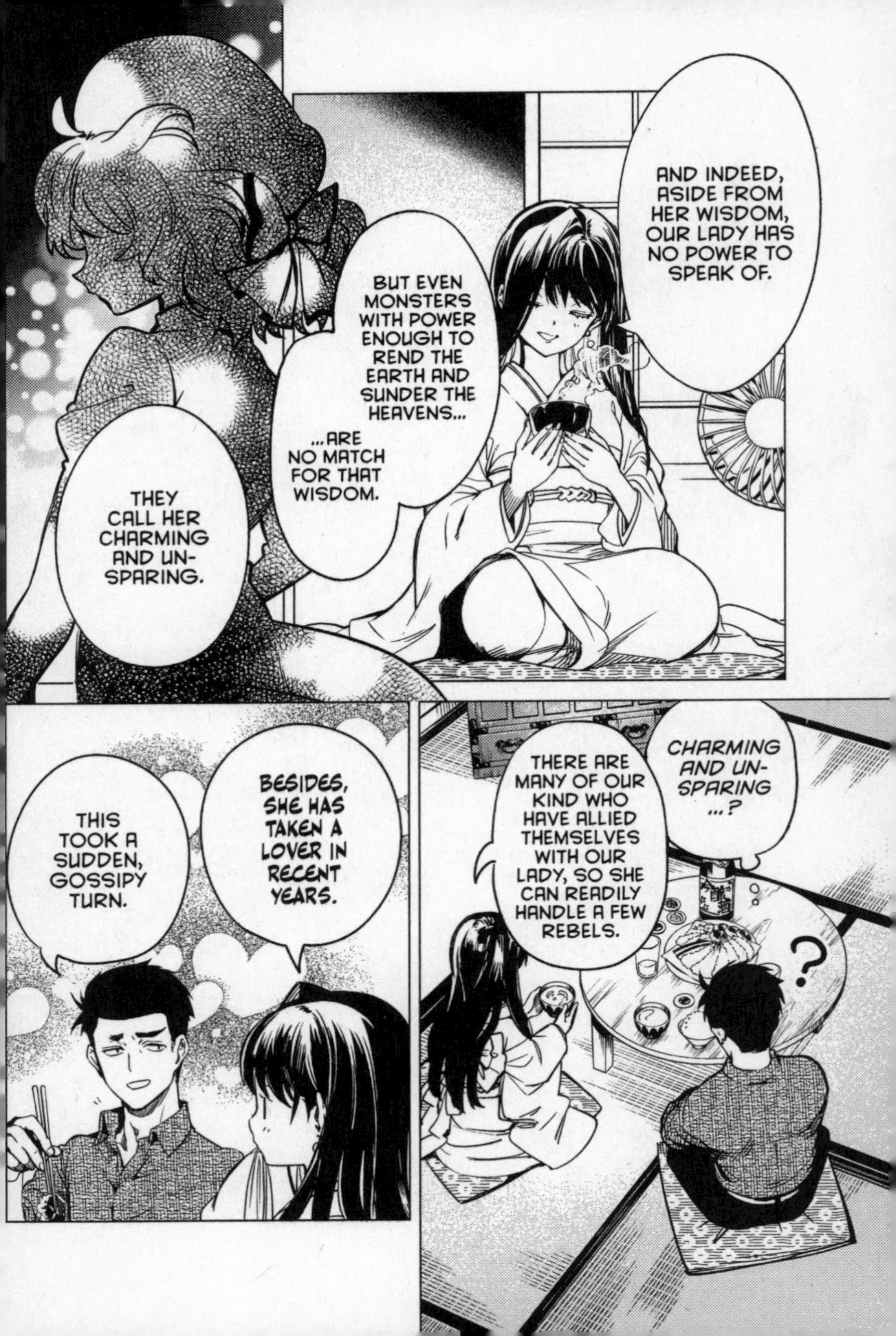
AND INDEED, ASIDE FROM HER WISDOM, OUR LADY HAS NO POWER TO SPEAK OF.
BUT EVEN MONSTERS WITH POWER ENOUGH TO REND THE EARTH AND SUNDER THE HEAVENS...
...ARE NO MATCH FOR THAT WISDOM.
THEY CALL HER CHARMING AND UN-SPARING.
CHARMING AND UN-SPARING ...?
THERE ARE MANY OF OUR KIND WHO HAVE ALLIED THEMSELVES WITH OUR LADY, SO SHE CAN READILY HANDLE A FEW REBELS.
BESIDES, SHE HAS TAKEN A LOVER IN RECENT YEARS.
THIS TOOK A SUDDEN, GOSSIPY TURN.
?

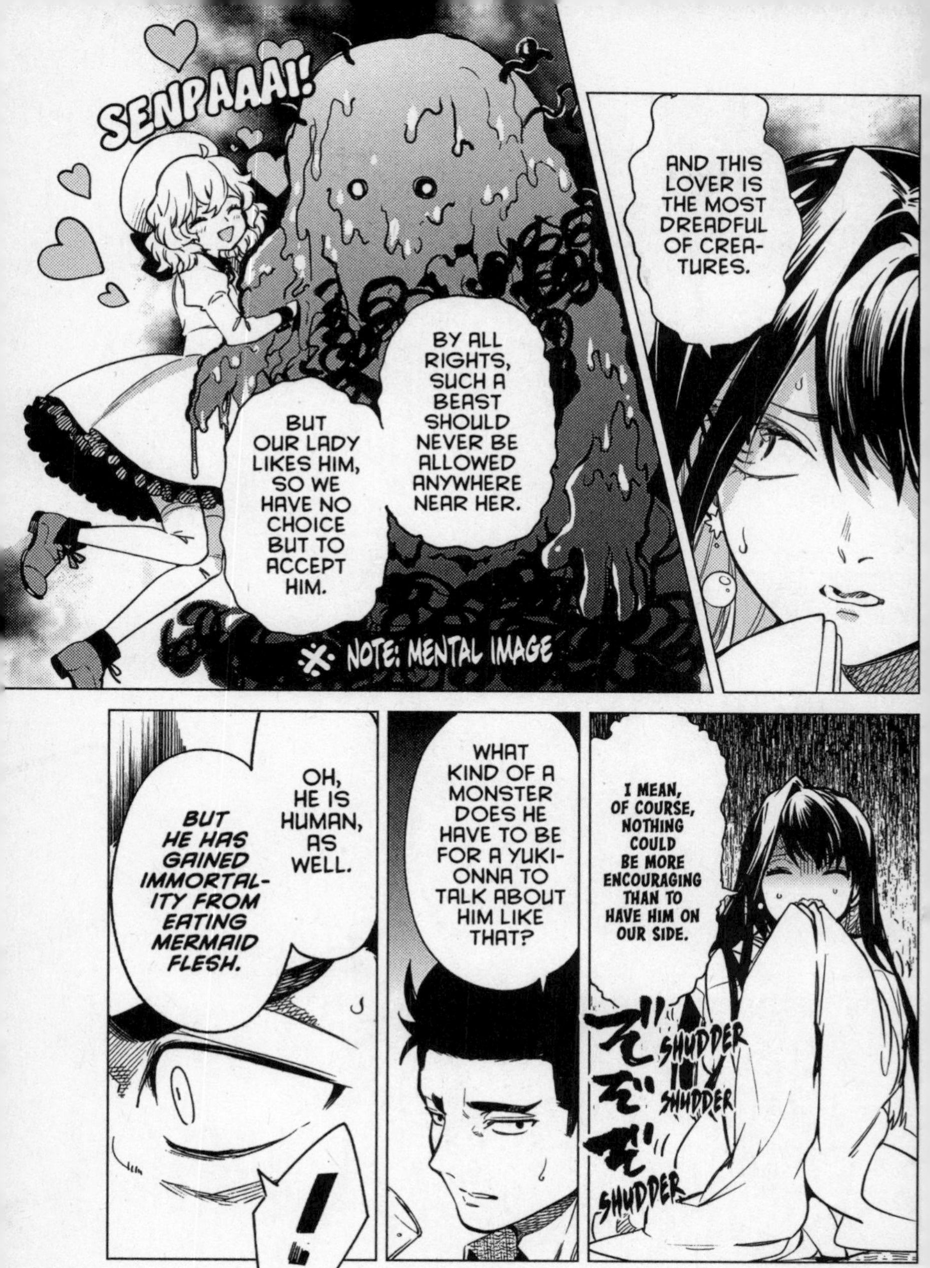
AND THIS LOVER IS THE MOST DREADFUL OF CREA-TURES.
SENPAAAI!
BY ALL RIGHTS, SUCH A BEAST SHOULD NEVER BE ALLOWED ANYWHERE NEAR HER.
BUT OUR LADY LIKES HIM, SO WE HAVE NO CHOICE BUT TO ACCEPT HIM.
※ NOTE: MENTAL IMAGE
I MEAN, OF COURSE, NOTHING COULD BE MORE ENCOURAGING THAN TO HAVE HIM ON OUR SIDE.
SHUDDER
SHUDDER
SHUDDER
WHAT KIND OF A MONSTER DOES HE HAVE TO BE FOR A YUKI-ONNA TO TALK ABOUT HIM LIKE THAT?
OH, HE IS HUMAN, AS WELL.
BUT HE HAS GAINED IMMORTALITY FROM EATING MERMAID FLESH.
!

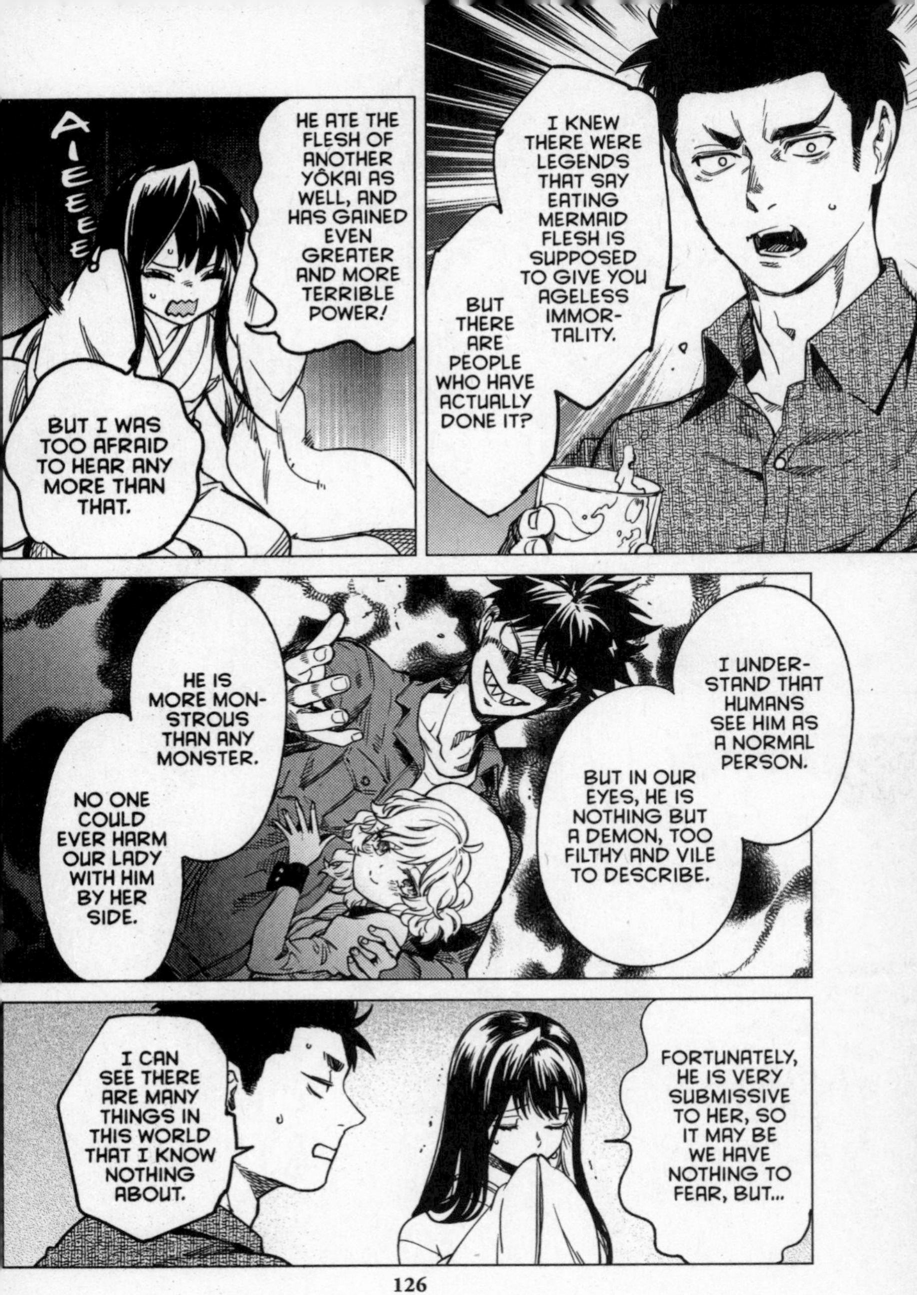
I KNEW THERE WERE LEGENDS THAT SAY EATING MERMAID FLESH IS SUPPOSED TO GIVE YOU AGELESS IMMORTALITY.
BUT THERE ARE PEOPLE WHO HAVE ACTUALLY DONE IT?
HE ATE THE FLESH OF ANOTHER YÔKAI AS WELL, AND HAS GAINED EVEN GREATER AND MORE TERRIBLE POWER!
AIEEEE
BUT I WAS TOO AFRAID TO HEAR ANY MORE THAN THAT.
I UNDERSTAND THAT HUMANS SEE HIM AS A NORMAL PERSON.
BUT IN OUR EYES, HE IS NOTHING BUT A DEMON, TOO FILTHY AND VILE TO DESCRIBE.
HE IS MORE MONSTROUS THAN ANY MONSTER.
NO ONE COULD EVER HARM OUR LADY WITH HIM BY HER SIDE.
FORTUNATELY, HE IS VERY SUBMISSIVE TO HER, SO IT MAY BE WE HAVE NOTHING TO FEAR, BUT...
I CAN SEE THERE ARE MANY THINGS IN THIS WORLD THAT I KNOW NOTHING ABOUT.

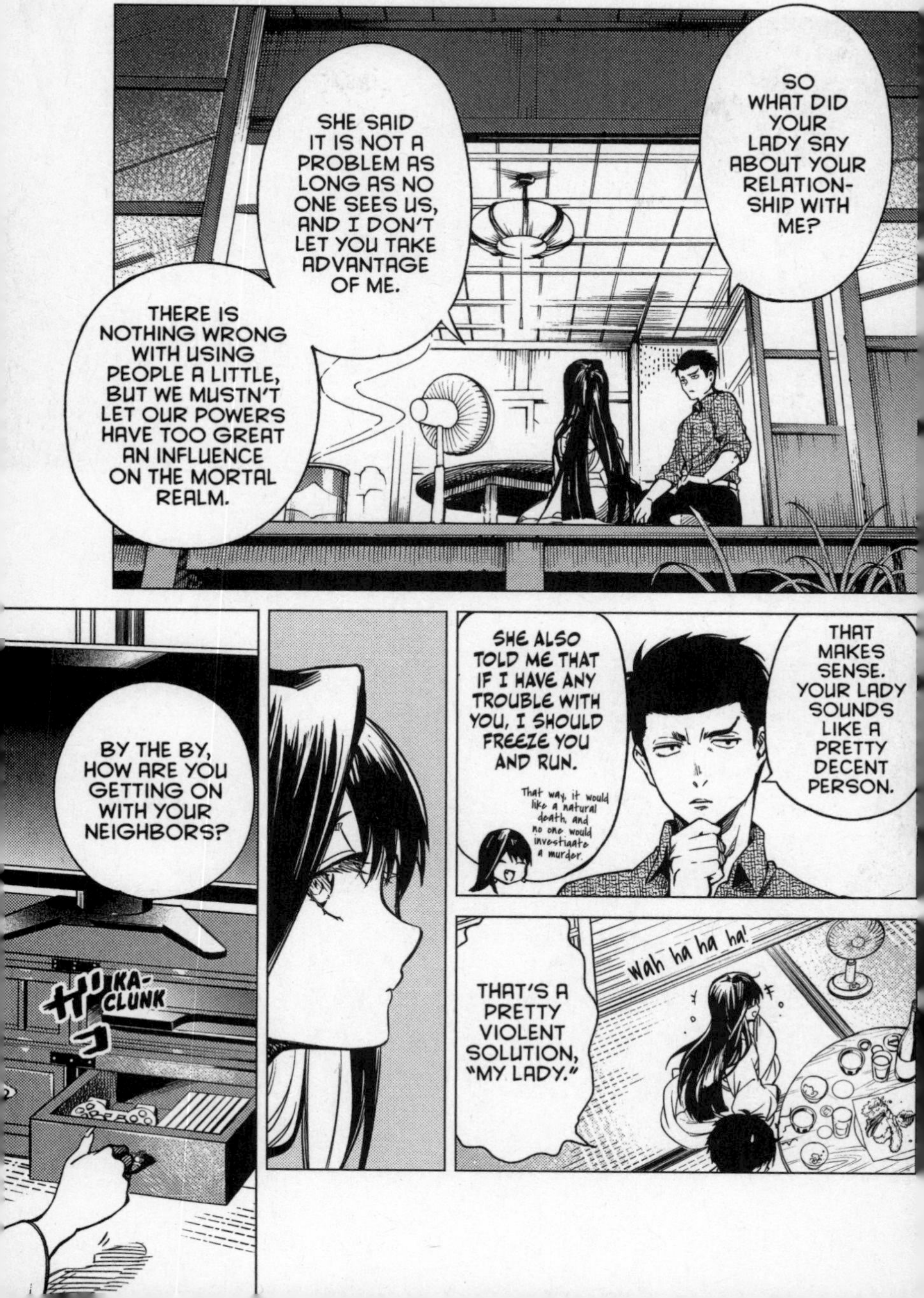
SO WHAT DID YOUR LADY SAY ABOUT YOUR RELATIONSHIP WITH ME?
SHE SAID IT IS NOT A PROBLEM AS LONG AS NO ONE SEES US, AND I DON'T LET YOU TAKE ADVANTAGE OF ME.
THERE IS NOTHING WRONG WITH USING PEOPLE A LITTLE, BUT WE MUSTN'T LET OUR POWERS HAVE TOO GREAT AN INFLUENCE ON THE MORTAL REALM.
THAT MAKES SENSE. YOUR LADY SOUNDS LIKE A PRETTY DECENT PERSON.
SHE ALSO TOLD ME THAT IF I HAVE ANY TROUBLE WITH YOU, I SHOULD FREEZE YOU AND RUN.
That way, it would like a natural death, and no one would investiaate a murder.
wah ha ha ha!
THAT'S A PRETTY VIOLENT SOLUTION, "MY LADY."
BY THE BY, HOW ARE YOU GETTING ON WITH YOUR NEIGHBORS?
KA-CLUNK

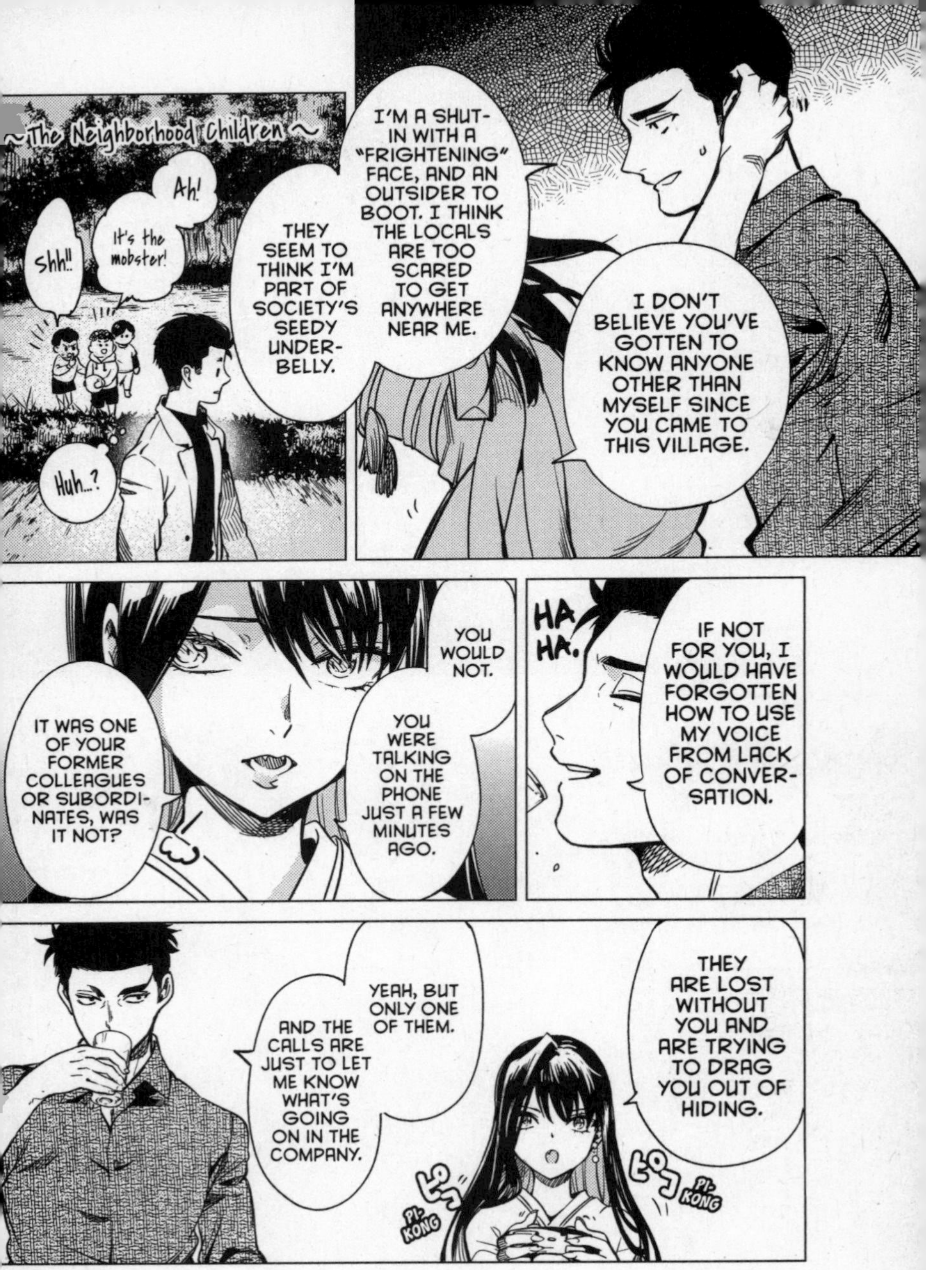
I DON'T BELIEVE YOU'VE GOTTEN TO KNOW ANYONE OTHER THAN MYSELF SINCE YOU CAME TO THIS VILLAGE.
I'M A SHUT-IN WITH A "FRIGHTENING" FACE, AND AN OUTSIDER TO BOOT. I THINK THE LOCALS ARE TOO SCARED TO GET ANYWHERE NEAR ME.
THEY SEEM TO THINK I'M PART OF SOCIETY'S SEEDY UNDER-BELLY.
~The Neighborhood Children~
Ah!
It's the mobster!
Shh!!
Huh...?
HA HA.
IF NOT FOR YOU, I WOULD HAVE FORGOTTEN HOW TO USE MY VOICE FROM LACK OF CONVER-SATION.
YOU WOULD NOT.
YOU WERE TALKING ON THE PHONE JUST A FEW MINUTES AGO.
IT WAS ONE OF YOUR FORMER COLLEAGUES OR SUBORDI-NATES, WAS IT NOT?
THEY ARE LOST WITHOUT YOU AND ARE TRYING TO DRAG YOU OUT OF HIDING.
YEAH, BUT ONLY ONE OF THEM.
AND THE CALLS ARE JUST TO LET ME KNOW WHAT'S GOING ON IN THE COMPANY.
PI-KONG
PI-KONG

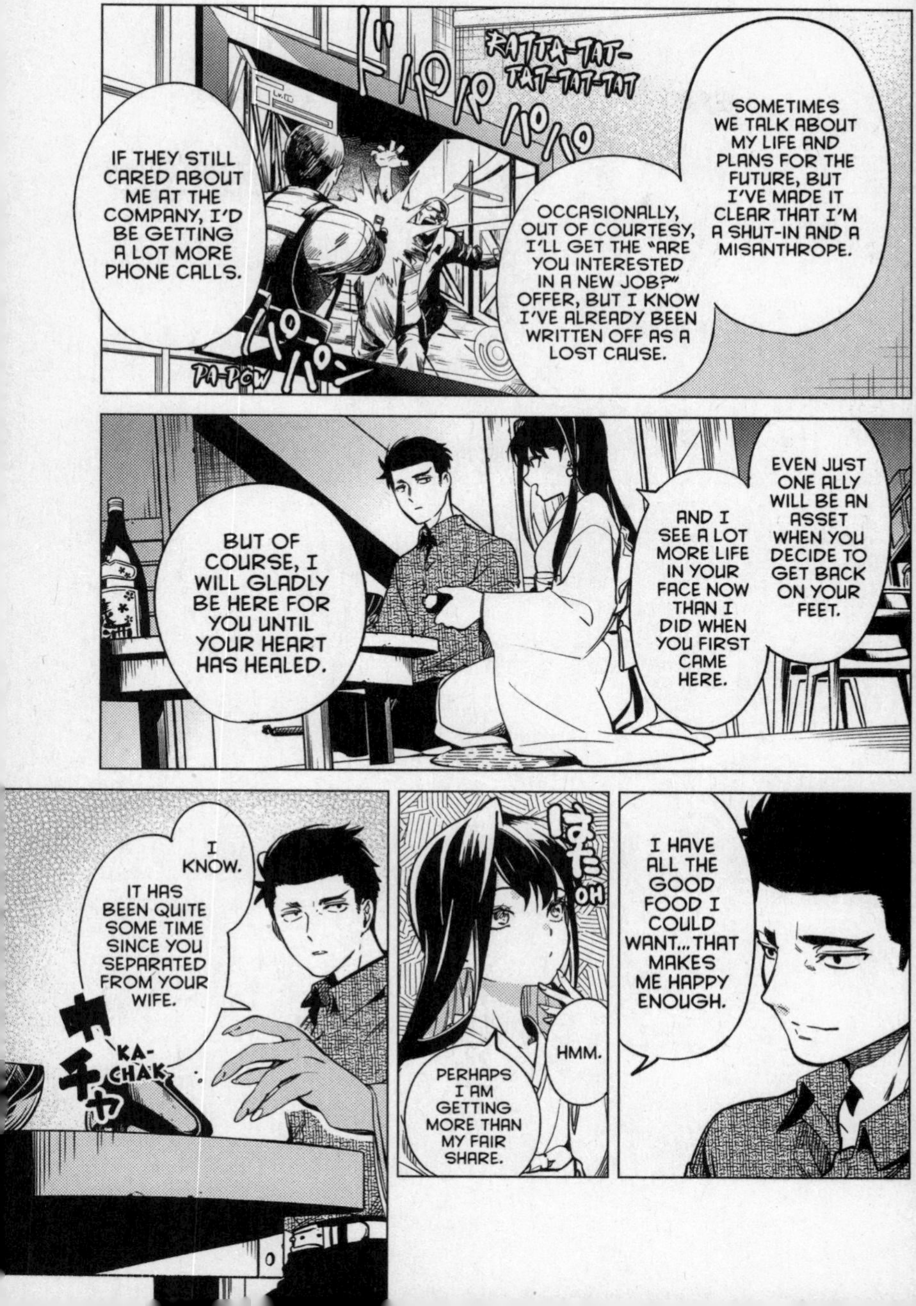
SOMETIMES WE TALK ABOUT MY LIFE AND PLANS FOR THE FUTURE, BUT I'VE MADE IT CLEAR THAT I'M A SHUT-IN AND A MISANTHROPE.
OCCASIONALLY, OUT OF COURTESY, I'LL GET THE "ARE YOU INTERESTED IN A NEW JOB?" OFFER, BUT I KNOW I'VE ALREADY BEEN WRITTEN OFF AS A LOST CAUSE.
RATTA-TAT-TAT-TAT-TAT
IF THEY STILL CARED ABOUT ME AT THE COMPANY, I'D BE GETTING A LOT MORE PHONE CALLS.
PA-POW
EVEN JUST ONE ALLY WILL BE AN ASSET WHEN YOU DECIDE TO GET BACK ON YOUR FEET.
AND I SEE A LOT MORE LIFE IN YOUR FACE NOW THAN I DID WHEN YOU FIRST CAME HERE.
BUT OF COURSE, I WILL GLADLY BE HERE FOR YOU UNTIL YOUR HEART HAS HEALED.
I HAVE ALL THE GOOD FOOD I COULD WANT... THAT MAKES ME HAPPY ENOUGH.
OH
HMM.
PERHAPS I AM GETTING MORE THAN MY FAIR SHARE.
I KNOW.
IT HAS BEEN QUITE SOME TIME SINCE YOU SEPARATED FROM YOUR WIFE.
KA-CHAK

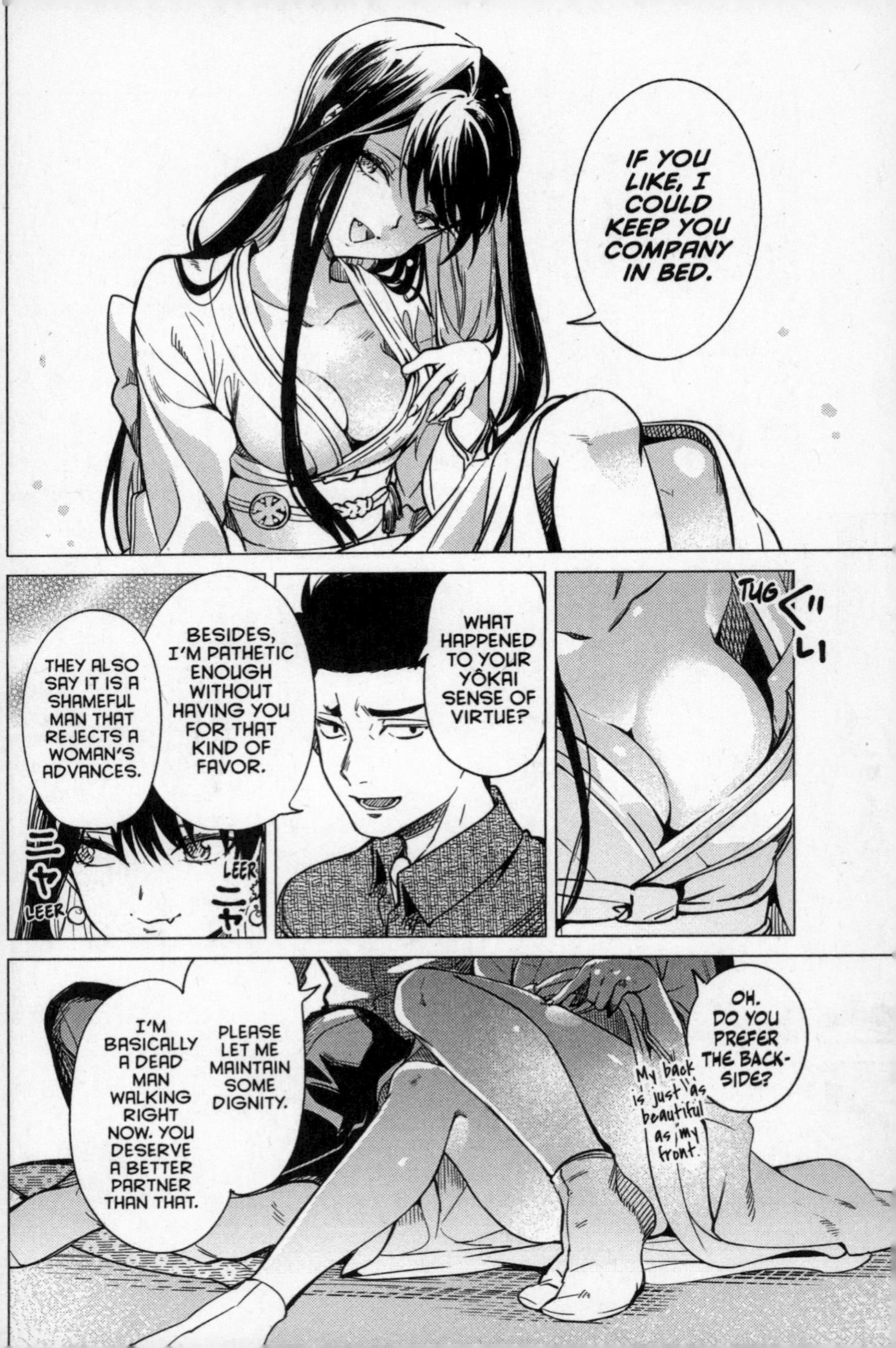
IF YOU LIKE, I COULD KEEP YOU COMPANY IN BED.
TUG
WHAT HAPPENED TO YOUR YÔKAI SENSE OF VIRTUE?
BESIDES, I'M PATHETIC ENOUGH WITHOUT HAVING YOU FOR THAT KIND OF FAVOR.
THEY ALSO SAY IT IS A SHAMEFUL MAN THAT REJECTS A WOMAN'S ADVANCES.
ニヤ
LEER
ニヤ
LEER
OH. DO YOU PREFER THE BACK-SIDE?
My back is just as beautiful as my front.
PLEASE LET ME MAINTAIN SOME DIGNITY.
I'M BASICALLY A DEAD MAN WALKING RIGHT NOW. YOU DESERVE A BETTER PARTNER THAN THAT.

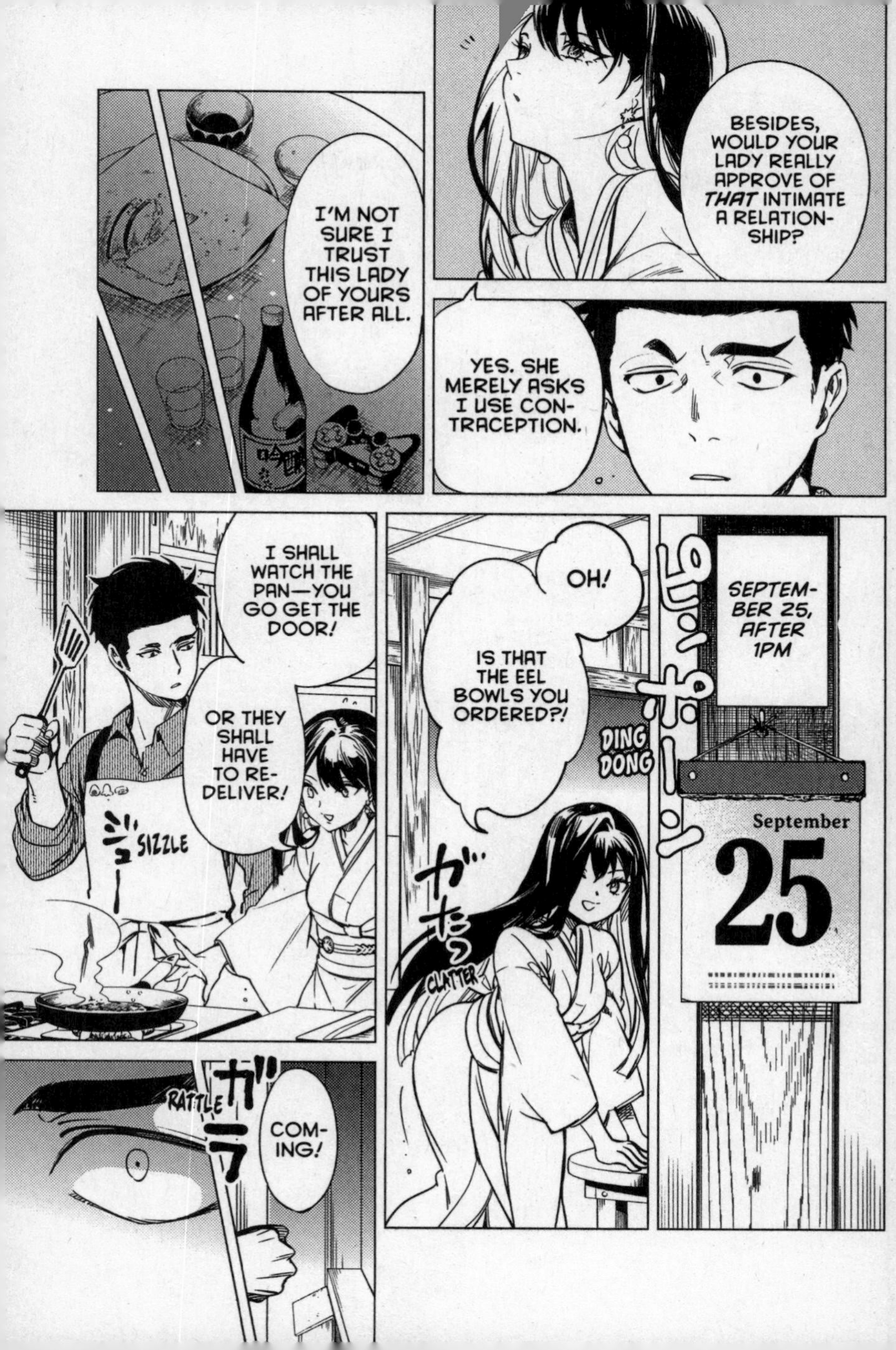

BESIDES, WOULD YOUR LADY REALLY APPROVE OF *THAT* INTIMATE A RELATION-SHIP?
YES. SHE MERELY ASKS I USE CON-TRACEPTION.
I'M NOT SURE I TRUST THIS LADY OF YOURS AFTER ALL.
ピンポーン
SEPTEM-BER 25, AFTER 1PM
September
25
OH!
IS THAT THE EEL BOWLS YOU ORDERED?!
DING DONG
ガたっ
CLATTER
I SHALL WATCH THE PAN—YOU GO GET THE DOOR!
OR THEY SHALL HAVE TO RE-DELIVER!
ジュー
SIZZLE
RATTLE
ガラ
COM-ING!

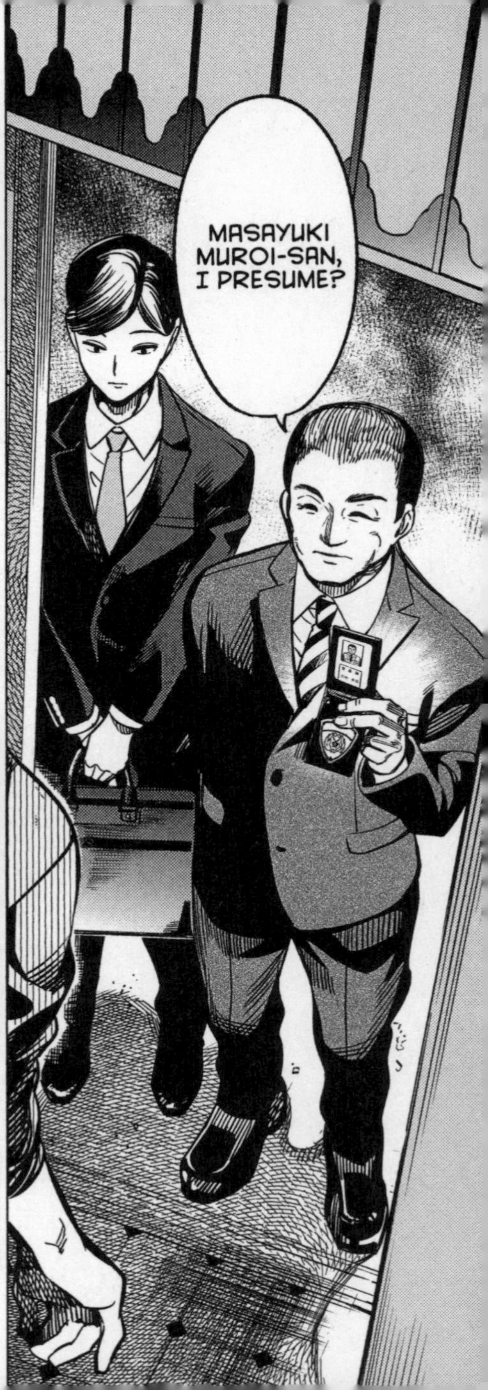
MASAYUKI MUROI-SAN, I PRESUME?
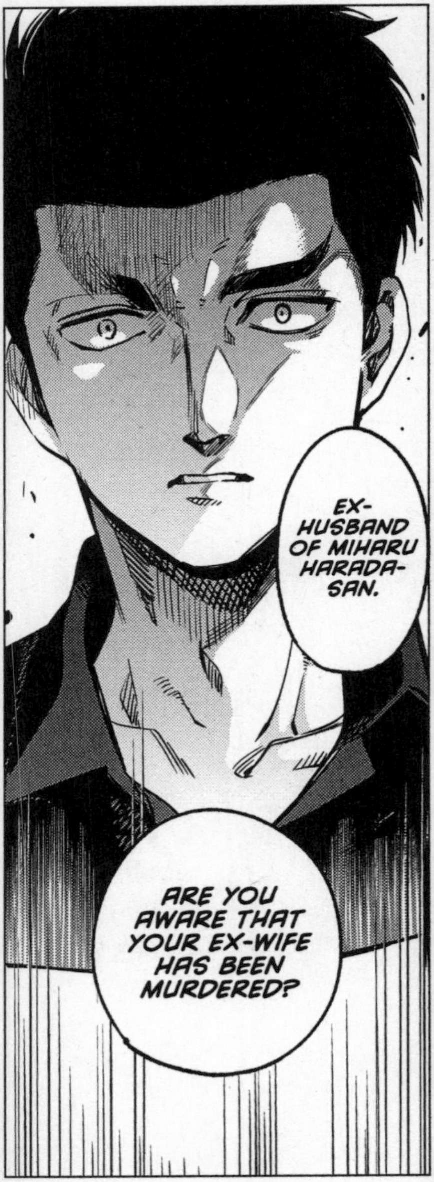
EX-HUSBAND OF MIHARU HARADA-SAN.
ARE YOU AWARE THAT YOUR EX-WIFE HAS BEEN MURDERED?

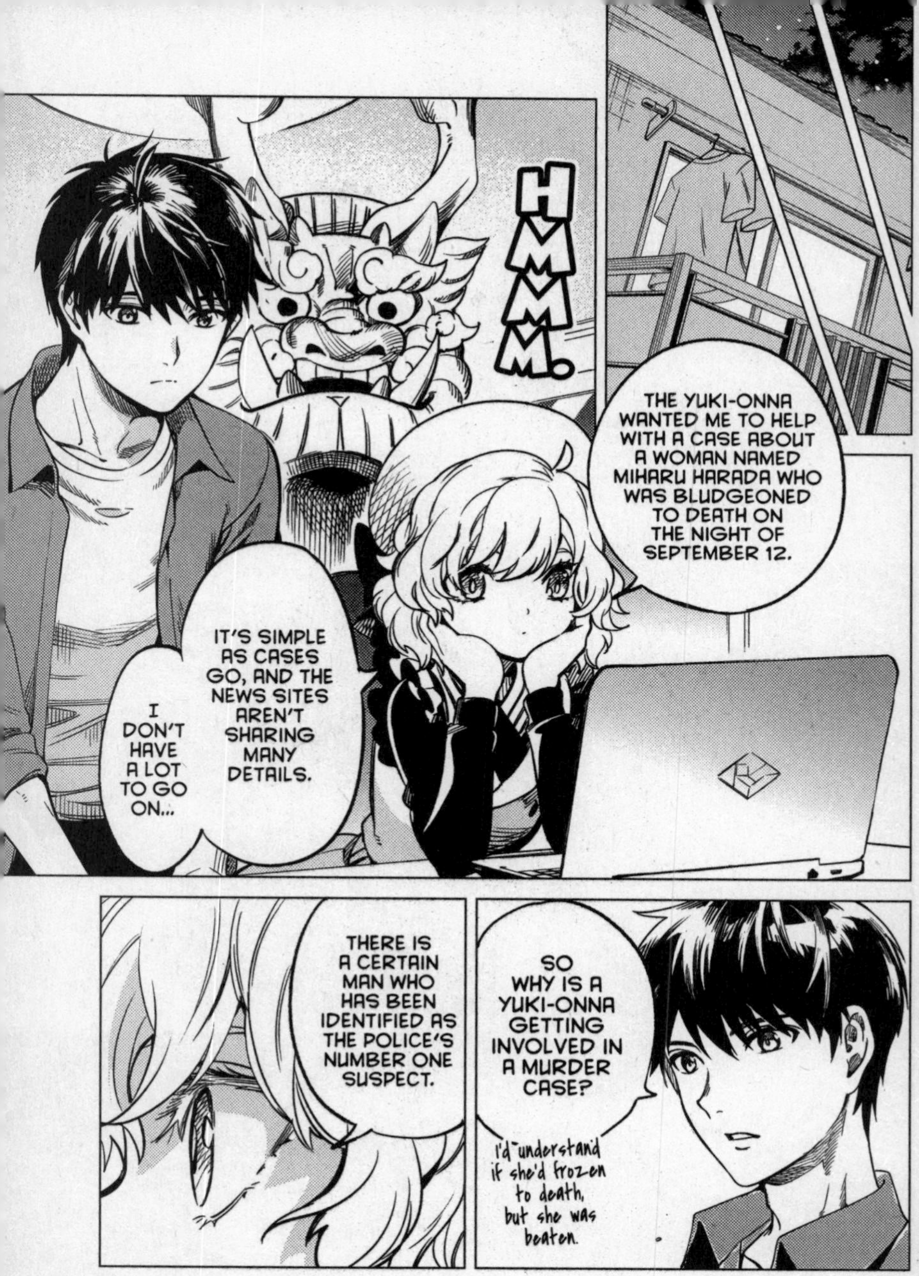
THE YUKI-ONNA WANTED ME TO HELP WITH A CASE ABOUT A WOMAN NAMED MIHARU HARADA WHO WAS BLUDGEONED TO DEATH ON THE NIGHT OF SEPTEMBER 12.
HMMMM.
IT'S SIMPLE AS CASES GO, AND THE NEWS SITES AREN'T SHARING MANY DETAILS.
I DON'T HAVE A LOT TO GO ON...
SO WHY IS A YUKI-ONNA GETTING INVOLVED IN A MURDER CASE?
I'd understand if she'd frozen to death, but she was beaten.
THERE IS A CERTAIN MAN WHO HAS BEEN IDENTIFIED AS THE POLICE'S NUMBER ONE SUSPECT.

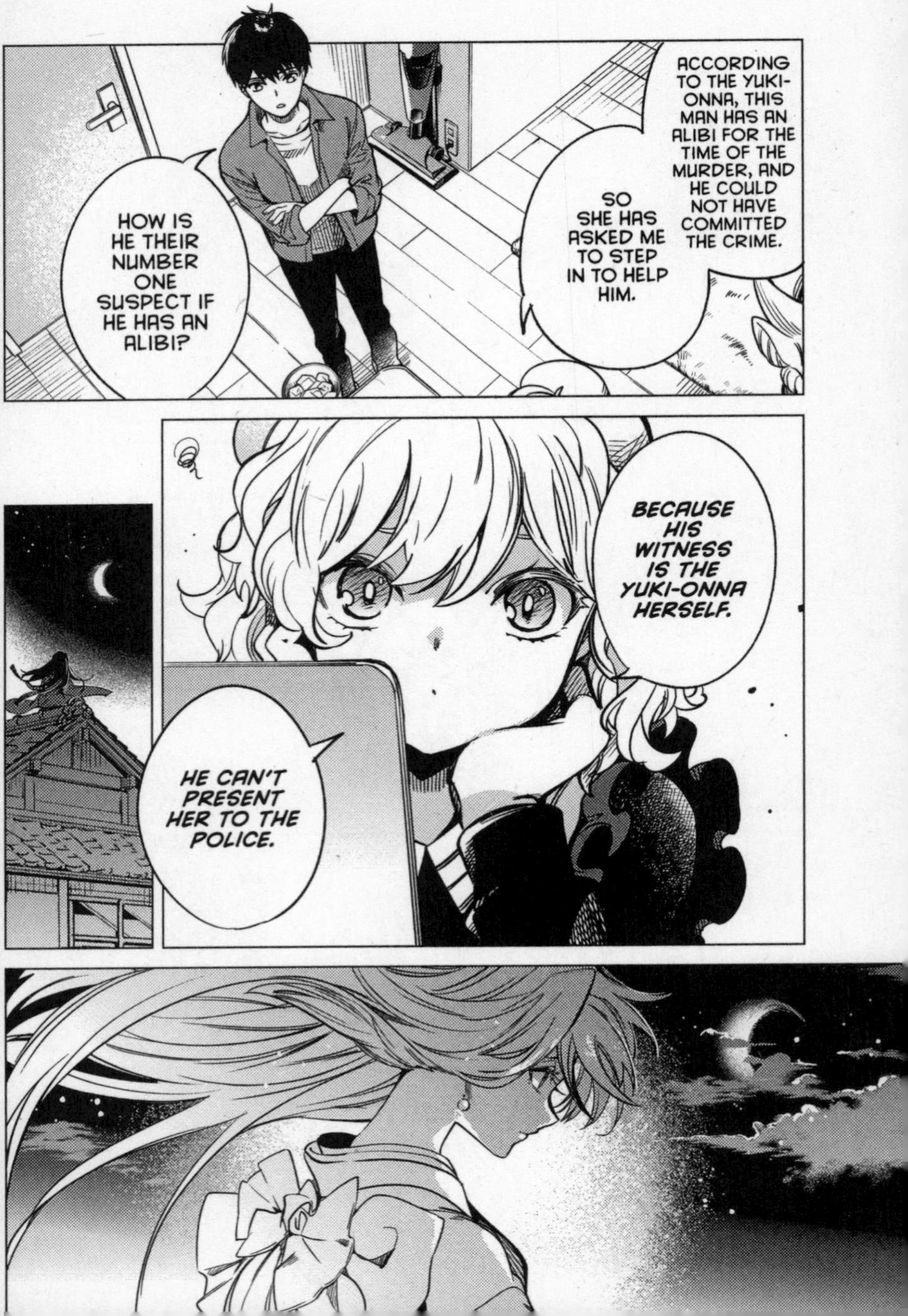
ACCORDING TO THE YUKI-ONNA, THIS MAN HAS AN ALIBI FOR THE TIME OF THE MURDER, AND HE COULD NOT HAVE COMMITTED THE CRIME.
SO SHE HAS ASKED ME TO STEP IN TO HELP HIM.
HOW IS HE THEIR NUMBER ONE SUSPECT IF HE HAS AN ALIBI?
BECAUSE HIS WITNESS IS THE YUKI-ONNA HERSELF.
HE CAN'T PRESENT HER TO THE POLICE.

IN/SPECTRE

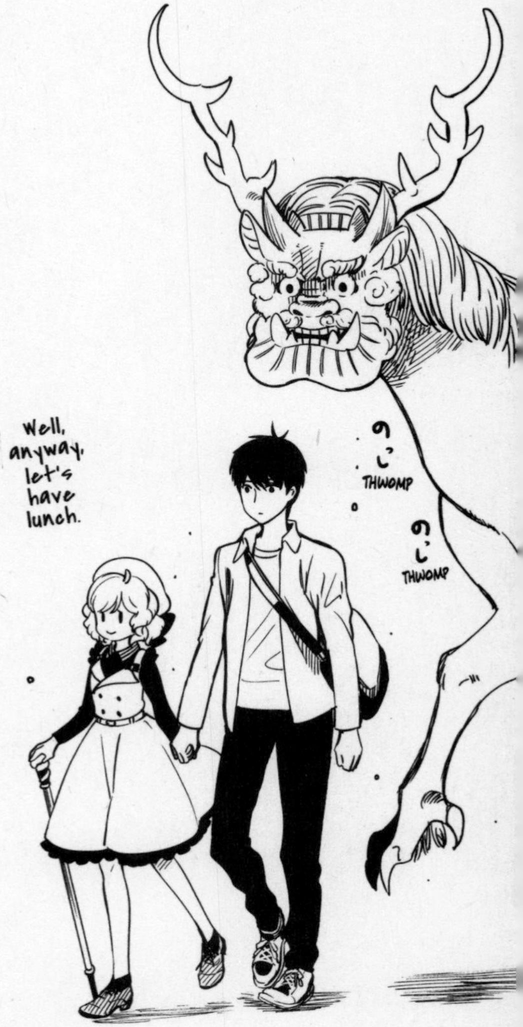
のし
THWOMP
のし
THWOMP
Well, anyway, let's have lunch.

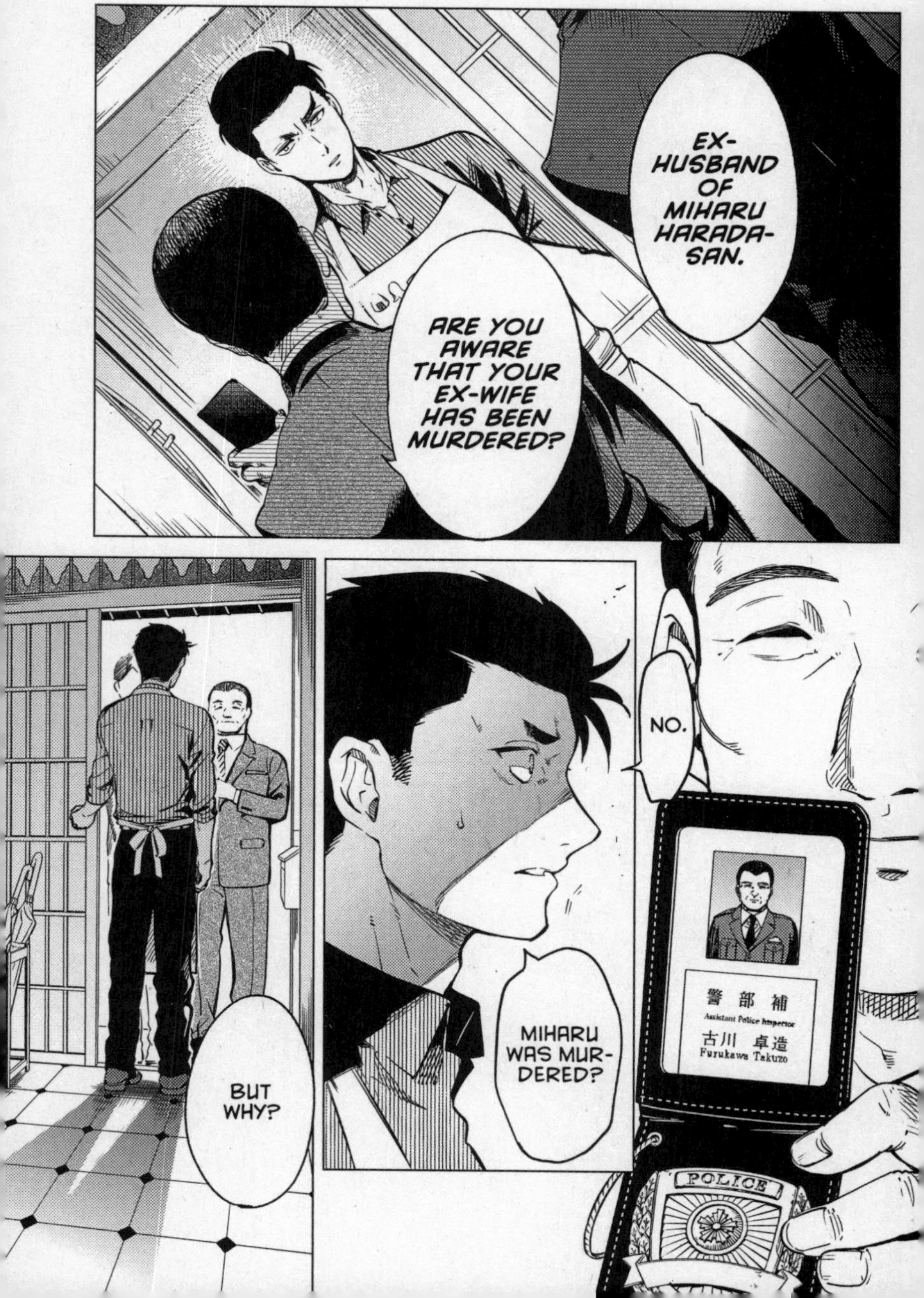
EX-HUSBAND OF MIHARU HARADA-SAN.
ARE YOU AWARE THAT YOUR EX-WIFE HAS BEEN MURDERED?
NO.
警部補
Assistant Police Inspector
古川 卓造
Furukawa Takuzo
POLICE
MIHARU WAS MURDERED?
BUT WHY?

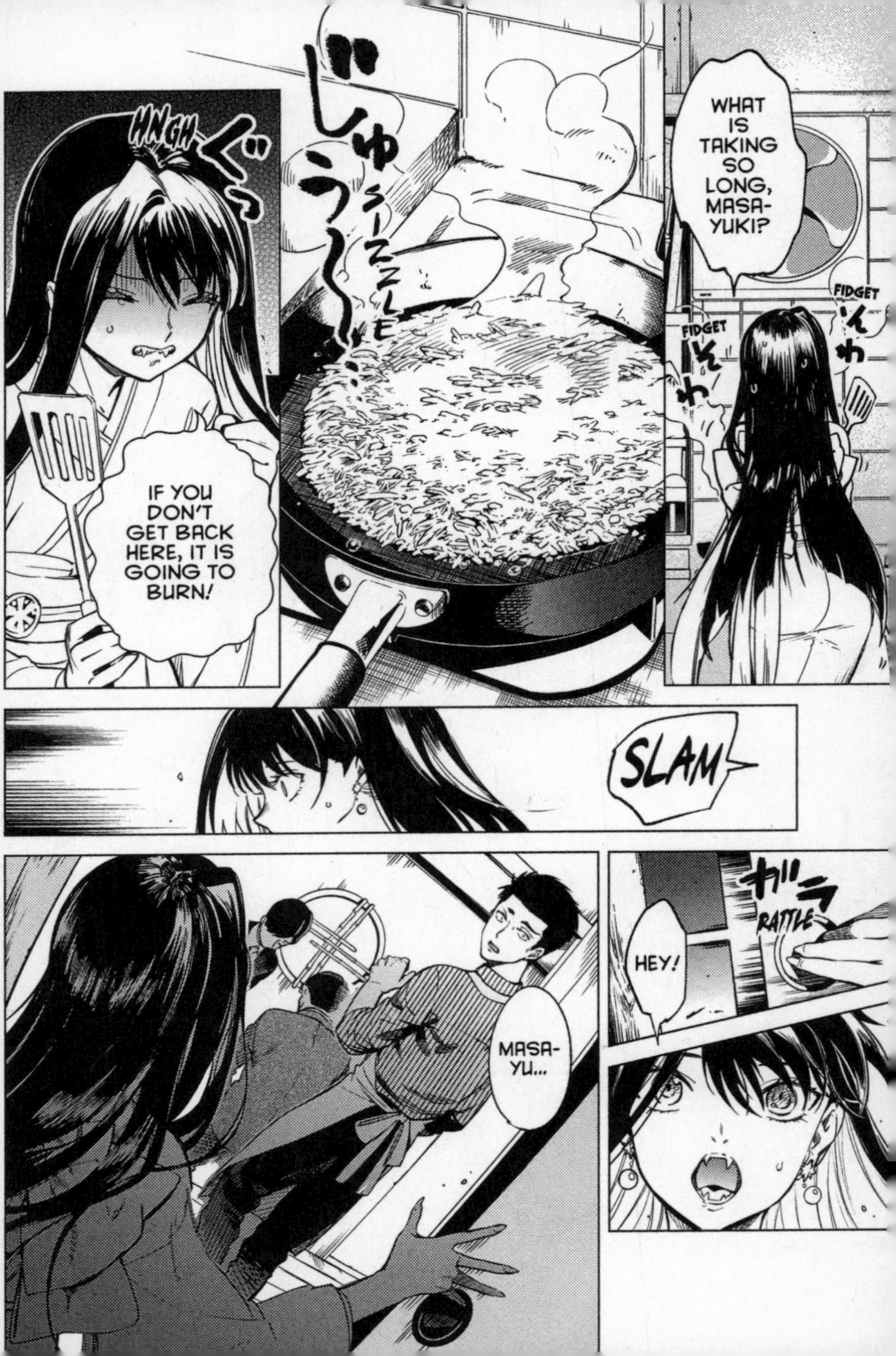
WHAT IS TAKING SO LONG, MASA-YUKI?
FIDGET そわ
FIDGET そわ
じゅう～
SIZZLE
HNGH ぐっ
IF YOU DON'T GET BACK HERE, IT IS GOING TO BURN!
SLAM
ガラ
RATTLE
HEY!
MASA-YU...

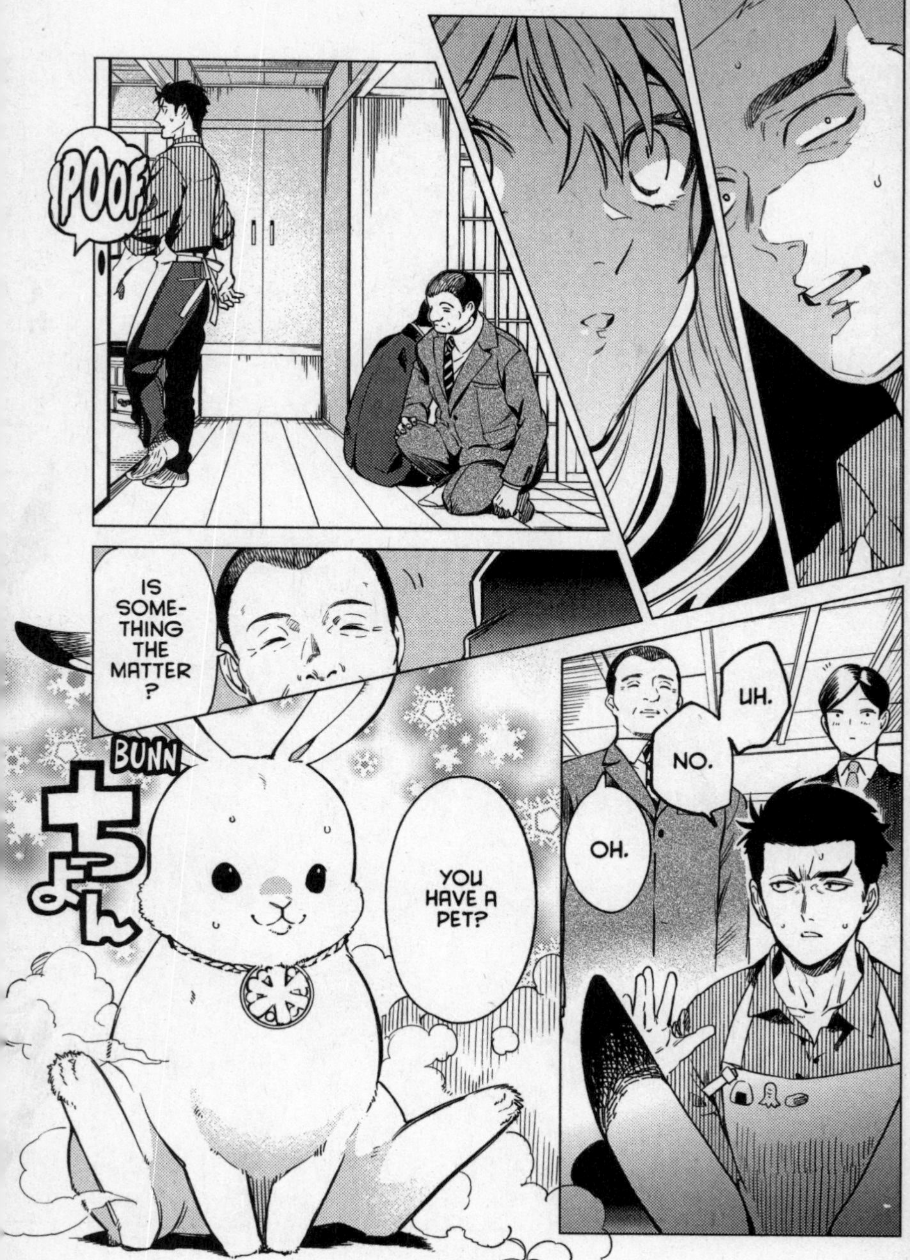
POOF
IS SOMETHING THE MATTER?
UH.
NO.
OH.
BUNN
ちょん
YOU HAVE A PET?

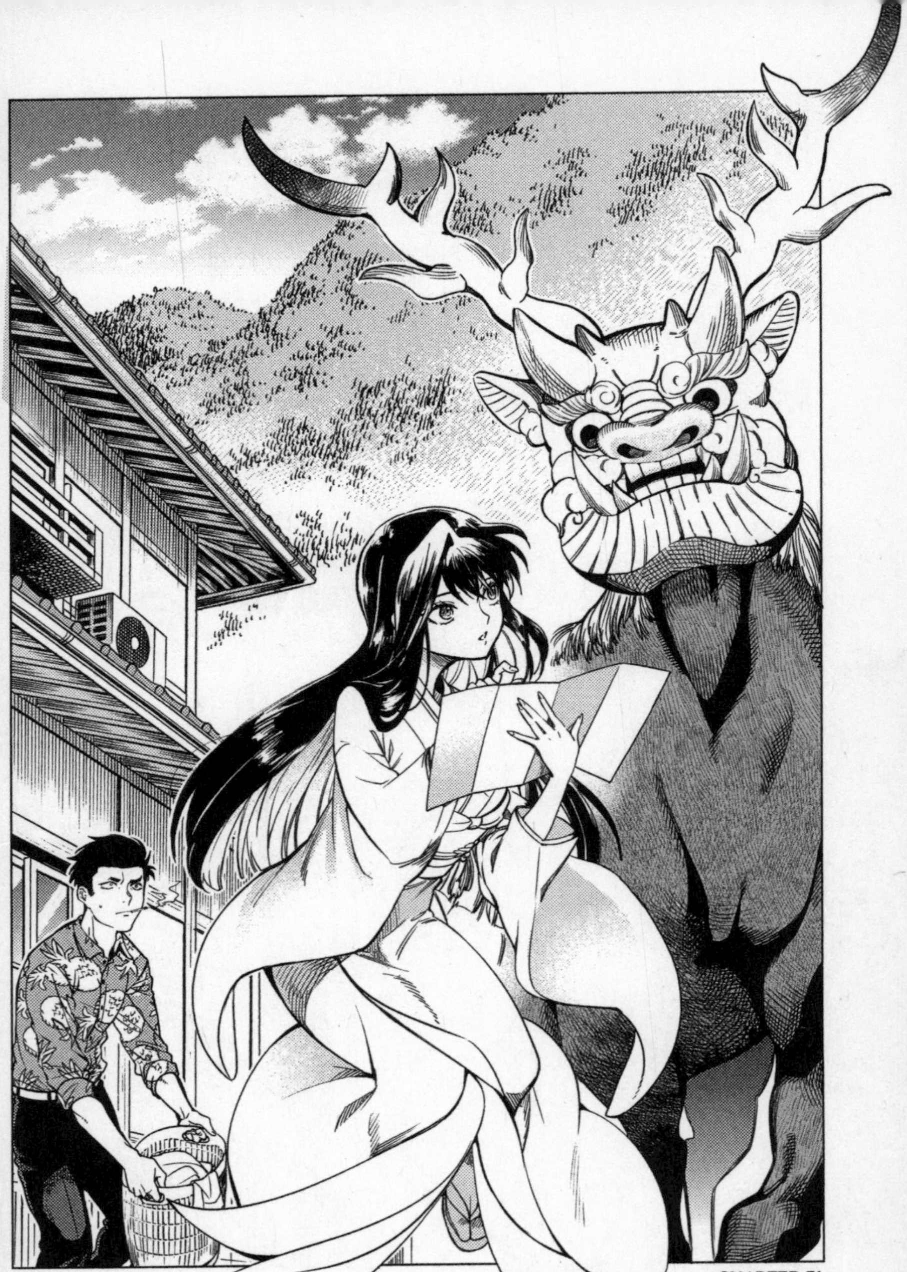

CHAPTER 31:
"THE YUKI-ONNA'S DILEMMA PART TWO"

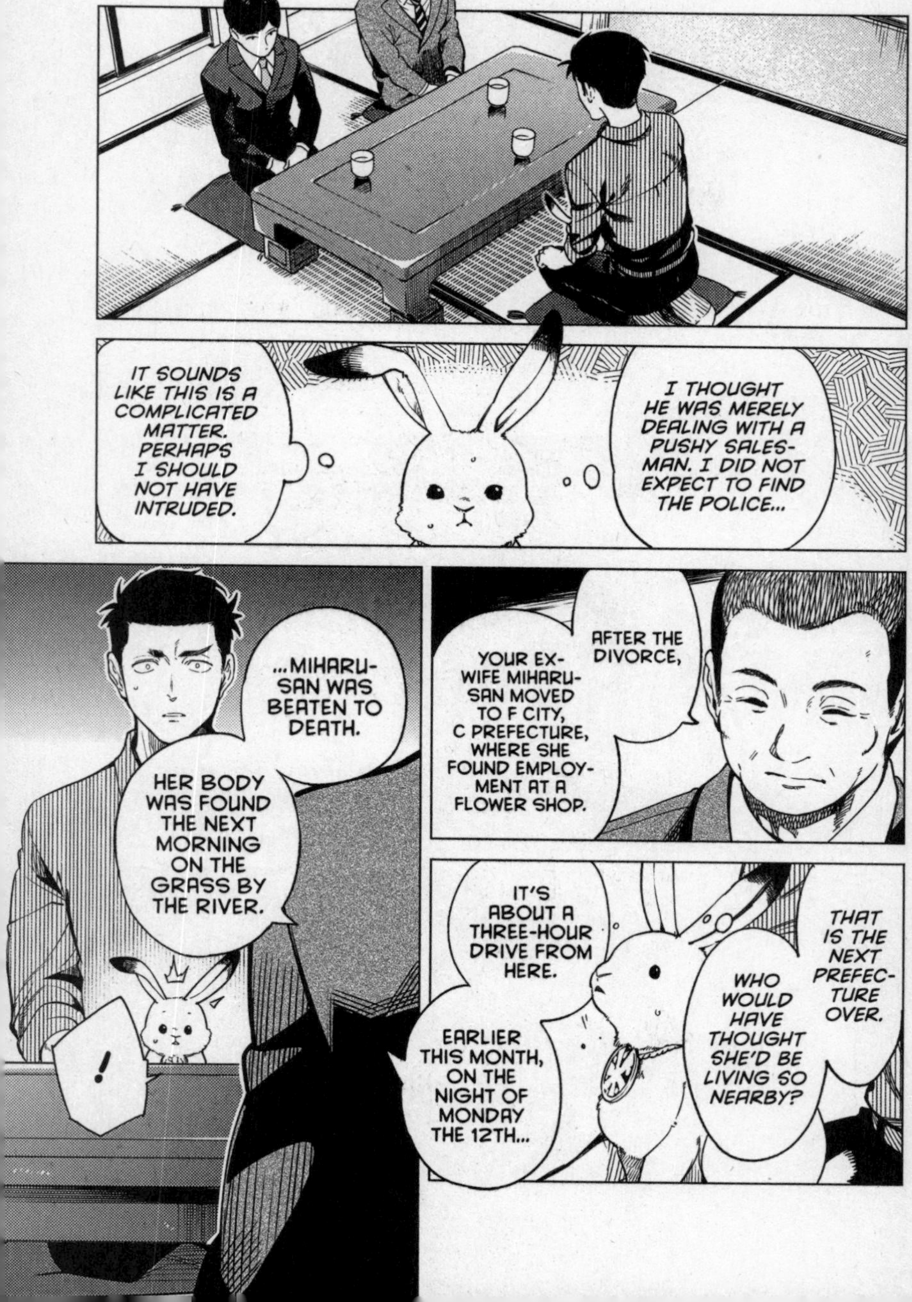
I THOUGHT HE WAS MERELY DEALING WITH A PUSHY SALES-MAN. I DID NOT EXPECT TO FIND THE POLICE...
IT SOUNDS LIKE THIS IS A COMPLICATED MATTER. PERHAPS I SHOULD NOT HAVE INTRUDED.
AFTER THE DIVORCE,
YOUR EX-WIFE MIHARU-SAN MOVED TO F CITY, C PREFECTURE, WHERE SHE FOUND EMPLOY-MENT AT A FLOWER SHOP.
THAT IS THE NEXT PREFEC-TURE OVER.
WHO WOULD HAVE THOUGHT SHE'D BE LIVING SO NEARBY?
IT'S ABOUT A THREE-HOUR DRIVE FROM HERE.
EARLIER THIS MONTH, ON THE NIGHT OF MONDAY THE 12TH...
...MIHARU-SAN WAS BEATEN TO DEATH.
HER BODY WAS FOUND THE NEXT MORNING ON THE GRASS BY THE RIVER.
!

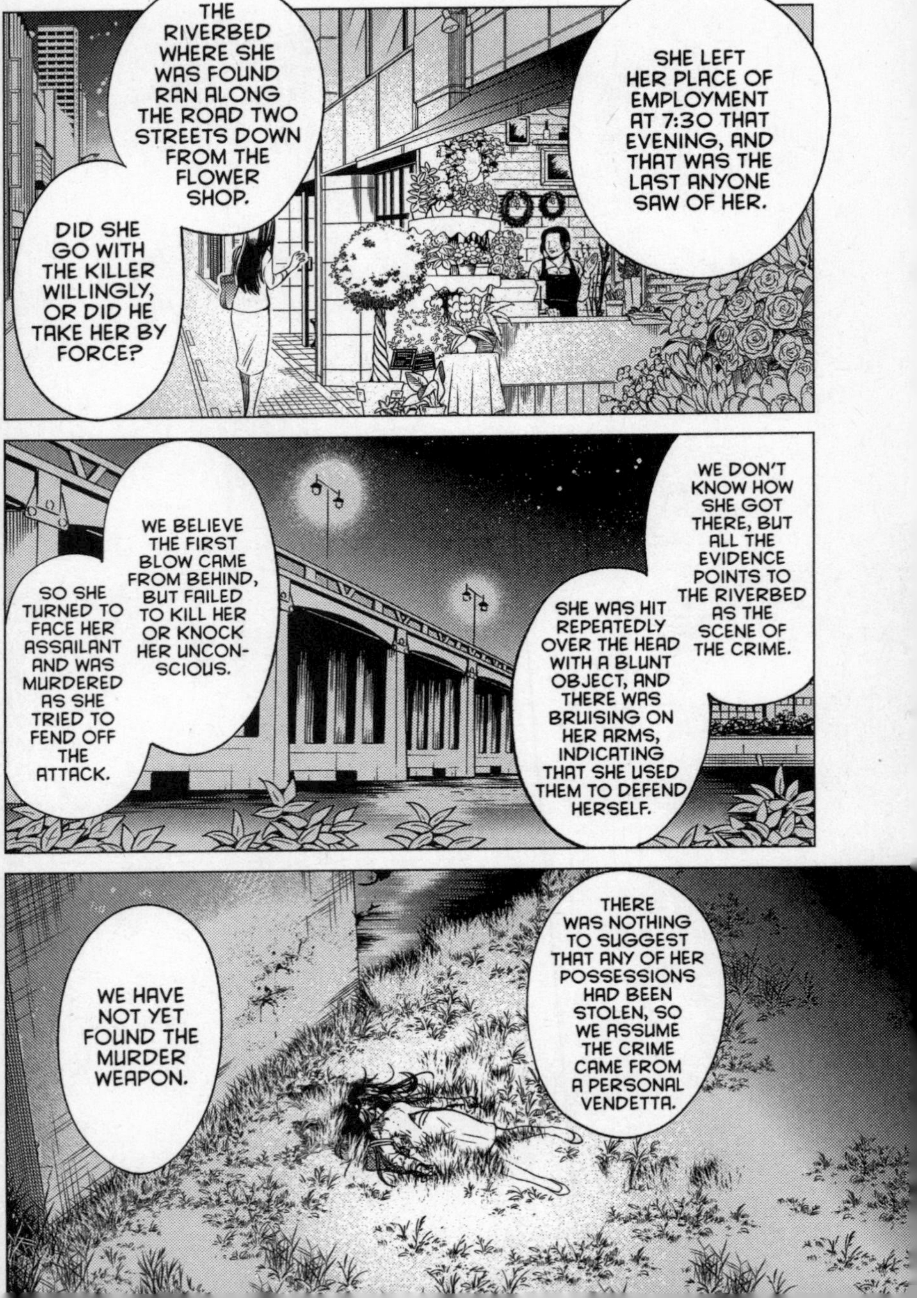
SHE LEFT HER PLACE OF EMPLOYMENT AT 7:30 THAT EVENING, AND THAT WAS THE LAST ANYONE SAW OF HER.
THE RIVERBED WHERE SHE WAS FOUND RAN ALONG THE ROAD TWO STREETS DOWN FROM THE FLOWER SHOP.
DID SHE GO WITH THE KILLER WILLINGLY, OR DID HE TAKE HER BY FORCE?
WE DON'T KNOW HOW SHE GOT THERE, BUT ALL THE EVIDENCE POINTS TO THE RIVERBED AS THE SCENE OF THE CRIME.
SHE WAS HIT REPEATEDLY OVER THE HEAD WITH A BLUNT OBJECT, AND THERE WAS BRUISING ON HER ARMS, INDICATING THAT SHE USED THEM TO DEFEND HERSELF.
WE BELIEVE THE FIRST BLOW CAME FROM BEHIND, BUT FAILED TO KILL HER OR KNOCK HER UNCONSCIOUS.
SO SHE TURNED TO FACE HER ASSAILANT AND WAS MURDERED AS SHE TRIED TO FEND OFF THE ATTACK.
THERE WAS NOTHING TO SUGGEST THAT ANY OF HER POSSESSIONS HAD BEEN STOLEN, SO WE ASSUME THE CRIME CAME FROM A PERSONAL VENDETTA.
WE HAVE NOT YET FOUND THE MURDER WEAPON.

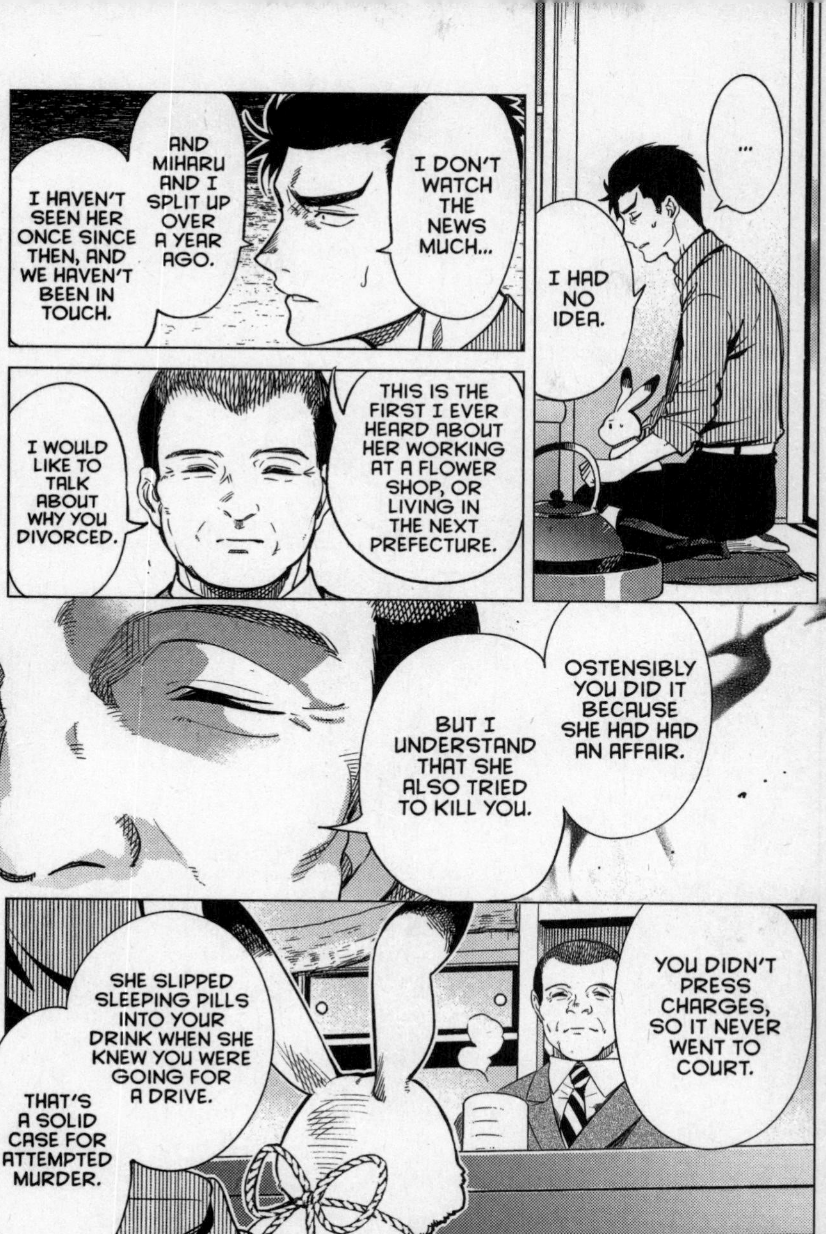
...
I HAD NO IDEA.
I DON'T WATCH THE NEWS MUCH...
AND MIHARU AND I SPLIT UP OVER A YEAR AGO.
I HAVEN'T SEEN HER ONCE SINCE THEN, AND WE HAVEN'T BEEN IN TOUCH.
THIS IS THE FIRST I EVER HEARD ABOUT HER WORKING AT A FLOWER SHOP, OR LIVING IN THE NEXT PREFECTURE.
I WOULD LIKE TO TALK ABOUT WHY YOU DIVORCED.
OSTENSIBLY YOU DID IT BECAUSE SHE HAD HAD AN AFFAIR.
BUT I UNDERSTAND THAT SHE ALSO TRIED TO KILL YOU.
YOU DIDN'T PRESS CHARGES, SO IT NEVER WENT TO COURT.
SHE SLIPPED SLEEPING PILLS INTO YOUR DRINK WHEN SHE KNEW YOU WERE GOING FOR A DRIVE.
THAT'S A SOLID CASE FOR ATTEMPTED MURDER.

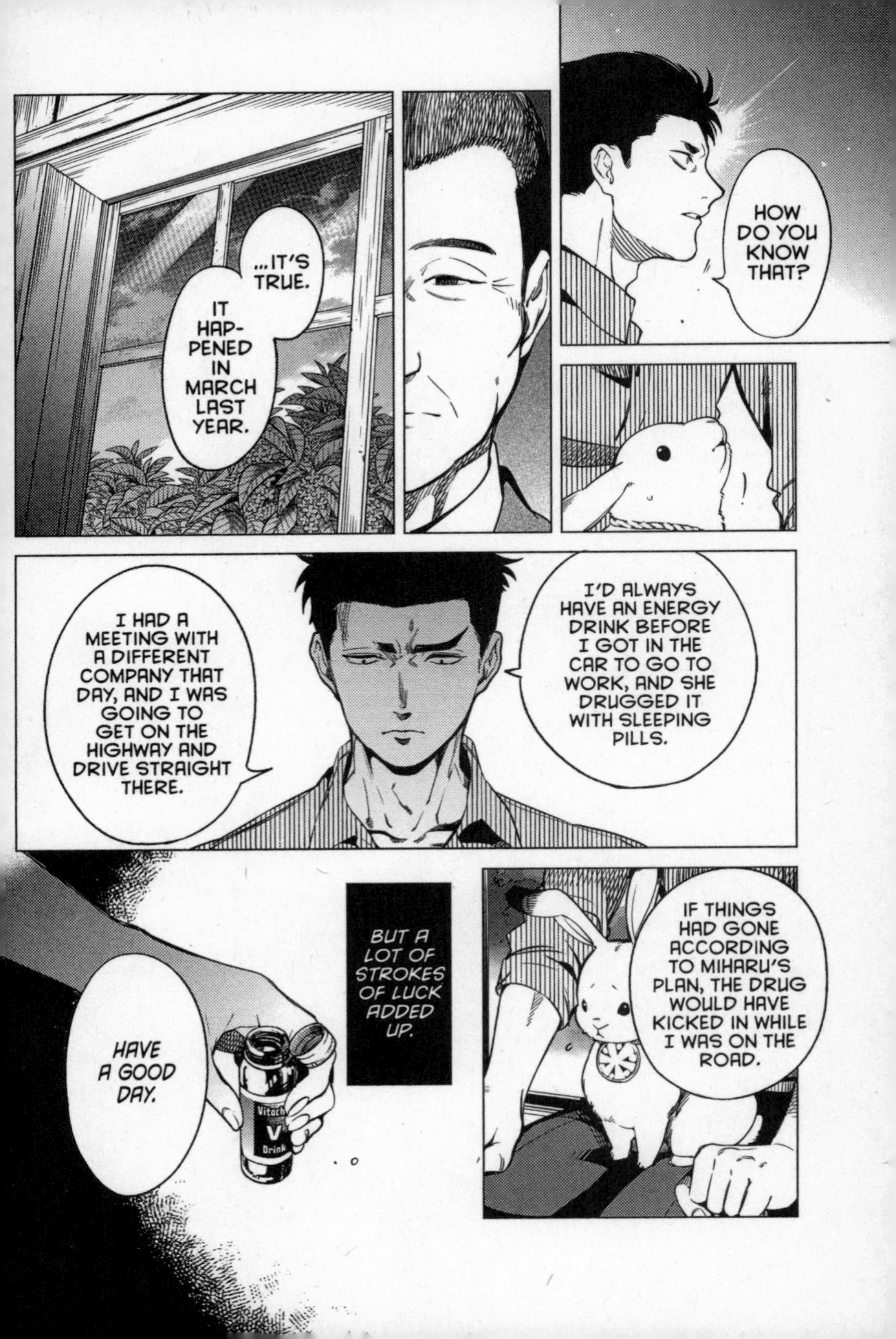
HOW DO YOU KNOW THAT?
...IT'S TRUE.
IT HAP-PENED IN MARCH LAST YEAR.
I'D ALWAYS HAVE AN ENERGY DRINK BEFORE I GOT IN THE CAR TO GO TO WORK, AND SHE DRUGGED IT WITH SLEEPING PILLS.
I HAD A MEETING WITH A DIFFERENT COMPANY THAT DAY, AND I WAS GOING TO GET ON THE HIGHWAY AND DRIVE STRAIGHT THERE.
IF THINGS HAD GONE ACCORDING TO MIHARU'S PLAN, THE DRUG WOULD HAVE KICKED IN WHILE I WAS ON THE ROAD.
BUT A LOT OF STROKES OF LUCK ADDED UP.
HAVE A GOOD DAY.
Vitach
V
Drink

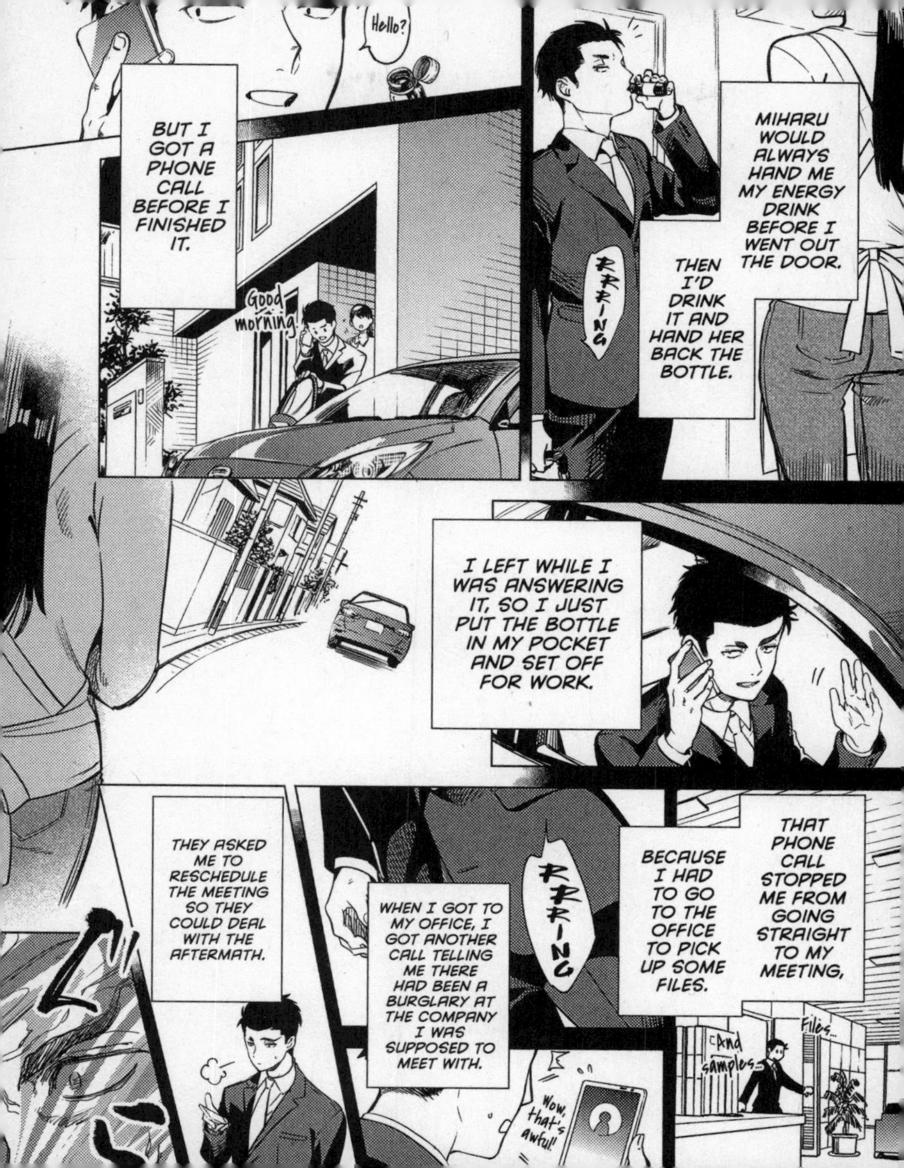
MIHARU WOULD ALWAYS HAND ME MY ENERGY DRINK BEFORE I WENT OUT THE DOOR.
THEN I'D DRINK IT AND HAND HER BACK THE BOTTLE.
RRRING
Hello?
BUT I GOT A PHONE CALL BEFORE I FINISHED IT.
Good morning!
I LEFT WHILE I WAS ANSWERING IT, SO I JUST PUT THE BOTTLE IN MY POCKET AND SET OFF FOR WORK.
THAT PHONE CALL STOPPED ME FROM GOING STRAIGHT TO MY MEETING,
BECAUSE I HAD TO GO TO THE OFFICE TO PICK UP SOME FILES.
Files...
And samples...
RRRING
WHEN I GOT TO MY OFFICE, I GOT ANOTHER CALL TELLING ME THERE HAD BEEN A BURGLARY AT THE COMPANY I WAS SUPPOSED TO MEET WITH.
Wow, that's awful!
THEY ASKED ME TO RESCHEDULE THE MEETING SO THEY COULD DEAL WITH THE AFTERMATH.

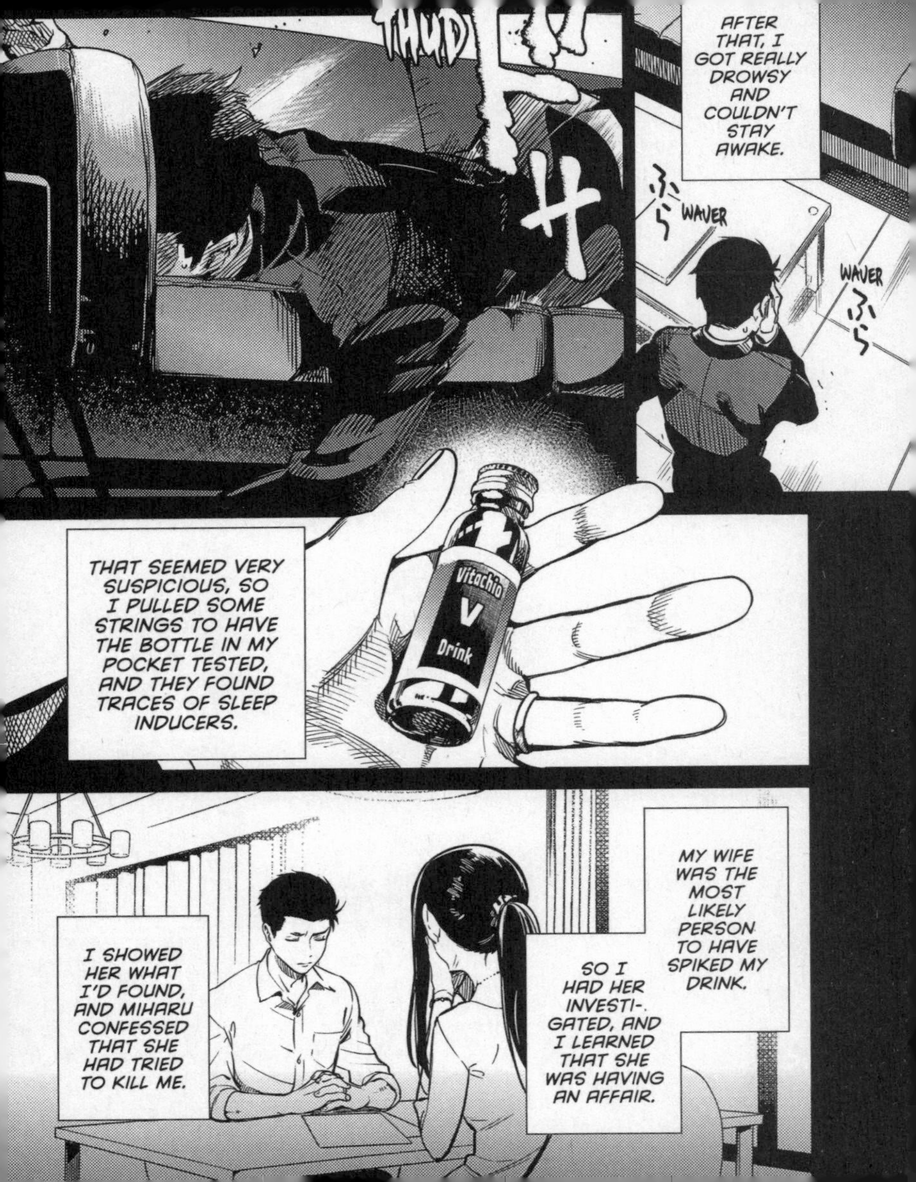
AFTER THAT, I GOT REALLY DROWSY AND COULDN'T STAY AWAKE.
ふら WAVER
WAVER ふら
THUD
THAT SEEMED VERY SUSPICIOUS, SO I PULLED SOME STRINGS TO HAVE THE BOTTLE IN MY POCKET TESTED, AND THEY FOUND TRACES OF SLEEP INDUCERS.
Vitachio
V
Drink
MY WIFE WAS THE MOST LIKELY PERSON TO HAVE SPIKED MY DRINK.
SO I HAD HER INVESTI-GATED, AND I LEARNED THAT SHE WAS HAVING AN AFFAIR.
I SHOWED HER WHAT I'D FOUND, AND MIHARU CONFESSED THAT SHE HAD TRIED TO KILL ME.

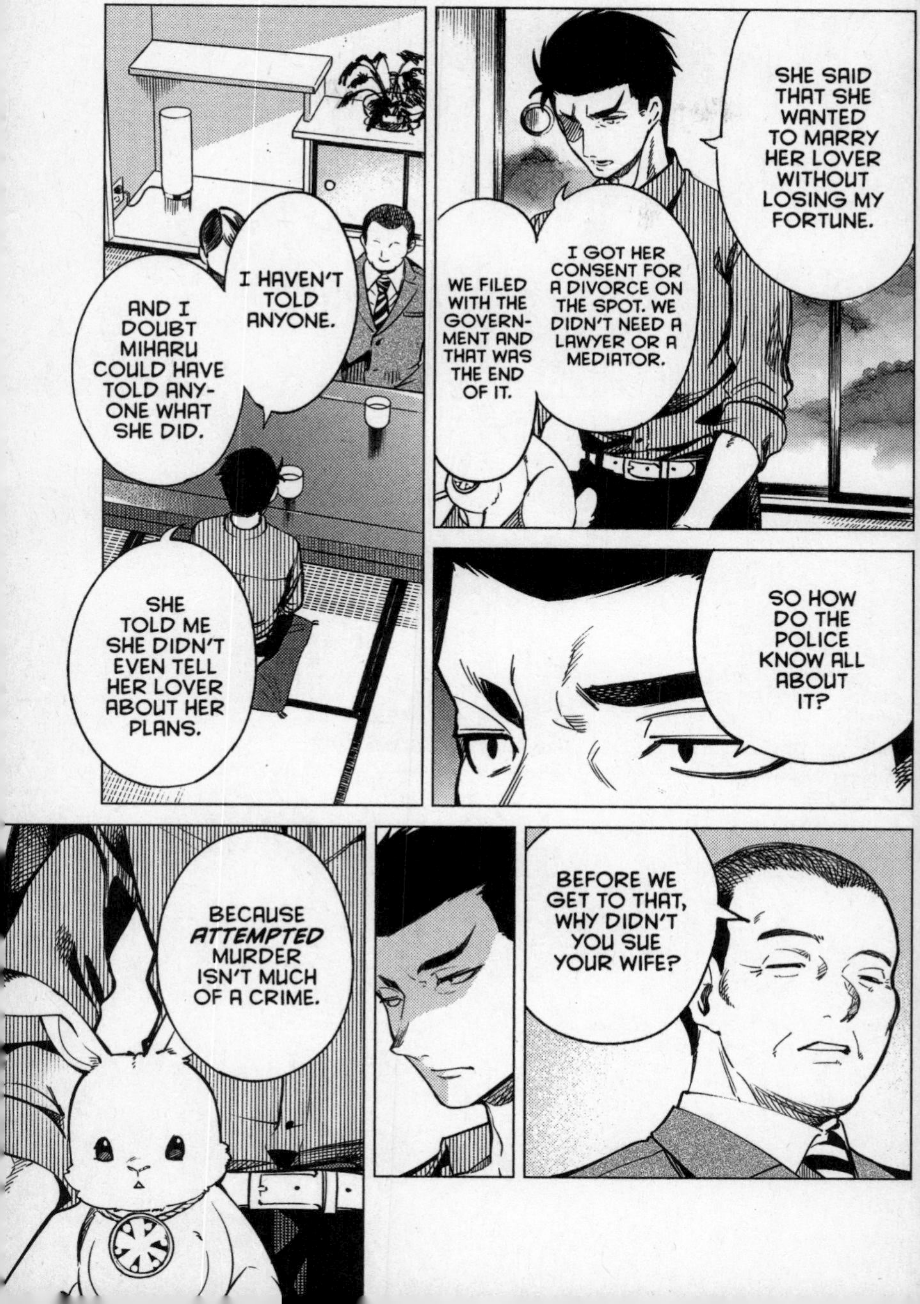
SHE SAID THAT SHE WANTED TO MARRY HER LOVER WITHOUT LOSING MY FORTUNE.
I GOT HER CONSENT FOR A DIVORCE ON THE SPOT. WE DIDN'T NEED A LAWYER OR A MEDIATOR.
WE FILED WITH THE GOVERN-MENT AND THAT WAS THE END OF IT.
SO HOW DO THE POLICE KNOW ALL ABOUT IT?
I HAVEN'T TOLD ANYONE.
AND I DOUBT MIHARU COULD HAVE TOLD ANY-ONE WHAT SHE DID.
SHE TOLD ME SHE DIDN'T EVEN TELL HER LOVER ABOUT HER PLANS.
BEFORE WE GET TO THAT, WHY DIDN'T YOU SUE YOUR WIFE?
BECAUSE *ATTEMPTED* MURDER ISN'T MUCH OF A CRIME.

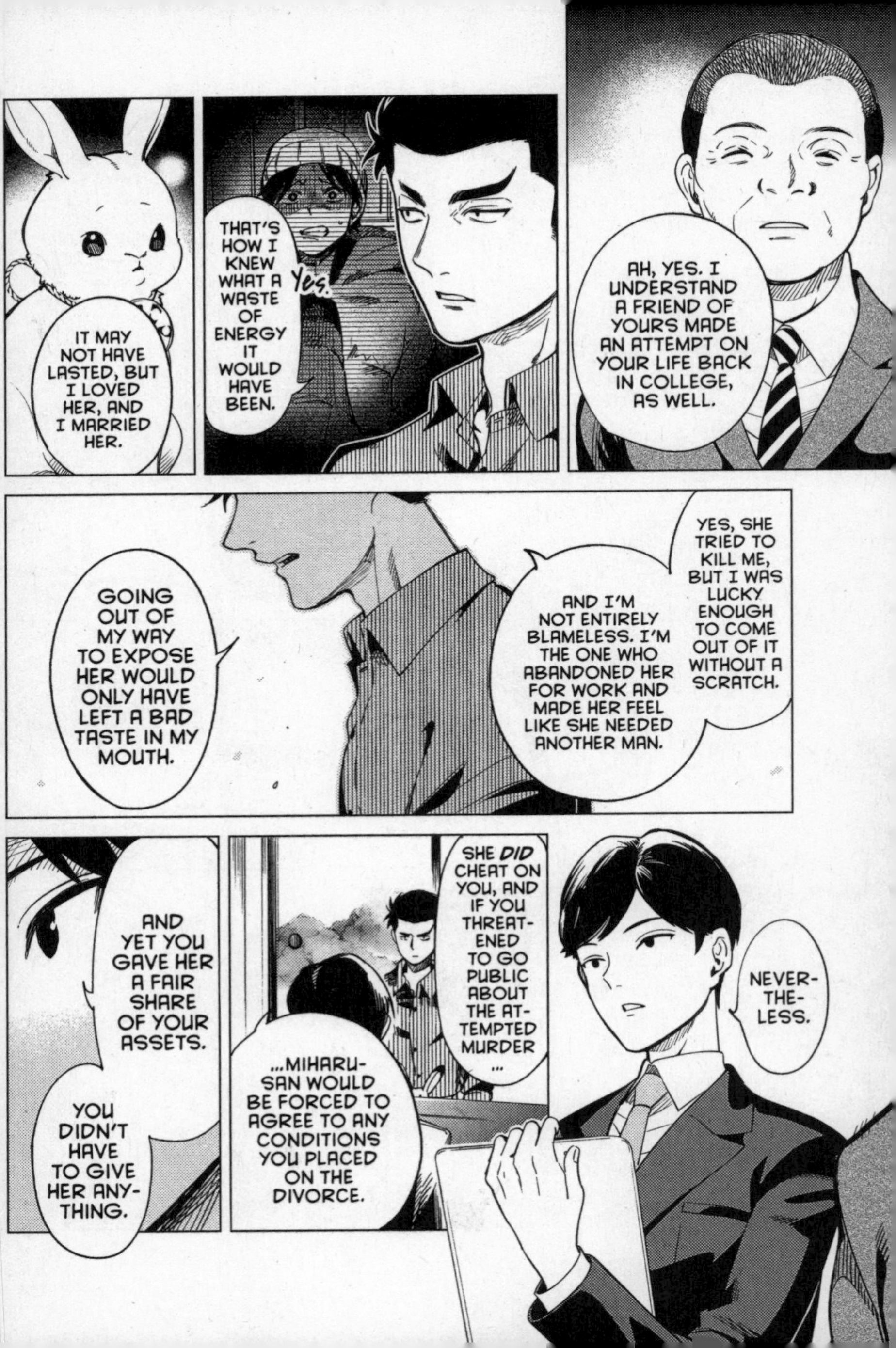
AH, YES. I UNDERSTAND A FRIEND OF YOURS MADE AN ATTEMPT ON YOUR LIFE BACK IN COLLEGE, AS WELL.
THAT'S HOW I KNEW WHAT A WASTE OF ENERGY IT WOULD HAVE BEEN.
Yes.
IT MAY NOT HAVE LASTED, BUT I LOVED HER, AND I MARRIED HER.
YES, SHE TRIED TO KILL ME, BUT I WAS LUCKY ENOUGH TO COME OUT OF IT WITHOUT A SCRATCH.
AND I'M NOT ENTIRELY BLAMELESS. I'M THE ONE WHO ABANDONED HER FOR WORK AND MADE HER FEEL LIKE SHE NEEDED ANOTHER MAN.
GOING OUT OF MY WAY TO EXPOSE HER WOULD ONLY HAVE LEFT A BAD TASTE IN MY MOUTH.
NEVER-THE-LESS.
SHE *DID* CHEAT ON YOU, AND IF YOU THREAT-ENED TO GO PUBLIC ABOUT THE AT-TEMPTED MURDER ...
...MIHARU-SAN WOULD BE FORCED TO AGREE TO ANY CONDITIONS YOU PLACED ON THE DIVORCE.
AND YET YOU GAVE HER A FAIR SHARE OF YOUR ASSETS.
YOU DIDN'T HAVE TO GIVE HER ANYTHING.

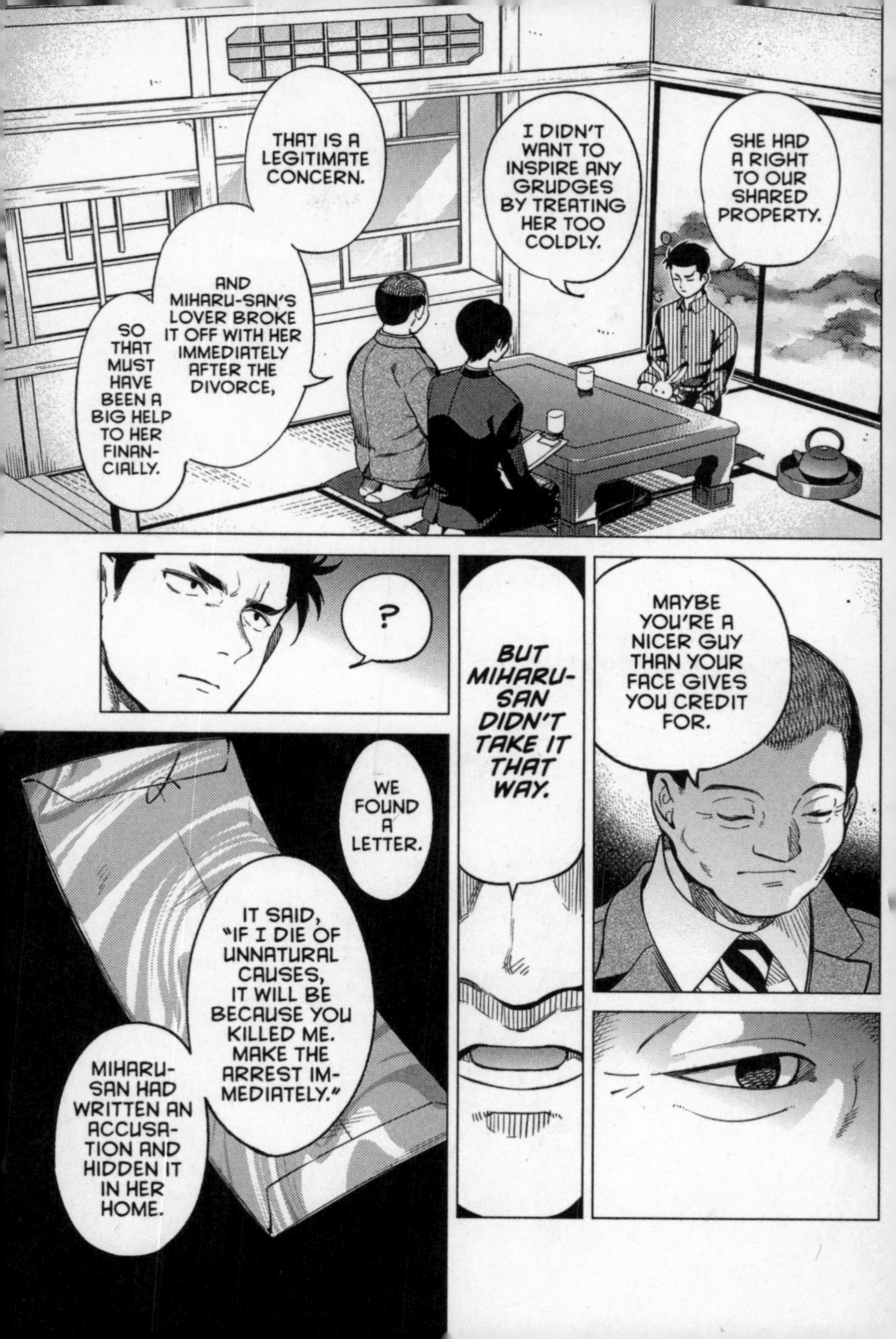
SHE HAD A RIGHT TO OUR SHARED PROPERTY.
I DIDN'T WANT TO INSPIRE ANY GRUDGES BY TREATING HER TOO COLDLY.
THAT IS A LEGITIMATE CONCERN.
AND MIHARU-SAN'S LOVER BROKE IT OFF WITH HER IMMEDIATELY AFTER THE DIVORCE,
SO THAT MUST HAVE BEEN A BIG HELP TO HER FINANCIALLY.
MAYBE YOU'RE A NICER GUY THAN YOUR FACE GIVES YOU CREDIT FOR.
BUT MIHARU-SAN DIDN'T TAKE IT THAT WAY.
?
WE FOUND A LETTER.
IT SAID, "IF I DIE OF UNNATURAL CAUSES, IT WILL BE BECAUSE YOU KILLED ME. MAKE THE ARREST IMMEDIATELY."
MIHARU-SAN HAD WRITTEN AN ACCUSATION AND HIDDEN IT IN HER HOME.

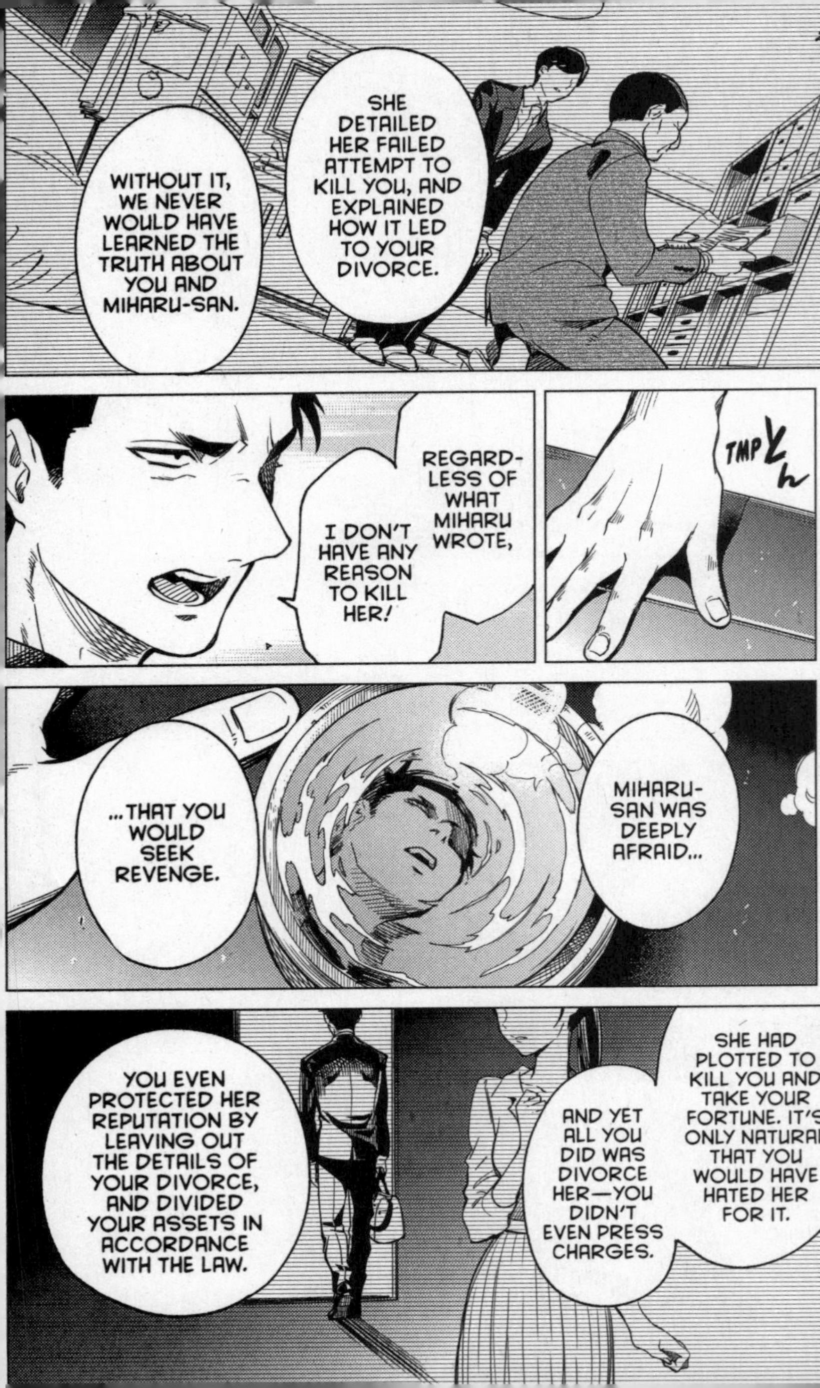
SHE DETAILED HER FAILED ATTEMPT TO KILL YOU, AND EXPLAINED HOW IT LED TO YOUR DIVORCE.
WITHOUT IT, WE NEVER WOULD HAVE LEARNED THE TRUTH ABOUT YOU AND MIHARU-SAN.
TMP
REGARDLESS OF WHAT MIHARU WROTE,
I DON'T HAVE ANY REASON TO KILL HER!
MIHARU-SAN WAS DEEPLY AFRAID...
...THAT YOU WOULD SEEK REVENGE.
SHE HAD PLOTTED TO KILL YOU AND TAKE YOUR FORTUNE. IT'S ONLY NATURAL THAT YOU WOULD HAVE HATED HER FOR IT.
AND YET ALL YOU DID WAS DIVORCE HER—YOU DIDN'T EVEN PRESS CHARGES.
YOU EVEN PROTECTED HER REPUTATION BY LEAVING OUT THE DETAILS OF YOUR DIVORCE, AND DIVIDED YOUR ASSETS IN ACCORDANCE WITH THE LAW.

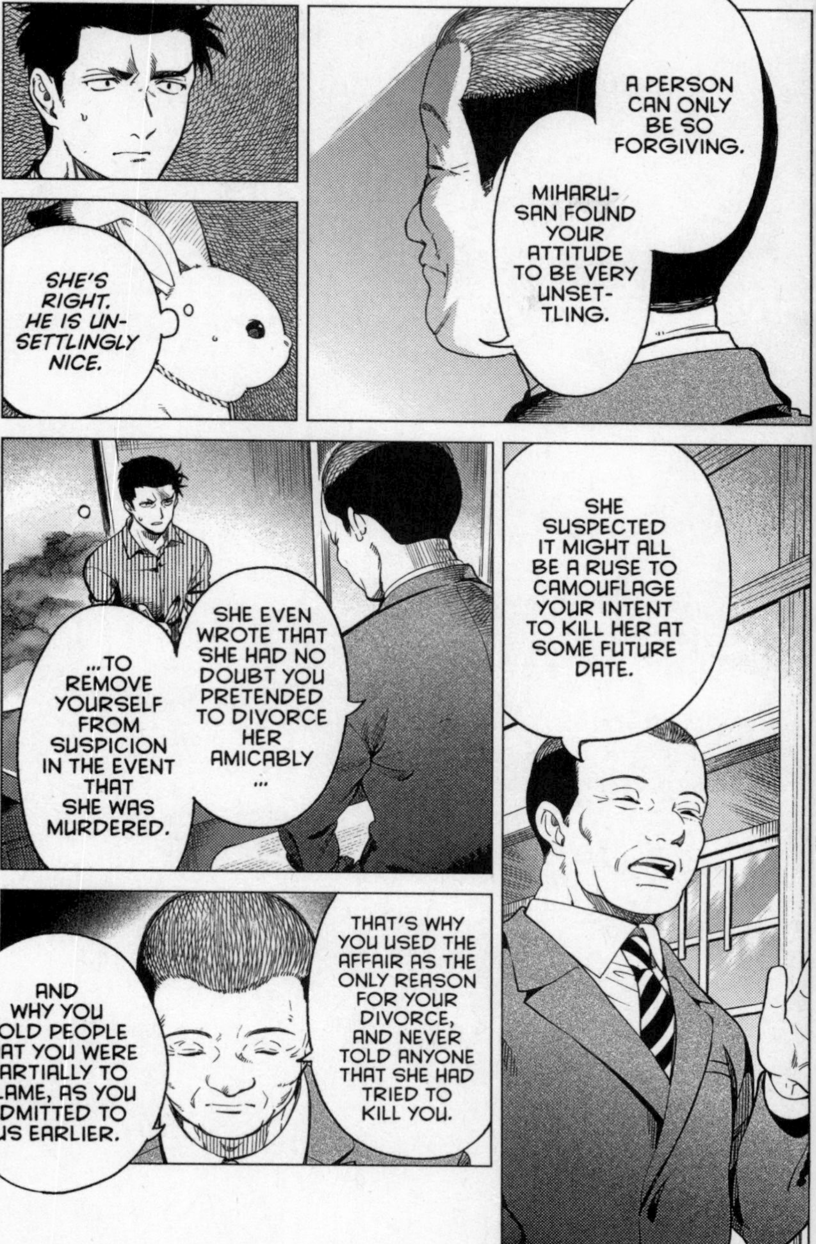
A PERSON CAN ONLY BE SO FORGIVING.
MIHARU-SAN FOUND YOUR ATTITUDE TO BE VERY UNSET-TLING.
SHE'S RIGHT. HE IS UN-SETTLINGLY NICE.
SHE SUSPECTED IT MIGHT ALL BE A RUSE TO CAMOUFLAGE YOUR INTENT TO KILL HER AT SOME FUTURE DATE.
SHE EVEN WROTE THAT SHE HAD NO DOUBT YOU PRETENDED TO DIVORCE HER AMICABLY ...
...TO REMOVE YOURSELF FROM SUSPICION IN THE EVENT THAT SHE WAS MURDERED.
THAT'S WHY YOU USED THE AFFAIR AS THE ONLY REASON FOR YOUR DIVORCE, AND NEVER TOLD ANYONE THAT SHE HAD TRIED TO KILL YOU.
AND WHY YOU TOLD PEOPLE THAT YOU WERE PARTIALLY TO BLAME, AS YOU ADMITTED TO US EARLIER.

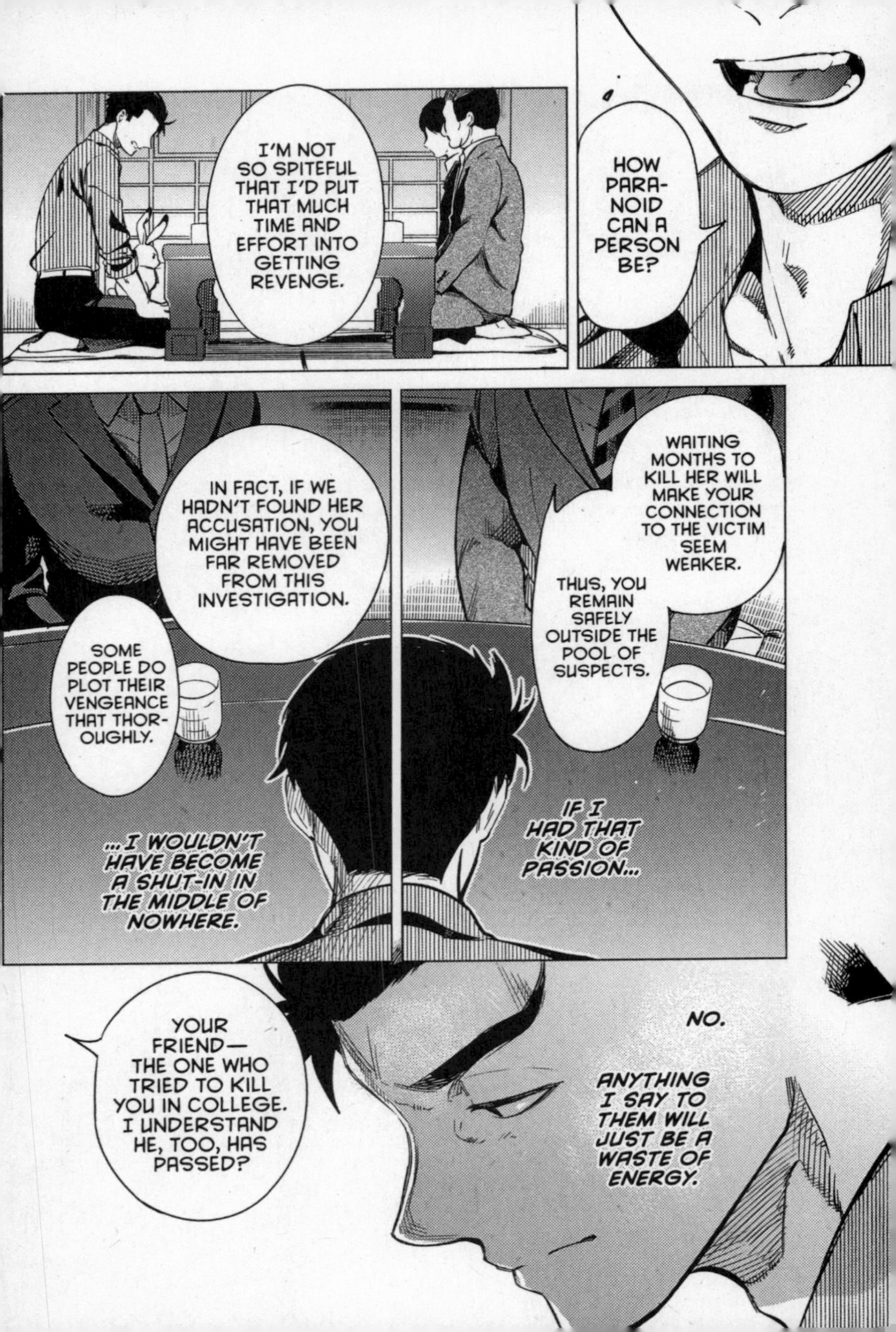
HOW PARANOID CAN A PERSON BE?
I'M NOT SO SPITEFUL THAT I'D PUT THAT MUCH TIME AND EFFORT INTO GETTING REVENGE.
WAITING MONTHS TO KILL HER WILL MAKE YOUR CONNECTION TO THE VICTIM SEEM WEAKER.
THUS, YOU REMAIN SAFELY OUTSIDE THE POOL OF SUSPECTS.
IF I HAD THAT KIND OF PASSION...
IN FACT, IF WE HADN'T FOUND HER ACCUSATION, YOU MIGHT HAVE BEEN FAR REMOVED FROM THIS INVESTIGATION.
SOME PEOPLE DO PLOT THEIR VENGEANCE THAT THOROUGHLY.
...I WOULDN'T HAVE BECOME A SHUT-IN IN THE MIDDLE OF NOWHERE.
NO.
ANYTHING I SAY TO THEM WILL JUST BE A WASTE OF ENERGY.
YOUR FRIEND—THE ONE WHO TRIED TO KILL YOU IN COLLEGE. I UNDERSTAND HE, TOO, HAS PASSED?

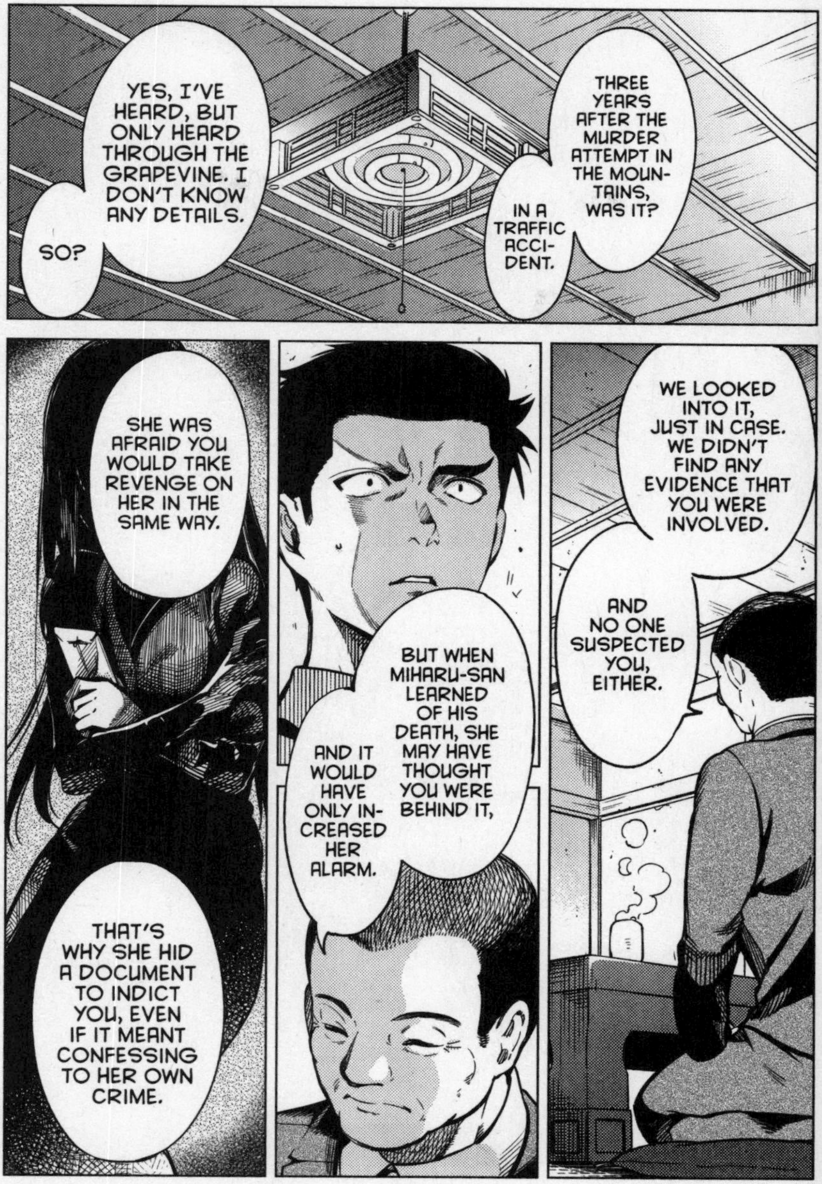
THREE YEARS AFTER THE MURDER ATTEMPT IN THE MOUNTAINS, WAS IT?
IN A TRAFFIC ACCIDENT.
YES, I'VE HEARD, BUT ONLY HEARD THROUGH THE GRAPEVINE. I DON'T KNOW ANY DETAILS.
SO?
WE LOOKED INTO IT, JUST IN CASE. WE DIDN'T FIND ANY EVIDENCE THAT YOU WERE INVOLVED.
AND NO ONE SUSPECTED YOU, EITHER.
BUT WHEN MIHARU-SAN LEARNED OF HIS DEATH, SHE MAY HAVE THOUGHT YOU WERE BEHIND IT,
AND IT WOULD HAVE ONLY INCREASED HER ALARM.
SHE WAS AFRAID YOU WOULD TAKE REVENGE ON HER IN THE SAME WAY.
THAT'S WHY SHE HID A DOCUMENT TO INDICT YOU, EVEN IF IT MEANT CONFESSING TO HER OWN CRIME.

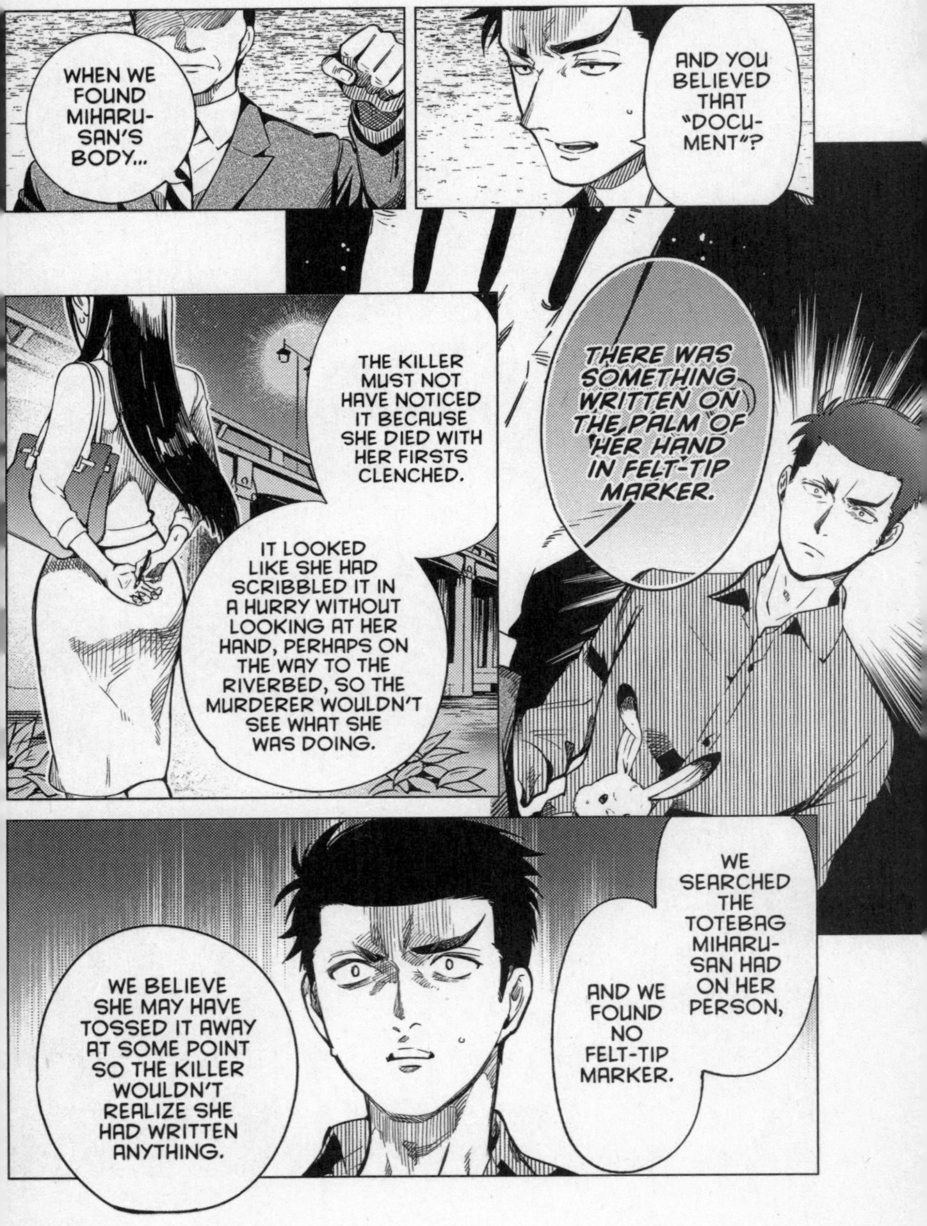
AND YOU BELIEVED THAT "DOCUMENT"?
WHEN WE FOUND MIHARU-SAN'S BODY...
THERE WAS SOMETHING WRITTEN ON THE PALM OF HER HAND IN FELT-TIP MARKER.
THE KILLER MUST NOT HAVE NOTICED IT BECAUSE SHE DIED WITH HER FIRSTS CLENCHED.
IT LOOKED LIKE SHE HAD SCRIBBLED IT IN A HURRY WITHOUT LOOKING AT HER HAND, PERHAPS ON THE WAY TO THE RIVERBED, SO THE MURDERER WOULDN'T SEE WHAT SHE WAS DOING.
WE SEARCHED THE TOTEBAG MIHARU-SAN HAD ON HER PERSON,
AND WE FOUND NO FELT-TIP MARKER.
WE BELIEVE SHE MAY HAVE TOSSED IT AWAY AT SOME POINT SO THE KILLER WOULDN'T REALIZE SHE HAD WRITTEN ANYTHING.

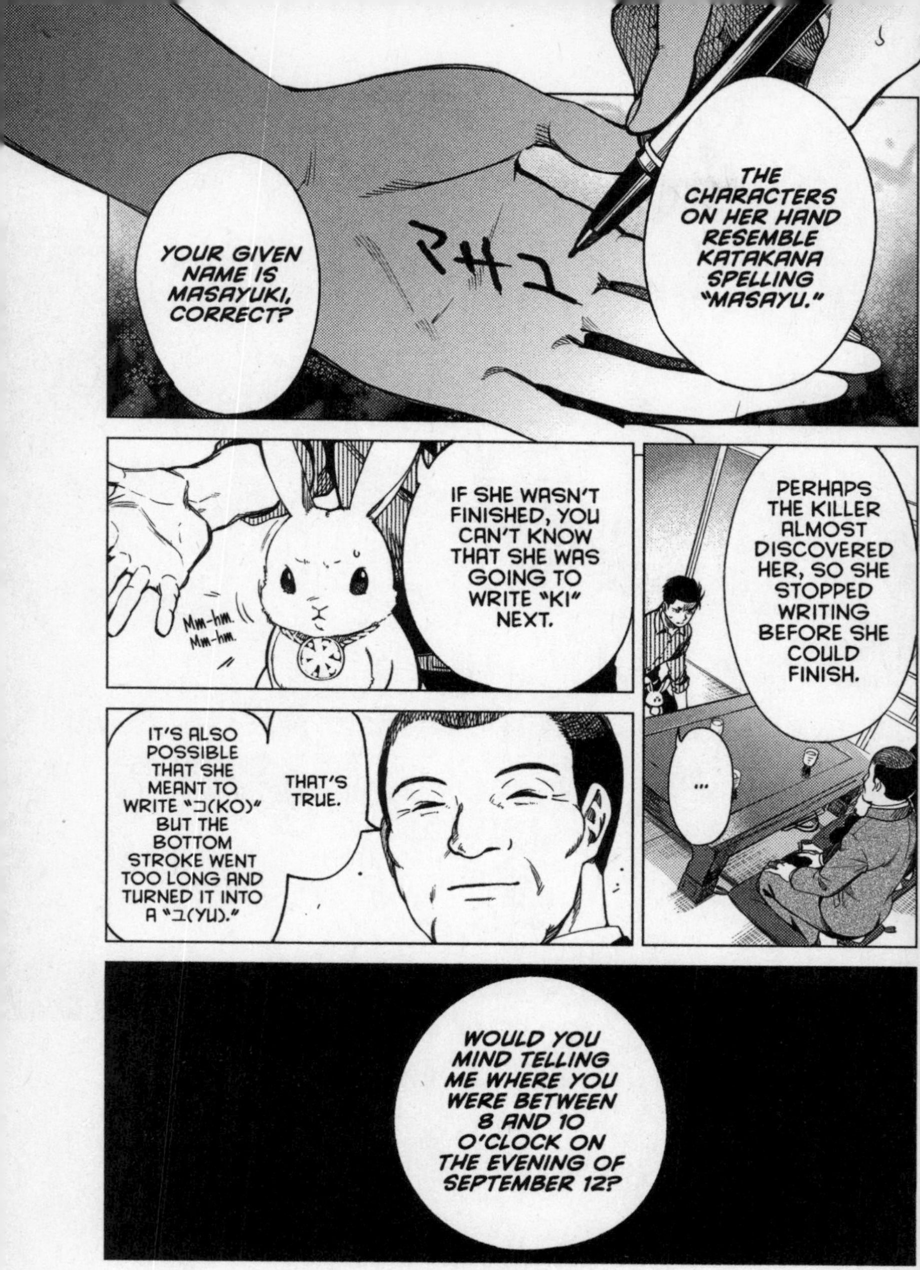
THE CHARACTERS ON HER HAND RESEMBLE KATAKANA SPELLING "MASAYU."
マサユ
YOUR GIVEN NAME IS MASAYUKI, CORRECT?
PERHAPS THE KILLER ALMOST DISCOVERED HER, SO SHE STOPPED WRITING BEFORE SHE COULD FINISH.
IF SHE WASN'T FINISHED, YOU CAN'T KNOW THAT SHE WAS GOING TO WRITE "KI" NEXT.
Mm-hm. Mm-hm.
...
IT'S ALSO POSSIBLE THAT SHE MEANT TO WRITE "コ(KO)" BUT THE BOTTOM STROKE WENT TOO LONG AND TURNED IT INTO A "ユ(YU)."
THAT'S TRUE.
WOULD YOU MIND TELLING ME WHERE YOU WERE BETWEEN 8 AND 10 O'CLOCK ON THE EVENING OF SEPTEMBER 12?

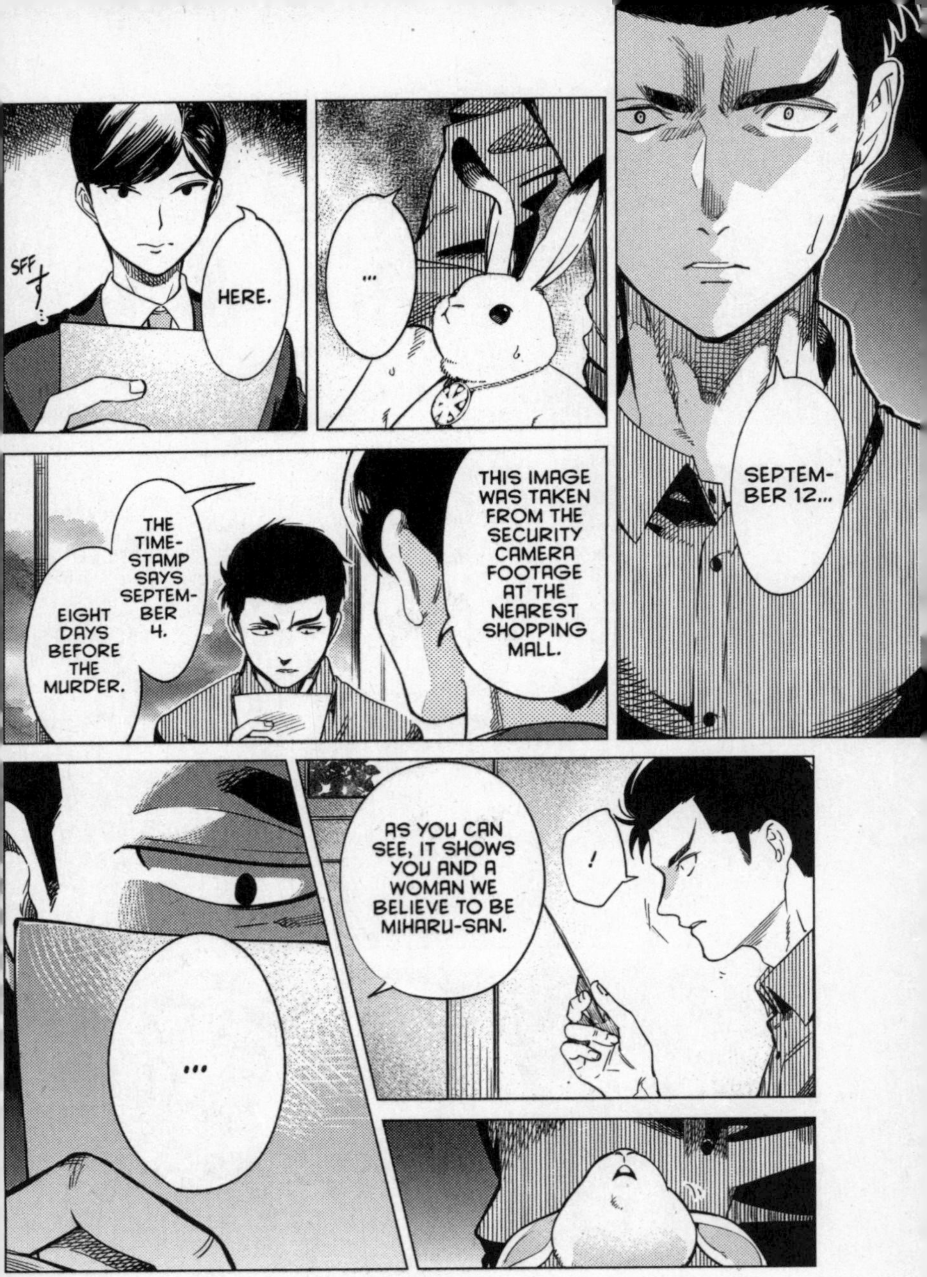
SEPTEMBER 12...
...
HERE.
SFF
す…
THIS IMAGE WAS TAKEN FROM THE SECURITY CAMERA FOOTAGE AT THE NEAREST SHOPPING MALL.
THE TIME-STAMP SAYS SEPTEMBER 4.
EIGHT DAYS BEFORE THE MURDER.
!
AS YOU CAN SEE, IT SHOWS YOU AND A WOMAN WE BELIEVE TO BE MIHARU-SAN.
...

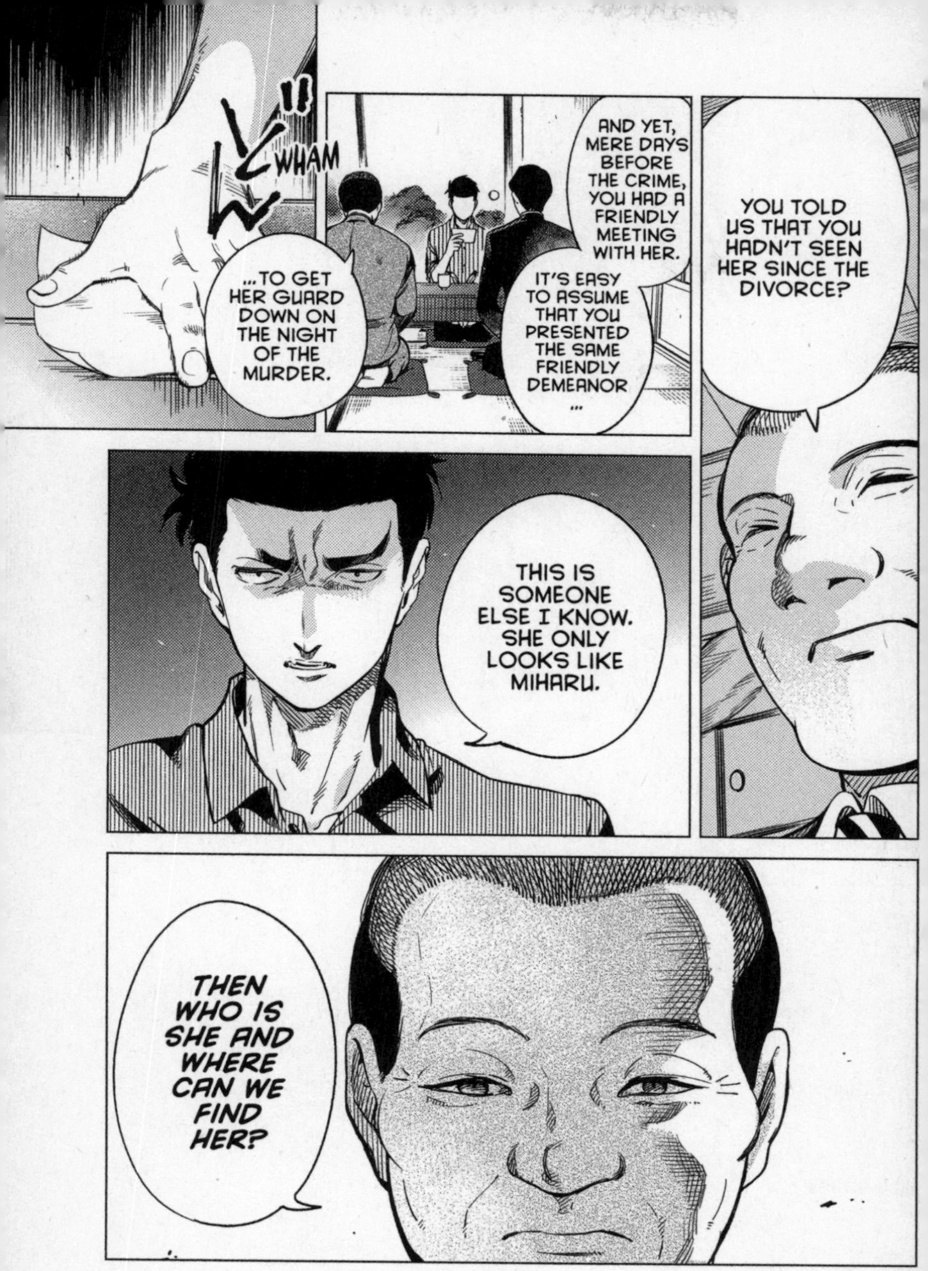
YOU TOLD US THAT YOU HADN'T SEEN HER SINCE THE DIVORCE?
AND YET, MERE DAYS BEFORE THE CRIME, YOU HAD A FRIENDLY MEETING WITH HER.
IT'S EASY TO ASSUME THAT YOU PRESENTED THE SAME FRIENDLY DEMEANOR ...
WHAM!!
...TO GET HER GUARD DOWN ON THE NIGHT OF THE MURDER.
THIS IS SOMEONE ELSE I KNOW. SHE ONLY LOOKS LIKE MIHARU.
THEN WHO IS SHE AND WHERE CAN WE FIND HER?

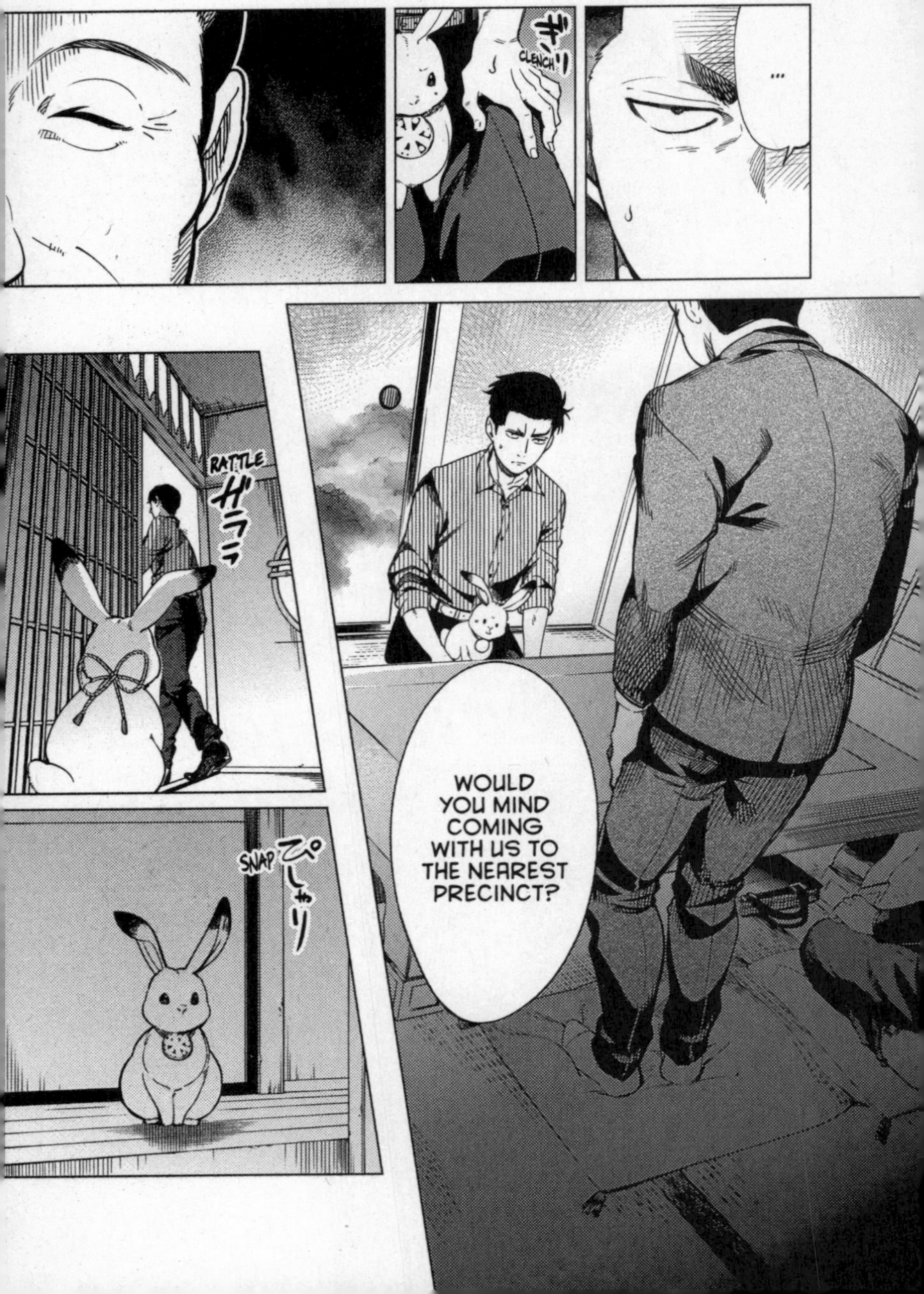
...
ギリ
CLENCH
WOULD YOU MIND COMING WITH US TO THE NEAREST PRECINCT?
RATTLE
ガララ
SNAP
ぴしゃり

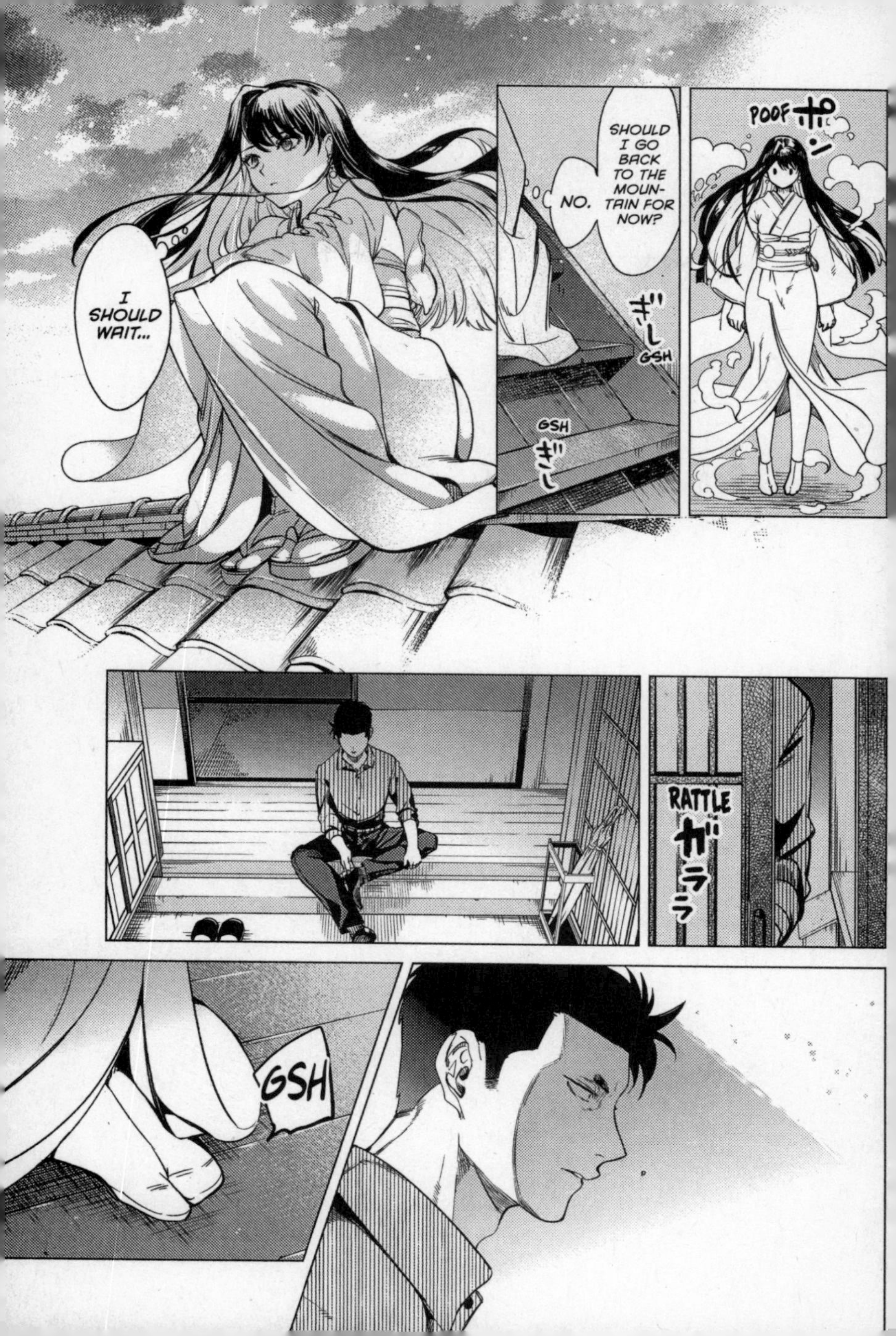
POOF ポン
SHOULD I GO BACK TO THE MOUN-TAIN FOR NOW?
NO.
ぎし GSH
GSH ぎし
I SHOULD WAIT...
RATTLE ガララ
GSH

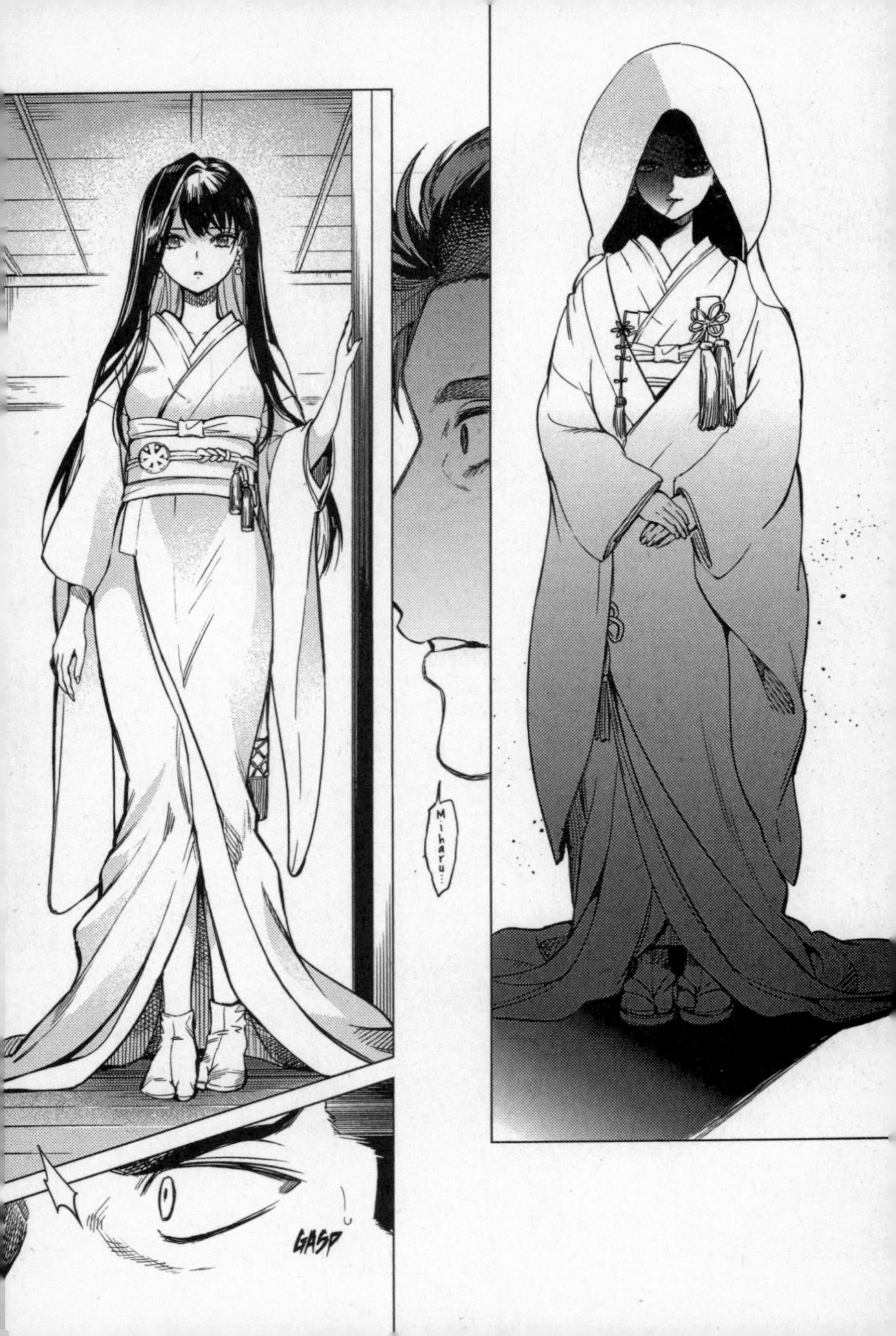
Miharu...
GASP

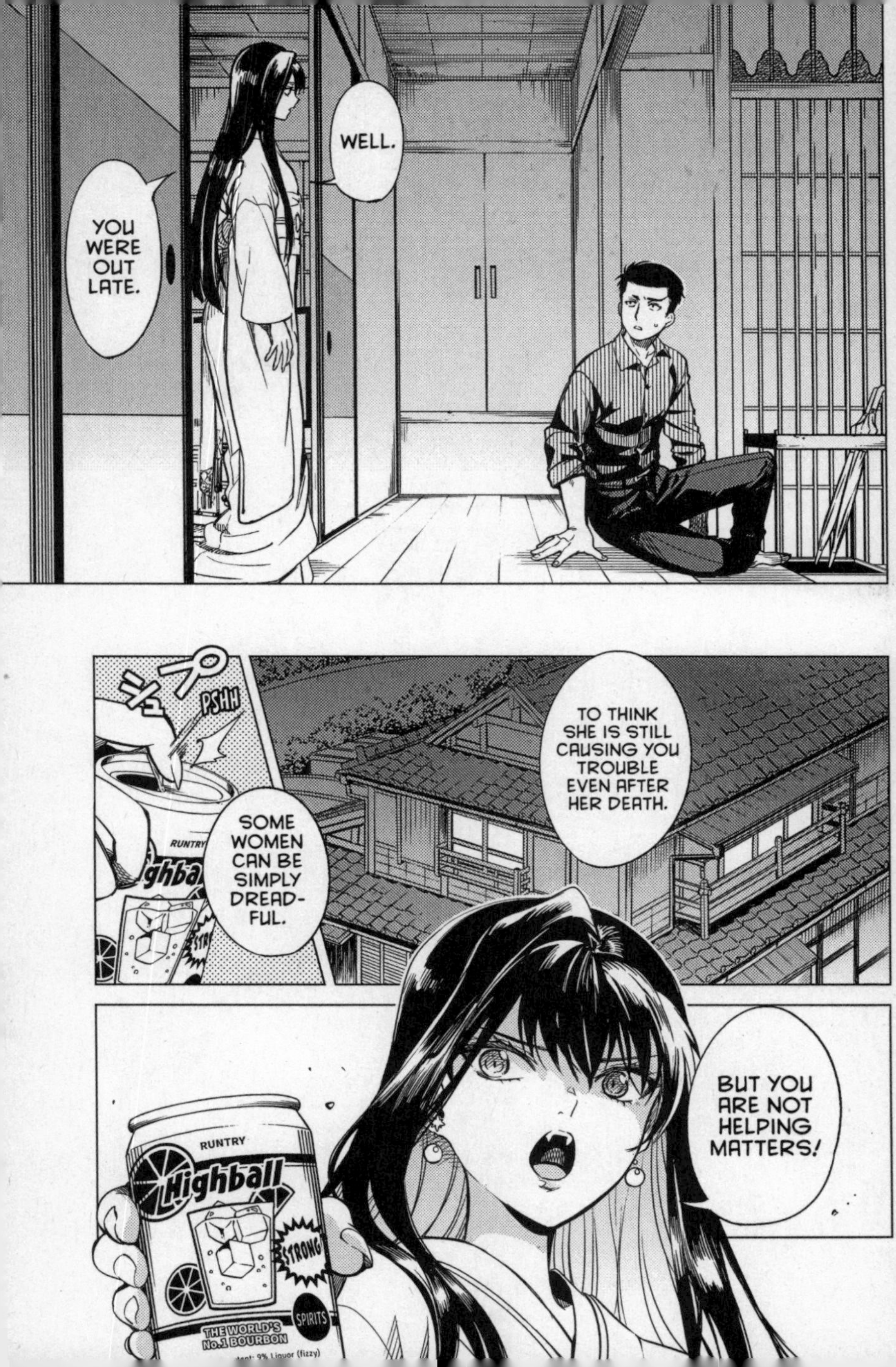
WELL.
YOU WERE OUT LATE.
TO THINK SHE IS STILL CAUSING YOU TROUBLE EVEN AFTER HER DEATH.
PSHH
シュ
RUNTRY
SOME WOMEN CAN BE SIMPLY DREAD-FUL.
BUT YOU ARE NOT HELPING MATTERS!
RUNTRY
Highball
STRONG
SPIRITS
THE WORLD'S No.1 BOURBON

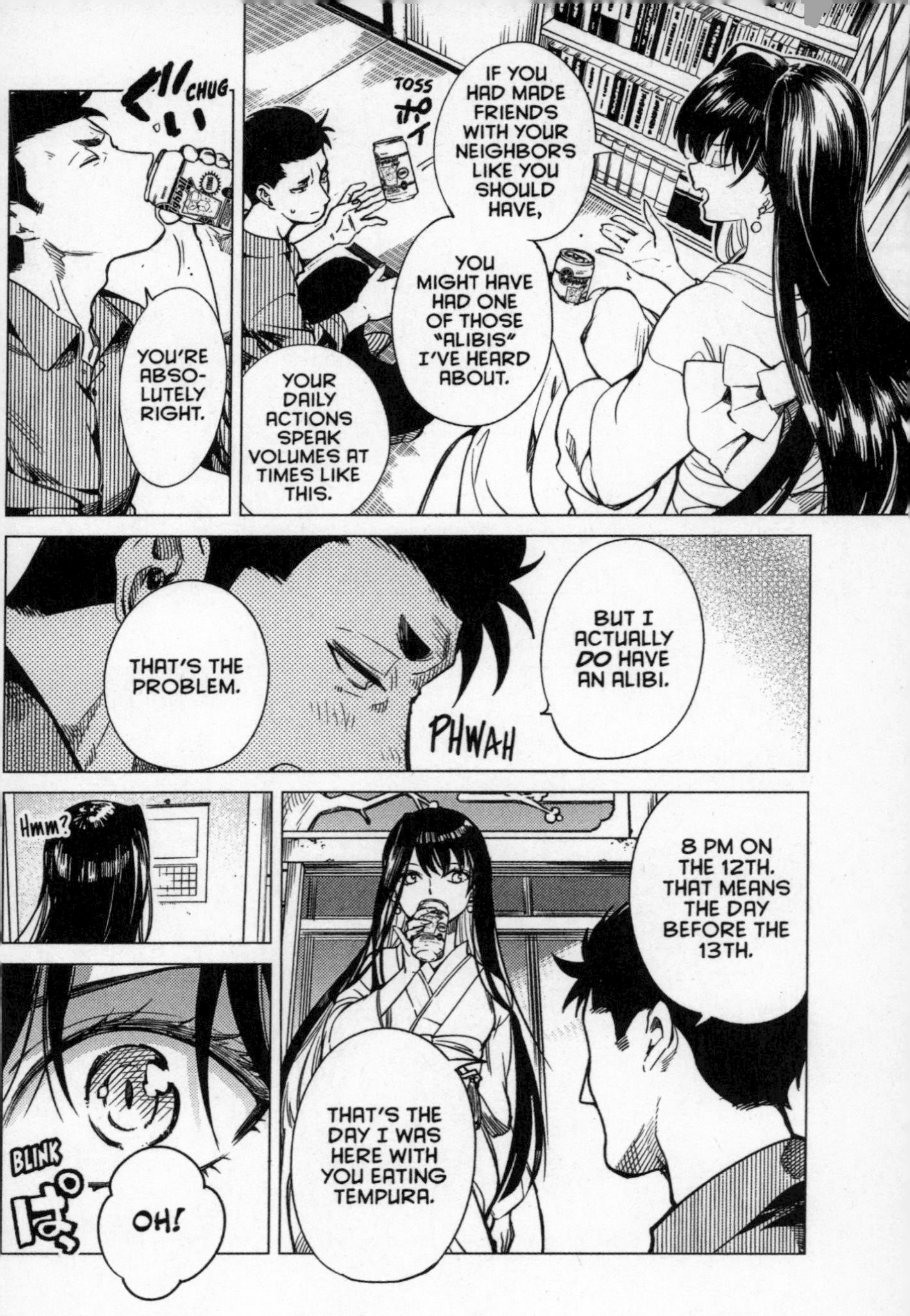
TOSS
IF YOU HAD MADE FRIENDS WITH YOUR NEIGHBORS LIKE YOU SHOULD HAVE,
YOU MIGHT HAVE HAD ONE OF THOSE "ALIBIS" I'VE HEARD ABOUT.
YOUR DAILY ACTIONS SPEAK VOLUMES AT TIMES LIKE THIS.
CHUG
YOU'RE ABSOLUTELY RIGHT.
BUT I ACTUALLY *DO* HAVE AN ALIBI.
PHWAH
THAT'S THE PROBLEM.
8 PM ON THE 12TH. THAT MEANS THE DAY BEFORE THE 13TH.
THAT'S THE DAY I WAS HERE WITH YOU EATING TEMPURA.
Hmm?
BLINK
OH!

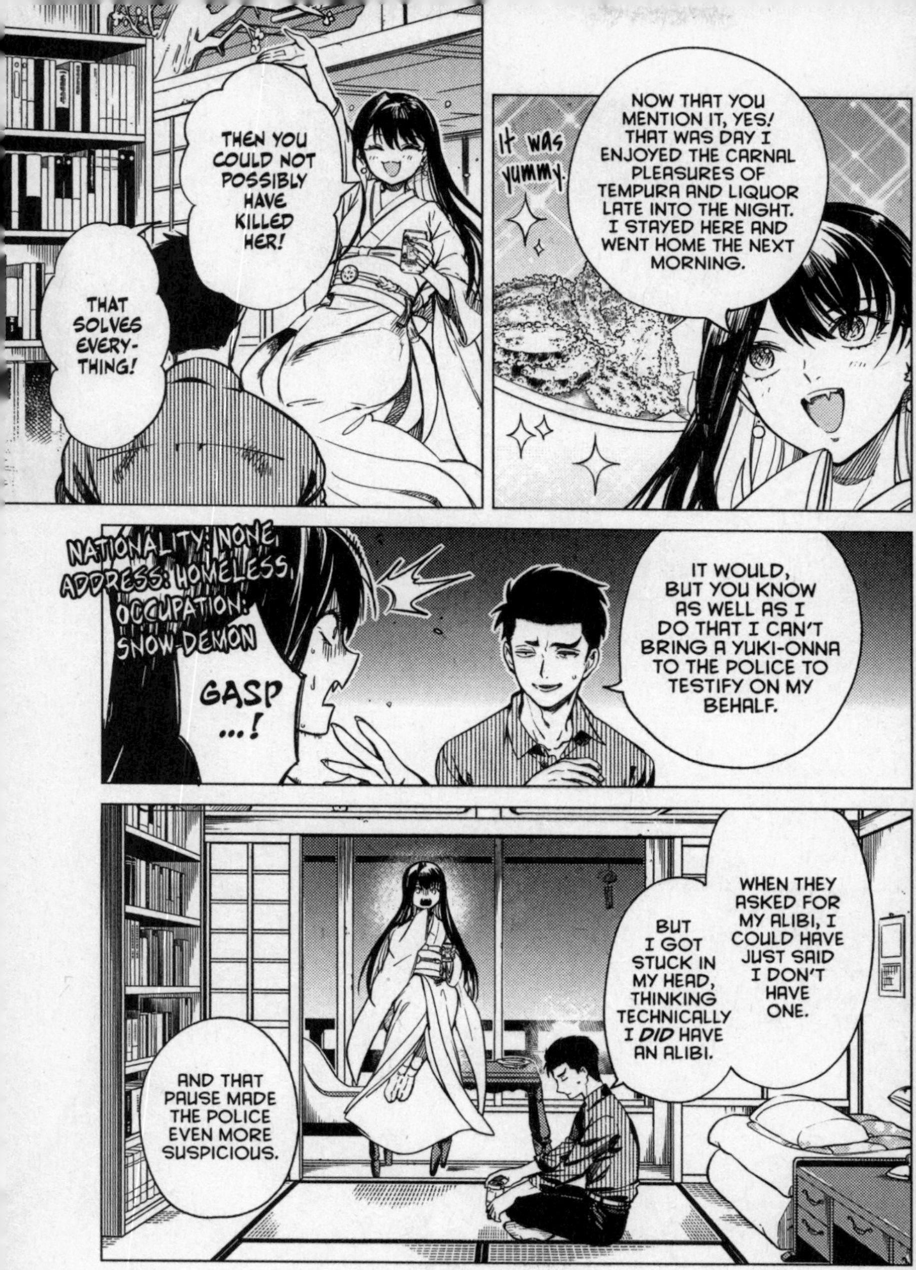
NOW THAT YOU MENTION IT, YES! THAT WAS DAY I ENJOYED THE CARNAL PLEASURES OF TEMPURA AND LIQUOR LATE INTO THE NIGHT. I STAYED HERE AND WENT HOME THE NEXT MORNING.
It was yummy.
THEN YOU COULD NOT POSSIBLY HAVE KILLED HER!
THAT SOLVES EVERY-THING!
IT WOULD, BUT YOU KNOW AS WELL AS I DO THAT I CAN'T BRING A YUKI-ONNA TO THE POLICE TO TESTIFY ON MY BEHALF.
NATIONALITY: NONE, ADDRESS: HOMELESS, OCCUPATION: SNOW-DEMON
GASP ...!
WHEN THEY ASKED FOR MY ALIBI, I COULD HAVE JUST SAID I DON'T HAVE ONE.
BUT I GOT STUCK IN MY HEAD, THINKING TECHNICALLY I *DID* HAVE AN ALIBI.
AND THAT PAUSE MADE THE POLICE EVEN MORE SUSPICIOUS.

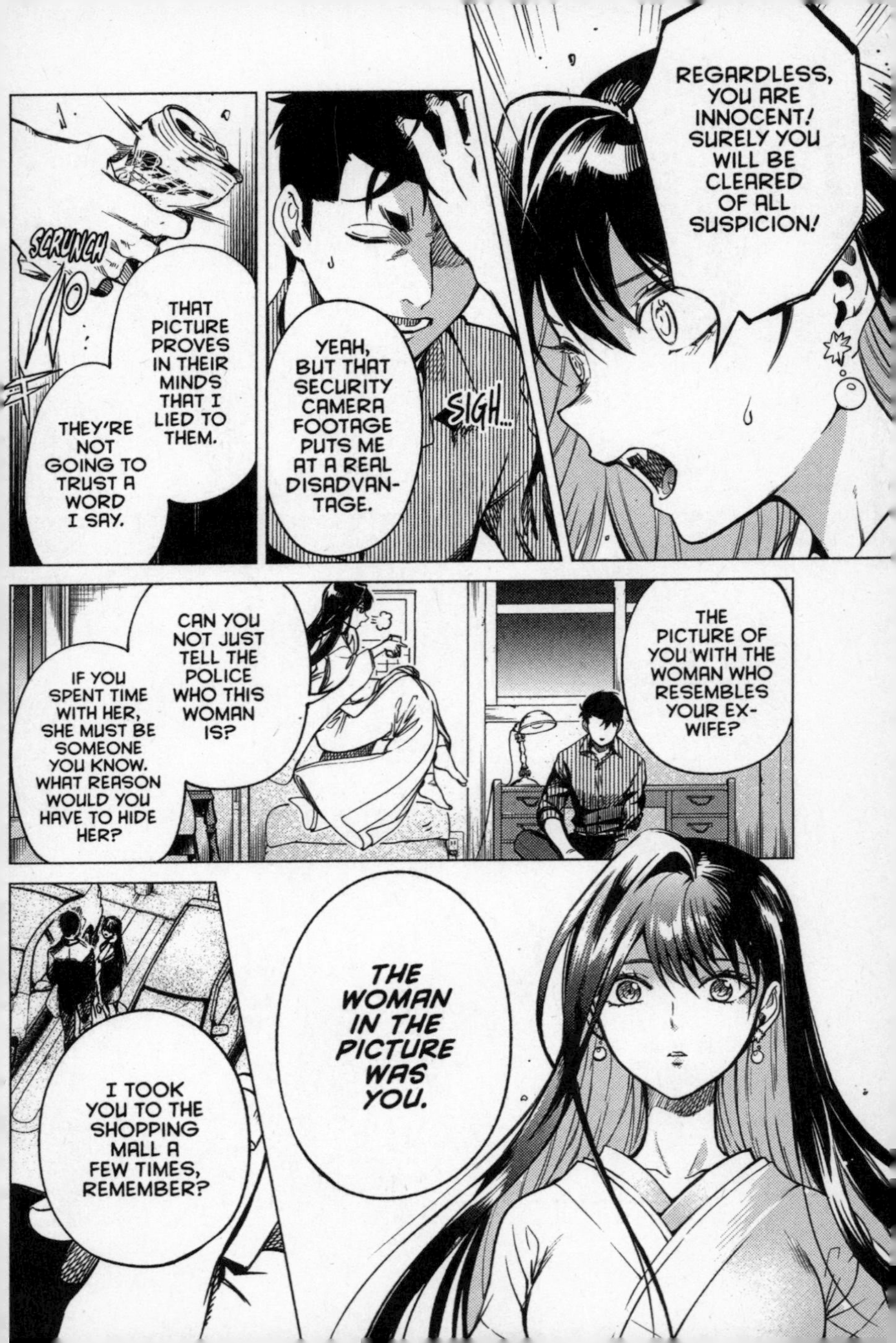
REGARDLESS, YOU ARE INNOCENT! SURELY YOU WILL BE CLEARED OF ALL SUSPICION!
SIGH...
YEAH, BUT THAT SECURITY CAMERA FOOTAGE PUTS ME AT A REAL DISADVANTAGE.
SCRUNCH
THAT PICTURE PROVES IN THEIR MINDS THAT I LIED TO THEM.
THEY'RE NOT GOING TO TRUST A WORD I SAY.
THE PICTURE OF YOU WITH THE WOMAN WHO RESEMBLES YOUR EX-WIFE?
CAN YOU NOT JUST TELL THE POLICE WHO THIS WOMAN IS?
IF YOU SPENT TIME WITH HER, SHE MUST BE SOMEONE YOU KNOW. WHAT REASON WOULD YOU HAVE TO HIDE HER?
THE WOMAN IN THE PICTURE WAS YOU.
I TOOK YOU TO THE SHOPPING MALL A FEW TIMES, REMEMBER?

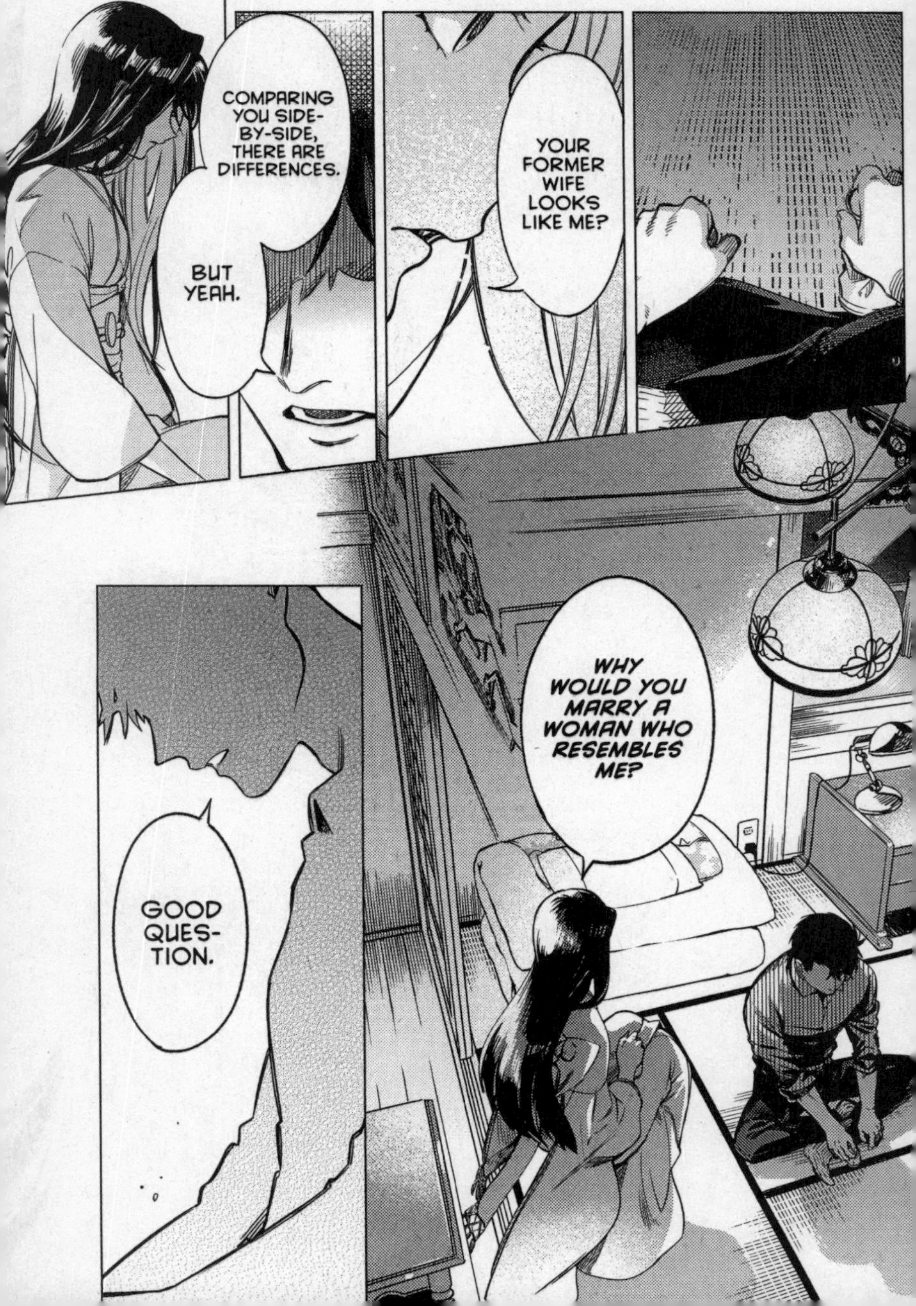
YOUR FORMER WIFE LOOKS LIKE ME?
COMPARING YOU SIDE-BY-SIDE, THERE ARE DIFFERENCES.
BUT YEAH.
WHY WOULD YOU MARRY A WOMAN WHO RESEMBLES ME?
GOOD QUES-TION.

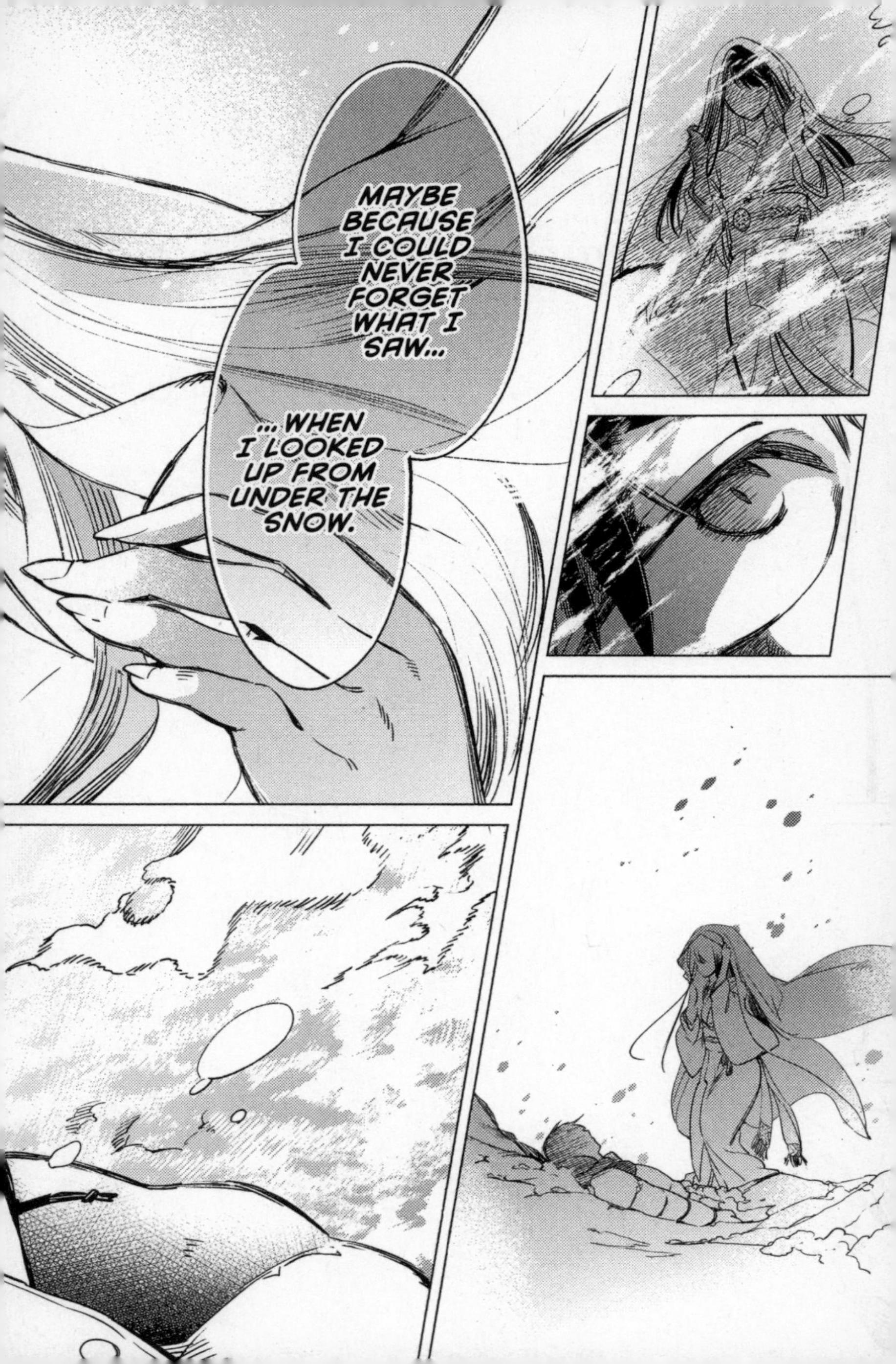
MAYBE BECAUSE I COULD NEVER FORGET WHAT I SAW...
...WHEN I LOOKED UP FROM UNDER THE SNOW.

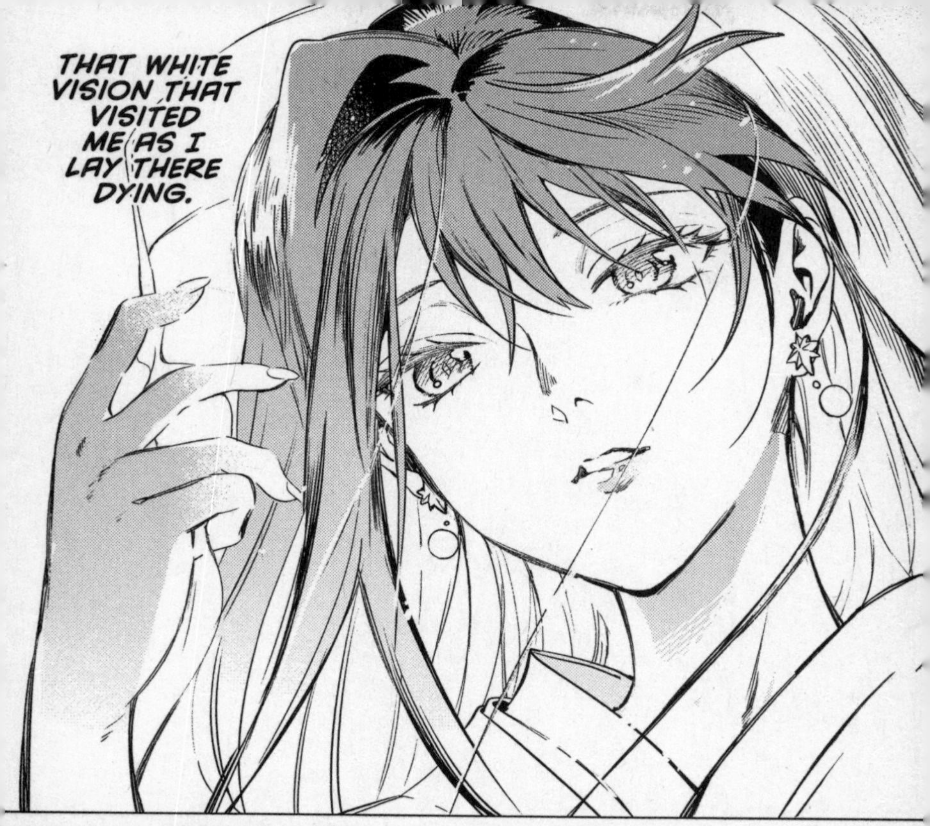
THAT WHITE VISION THAT VISITED ME AS I LAY THERE DYING.
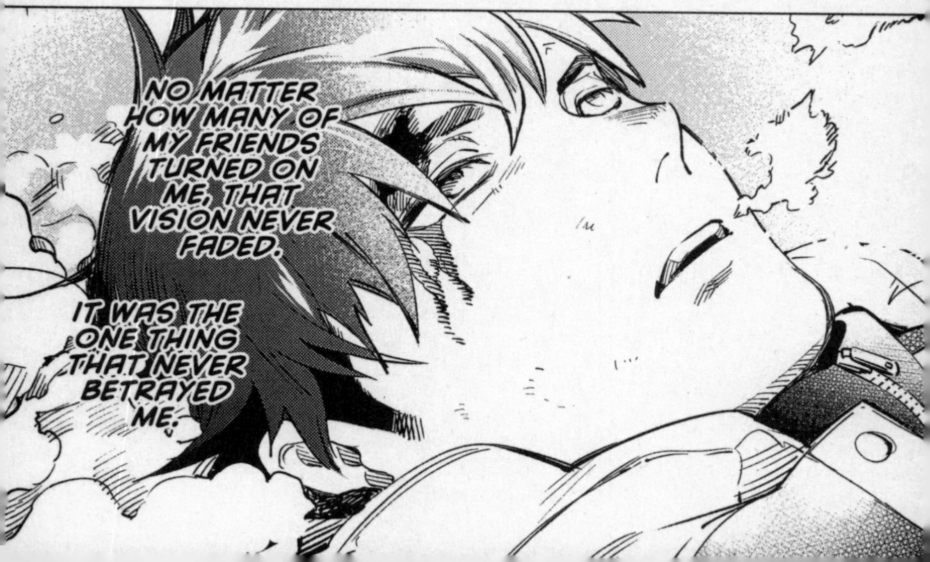
NO MATTER HOW MANY OF MY FRIENDS TURNED ON ME, THAT VISION NEVER FADED.
IT WAS THE ONE THING THAT NEVER BETRAYED ME.
...

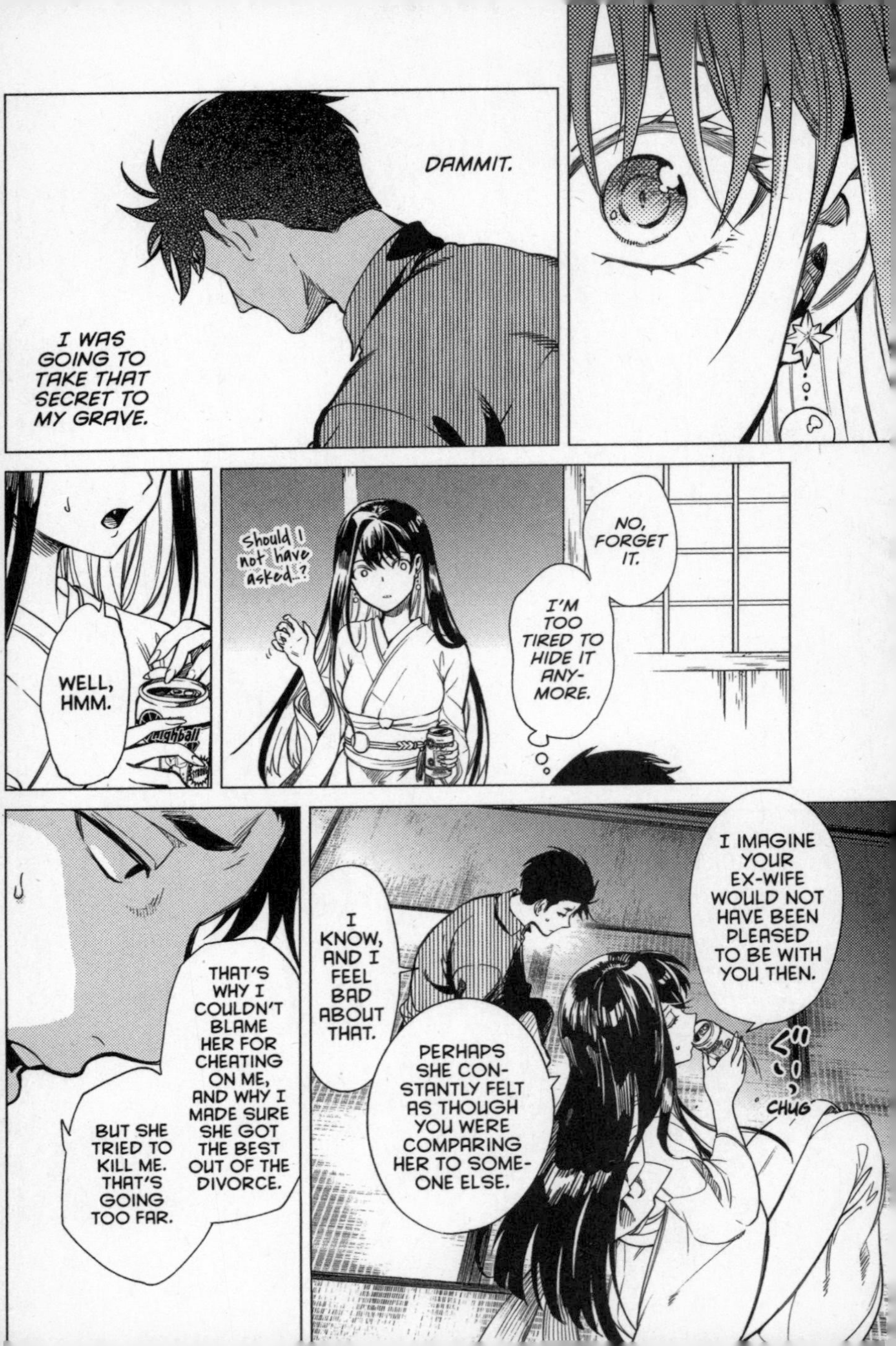
DAMMIT.
I WAS GOING TO TAKE THAT SECRET TO MY GRAVE.
NO, FORGET IT.
I'M TOO TIRED TO HIDE IT ANYMORE.
should I not have asked...?
WELL, HMM.
I IMAGINE YOUR EX-WIFE WOULD NOT HAVE BEEN PLEASED TO BE WITH YOU THEN.
CHUG
I KNOW, AND I FEEL BAD ABOUT THAT.
PERHAPS SHE CONSTANTLY FELT AS THOUGH YOU WERE COMPARING HER TO SOMEONE ELSE.
THAT'S WHY I COULDN'T BLAME HER FOR CHEATING ON ME, AND WHY I MADE SURE SHE GOT THE BEST OUT OF THE DIVORCE.
BUT SHE TRIED TO KILL ME. THAT'S GOING TOO FAR.

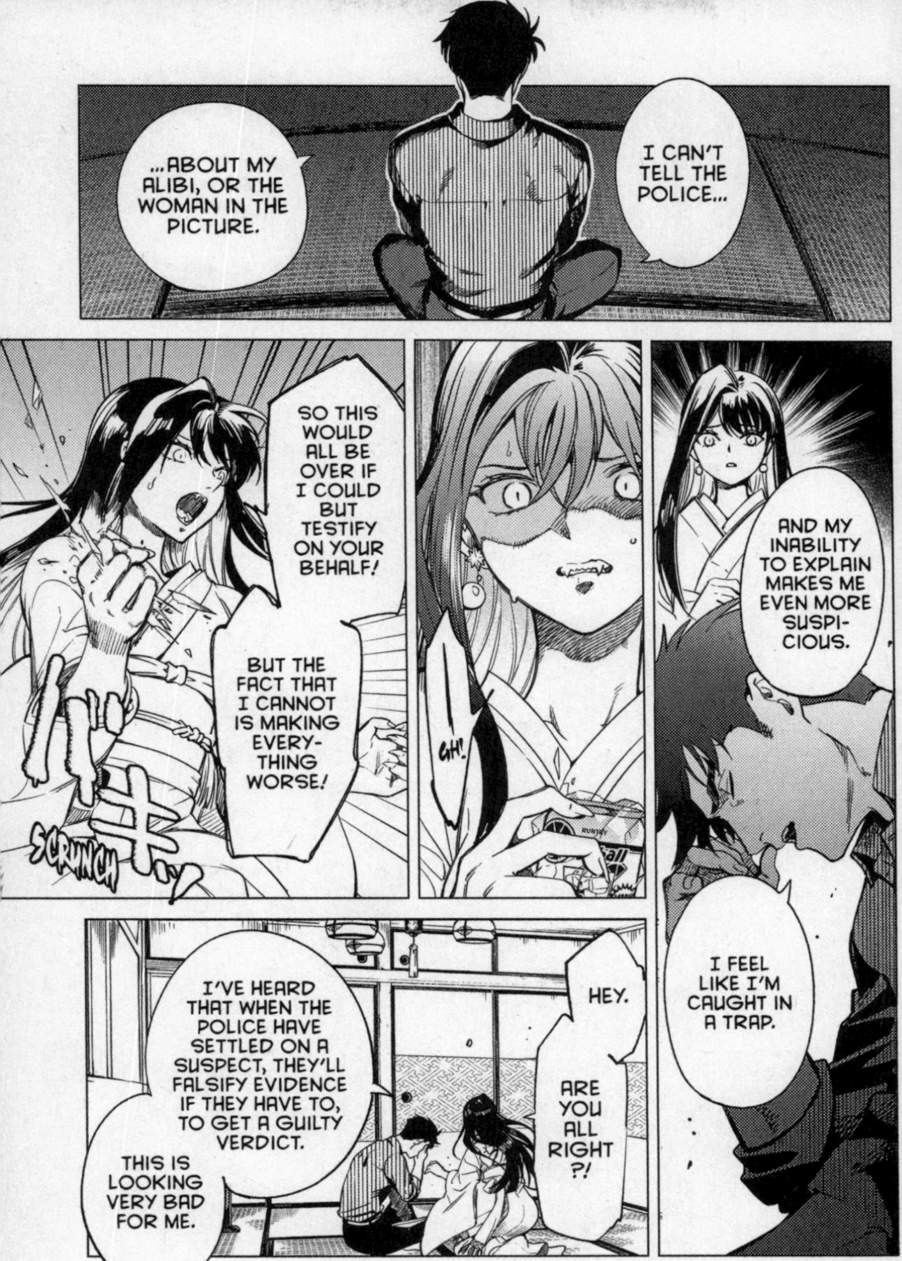
I CAN'T TELL THE POLICE...
...ABOUT MY ALIBI, OR THE WOMAN IN THE PICTURE.
AND MY INABILITY TO EXPLAIN MAKES ME EVEN MORE SUSPI-CIOUS.
I FEEL LIKE I'M CAUGHT IN A TRAP.
GH!
SO THIS WOULD ALL BE OVER IF I COULD BUT TESTIFY ON YOUR BEHALF!
BUT THE FACT THAT I CANNOT IS MAKING EVERY-THING WORSE!
SCRUNCH
HEY.
ARE YOU ALL RIGHT?!
I'VE HEARD THAT WHEN THE POLICE HAVE SETTLED ON A SUSPECT, THEY'LL FALSIFY EVIDENCE IF THEY HAVE TO, TO GET A GUILTY VERDICT.
THIS IS LOOKING VERY BAD FOR ME.

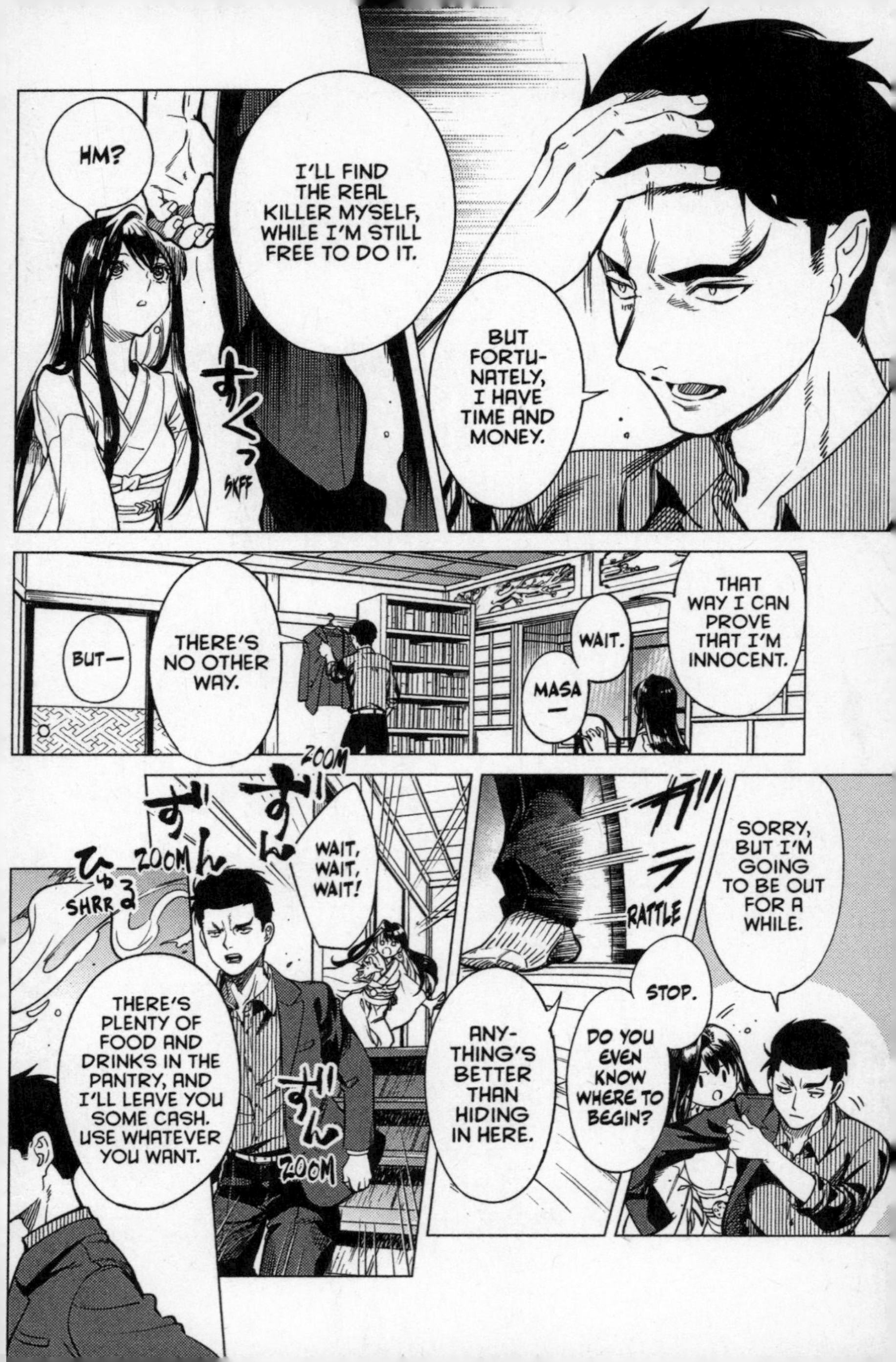
BUT FORTUNATELY, I HAVE TIME AND MONEY.
I'LL FIND THE REAL KILLER MYSELF, WHILE I'M STILL FREE TO DO IT.
HM?
すくっ
SKFF
THAT WAY I CAN PROVE THAT I'M INNOCENT.
WAIT.
MASA—
THERE'S NO OTHER WAY.
BUT—
SORRY, BUT I'M GOING TO BE OUT FOR A WHILE.
STOP.
DO YOU EVEN KNOW WHERE TO BEGIN?
ガラ
RATTLE
ANYTHING'S BETTER THAN HIDING IN HERE.
ずん
ZOOM
WAIT, WAIT, WAIT!
ずん
ZOOM
ひゅる
SHRR
THERE'S PLENTY OF FOOD AND DRINKS IN THE PANTRY, AND I'LL LEAVE YOU SOME CASH. USE WHATEVER YOU WANT.
ずん
ZOOM

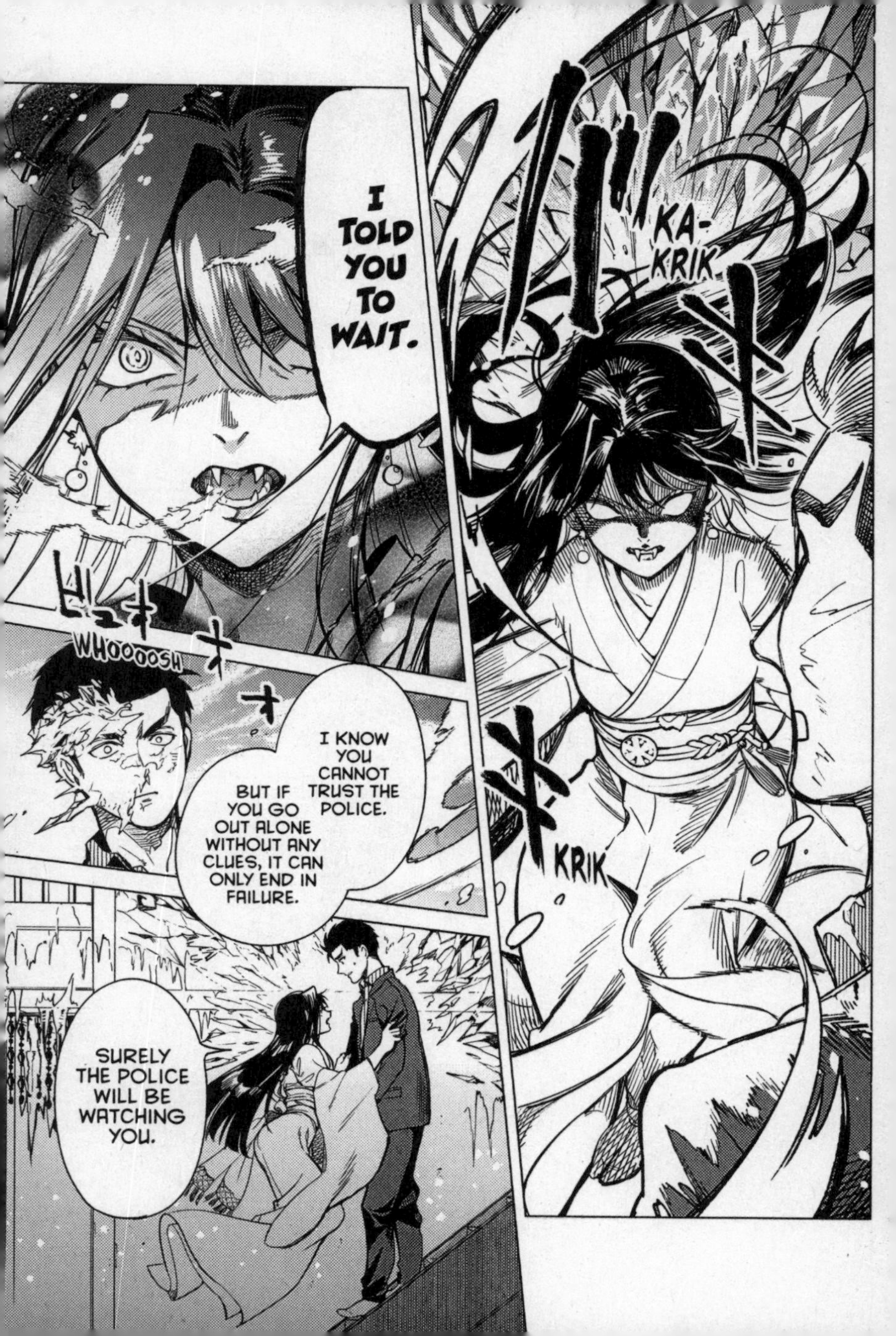
KA-KRIK
KRIK
I TOLD YOU TO WAIT.
WHOOOOSH
I KNOW YOU CANNOT TRUST THE POLICE.
BUT IF YOU GO OUT ALONE WITHOUT ANY CLUES, IT CAN ONLY END IN FAILURE.
SURELY THE POLICE WILL BE WATCHING YOU.

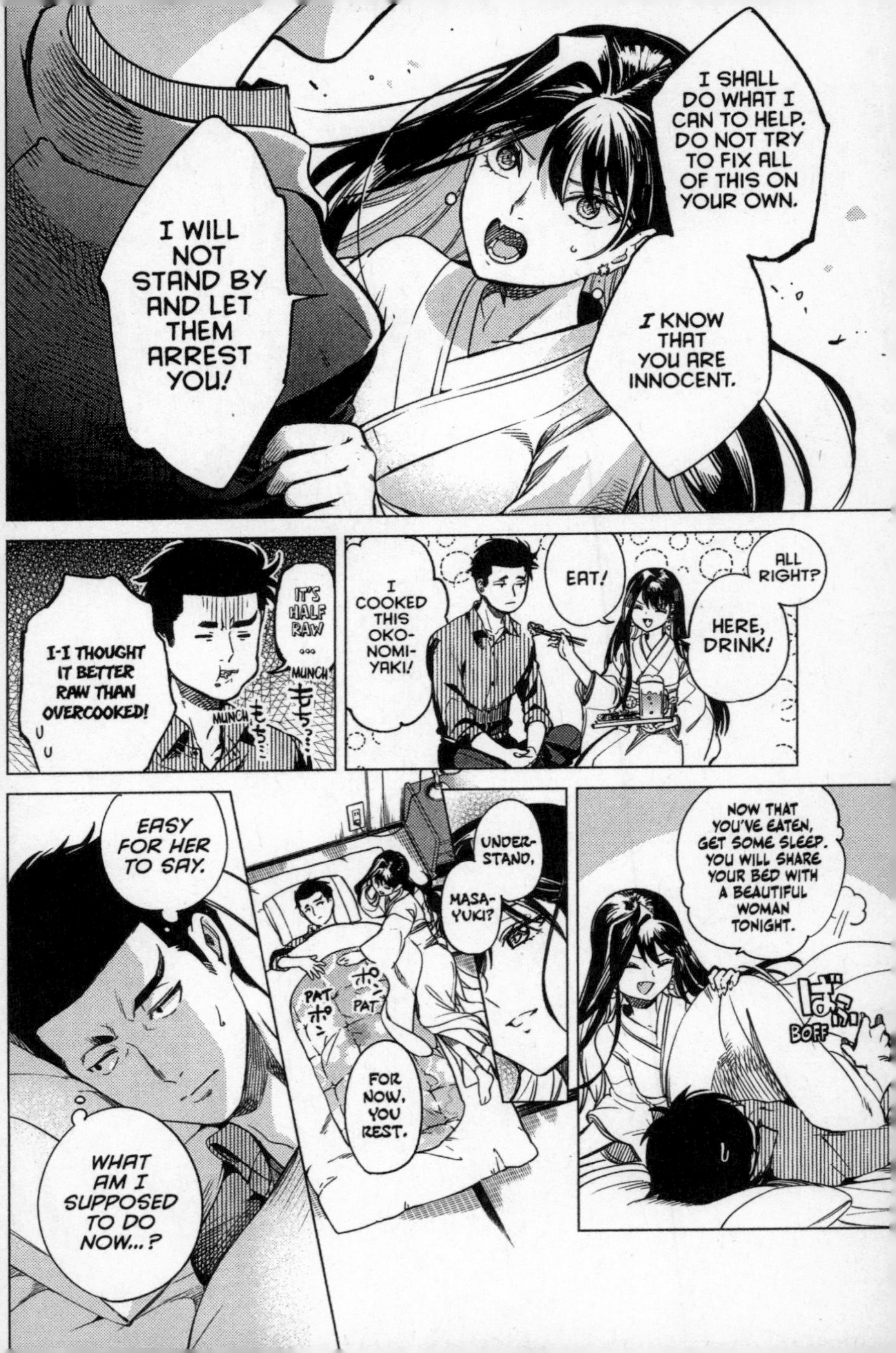
I SHALL DO WHAT I CAN TO HELP. DO NOT TRY TO FIX ALL OF THIS ON YOUR OWN.
I KNOW THAT YOU ARE INNOCENT.
I WILL NOT STAND BY AND LET THEM ARREST YOU!
ALL RIGHT?
HERE, DRINK!
EAT!
I COOKED THIS OKO-NOMI-YAKI!
IT'S HALF RAW...
MUNCH もち
MUNCH もち…
I-I THOUGHT IT BETTER RAW THAN OVERCOOKED!
NOW THAT YOU'VE EATEN, GET SOME SLEEP. YOU WILL SHARE YOUR BED WITH A BEAUTIFUL WOMAN TONIGHT.
ばふっ BOFF
UNDER-STAND,
MASA-YUKI?
ポン PAT
PAT ポン
FOR NOW, YOU REST.
EASY FOR HER TO SAY.
WHAT AM I SUPPOSED TO DO NOW...?

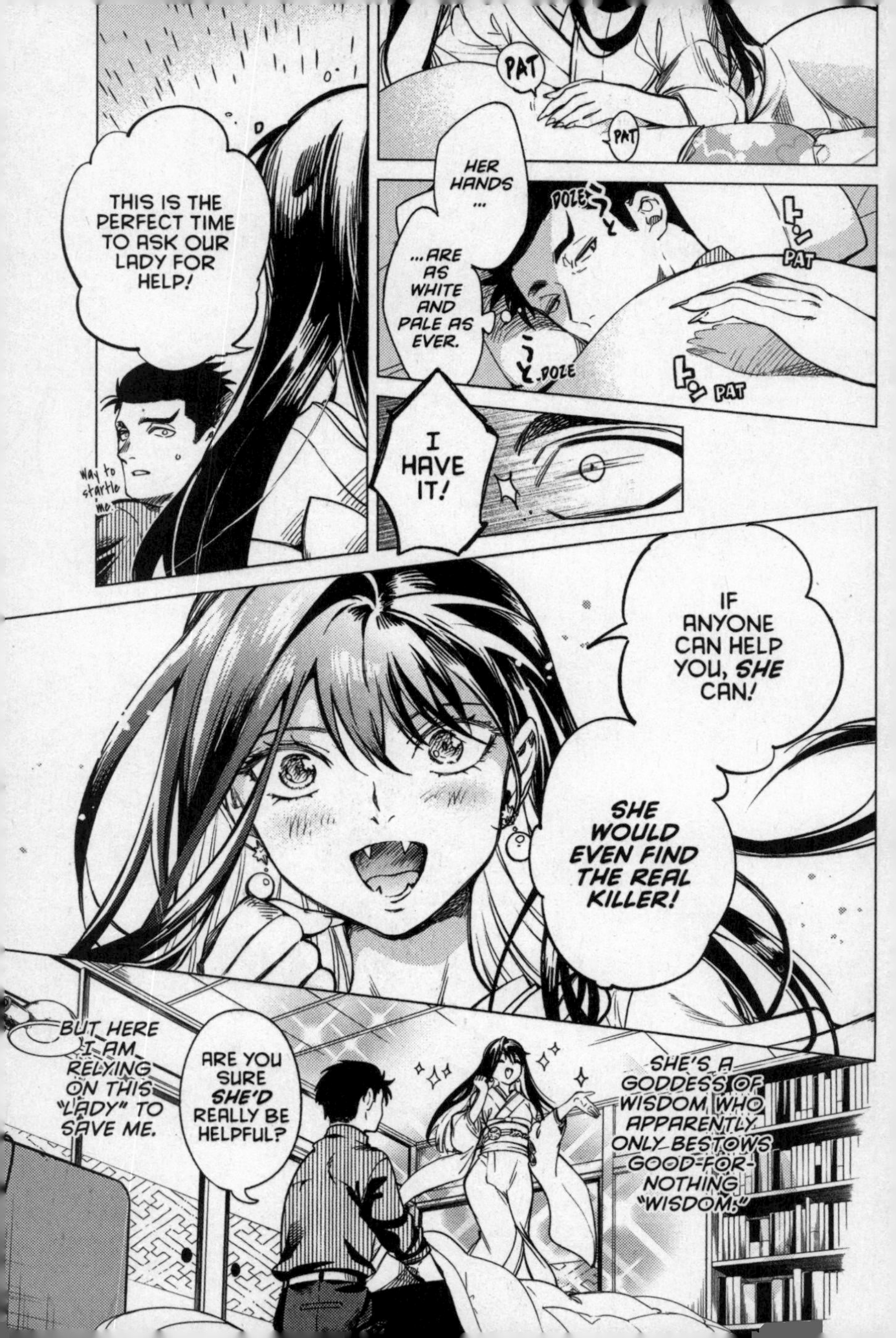
PAT
PAT
HER HANDS ...
...ARE AS WHITE AND PALE AS EVER.
DOZE
PAT
DOZE
PAT
I HAVE IT!
THIS IS THE PERFECT TIME TO ASK OUR LADY FOR HELP!
Way to startle me.
IF ANYONE CAN HELP YOU, SHE CAN!
SHE WOULD EVEN FIND THE REAL KILLER!
SHE'S A GODDESS OF WISDOM WHO APPARENTLY ONLY BESTOWS GOOD-FOR-NOTHING "WISDOM."
ARE YOU SURE SHE'D REALLY BE HELPFUL?
BUT HERE I AM RELYING ON THIS "LADY" TO SAVE ME.

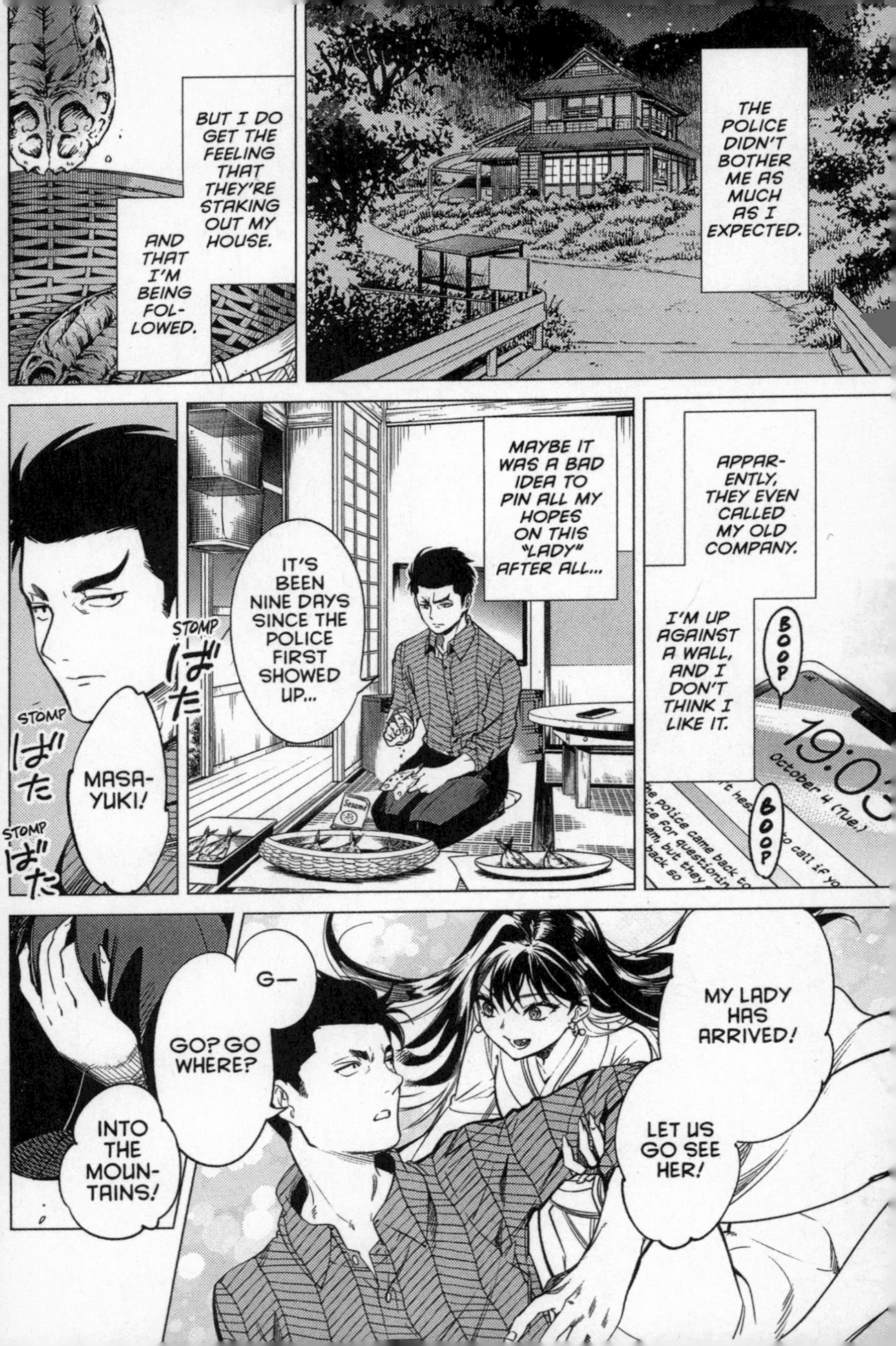
THE POLICE DIDN'T BOTHER ME AS MUCH AS I EXPECTED.
BUT I DO GET THE FEELING THAT THEY'RE STAKING OUT MY HOUSE.
AND THAT I'M BEING FOL-LOWED.
APPAR-ENTLY, THEY EVEN CALLED MY OLD COMPANY.
I'M UP AGAINST A WALL, AND I DON'T THINK I LIKE IT.
BOOP
October 4 (Tue.)
BOOP
MAYBE IT WAS A BAD IDEA TO PIN ALL MY HOPES ON THIS "LADY" AFTER ALL...
IT'S BEEN NINE DAYS SINCE THE POLICE FIRST SHOWED UP...
Sesame
STOMP ばた
STOMP ばた
MASA-YUKI!
STOMP ばた
MY LADY HAS ARRIVED!
LET US GO SEE HER!
G—
GO? GO WHERE?
INTO THE MOUN-TAINS!

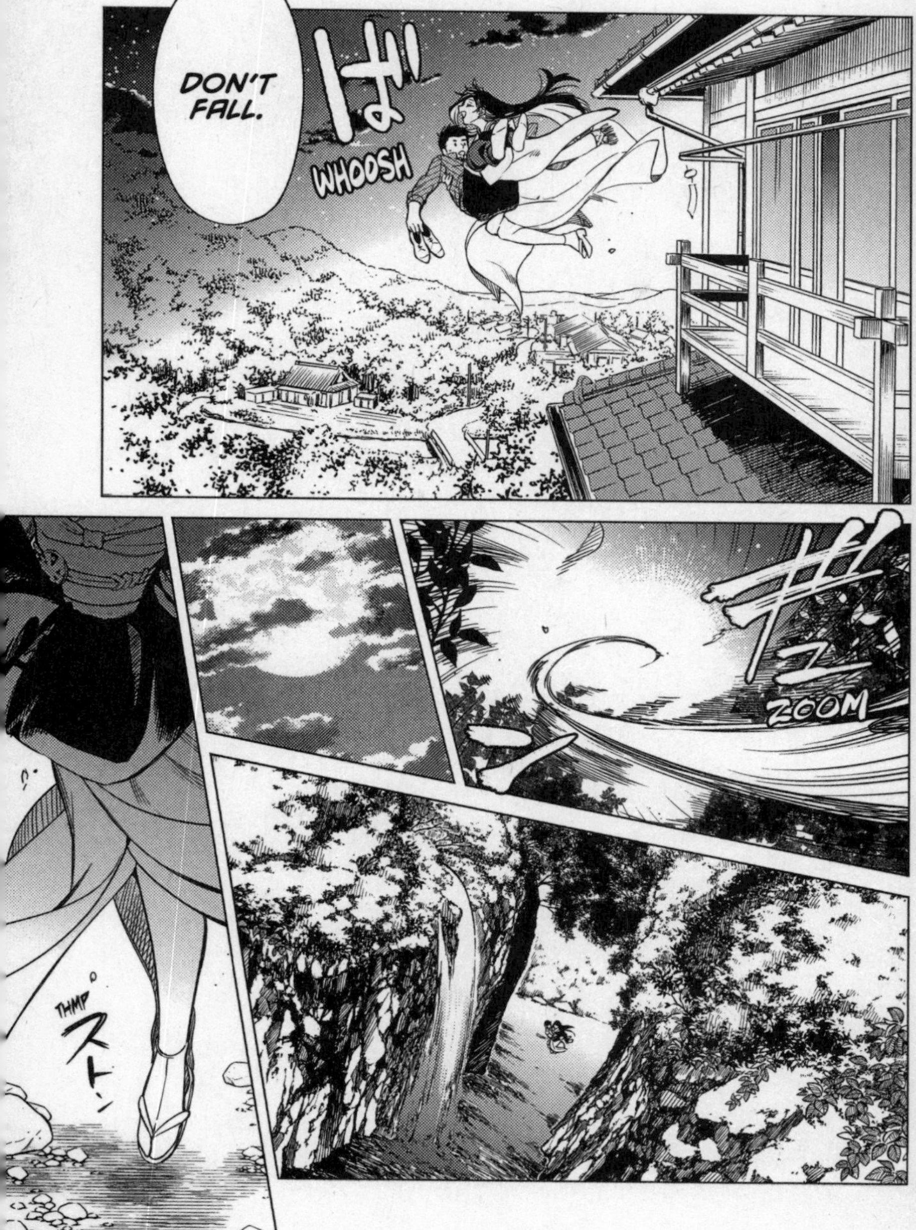
DON'T FALL.
WHOOSH
ZOOM
THMP
ストン

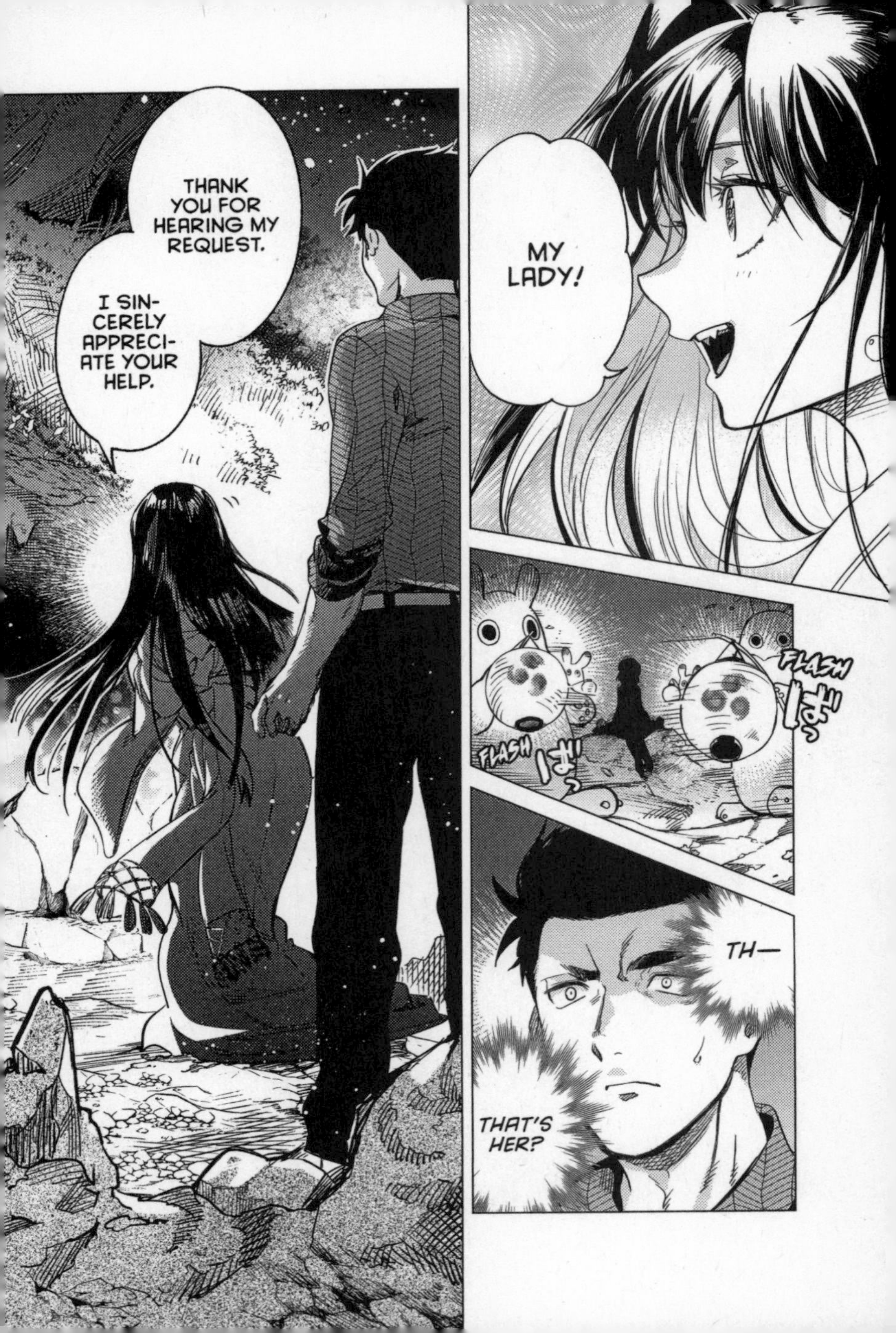
MY LADY!
FLASH
FLASH
TH—
THAT'S HER?
THANK YOU FOR HEARING MY REQUEST.
I SINCERELY APPRECIATE YOUR HELP.

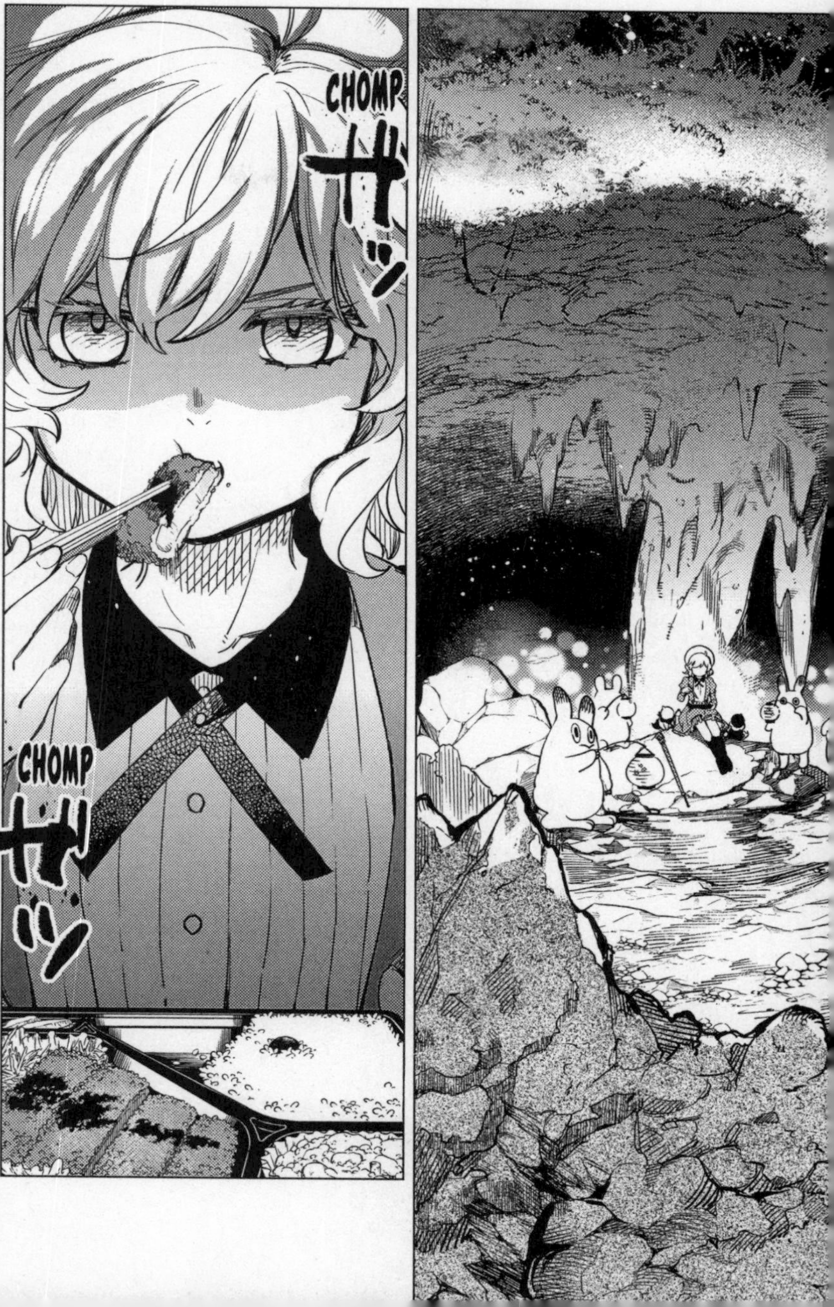
CHOMP
ザッ
CHOMP
ザッ

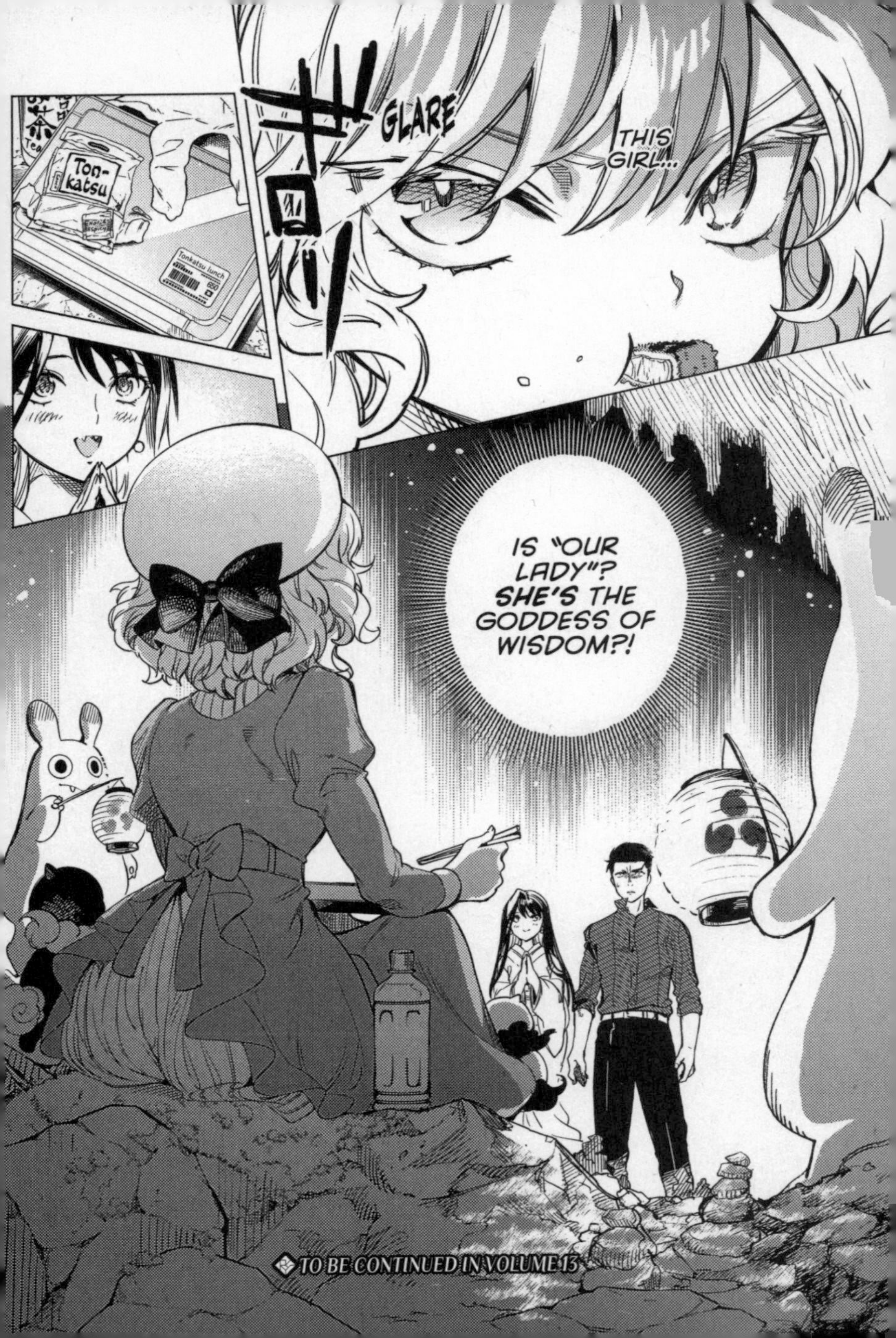
GLARE
THIS GIRL...
Ton-katsu
Tonkatsu lunch
IS "OUR LADY"? SHE'S THE GODDESS OF WISDOM?!
TO BE CONTINUED IN VOLUME 13

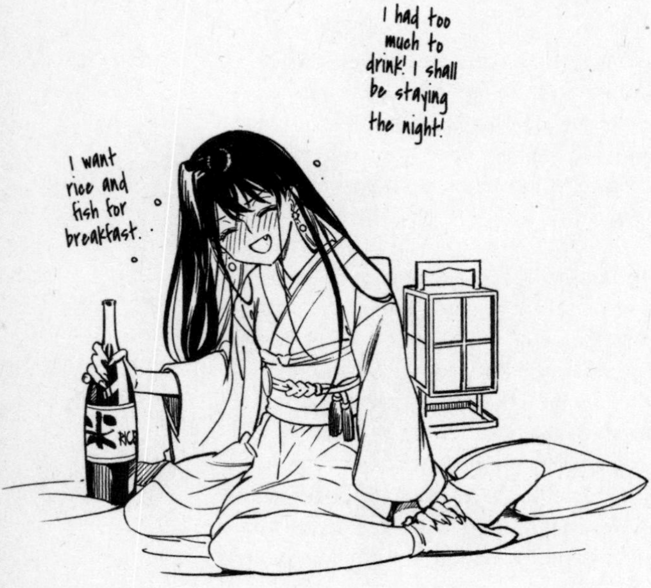
I had too much to drink! I shall be staying the night!
I want rice and fish for breakfast.
RICE

Thoughts on Dying Messages and Such from the Author

I am the author, Kyo Shirodaira, and this is volume 12. The volume count has gotten high enough that even I have to review volume one to see what I wrote. And there are differences between the novel and the manga versions, so my memories are even fuzzier.

That's not exactly why, but I did re-explain Iwanaga and Kurô in the first chapter of "The Yuki-Onna's Dilemma." As a matter of fact, this chapter marks the beginning of a simultaneous serialization in another magazine, so I did it out of consideration for readers who would be coming across the series for the first time.

Now then, I didn't do it intentionally, but both of the cases in this volume feature a dying message. I didn't intend to make the victim's deaths similar, either; it was an accident. These things happen when you've been working on something for a long time, so it's something I need to watch out for.

I wrote about this in the story, too, but, for as often as you see them in mysteries, a dying message is the prime example of an "unreliable clue." On the other hand, they leave a strong impression, and they can make anybody into the killer, which may be why they're used so often. It also makes a good visual to have letters in blood or a significant-looking object near the body. Nevertheless, they remain an unreliable clue that can be interpreted any number of ways, and even when the true meaning of the message is revealed at the end, it's not always convincing.

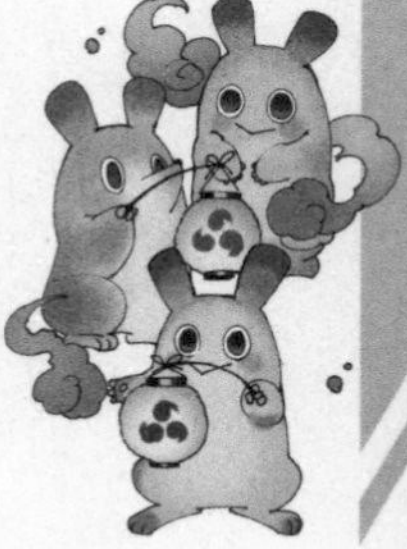

These days, authors don't always focus on what the message says, but on why the victim left the message, and how they had the chance to write it. Or if the killer left a fake message, they'll have the story revolve around why they did that. Sometimes they'll narrow down the list of suspects based on who could have left a fake message, and that will lead to finding the murderer.

In some stories, they find evidence that the victim wrote a message and the killer erased it, and they use that to find the culprit based on who had means and opportunity to erase it. The content of the dying message has lost its significance, but you might say that they can be trusted as a way of using an unreliable clue to find the guilty party. But then, it's possible that someone else faked the message or erased it, so it's still imperfect.

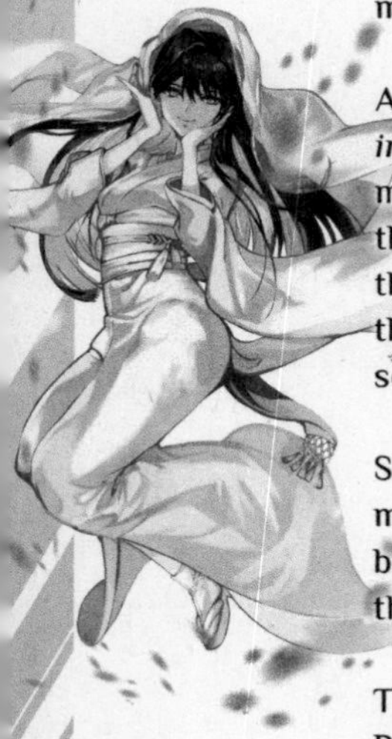

Also, there's a novel (a short one) called *The Last Woman in His Life* by Ellery Queen, which involved a dying message, and it makes me shudder at the way it sets up the story so that the dying message can only mean one thing. And yet, I do feel a little like the victim who left that message must have been possessed by a god or something.

So how will the readers feel about the handling of dying messages in this volume? One of the mysteries hasn't been solved yet, but I do hope you get the sense that there's some trick to it.

The next volume will have some things leading up to Rikka-san's return to action. Her reunion with Iwanaga and Kurô doesn't seem far off.

Well, I hope to see you again.

Kyo Shirodaira

Bonus Manga 1: "Clothing for a Special Occasion"

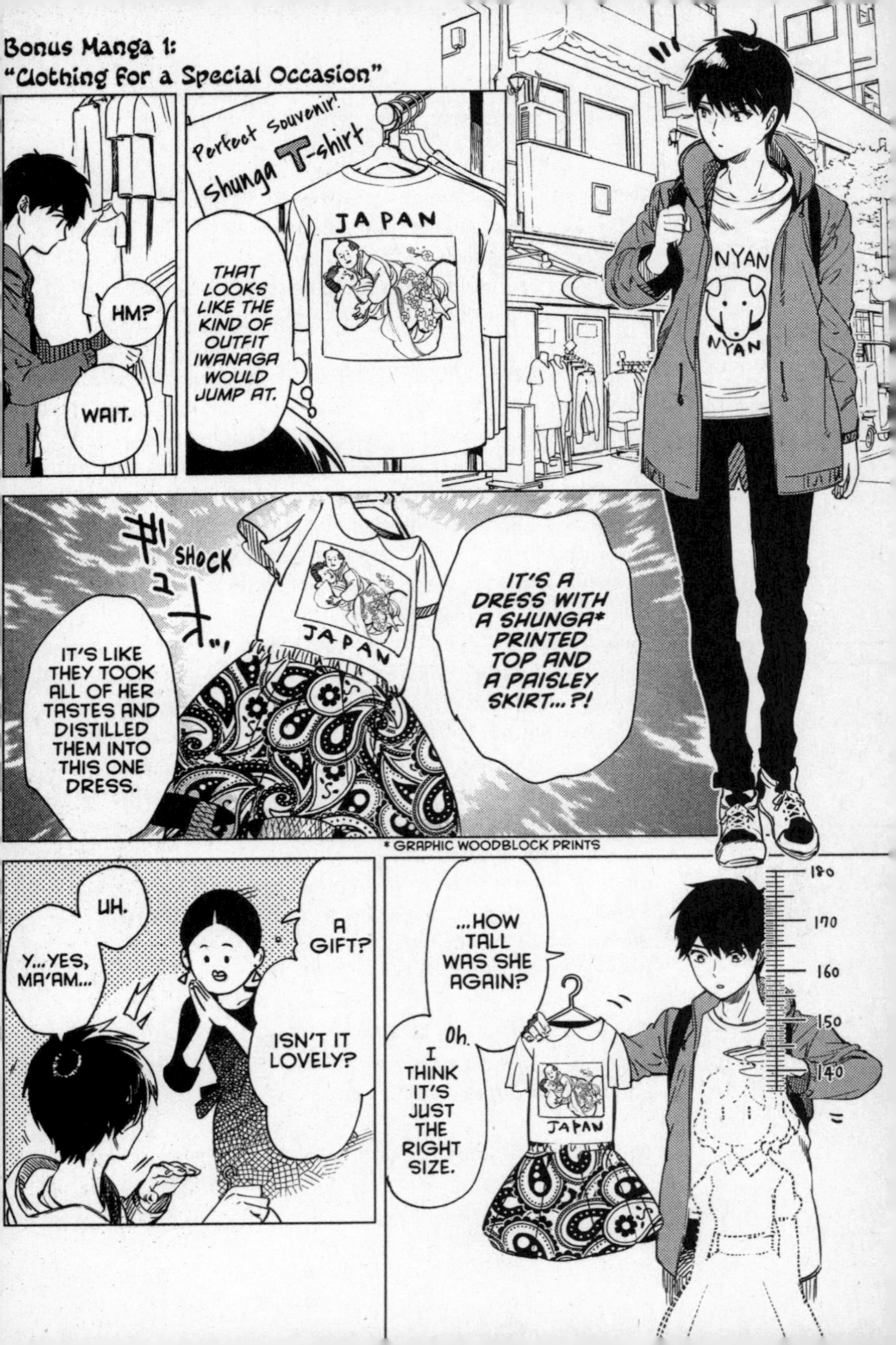

NYAN
NYAN
Perfect Souvenir! Shunga T-shirt
JAPAN
THAT LOOKS LIKE THE KIND OF OUTFIT IWANAGA WOULD JUMP AT.
HM?
WAIT.
IT'S A DRESS WITH A SHUNGA* PRINTED TOP AND A PAISLEY SKIRT...?!
JAPAN
SHOCK
IT'S LIKE THEY TOOK ALL OF HER TASTES AND DISTILLED THEM INTO THIS ONE DRESS.
* GRAPHIC WOODBLOCK PRINTS
...HOW TALL WAS SHE AGAIN?
Oh.
I THINK IT'S JUST THE RIGHT SIZE.
180
170
160
150
140
JAPAN
A GIFT?
ISN'T IT LOVELY?
UH.
Y...YES, MA'AM...

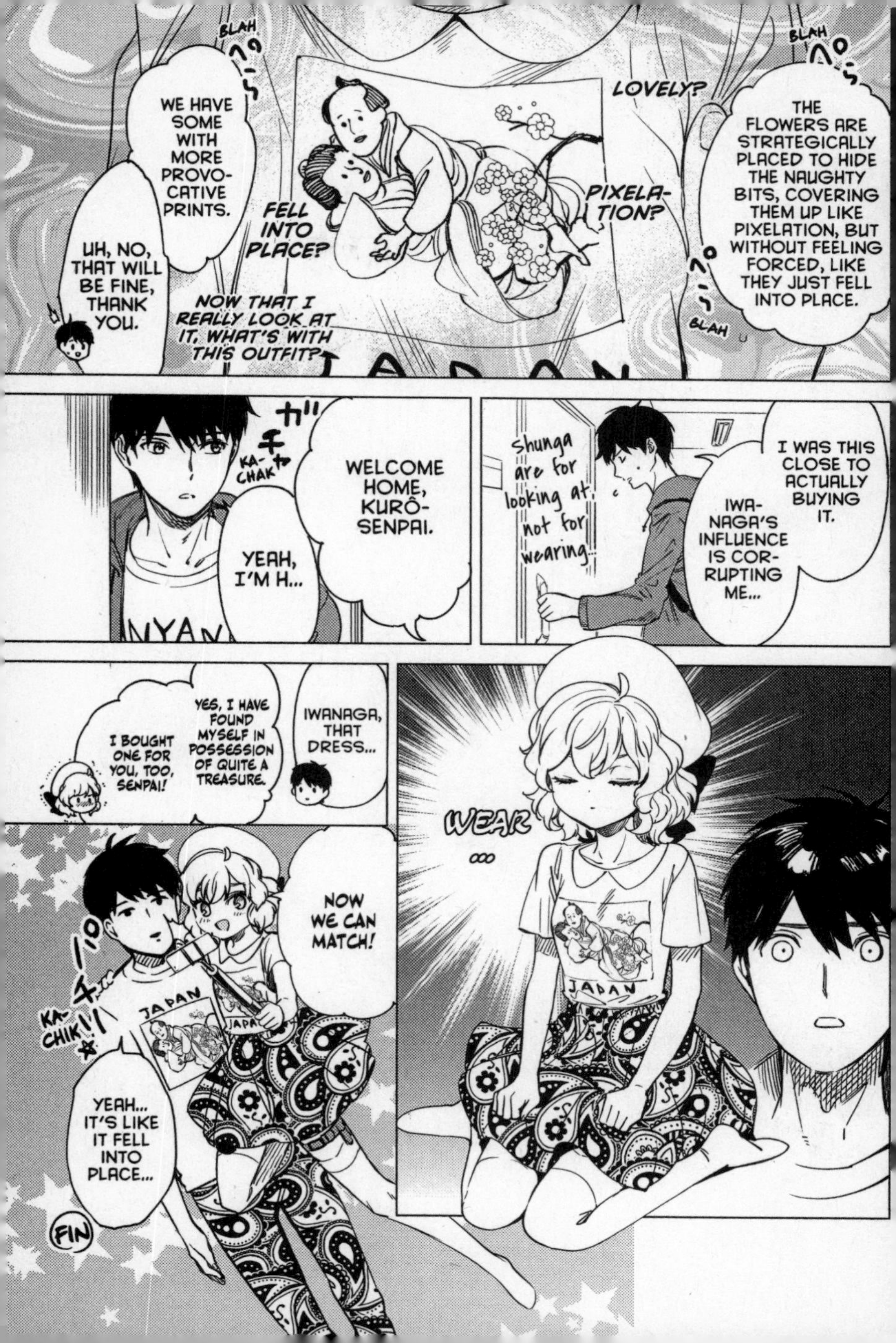
BLAH
THE FLOWERS ARE STRATEGICALLY PLACED TO HIDE THE NAUGHTY BITS, COVERING THEM UP LIKE PIXELATION, BUT WITHOUT FEELING FORCED, LIKE THEY JUST FELL INTO PLACE.
BLAH
LOVELY?
PIXELATION?
FELL INTO PLACE?
BLAH
WE HAVE SOME WITH MORE PROVOCATIVE PRINTS.
UH, NO, THAT WILL BE FINE, THANK YOU.
NOW THAT I REALLY LOOK AT IT, WHAT'S WITH THIS OUTFIT?
I WAS THIS CLOSE TO ACTUALLY BUYING IT.
IWANAGA'S INFLUENCE IS CORRUPTING ME...
Shunga are for looking at, not for wearing...
KA-CHAK
WELCOME HOME, KURÔ-SENPAI.
YEAH, I'M H...
WEAR...
IWANAGA, THAT DRESS...
YES, I HAVE FOUND MYSELF IN POSSESSION OF QUITE A TREASURE.
I BOUGHT ONE FOR YOU, TOO, SENPAI!
NOW WE CAN MATCH!
KA-CHIK!
YEAH... IT'S LIKE IT FELL INTO PLACE...
FIN

Bonus Manga 2: "It Happens with Ice Types"

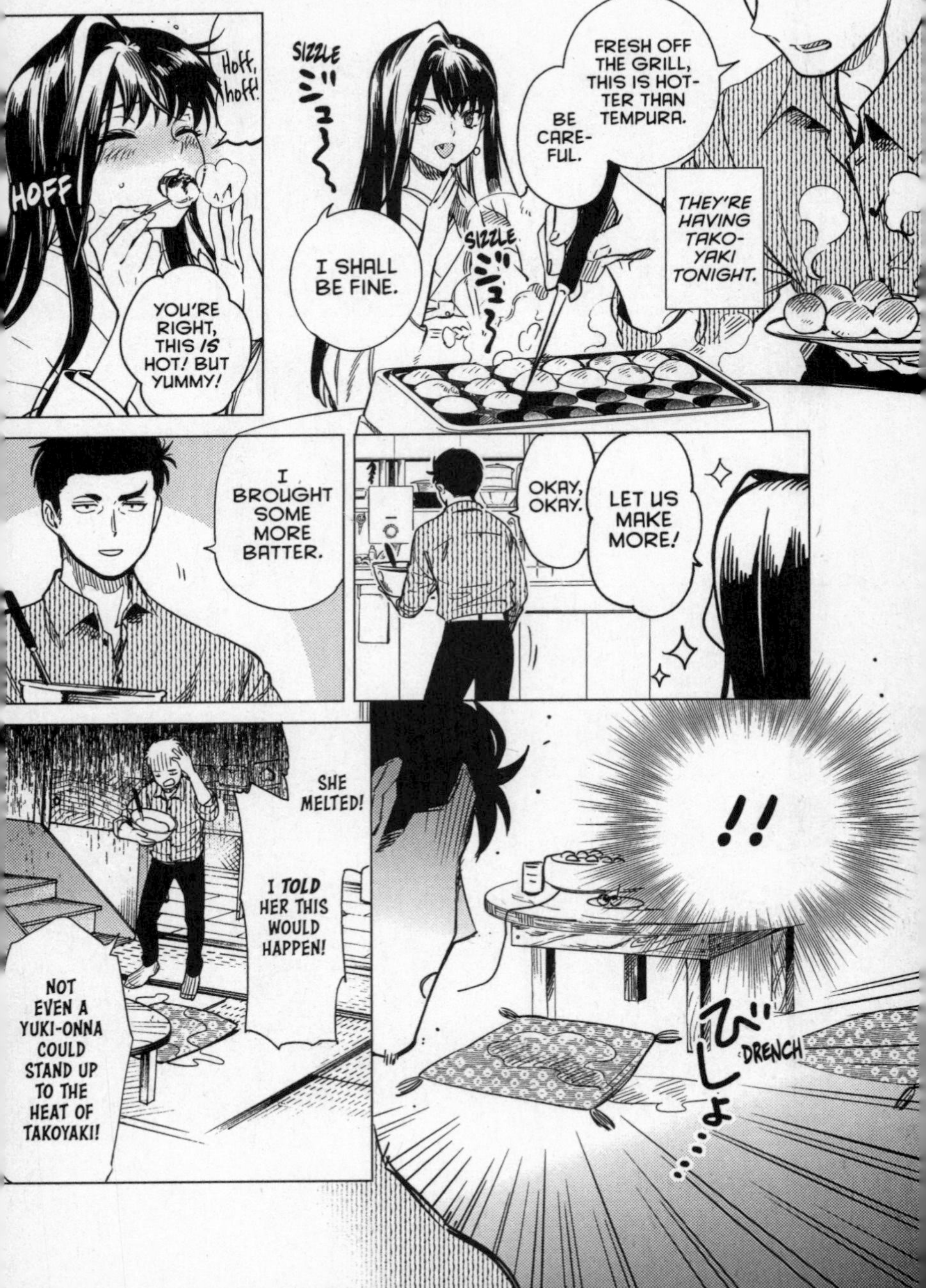
FRESH OFF THE GRILL, THIS IS HOTTER THAN TEMPURA.
BE CAREFUL.
THEY'RE HAVING TAKOYAKI TONIGHT.
SIZZLE
ジュ〜
I SHALL BE FINE.
SIZZLE
ジュ〜
Hoff, hoff!
HOFF
YOU'RE RIGHT, THIS *IS* HOT! BUT YUMMY!
LET US MAKE MORE!
OKAY, OKAY.
I BROUGHT SOME MORE BATTER.
!!
DRENCH
びしょ…
SHE MELTED!
I *TOLD* HER THIS WOULD HAPPEN!
NOT EVEN A YUKI-ONNA COULD STAND UP TO THE HEAT OF TAKOYAKI!

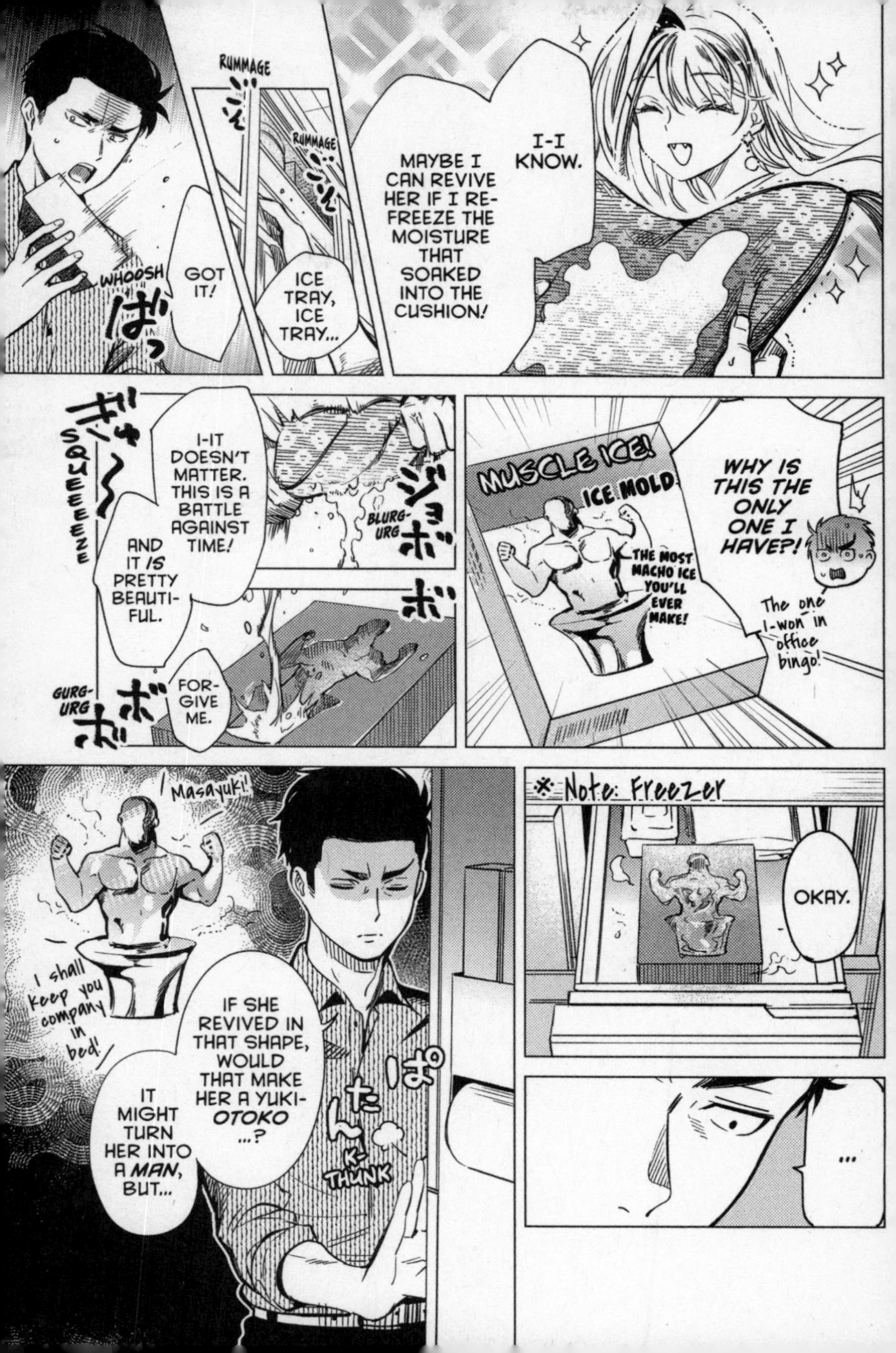
I-I KNOW.
MAYBE I CAN REVIVE HER IF I RE-FREEZE THE MOISTURE THAT SOAKED INTO THE CUSHION!
RUMMAGE
RUMMAGE
ICE TRAY, ICE TRAY...
GOT IT!
WHOOSH
MUSCLE ICE!
ICE MOLD
THE MOST MACHO ICE YOU'LL EVER MAKE!
WHY IS THIS THE ONLY ONE I HAVE?!
The one I won in office bingo!
BLURG-URG
I-IT DOESN'T MATTER. THIS IS A BATTLE AGAINST TIME!
AND IT *IS* PRETTY BEAUTIFUL.
SQUEEEEEZE
FOR-GIVE ME.
GURG-URG
※Note: Freezer
OKAY.
...
K-THUNK
IF SHE REVIVED IN THAT SHAPE, WOULD THAT MAKE HER A YUKI-*OTOKO*...?
IT MIGHT TURN HER INTO A *MAN*, BUT...
Masayuki!
I shall keep you company in bed!

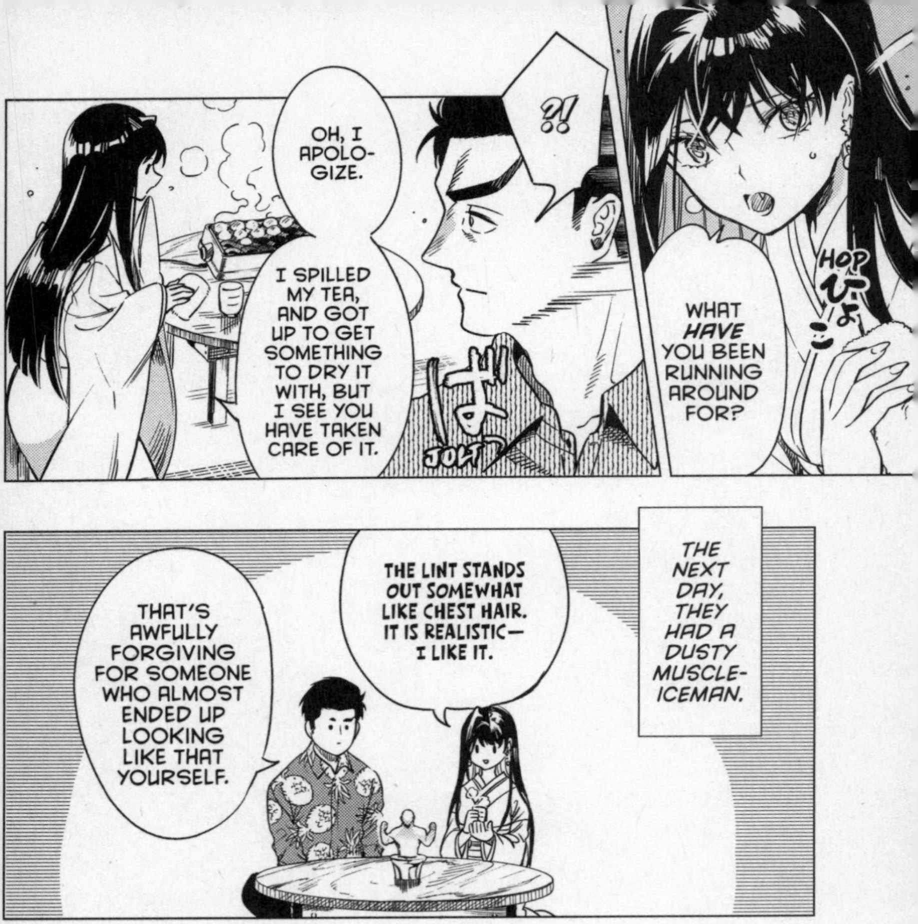
HOP
WHAT HAVE YOU BEEN RUNNING AROUND FOR?
?!
OH, I APOLOGIZE.
I SPILLED MY TEA, AND GOT UP TO GET SOMETHING TO DRY IT WITH, BUT I SEE YOU HAVE TAKEN CARE OF IT.
JOLT
THE NEXT DAY, THEY HAD A DUSTY MUSCLE-ICEMAN.
THE LINT STANDS OUT SOMEWHAT LIKE CHEST HAIR. IT IS REALISTIC— I LIKE IT.
THAT'S AWFULLY FORGIVING FOR SOMEONE WHO ALMOST ENDED UP LOOKING LIKE THAT YOURSELF.

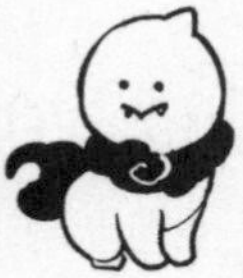

Thank you for picking up volume 12!
I hope you'll read the next one, too.

Staff: Asai, Shimameguri, Gomakurô
Editors: O-kawa, T-da (honorifics excluded)

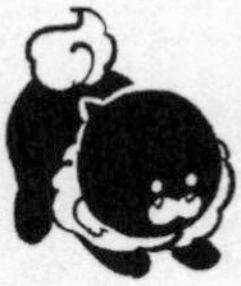

IN/SPECTRE

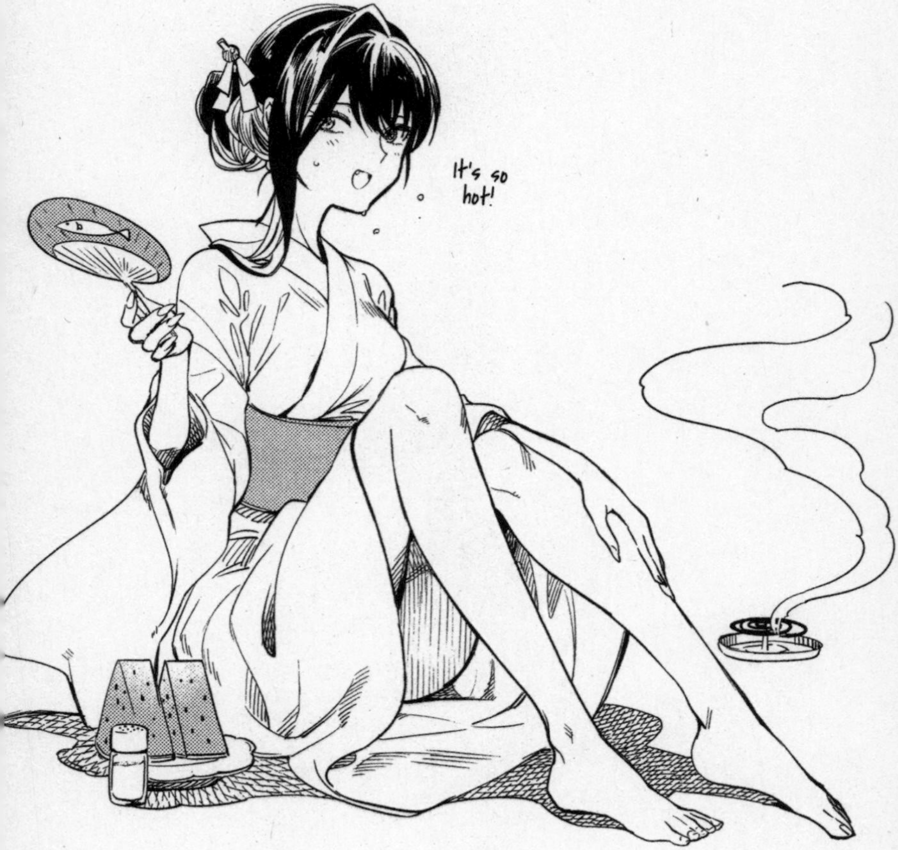
It's so hot!

A Yuki-Onna in summer

Senpai had so little to do in this volume that he started cooking some pork bone broth.

Let's make ramen from scratch.

TRANSLATION NOTES

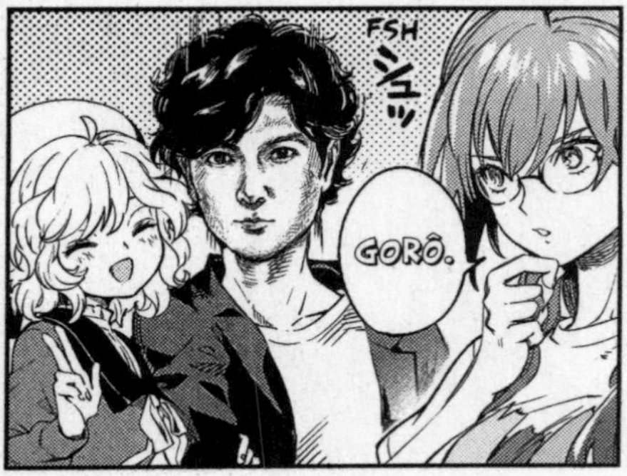
FSH
シュッ
GORÔ.

Gorô, page 14
Upon remembering what she thinks is Kurô's name, Rena remembers the face of Gorô Inagaki, member of the ultra-popular boyband SMAP.

Funazushi, page 16
Funazushi is sushi made out of extremely fermented fish. The taste has been likened to very tangy cheese as well as ammonia.

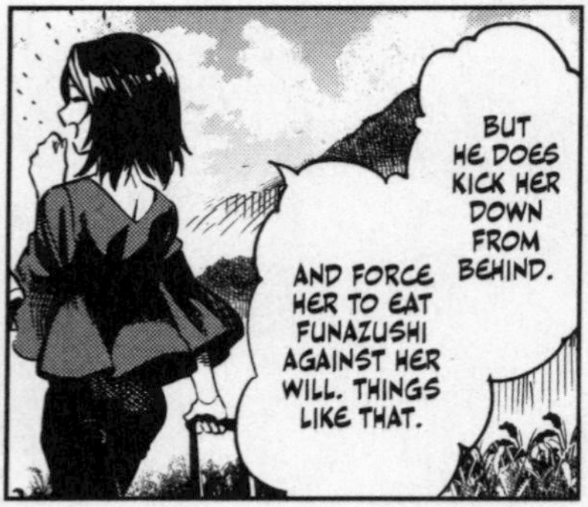
BUT HE DOES KICK HER DOWN FROM BEHIND.
AND FORCE HER TO EAT FUNAZUSHI AGAINST HER WILL. THINGS LIKE THAT.

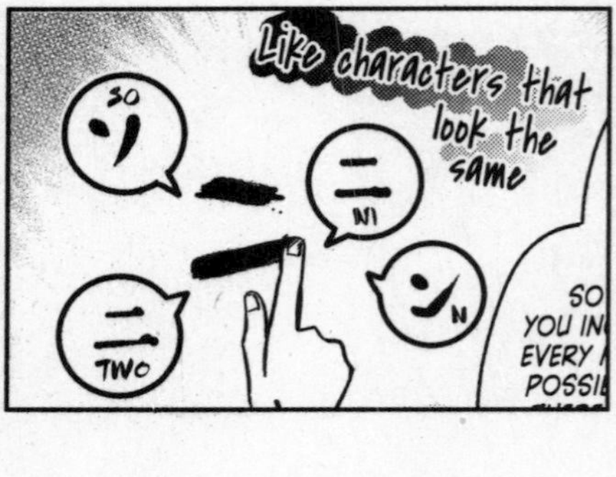
Like characters that look the same
SO
ソ
ニ
NI
ン
N
二
TWO

Characters that look the same, page 21
As shown in the picture, the two lines drawn by the hypothetical murder victim can represent any of several similarly written Japanese characters. Most of them are from the *katakana* syllabary, which uses one character to represent one syllable. The one on the lower left is a *kanji* character, representing the number two, which is pronounced *ni* in Japanese.

Ooooh dun dun dun dun, page 42

Written "*hyuu doro doro*" in Japanese, this is the sound of ghostly apparitions. It's a sound effect used in Japanese theater (mainly kabuki) when specters appear on stage. The "oooh" is created by a high-pitched flute and sounds like a ghostly wail. The "dun-dun-dun-dun" is the beating of a large drum. This sound effect can be accompanied by pyrotechnic effects, also called "*hyuu doro doro*," representing ghost fire.

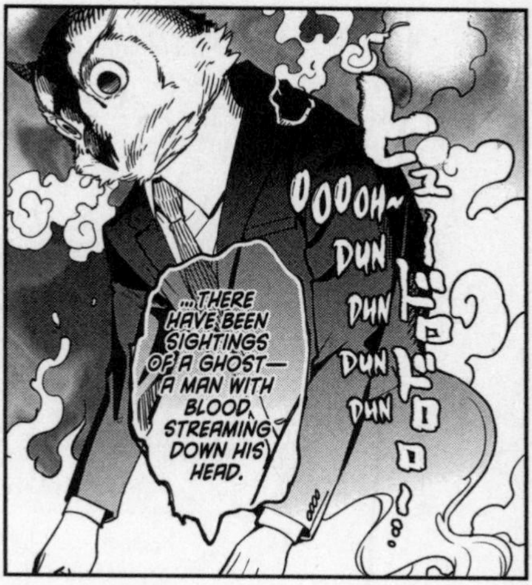
OOOOH~ DUN DUN DUN DUN
...THERE HAVE BEEN SIGHTINGS OF A GHOST—A MAN WITH BLOOD STREAMING DOWN HIS HEAD.

Yuki-Onna, page 82

In Japanese folklore, a *yuki-onna*, or "snow woman," is an ethereal woman who appears in snowy places. She is known for her beauty, as well as for ruthlessly killing people with her coldness.

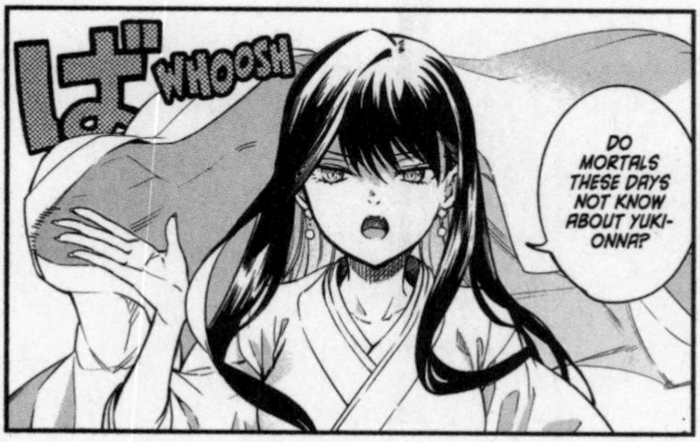
ば
WHOOSH
DO MORTALS THESE DAYS NOT KNOW ABOUT YUKI-ONNA?

Ginjô saké, page 117

Ginjô saké is a premium type of rice wine made from rice that has been polished down to no more than 60% of its original size.

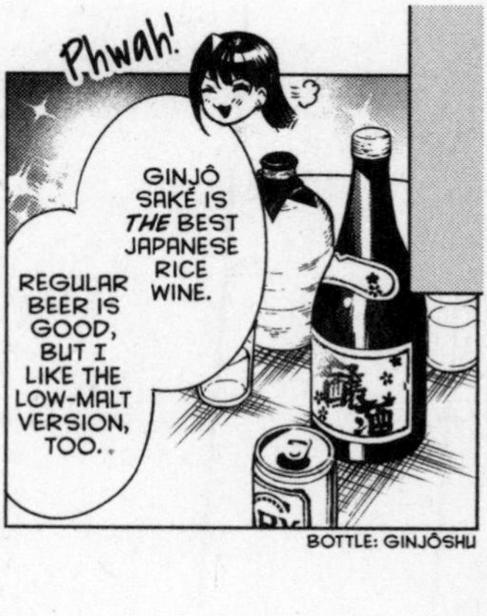
Phwah!
GINJÔ SAKÉ IS *THE* BEST JAPANESE RICE WINE.
REGULAR BEER IS GOOD, BUT I LIKE THE LOW-MALT VERSION, TOO..

BOTTLE: GINJÔSHU

A Kodansha Comics Trade Paperback Original

In/Spectre 12 copyright © 2020 Kyo Shirodaira/Chashiba Katase
English translation copyright © 2020 Kyo Shirodaira/Chashiba Katase

Published in the United States by Kodansha Comics, an imprint of
Kodansha USA Publishing, LLC, New York.

Publication rights for this English edition arranged through
Kodansha Ltd., Tokyo.

First published in Japan in 2020 by Kodansha Ltd., Tokyo
as *Kyokou Suiri*, volume 12.

ISBN 978-1-63236-987-1

Original cover design by Takashi Shimoyama and Mami Fukunaga (RedRooster)

Printed in the United States of America.

www.kodanshacomics.com

9 8 7 6 5 4 3 2 1

Translation: Alethea Nibley & Athena Nibley
Lettering: Lys Blakeslee
Editing: Vanessa Tenazas
Kodansha Comics edition cover design by Phil Balsman

Publisher: Kiichiro Sugawara

Director of publishing services: Ben Applegate
Associate director of operations: Stephen Pakula
Publishing services managing editor: Noelle Webster
Assistant production manager: Emi Lotto, Angela Zurlo